Natural Language Processing

NATURAL LANGUAGE PROCESSING

A Knowledge-Engineering Approach

RICHARD E. CULLINGFORD

SCHOOL OF INFORMATION AND COMPUTER SCIENCE
GEORGIA INSTITUTE OF TECHNOLOGY

ROWMAN & LITTLEFIELD
Publishers

ROWMAN & LITTLEFIELD

Published in the United States of America in 1986
by Rowman & Littlefield, Publishers
(a division of Littlefield, Adams & Company
81 Adams Drive, Totowa, New Jersey 07512

Library of Congress Cataloging-in-Publication Data

Cullingford, Richard E., 1946–
  Natural language processing

  Bibliography: p. 335
  Includes index.
  1. Linguistics—Data processing. 2. Artificial
intelligence. I. Title
P98.C85 1986   402.8'5   85-26139
ISBN 0-8476-7358-8

88 87 86
10 9 8 7 6 5 4 3 2 1

Printed in the United States of America

Contents

Part II Building a Conversationalist

Chapter 7 Summarizing Knowledge Bases   203

Chapter 8 Knowledge-Base Management   224

Chapter 9 Commonsense Reasoning   234

Illustrations

Figures

Preface

The scientific goal of making digital computers fluent users of human language is probably as old as the computer itself. In the past quarter century, various aspects of natural language processing by computer have been pursued by workers in a number of fields. For example, library scientists have been interested in the automated indexing and retrieval of documents; computational linguists have studied the syntactic analysis and machine translation of languages; psychologists have built computer models of certain aspects of human language behavior; and recently computer scientists have begun constructing language interfaces to commercial database management systems.

By and large, these efforts have utilized the computer as a tool for exploring isolated facets of language use. Beginning in the late 1960s, workers in the new field of Artificial Intelligence (AI), which regards the computer as a potentially sentient entity in its own right, began research aimed at providing the machine with language-processing capabilities comparable to those of people. The possibilities for high-quality computer language understanding were explored in the decade of the '70s by work on theories of meaning and the structuring of world knowledge; on models of language analysis and generation; and on methods for commonsense reasoning and inference. Since AI is interested in process models, these theories have been realized in programs that perform tasks such as question-answering, story understanding, machine translation, and conversational interaction.

As a side-effect, a body of ideas and a collection of tools for building language-using systems have gradually been accumulating in AI. No one who has worked seriously in this field believes that all, or even most of, the problems have been solved, or that we will see practical, intelligent, general-purpose conversational systems in the near future. The past few years, however, have witnessed the growing conviction that enough has been learned that progress toward a *methodology* for constructing practical language-using systems may now be possible.

This book is an introduction to an emerging AI technology of natural language processing. The technology is based on what has come to be called the *Conceptual Information Processing* approach to language, largely, although not exclusively, associated with the work of Roger Schank and his students at Stanford University, Yale University, and elsewhere. I have chosen to present this important body of work in depth rather than to survey the various alternatives. (There are good surveys available; see, for example, Char76; Tenn80; Barr81; Wino83.)

The book is written from a *knowledge-engineering* viewpoint. If the computer is to cope robustly with its users in some application, it seems obvious that it will need to "know," in some reasonably deep sense, many things about that application. The knowledge the computer requires, of course, has to be provided by the experts at natural language: ourselves. Thus, the first part of the book discusses some simple techniques for representing commonsense knowledge and for building application-specific knowledge structures. Then follows a description of a general-purpose language understanding and generating interface that works with such representations.

Neither the representation scheme nor the language-processing programs is claimed to be anything more than a reasonable starting point for the engineering of an interface. The practice of engineering is largely concerned with the creation and elaboration of tools for solving increasingly complex problems. My intention has been to present the key algorithms and data structures used by these programs in sufficient detail that a software engineer would be convinced that the approach is practical and extensible. Along the way, I have tried to illustrate some of the characteristic ways that AI workers think about complicated symbolic computing problems.

The second half of the book consists of a series of case studies of programs that either use the interface to perform some task, or that support the interface's operation in some way. All the example programs are drawn from two text-processing systems that are typical of current work in AI. One *converses* with its users in a complex task: academic counseling of undergraduates. The other *explains* the operation of a computer-aided design system to its user by generating descriptive text coordinated with a graphical display. The case studies are designed to illustrate some of the practical details of tailoring a language-processing system to an application.

The counseling and explaining programs are both typical AI research products: large, fragile, and narrow in their coverage. Neither has been exhaustively tested with real users. Nevertheless, from the standpoint of a *methodology* for developing systems of this kind, they work well enough to establish confidence in their basic approach. What we have, therefore, is a viewpoint, a blueprint, and a set of tools we can use to begin the design of truly intelligent, human-usable language-processing systems.

Notes on the Use of This Book

As a text, this book is suitable for an advanced undergraduate or graduate course on the natural language-processing subfield of AI. The book is also intended for programmers and engineers who want to see what's involved in developing a natural language interface to an expert reasoning or database management system. In addition to a *theory* of natural language processing, I present, and try to motivate, a unified set of data structures and functions that can be used to experiment with language interfaces. A variety of exercises is also included that extend the programs in useful ways. For those who wish to look further into the field, there are a number of references to the research literature. I introduce a fair amount of technical jargon during the discussion; definitions for these words and phrases can be found in the Glossary of Terms (Appendix III).

Normally, a chapter introducing some theoretical aspect of language processing will have several sections describing concrete implementation details. All that's required to understand the technical discussion here is a working knowledge of grade-school grammar and of Lisp, a symbolic computing language that is widely used in Artificial Intelligence work. (For descriptions of Lisp, see Wins81, Abel85 or Wile84, the latter being especially good for Franz Lisp [Fode81], the dialect used in this book. Char80 is an excellent overview of AI programming techniques in Lisp.)

A complete AI program is a huge, complicated system. Not all the details of an implementation can, or should, be described in an introductory book of this kind. For those adventurous readers who want hands-on experience with actual software, I have packaged a version of the interface described in Part I into a Natural Language Processing Toolkit. This software package, which is available from Rowman & Littlefield, includes versions of the representation design, language analysis, language generation and knowledge-base management programs discussed in the text. The Toolkit is a collection of Franz Lisp programs for computer systems, such as the DEC VAX, the Pyramid 90x, or the Sun Workstation, running Version 4.2 of the Berkeley Software Distribution of the Unix Operating System.* I've also provided a variety of example files that exercise the Toolkit, which were developed for courses that used the software. I hope that the availability of these tools will lure more people into the study of the many fascinating problems encountered in the attempt to give the machine a human language.

---

* DEC and VAX are registered trademarks of Digital Equipment Corp. Pyramid is a registered trademark of Pyramid Technology Corp. Sun is a registered trademark of Sun Microsystems, Inc. Unix is a registered trademark of AT&T Bell Laboratories, Inc.

Acknowledgments

This book is a practical introduction to more than a decade's research by my colleagues, my students, and myself. The pioneering work in semantics-based natural language processing was done by Charniak, Schank, Wilks and Winograd. I have been heavily influenced, in particular, by the ideas of Roger Schank, with whom I did my graduate work at Yale University. Many of my friends at the Yale AI Project have contributed ideas and software over the years. Larry Birnbaum and Mal Selfridge deserve special mention for their implementation of the conceptual analyzer, CA (Birn81), from which the analysis program described in this book is lineally descended. A special note of thanks also must go to Eugene Charniak, Chris Riesbeck and Drew McDermott, the authors of *Artificial Intelligence Programming* (Char80), for collecting in one place many major AI programming ideas.

Colleagues and students in the Intelligent Systems Design Group at the University of Connecticut have also collaborated on the work discussed in this book. Professors Bill Krueger and Mal Selfridge shared in the design of CADHELP, the self-explaining CAD system (Cull81, Cull82a). Marie Bienkowski, Danielle Bellavance, and Daniel Neiman were responsible for the major portion of its implementation. This work was supported by the Defense Advanced Research Projects Agency and monitored by the Office of Naval Research under contract N00014-79-C-0807. Bienkowski, Bruce Dawson, Leonard Joseph, James Milstein, Michael Pazzani, and Jeff Staley designed and programmed major pieces of the counseling system ACE (Cull82b).

Faculty and students at the EECS Department, Princeton University, made many valuable suggestions for improvements to the manuscript when it was used as a textbook during the spring of 1984 and 1985. Professors Bob Freidin, Gil Harman, and George Miller of the Cognitive Studies Group at Princeton made useful comments on the book from various non-AI perspectives of Cognitive Science. Marie Bienkowski was of tremendous assistance in the preparation of the final draft of the manuscript, especially the material on language generation. Oleh Sochan of the Institute for Defense Analyses contributed the Glossary of Terms (Appendix III). Finally, I owe a vote of thanks to Prof. Jaime Carbonell of Carnegie-Mellon University for a thoughtful and thorough review of the manuscript. The remaining errors are, of course, my responsibility.

To all these people, my friends, this book is affectionately dedicated.

Atlanta, Georgia

Natural Language Processing

1

Natural Language Processing: An Overview

1.0 Introduction

Scientists and engineers usually view the digital computer as a tool for solving problems based on a mathematical model of a physical process (e. g., a set of differential equations). Programs written for such applications perform *numerical processing:* they do arithmetic calculations on bodies of numerical data. Programs for business applications, on the other hand, must deal with a whole range of data types in addition to simple numbers. For example, their input may be streams of employee names or product inventories. These applications are of a primarily *non-numeric* or *symbolic computing* nature. Symbolic computing applications have grown rapidly in recent years, as the user community has come to understand the machine's power as a general information-processing device.

Ordinary written language is an extremely flexible and compact encoding of information in a symbolic form. Even in this digital age, written records are the most important form of mankind's "external memory," which allows us to progress in a cumulative manner. Thus, the processing of natural language by the machine as a means of interacting with its users is, in a sense, the ultimate symbolic computing problem.

The object of the field of *natural language processing* is to make the computer a fluent user of ordinary language in all kinds of conversational tasks. This book is an introduction to the theory and methodology of an important modern approach to natural language processing.

The computer will not be able to communicate effectively with its users in language unless it has a reasonably deep "knowledge" of the domain being discussed. Natural language processing (henceforth NLP) is therefore a branch of *artificial intelligence,* because it is based upon computer models of cognition, which are concerned with the structuring and application of knowledge.

The work is meant for two different audiences. It can be read by computer science students interested in a fascinating subfield of AI. It can also be usefully studied by software system designers who want to see what's involved in providing natural language interfaces to large information-processing systems. My intention is to describe a particular approach to NLP through case studies of experimental text-processing systems. For both types of readers, a large number of program fragments

1

from running systems are included to illustrate the key features of systems able to "understand" their inputs. Although none of the programs is in any way a complete solution to the problems it addresses, each contains certain key elements that workers in the field agree will have to be in the solution.

1.1   Related Fields: An Overview

1.1.1   NLP, Artificial Intelligence, and Knowledge Engineering

Artificial intelligence is concerned with understanding the *process* of cognition. Researchers "do" AI by building symbolic computing models, embodied in software programs, of information-processing tasks. The adequacy of these process models is judged by how well they mimic the corresponding natural behavior. As practiced today, AI can be divided into such subfields as robotics, computer vision, problem solving, machine learning, and NLP.

In this book, I will be concerned with the understanding and generation of natural language *text,* not with the wider (and much more difficult) problems of speech understanding. Viewed in this way, NLP is perhaps the most accessible approach to the understanding of cognition. First, essentially any knowledge can be described in natural language, which, after all, presumably developed primarily as a means of communicating information. Moreover, native speakers can agree that a description of an item of knowledge is appropriate, accurate, and complete. Since language is general purpose and adaptable, new kinds of knowledge are always describable.

Cognitive functions involve the processing of large amounts of symbolic information. NLP, a symbolic computing activity, allows us to study cognition without the distraction of hardware such as is found, for example, in machine vision or robotics. In NLP, we can use the research strategy of studying an existing solution to the problem of language use, viz., human language behavior. Finally, an empirical test of the solution is possible in real-world situations. We can try to design an intelligent, language-using artifact that interacts effectively with human users.

The processes that manifest themselves in intelligent behavior are elusive and very complex. While the study of these processes in AI is really only beginning, it seems clear that intelligent language behavior must be directed by application of large amounts of knowledge about the world: about people's beliefs, plans and goals; about machines and natural phenomena; about rules of thumb for special situations; and the like.

Knowledge engineering is the name given to the process of designing a system that, by use of carefully crafted structures of knowledge, exhibits a high level of intelligent performance in a solving a problem. The knowledge that a system requires to exhibit expertise in, say, a medical diagnosis needs to be extracted from the human expert and made explicit in the program. For NLP, we, the native speakers of a language, are the experts. Therefore, the knowledge-engineering task is to make explicit what we know about the meanings of words, how individual meanings contribute to a composite meaning structure, and how meanings are related to the real-world application domain. This book is an introduction to principles for explicating such knowledge to support the design of intelligent text-processing systems, and thus is written from a knowledge-engineering standpoint.

1.1.2 NLP and the Sciences of Language

Philosophy, linguistics, psychology, and the neural sciences have all contributed valuable insights to NLP. None of these fields, however, except for recent cognitive psychology, is oriented toward process models. Moreover, many of the research results, valuable as they are, are focused at much too fine a level of detail to be usable in an AI process model of the kind we want. The upshot has been that AI has had to develop its own distinctive approach to the study of language.

Philosophy (specifically logic) has traditionally been concerned with the relation between formal structures and meaning, and with *valid* inference methods for manipulating these structures. Human language users, on the other hand, appear to engage in a continuous, intricate process of *natural* inference as they attempt to understand what they are being told (cf., for example, Char72). They use contingent, plausible reasoning methods, based on their commonsense knowledge of the world. Thus, although there is an important place for purely logical methods in AI models, new, machine-usable methods of commonsense reasoning have had to be devised.

Cognitive psychology and psycholinguistics typically study use of language under carefully controlled experimental conditions. While experimental controls are essential for valid results, psycholinguists in many cases have had to constrain their experiments so severely that the language tasks undertaken often look extremely unnatural in comparison with ordinary reading or conversation (cf. Spir75, p. 11). The facts that emerge from such experiments, such as the detailed constraints on vision during reading, tend to be at too low a level to be incorporated directly into AI process models. At the other extreme, theories of memory structure and belief systems, two recent popular areas in cognitive and social psychology, tend to be so broad-brush, speculative, and lacking in detail that it is again difficult to see how to construct a process model exhibiting the desired behavior.

The neural sciences study the details of the structure and functioning of the human nervous system. Again, because of the complexity of the phenomena, the facts that emerge do not directly address cognitive processing issues. For example, neuroanatomists and neurophysiologists have discovered a number of facts about the stages of processing of visual data. Nearly all these facts, however, are really about *pre-processing,* the transformation of raw visual information into a (pre-)symbolic form. The nature of the higher-level processes of recognition and interpretation, and how the processed visual form is stored in long-term memory, remains mysterious.

Linguistics has been a major source of insight and examples for NLP. It must be said, however, that there has been a resistance to process models in the field. For their own methodological reasons, linguists have tended to assume that language can be studied in isolation from its use by an intelligent, problem-solving, knowledge-using entity. Linguistics and much of computational linguistics have been dominated by the search for pan-linguistic generalizations, and have emphasized grammatical, morphological, and phonological phenomena. The approach to NLP described in this book, on the other hand, has from the first tried to deal with the semantic and pragmatic details of actual language use, on a case-by-case basis. The overriding concern has been with issues of meaning and the application of knowledge, in various realistic language-processing tasks.

As a result of these factors, this brand of NLP has been pursued as a distinct research enterprise within AI. The primary research "tool" has been an introspective feeling for how language processing proceeds. These processes are extremely intricate, so the computer models tend to be very complicated. Thus, the research has largely been an engineering enterprise, but with a scientific purpose. Workers in NLP have been building larger and larger programs in an attempt to produce scientifically sound process models. NLP's methodological standpoint has definitely been toward the "theory development" (or "scruffy") side of Cognitive Science, as opposed to the "theory demonstration" (or "neat") side (cf. Mill78).

1.2 NLP Efforts in AI

As in other parts of AI, in NLP there is considerable controversy about research goals, methodology, and results. Nevertheless, it seems clear from its history that the main line of development in NLP has been in the elucidation and incorporation of more and more knowledge of disparate kinds in support of intelligent language-processing tasks.

1.2.1 Early Efforts

Early efforts in NLP were exploratory in nature, and sought to achieve only limited performance in tightly constrained tasks. Programs such as Weizenbaum's ELIZA (Weiz66) and Bobrow's STUDENT (Bobr68) stored information about their domains in an admittedly ad hoc manner, and scanned their input sentences (simple declaratives or interrogatives) for keywords or simple patterns. Since these predefined items were associated with known objects and relationships, appropriate responses could be generated on the basis of domain-dependent heuristic rules. Their domains were so limited that these systems were able to ignore many of the real problems of language understanding, and sometimes to achieve superficially impressive performance (cf. Weiz76).

Another well-publicized early effort in NLP was concerned with the machine translation of languages. Computational linguists hoped that the translation of texts between languages in a meaning-preserving manner could be effected solely on dictionary-driven, morphological or syntactic grounds. By 1960, however, it was clear (for example, BarH60) that automatic translation would require that the machine *understand* its input at a level comparable to a person. People's understanding is based upon huge amounts of world knowledge, and in particular upon the capability to make *inferences* about objects, intentions, relations, etc., that aren't lexically "there" in the input. Since no solid theories of inference or knowledge structuring were available at the time, attempts at producing practical translation systems were clearly premature. The next significant step in machine translation in AI did not occur until the early '70s and Yorick Wilks's English-French translation system, based upon his well-developed Preference Semantics representational and inferencing scheme (Wilk73, Wilk75).

The results of these early efforts were limited in large part because the programs really didn't "know" anything, in any reasonable sense.

1.2.2 Second-Generation Systems

The second-generation systems of the '70s and early '80s can be thought of as embodying a series of claims about the kinds of knowledge and the modes of processing needed by sentient language-using systems. The following brief descriptions of a few representative systems of this era make some of these claims explicit.

The program SHRDLU (Wino72) interacted with its user in the task of manipulating simulated toy blocks on a table. Developed by Terry Winograd at the MIT AI Laboratory, the system would accept statements and commands and answer questions about the state of its world and the reasons for its actions. The design of the system was based on the belief that language understanding requires an integration of syntactic, semantic, and reasoning processes. The particular approach to the problems of meaning and knowledge is based on the *Procedural Representation Hypothesis:* the meanings of sentences and their components are embodied in procedural structures (runnable programs), and language understanding is the means by which the appropriate procedures are activated in the hearer. Using an extensive model of its simple task domain and a large procedurally encoded grammar of English, SHRDLU was able to achieve unprecedented levels of performance. This was also the beginning of two of the mainstreams of further development in NLP: the elaboration of knowledge sources and the stress on integration.

The MARGIE (Memory, Analysis, and Response Generation in English [Scha75a]) system was developed by Roger Schank and his students Neil Goldman, Charles Rieger, and Christopher Riesbeck at the Stanford AI Laboratory to test two basic assumptions about language understanding. The first is the *Primitive Decomposition Hypothesis:* for any two sentences of identical meaning, in any language, a single underlying symbolic representation can be assigned, composed of structures encoded in terms of a relatively small set of "primitive elements." Conceptual Dependency (CD [Scha73a]) is the theory, with an associated primitive set, of how such representations are to be assigned. (Wilks's Preference Semantics is based on essentially the same principle.) The second claim is the *Understanding as Spontaneous Inference Hypothesis:* the process of understanding is at least partly that of computing the inferences that follow, in an asynchronous, forward-chaining manner, from a conceptual form representing the meaning of a sentence. Rieger (Rieg75) identified sixteen classes of such inferences, which were used in MARGIE to draw conclusions from, and form paraphrases for, English inputs presented to the system.

In the latter part of the '70s, the notion of understanding as *activation and search of various knowledge structures* was explored in the task of story understanding by the programs SAM (Scha75b), Ms. Malaprop (Char77), PAM (Wile78) and POLITICS (Carb79). Developed by Schank and his students at the Yale AI Project, SAM (Script Applier Mechanism) introduced the notion of the *situational script* as a means of structuring large amounts of information about stereotyped episodes, such as riding subways and eating in restaurants, in a form that would allow the machine to read stories involving such episodes. The program could then demonstrate its understanding by generating a summary or paraphrase of the story, by answering questions about it (Lehn78), or by translating a summary or paraphrase into another language (Carb81). A later development of SAM (Cull77) allowed the program to understand actual newspaper stories drawn from a variety of domains, such as car accidents and state visits. The system CADHELP (Cull82a), which will be used as a source of examples later in this book, also used the script formalism to allow a computer-aided design system to *explain* its operation to its user, including how to make and recover from mistakes.

In each of these cases, the scriptal knowledge structure was built up from *causal chains* (Scha77) interconnecting characteristic actions and states represented using the CD formalism. Access to the chains was managed through a hierarchical structure representing such items as the usual goal achieved by the episode, the actors and objects one could expect to find there, and the means by which *expectations* could be set up for further inputs in a story based on what had already been seen.

The program Ms. Malaprop used a representational idea similar to, but somewhat more general than, scripts, the so-called *frame system* (Mins75), to deal with stories about routine episodes, such as eating or painting a chair. Developed at Yale and later at Brown University by Eugene Charniak, Ms. Malaprop stressed issues of modularity and sharing among knowledge structures called "frames," interconnected into a system representing the typical ways that states change in a ritualized activity.

Wilensky's PAM system went beyond SAM and Ms. Malaprop by positing the existence of *plans* (Scha77) as a knowledge structure representing people's typical goals and the characteristic means they possess to achieve those goals. The program was able to handle a much wider variety of stories about goal-following individuals than earlier systems had, because of the flexibility provided by such knowledge structures.

Finally, Carbonell's POLITICS program took another step in the direction of new knowledge structures by basing the process of *interpreting* a story from various idiosyncratic or ideological viewpoints on a model of human *belief systems*. Such knowledge structures allowed the program to read newspaper headlines about foreign affairs and to produce different depictions of the motives and likely actions of the actors based, for instance, on a liberal or conservative ideology. Both PAM and POLITICS were developed while their authors were at Yale.

A dissatisfaction with the compartmentalized, modular organization of earlier systems led to the development of IPP (Lebo80) and BORIS (Dyer82). Lebowitz's IPP (Integrated Partial Parsing) used a variant of the script formalism to combine the processes of language analysis and knowledge structure search in a system that reads large numbers of newspaper stories about the domain of international terrorism. IPP incrementally forms various kinds of *generalizations* about the typical actors and activities in such stories (such as how the locale of the incident or nationality of the terrorist could predict what the demands might be). The generalization process (a kind of machine learning) forms an additional source of expectations that the system can bring to bear in an integrated fashion to deal with ongoing inputs.

Michael Dyer's BORIS represents the most ambitious attempt to date to combine a large variety of knowledge structures in a closely integrated manner to understand extremely complicated narratives about divorces, kidnappings, and other involved situations. The program combines elements of scriptal, planning, and belief-driven processing into a very general kind of knowledge structure called a TAU (Thematic Abstraction Unit). These contain an abstracted intentional structure based upon *planning failures,* including the plan used, its intended effect, why it failed, and how to avoid or recover from such failures in the future. It is interesting that many TAUs can be summarized by adages, such as "the pot calling the kettle black," which is really about the behavior pattern called "hypocrisy." TAUs can be used to index episodes across widely different episodic contexts and thus account for cross-contextual reminding phenomena. Both IPP and BORIS were developed at the Yale AI Project.

A parallel stream of research in NLP has been concerned with the extremely difficult problems of *conversational interaction.* Here, too, we see the interplay of control (i.e., integration) and structuring of knowledge. To illustrate three representative examples of conversational systems exhibiting these tendencies, I will briefly consider GUS (Bobr77a), ARGOT (Alle82) and ACE (Cull82b). GUS (Genial Understanding System) was developed at Xerox Palo Alto Research Center as a simulated airline reservation assistant, which could interact with its user to plan a trip. The main control notion is the idea of a *conversational frame,* a fairly rigid declarative structure used to guide the stages of the interviewing conversation, to propagate information needed later in the interaction, and to deal with discourse phenomena such as anaphora and ellipsis. The latter kinds of processing were facilitated by the ability to make expectations and defaults available with frames.

Allen's ARGOT is a conversational system under development at the University of Rochester that is intended to engage in extended dialogue with its user on a variety of topics. (Initially, the conversation is between a computer user and the machine's operator.) The model of conversational control the system uses is explicitly *plan-based;* that is, it is assumed that the participants are conversing so as to cooperatively achieve certain goals. Two different types of goals are used as the conversation proceeds: *task goals,* which represent desired states of affairs in the application domain (such as mounting a magnetic tape); and *communicative goals,* which represent discourse segments in which topics are introduced, previous utterances are clarified or elaborated, or the topic is modified. A difficult problem in maintaining a discourse is handled by a model of *time* (Alle81), which yields a general representation of events and acts. The representation is based on time intervals rather than a time-line, and thus allows a partially ordered set of time spans of indefinite duration.

ACE (Academic Counseling Experiment) also uses a goal-directed regime of processing to handle mixed-initiative conversations typical of a faculty advisor talking to a student. Tasks such as question answering, preregistration, and setting up a plan of study are intensely *purposive* ones, and thus the goal-following mode of conversational control is an appropriate one. Another feature of ACE is the extensive, detailed model of the academic curriculum and scheduling rules that the system consults to both analyze and generate answers and questions about proposed course offerings and schedules. (ACE's approach to conversational control and knowledge base management will be discussed in Chapter 10.)

1.2.3 Third-Generation Systems: A Look into the Future

I will use the term "third generation" for knowledge-based text-processing systems intended for a relatively long lifetime spent interacting with their users in complex applications. Although no such systems yet exist, it seems clear from the foregoing that their design will have to be based on the close integration of language understanding, generation, inference, and knowledge-base management; the commitment to robust interaction; and the application of a methodology transportable across knowledge domains.

My expectation of the characteristics of third-generation systems is conditioned by the so-called *Conceptual Information Processing* approach to NLP, as developed by Roger Schank, Robert Abelson and their students (and many others!). This view of NLP tries to take seriously the rather intuitive claim that the important processes in understanding and generation go on at a deep conceptual level, rather than, for example, at the more superficial levels of syntax and morphology. Thus, questions of memory structure and access, active problem solving, the formation of expectations, etc., are taken to be central to successful language use by humans, and therefore by the computer. AI research certainly includes other approaches to NLP, which share these attitudes to a greater or lesser extent. This book presents this one outlook on NLP in some depth, rather than surveying the alternative approaches. (But see, for example, Char76; Tenn80; Barr81; Wino83.)

A typical application for a third generation system of the sort we would like to design would be as an expert "consultant" for decision-makers in fields such as medicine, finance, geology, or manufacturing. A simple block diagram of a possible architecture for systems of this type is given in Diagram 1.1, in which a natural language interface accepts user queries, translates them into a meaning structure, and sends them on to some sort of expert reasoning system. The reasoning system contains symbolic representations for the knowledge of its application plus an inference mechanism for drawing conclusions based on that knowledge. The language interface, which maintains a model of the dialogue stream, also

Diagram 1.1
General Block Diagram for a Conversational System

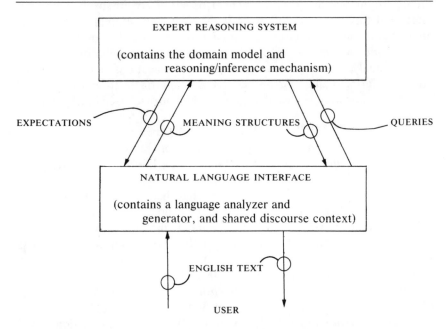

translates meaning structures produced by the reasoning system back into language. These structures might correspond to answers to the user's queries or to questions that the system might want to put to the user.

The reasoning system is also a source of two major kinds of assistance for the interface. As the repository for the structure of knowledge that models the application domain, the reasoning system can provide *expectations* about the conceptual form of the user's inputs, which the interface can use to make decisions about meaning. Since the interface and reasoner presumably share a representational vocabulary, the reasoning system can answer the interface's *questions* about the world model, to move it past various decision points.

How might a system be structured to allow all this functionality? A simple but serviceable model is sketched in Diagram 1.2. Certainly, the diagram's modular, hierarchical organization cannot correspond directly to how people use language. (This is true of Diagram 1.1, as well.) Our language use seems introspectively to be unitary: while speaking or listening, we don't have any sensation of cooperating or sequenced activities.

Part of the motivation for a modular approach is the usual software engineering one: modular systems, if developed properly, tend to be

Diagram 1.2
Functional Block Diagram for a Conversational System

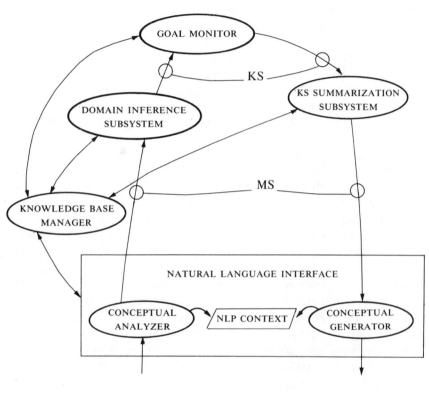

easier to implement, understand, and maintain. More important, however, language-processing tasks can be most easily understood as involving a coordination among a number of conceptually distinct processes.

Of the functions that seem to be at work in language processing, one of
the most important is the notion of *goal directedness*. A conversational
system, for example, must have not only things to talk about, but the *need*
to talk about them. I am positing a fundamental model of language
processing in which all the system's behavior, including in particular its
language behavior, follows from the processing of goals and subgoals.
This fits well with the hierarchical structure of Diagram 1.2, which has the
module labeled "Goal Monitor" at the top of the hierarchy. I envision a
system that is started with a goal supplied by its designer (such as "help
a student" or "interview a candidate").

The module labeled "Natural Language Interface" is the means by which the Goal Monitor communicates with the user of the system. In a general conversational system, this interface has three parts. The input process to the system is a *Conceptual Analyzer,* which maps NL strings into a representation of their *meaning.* These Meaning Structures (MSs) are examined by the other parts of the system in the current conversational context.

Often in NLP, the analysis process is modeled by a grammatical analyzer (or parser), which produces a syntactic description of the sentence. This description in turn is interpreted by a semantic analysis module that determines the meaning of the utterance. The particular model of analysis I will present is typical of the Conceptual Information Processing view of NLP. The analyzer's job is to form a meaning structure directly from an input sentence and, as such, it has no separate syntactic processing phase. Practically speaking, an analyzer that relies on an explicit grammar will clearly have trouble with ungrammatical or fragmented input, which users tend to produce. Our model uses syntactic and morphological cues solely to guide the extraction of meaning.

I don't want to sound dogmatic about this. Grammar-directed analyzers have had a long and productive history. Indeed, the commercially available NL interfaces are all based on grammatical processing. My intention is simply to present an alternative style of analysis in which the processing of grammatical features is handled at the level of the individual word. As we shall see, the result is a powerful, incremental, flexible analysis scheme that has good promise of robustness.

Meaning structures are mapped into NL strings by the reverse process of *conceptual generation.* The Conceptual Generator module shown in Diagram 1.2 is a MS-at-a-time generator. It receives a stream of conceptualizations from the module labeled "KS Summarizer," and generates a sentence per MS. Certain discourse-level phenomena, such as anaphora, are handled by the generator itself by reference to a data structure called the NLP Context. The conceptual generator process need not in any sense be the processing inverse of analysis (as is claimed in many purely syntactic approaches). Analysis is a bottom-up discovery of the concept in the mind of the speaker. Generation can be more top-down, since the idea to be expressed, or at least a major part of it, is initially available in a more or less complete form as generation begins. Like our analyzer, most of the generator's processing will be focused at the level of the lexicon; there's no explicit grammar present.

When the Goal Monitor wishes to "speak" to the user, it sends the Summarizer a Knowledge Structure (KS) that packages up its request and the expectations it has about what the user may say in response. The Summarizer extracts the concept(s) actually needing to be expressed and sends them on to the generator. It also "primes" the analysis module with the expectations.

Even in the presence of strong expectations, accounting for real language input in context often requires a process of inference to fill in missing information about entities, actions, and intentions. This is the job of the module labeled "Domain Inferencer" in Diagram 1.2. The completed meaning structure assembled by the inference module is then sent back to the Goal Monitor, to become the basis for further decisions. Inference processes needed for language understanding do not appear to be substantially different from general reasoning processes. Thus, the Domain Inference module to be discussed in this book is based upon a general-purpose backward-chaining Deductive Retriever, similar to the one described in (Char80).

Finally, the actual problem-solving process must have recourse to large amounts of both general-purpose and domain-specific knowledge. The speed with which the Domain Inferencer has access to needed facts, rules, plans, etc., will be a fundamental determinant on how fast the system can be made to respond. Therefore, I have identified an independent Knowledge-Base Manager in Diagram 1.2 that implements this crucial function.

Each chapter of this book discusses one or another of these important processes and the problems they present. I discuss solutions that either originated with myself or my students, or that represent substantial improvements on ideas proposed by others. Despite differences in detail, I believe that the overall approach taken here is representative of the approach of people who think this way.

1.3 Outline of the Book

This book is a broad introduction to principles for the design of practical, robust conversational systems, based on the insights of the Conceptual Information Processing approach to NLP. It can be studied simply as a text, but is better read in coordination with the software modules from the NLP Toolkit.* The book has two parts, corresponding to the overview sketch of Diagram 1.1. Part I describes a general-purpose understanding and generation interface that can communicate with a reasoning/database system dealing in conceptual structures. I develop a simple system for representing word and sentence meanings and items of world knowledge in symbolic form. Although this system is not nearly complete enough for direct use in an application, it does contain many representative ideas

---

* This package of Franz Lisp programs, available from Rowman & Littlefield, includes versions of the analyzer, generator, and representation design modules that are designed to be compatible with the text.

from the research literature, and can be handled cleanly by the analysis and generation algorithms presented. Throughout, I try to motivate the approach by presenting fragments of code from actual programs. If readers have access to the NLP Toolkit, they can actually try out the suggested modifications to these programs, and invent their own extensions.

Part II discusses the use of the interface with two existing second-generation text-processing systems, CADHELP and ACE. Since these systems are research vehicles, and thus moving targets, I will have much less to say about the actual implementation, focusing instead on design ideas for crucial pieces of such systems. The presentation culminates in a detailed discussion of a session with ACE, the counseling program. The description is intended to drive home to the reader the tremendous complexity of the phenomena that conversational systems must handle. Integration of knowledge and problem-solving power is clearly the most serious problem to be faced in the design of third-generation systems.

The topics to be covered include:

1. design principles for meaning and knowledge representations for the domain information shared by parts of a conversational system (Chapters 2 and 3);
2. techniques for achieving robust natural language understanding (Chapters 4 and 5);
3. methods for generating fluent natural language text, including explanations of knowledge structures (Chapters 6 and 7);
4. automated construction and management of domain knowledge bases (Chapter 8);
5. reasoning processes in support of understanding (Chapter 9); and
6. goal-directed conversational control (Chapter 10).

Readers wishing to gain an overview of the style of language processing presented here can read Sections 2.1 through 2.9, 4.1 through 4.3, and 6.1 and 6.2.

Part I
A General-Purpose Language-Processing Interface

2

An Introduction to Representation Design

2.0 The Representation Problem

In Chapter 1, a model of language processing was introduced in which the activities of a conversational system are directed by a series of goals. These goals are so-called "conceptual" structures representing desired states of the world, accompanied by sequences of subgoals and actions to achieve these states. The goal-following module also communicates with the language-processing interface (see Diagram 1.2) in a stream of conceptual structures. For the computer implementation to work properly, these structures must be well defined and interpreted in a consistent manner by the various system modules. Thus the *representation problem,* specifying the rules by which conceptual structures are formed and associated with utterances, is a key one for any language-processing scheme.

Let us clarify the meanings of these terms. By "conceptual," I mean that the structures have no direct association with the words or syntax of a natural language, but instead express a meaning or item of knowledge in a language-free form. Of course, the structures will be built up out of a primitive vocabulary that will, if only for purposes of readability by the designer, *look like* ordinary English words. The point is that this vocabulary is not directly used by the system to create sentences for presentation to the user.

By "meaning," I refer to the encoding of the *real-world content* of a sentence, in its conversational or textual context, in a symbolic structure constructed systematically according to the formal rules of some notational system. "Knowledge item" means the encoding of some unit of information (a fact or rule, perhaps) from a real-world domain, again in a formal structure. Let's agree at the outset that no computer representation of knowledge will ever contain the immediacy and richness of detail of any individual's knowledge: what we know is acquired, sometimes painfully, nearly always haltingly, by living and acting through many years. But we can hope, and this is an entirely different matter, to put enough content into the machine's internal forms that we can engineer the system for a reasonable level of interaction with us.

The ordinary formulas of algebra and arithmetic are familiar examples of a formal encoding. For example, the structure

$$3 + 1 = 4$$

is an encoding (or *representation*) of (part of) the meaning of the sentence "Four is the sum of three and one," using the notational rules of arithmetic. It is also an encoding of a fact from the knowledge domain of arithmetic. Similarly, the structure

$$x + y .= y + x$$

represents a rule (or theorem) from the same domain of knowledge (viz., commutivity): a form encoding a relation that is true of many sets of the primitive objects (the numbers) of the domain simultaneously.

Representing meaning and knowledge in a precise, computer-usable form presents a multitude of extremely difficult problems. Partly this is because of the huge number of different kinds of things that people know about, which expands at a dizzying rate. Another set of problems is caused by the expression of knowledge in language. The meaning of an utterance can be extraordinarily elusive, especially when the intent of the speaker and the beliefs of the listener are taken into account.

A final problem faced by designers of AI programs is to convince skeptics that the program actually "knows" something, in some reasonable sense. This problem is made more difficult by the fact that knowledge can be expressed at many *levels of detail*. For example, should a program that "knows" about arithmetic contain knowledge at the level of a second-grader or of a number theorist?

This chapter is an introduction to the design of representations suitable for automated language-processing systems. There is no complete agreement in AI on how this is to be done. Systems such as KL-ONE (Brac79), KRL (Bobr77b), Active Structural Networks (Norm75), Preference Semantics (Wilk75), Commonsense Algorithms (Rieg76), Conceptual Dependency (Scha73a), Semantic Network representations (e.g., Wood75; Hend76; Brac78; and Stef80), and the proposals based on the First-Order Predicate Calculus (e.g., McCa77; Haye77; and Film79) all take decidedly different approaches to representation. Nevertheless, certain simple notions about representation do seem to be shared by a number of the important schemes that have been proposed. These notions are included in this chapter.

First to be discussed are a number of features which, it is generally agreed, a representational scheme must incorporate. Next the syntax and semantics of a simple representational system are introduced, which will be used for illustrative purposes throughout the rest of the book. Then follow a number of examples of the system's use, as I try to motivate a process by which one can systematically cover the knowledge content of an intended application. Although far too simple for direct use in an application, the representational system is a reasonable starting point for thinking about the problem.

2.1   The Need for a Formal Representational System

A formal encoding of meaning is desirable for several reasons. Foremost is to make formal structures *unambiguous* and *unique*. If native speakers of a language agree that a sentence (or *surface form*) can have several meanings (i.e., that the sentence is ambiguous), it should be possible to assign a different formal structure to each reading. Similarly, if two sentences have disparate meanings, a distinct structure should be assignable to each. The requirement of uniqueness means that there can be exactly one formal structure for each possible meaning.

A representational system allowing unambiguous, unique assignments of structures to meanings has a number of advantages for an intelligent system. First, it automatically provides for *paraphrase equivalence* in natural language; that is, any number of surface forms having an identical meaning will be assigned the same, *canonical* meaning structure. Or, to express the same idea in the opposite direction, a canonical meaning structure can be the starting point for a number of paraphrases, different surface forms having an identical meaning.[1]

Formal structures are also necessary for the *inference* and *reasoning* processes that fill out and account for "real" (i.e., agrammatical, ellipsed, etc.) input in a conversational context. For example, a single inference process can be keyed to a single type of formal structure (as in Rieg75), instead of a process that has to recognize many surface forms of identical meaning.

Such structures can also allow the system to express its understanding of what it was told in a variety of modalities. In addition to generating NL strings, for example, the structures can be used to create a graphical display (e.g., Neim82) or cause some motor activity to take place (by driving a robot arm, for example Enge84). Finally, and perhaps most important, these structures can be used to represent the system's own knowledge of its domain of discourse, and of how to achieve its internal goals. Thus, the choice of a formal system to express what an intelligent system knows is a crucial one.

Representation is the process by which formal, surface-language-free structures are assigned to items of meaning and knowledge. In devising a representation for a sentence, we are always trying to answer the question "What are the facts?" We're not concerned with the *form* of the sentence, but with the real-world condition the sentence is trying to describe. Thus, I will constantly be playing with sentences, changing the form slightly, coming up with near paraphrases, etc., in an attempt to uncover the underlying meaning.

Clearly, no single representational system can be expected to span the myriad of knowledge domains in which an intelligent system might be called upon to work. Even a single domain has many levels of detail at which the system's knowledge might be encoded. For these reasons, *design principles* are needed to help formulate the representation of the knowledge in a domain to a sufficiently deep level.

The basis for the design rules suggested in this book is the idea of selecting certain key items out of the application domain. These key items are the units in which the rest of the domain knowledge is phrased. Once the domain knowledge has been expressed, the system designer can concentrate on the required language phenomena by using the techniques to be described in subsequent chapters. Choosing the "key" items, of course, is a matter of judgment: many different selections are possible. Thus, the critical representation process is an *engineering* one, since one needs to choose a set of key elements from many alternatives. The basis of the choice is the level of detail we wish to build into the system being designed.

This chapter presents a simple core representational system, called ERKS (Eclectic Representations for Knowledge Structures). It is intended primarily as a pedagogical vehicle for the examples and programs to come later. It can also be used as a starting point for thinking about representation in specialized domains.

2.2   Requirements on a Representational System

Consider the process of assigning a meaning structure (conceptualization) to a sentence (surface form). We need rules defining the interpretation of not only "normal" but "anomalous" sentences. In particular, ungrammatical and heavily ellipsed sentences must be handled. For example, a NL interface to a database retrieval system can expect to see queries such as

What E coast data I have

in which "E" is presumably a shorthand for "East," and the auxiliary "do" (not to mention the question mark) have been left out. Similarly, following execution of an imperative command such as

print values for los angeles and portland, in spring quarter 83, for blue widgets

the system might receive a shorthand input such as

boston, philadelphia, NYC

To handle such cases, the representation must direct the inference scheme, e.g., cope with variant syntax in an input or fill in defaults for items not mentioned.

Each word of a natural language has at least one distinct meaning. For a NL analyzer, the problem is to fit together the meanings carried by the words, in the order in which they appear in an utterance, into a single, well-formed structure representing the overall meaning. For a generator, the problem is to assign pieces of a large meaning structure to a set of words, and to ensure that the words are "spoken" in the correct order.

In an approach that is heavily concerned with word meanings, it is natural to think of the individual word as the language unit that carries the heaviest burden of meaning. (Phrasal units [cf. Wile80] can also be thought of as representing "words".) Information about word meanings, for use by the analyzer and generator, will be found in *dictionaries,* accessed when a word is seen in the input stream, or when it is to be inserted into the output stream.

Because of the basic requirement of paraphrase equivalence, any representation scheme must break down related word meanings to explicate underlying *common elements*. The simplest way to ensure that identical meanings of two different words are assigned an identical structure is to base the representational system on a collection of *primitive units,* each expressing some fundamental component of meaning shared by a number of the objects, actions, or relationships in the knowledge domain. The units are called "primitive" because their meaning is not further analyzed; all other meanings are encoded in terms of them. For example, the sentences beginning "John asked," "John advised" and "John admitted" share an element of communication, plus *nuances*.

The claim that word meanings can be broken down by similarities and nuances is the Primitive Decomposition Hypothesis (Scha73a; Wilk75):

> The basic strategy behind primitive decomposition of similar word meanings is to select an appropriate primitive element to encode the major similarity, then to add on auxiliary meaning structures, expressed in terms of other primitives, to represent the nuances.

I said that NL analyzers and generators needed to be concerned at bottom with associations, called *word senses,* between words and meaning structures. This suggests that both modules might be designed to operate in a data-driven manner, using processing information stored (as data structures) in dictionaries. Above the basic word-at-a-time processing scheme, sentences must be accounted for in context, which normally removes the surface ambiguities to be found in isolated sentences. The representation must be able, therefore, to express contextual features. In particular, it must be possible to build complete *knowledge structures,* since such structures encode various important kinds of context.

2.3   Introduction to ERKS

ERKS is an amalgam of ideas from Conceptual Dependency, Commonsense Algorithms, and Preference Semantics. Like these systems, ERKS is designed to explicate the relationships among parts of a conceptual structure. In particular, ERKS forms can be used to guide inference processes that fill in missing parts of structures expressing, for example, sentence meanings. The system is built on top of a collection of representational *primitives* that comprise a kernel of knowledge and inferencing power about classes of related entities. ERKS represents meaning at the level of *naive physics* and *psychology*. In this book, I will model the understanding of non-specialists, rather than the detailed knowledge possessed by specialists of various kinds. Thus, the primitives refer to the commonsense world of actors, objects, actions, states, and other relationships, as we see them every day. As we shall see, models posed in these terms are sufficiently expressive to support a reasonable level of conversational interaction.

2.3.1   The ISA–Hierarchy of the Core System

The basic classification scheme ERKS imposes on common sense knowledge is a straightforward one. First, there are *entities,* substantial, long-lasting physical objects (some of which, like people, are animate). The animate entities engage in *actions,* by which the state of the world (and other entities) is changed. The state of the world is expressed in terms of *relationships* among the entities and/or actions. Some of the relationships encode attributes of the entities (or changes in these attributes), some encode physical or abstract connections among several entities, and some encode a causal, temporal, or logical condition on several actions or states. Many of the relationships express *enabling* or *resultative* conditions of the actions. Thus, a basic use of the representational system will be to support the *inferring* of likely actions from current conditions in the world, or the changes in these conditions due to some act's being carried out.

The entities, acts, and relationships in ERKS are subdivided into a number of *primitive types*. These types are organized into the simple inheritance hierarchy (or ISA–hierarchy, so-called because elements grouped below a given element share, or inherit, certain attributes of that element) shown in Diagram 2.1.[2] For example, people and buildings share some of the properties of "physical objects:" they both have weight and physical extent. Thus, when we say "a person IS A physical object," what we mean is that certain things true of objects are also true of people; that is, people inherit relationships such as "has weight" from objects in general.

Organizing the primitive classes in this way is a standard, useful means

Diagram 2.1
A Tangled ISA–Hierarchy for ERKS

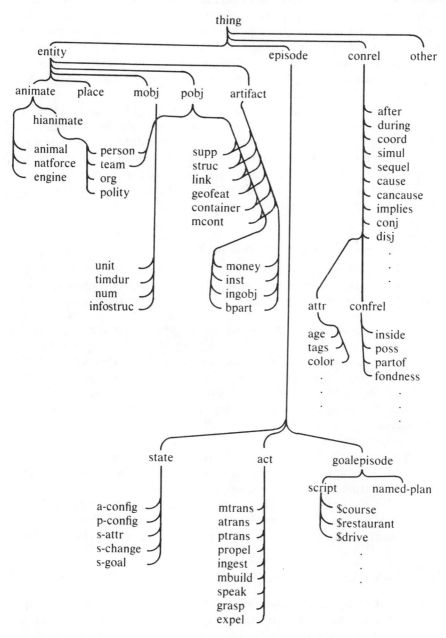

Note: Links are bi-directional as implemented

of controlling the inference processes that are concerned with reasoning about the primitive classes. The facts that both people and buildings have weight and extent can be stored once and for all with the primitive class called *pobj* (physical object) in Diagram 2.1, rather than separately for each class below it. Then, problem-solving processes trying to determine, for example, whether a person is a suitable "recipient" of a hitting action (as in the sentence "John punched Irving") can follow the bi-directional link (called the ISA link) between the primitive class *person* and *pobj* to get access to the necessary fact.

Note that the inheritance hierarchy of Diagram 2.1 is a *tangled* one: a primitive class may occur in the dependent subtree (called the ISA–subset) of more than one primitive class. For example, in Diagram 2.1, a person is simultaneously an example of a physical object and a "higher animate" entity. Thus, there may be more than one ISA link for the problem-solving process to follow given an instance of the primitive class. (Concrete implementations of such processes will be discussed in Chapter 3.)

2.3.2   Criteria for Selection of Primitive Items

The primitive types in Diagram 2.1 have been chosen to provide a reasonable balance among the following three informal representational criteria, in an ordinary commonsense domain of discourse:

1. *coverage:* Are all the important entities and phenomena represent-able? If certain facts or rules about some entities are not represented, and these structures are needed in some reasoning process, an essential component of the knowledge domain is missing.
2. *economy:* Can related entities, actions, etc., be classed together so that a reasonably small set of primitive types results? The rule of economy is simply to avoid providing unnecessary representations and inference machinery.
3. *orthogonality:* Do the types selected represent mutually exclusive sets of inferences? If the same or a similar inference can be drawn from structures based on two primitive types, they are probably better merged into a single class. By the same reasoning, objects need to be classified under separate primitive classes when a distinct rule of reasoning seems to be needed for one, but not the other.

2.4   ERKS in Lisp

Before describing the primitive types, we need to consider what meaning representations built up using the types will look like in the running programs. The example systems to be discussed later are programmed in the symbolic computing language Lisp, as is typical in AI applications.

Thus, the computer-usable versions of ERKS meaning representations are encoded as Lisp data structures.

The most popular format for structures of this kind is the "predicate with arguments" form familiar from mathematics. The predicates are the primitive types. Each predicate comes with a set of *mandatory* arguments, all of which must, in principle, be specified if the predicate expression is to correspond to a meaningful statement about the world. Note that the arguments may be items of meaning in their own right, i.e., they may also be predicate/arguments forms.

One possibility for such a predicate-arguments structure is the usual *indexed* one. Relations are expressed in a form such as $P(x,y,z)$, where the position or index of an argument tells how it fits into the relationship labeled by the predicate, or primitive type, P. Thus, in general, the form $P(x,y,z)$ expresses a different condition than $P(y,x,z)$, because the arguments x and y have different positions. Note that in an indexed form, all the positions must be filled even though many of the arguments may not be explicitly known, or may even be irrelevant.

Another possibility for a formalism, the one I will pursue in this book, is to *label* each argument explicitly. Structures built up from predicates whose arguments are labeled and may themselves be meaning structures are called *recursive, role-filler structures*. (These are also sometimes called "slot-filler" structures [Char80].) Role-filler structures are often used in AI representation work because they are easily understood, easily manipulated by symbolic computing languages such as Lisp, and economical of storage by comparison with indexed forms when many of the arguments are unknown or "don't cares."

In an ERKS role-filler structure, the predicates (types) come with a predetermined set of names, the roles, which label the required arguments, the fillers. The set of roles with required fillers constitutes the basic structural specification of the primitive type, and thus is called its *role-frame*. Note that the existence of labels means that the role-filler pairs may occur in any order. Clearly, a given argument of the type can occur exactly once, so there should be no more than one occurrence of a role among the role-filler pairs defined for an instance of a type.

The role-filler structures constructed in ERKS conform to the following syntax:

```
struct  —> (header body)
header —> "atom" | nil
body   —> role filler | role filler body
filler  —> struct | <struct>
role   —> "atom"
```

The syntactic class *struct* designates an ERKS role-filler structure. The class "atom" is a Lisp atomic form other than a number or the reserved symbols t ("true") and nil ("false"). The class <struct> is a pointer to an ERKS form rather than the form itself, e.g., an "atom" bound to an ERKS form. (So-called "atomized" forms are discussed further in Chapter 3.)

An example of a legal role-filler structure is

Example 2.1:
(ptrans actor (person persname (Marie) gender (fem))
    obj (inst insttype (wrench))
    from (nil)
    to (inside part (polity polname (Peoria))))

This means something like "Marie sent a wrench to Peoria," as we will see later. In (2.1), *actor, persname, gender, object, insttype, from, to, part* and *polname* are the roles. Of these, *actor, obj* and *to* belong to the role-frame of the primitive type *ptrans; persname* and *gender* to *person; polname* to *polity; part* to *inside;* and *insttype* to *inst.* (The complete role-frames for the primitive types discussed in this book are documented in Appendix I.)

All atoms to the immediate right of a left parenthesis designate either primitive types, or a selection from a predefined *contrast set* specified for a particular role of a primitive type. Thus, for example, the filler of the *gender* role of the type *person* in (2.1) has been selected from the set {(masc), (fem), (other)}. That is, all persons must have one of these genders.

The structures

(ptrans actor)
(ptrans actor ( ))

are illegal, the first because no filler is given for the role *actor*, the second because no primitive type is specified in that filler. However, structures such as

(ptrans)
(nil)
(ptrans actor (nil))

are legal. In the first, no role-filler pairs are specified at all. (All the legal roles of this primitive type are known implicitly through the role-frame, however, as discussed in Chapter 3.) In the second, the special primitive type *nil,* which stands for "don't care," "unknown" or "irrelevant," is used to create an instance of the "null" conceptualization (nil). In the third, the null conceptualization is given as the filler associated with the *actor* role.

To manipulate ERKS role-filler structures, we need a way of uniquely specifying each filler in the structure. A role *path* is a list of roles leading from the top level of a structure to a filler nested somewhere inside it. In (2.1), the path (to) specifies the filler (inside part (polity polname (Peoria))); the path (to part polname) specifies (Peoria); and the null path ( ) specifies the entire role-filler structure.

I said that the role-frame of a primitive type specifies a *mandatory* set of roles. These define paths to fillers that conceptually must be present for the ERKS structure to have meaning. Often certain fillers will not be known at the time the ERKS form is created. The associated paths, such as (actor surname) in (2.1), are treated as if the filler pointed to was present, and had *nil* as its type. That is, the structure is assumed to have the form:

(ptrans....actor (persname....surname (nil)...)......)

I adopt this default so that unknown and irrelevant slot filler pairs can be left out of the structure, thus minimizing storage needs for ERKS structures in the running program.

It is important to understand that an ERKS structure such as (2.1) is really only a *description* of a real-world entity, action, or relationship, such as would be built by a conceptual analyzer on the basis of dictionary definitions for generic concepts associated with words. For example, the same description is built for the word "John" each time it is seen in an input, even though different persons might actually be meant in different utterances. The process of understanding consists, in part, of linking such descriptions with the real objects being described.

For this reason, a structure such as (2.1) is called a *surface-semantic form*. When the surface structure is actually understood (or "absorbed"), the surface form for "John" is replaced by a pointer to the memory structure containing what is known about the real-world referent of "John," say JOHN310. Similar statements can be made about "wrench," "Peoria," and "ptrans." Thus, an ERKS form is a shorthand description, expressed in the core notation, for a deeper memory structure (which will be much richer, in general).

2.5 The Maximal Inference-Free Paraphrase

Now that we have a reasonable idea of what a meaning structure looks like, I can begin describing how one goes about forming such structures for sentences. The techniques I will propose can be sketched as follows:[3]

1. Meaning structures should be constructed from the *bottom-up* (in a sense to be defined). Thus, simple structures can be composed into more complex ones.
2. The meaning structure for a sentence should be derived from an "equivalent" set of sentences called the *maximal inference-free*

paraphrase (MIFP). The MIFP yields a set of assertions called *nuances* that serve to distinguish sentences of similar meaning.

3. The knowledge content of an intended application domain should be embodied in a set of sentences called the *model corpus*. Each sentence should be representative of a large class of "equivalent" sentences, varying, for example, only in the entities mentioned.

4. The model corpus should be formed from a *base sentence,* from which related sentences are derived by a process of *continuous deformation*.

A meaning representation for a given sentence is normally derived from what I will call a *maximal inference-free paraphrase* (MIFP) of the sentence. In an MIFP, one tries to re-express the sentence in the most verbose or circumlocuted form possible, expanding it in terms of clauses (assertions) based on the primitive types. The conjunction of the clauses is to be a restatement of the "exact" meaning of the original sentence. (The word "paraphrase" has a stricter meaning here than in ordinary usage.) By this I mean that none of the clauses should involve a *substantive inference* from the meaning of the sentence. They should only re-express what seems to be contained in the words of the sentence themselves.

By "substantive inference" I mean an assertion drawn from the real-world context surrounding the utterance, or an auxiliary concept formed from the hearer's mental model or belief system. "Surface semantic" inferences based on the ordinary meaning of words are, however, legitimate parts of an MIFP. For example, if I hear

Ronald took an aspirin from the bottle and ate it,

I am entitled to conclude on surface-semantic grounds that "it" refers to "aspirin" rather than "bottle." This is because the ordinary meaning of "eat" demands an ingestible object, and aspirins are ingestible while bottles are not. On the other hand, concluding that Ronald did this because he had a headache is a substantive inference. I need to know the real-world facts to draw the conclusion.

Clearly, the selection of referents for words such as "it" must be guided by semantic demands, rather than syntactic or morphological features. For example, the sentence

Ronald took the wrapper from the sandwich and ate it,

has an identical syntactic structure to the above, but the referent of "it" is different.

Having formed the MIFP, one selects the clause that expresses the "main" or most important component of the event being described as the *kernel* of the representation. The other clauses function as *nuances* serving to distinguish this particular event from others of the same type.

Obviously, the point of maximizing the number of nuances formed from a given sentence is to maximize the total number of assertions that can be distinguished.

Thus, for example, in the sentence

(1) Olivia punched Muhammed in the nose.

the following clauses all seem to be reasonable components of an exact paraphrase of (1):

(1a) The female person named Olivia propelled a hand into physical contact with a nose.
(1b) This event was forceful.
(1c) The event transpired in the past.
(1d) The hand was in the form of a fist.
(1e) The hand was part of Olivia.
(1f) The nose was part of Muhammed.
(1g) Olivia was facing Muhammed, and was within arm's reach when this event took place.

(There are several others, of course, but let's keep things simple for now.) However, assertions such as:

(2a) Olivia was mad at Muhammed.
(2b) Muhammed had done something to make Olivia punch him.
(2c) Both parties were wearing clothes when the event took place.

are clearly *inferences* from the described behavior; that is they are only plausibly true. It's quite possible, for example, that the two were only rough-housing, and Olivia wasn't mad at all. (If we knew that both were football players warming up for a game, we might infer that they were, in fact, getting mad at the other team.) In (2b), perhaps Olivia was frustrated for some reason, and Muhammed was the first person to come along. The wearing of clothes, finally, is a *social* fact having nothing to do with incidents of punching.

A good rule of thumb for distinguishing the exact parts of an MIFP from assertions that involve a substantive inference is the so-called "but" test (Scha75a). In using this test, we say that a statement Y must be part of the MIFP for a statement X if the statement "X but not Y" is absurd. Thus, we can have

John drove to New Haven, but he didn't get there

but not

John arrived in New Haven, but he didn't get there.

In the former, "but" is functioning to point out that the usual real-world inference from "drive" isn't valid. The latter makes no sense at all, unless "there" refers to some place other than New Haven. The "but" test clearly distinguishes (1a–g) from (2).

Of the parts of the exact paraphrase of Sentence (1), the first, (1a), can be taken to be *basic* for most purposes, since it is the one from which the most interesting consequences flow. Looking at (1a), one can speculate on the likely reasons for such an episode, how Muhammed might react, how relations between the two may change, etc.

Speculations of these sorts for the other components of the MIFP lead to much less interesting conclusions. It's nearly always the case, for example, that people have hands and noses. Thus, I will make (1a) the kernel of the representation of (1). The other assertions are nuances of various kinds.

Exercise I

Write down the MIFP for the following sentences:

1. Olivia kissed Muhammed on the cheek.
2. Olivia kissed Muhammed.
3. Olivia tapped Muhammed on the shoulder.
4. Ronald pushed the button.
5. Ronald hit the ball into center field.
6. Ronald threw the ball to Olivia.

The kernel assertion for Example 1, "Olivia propelled a hand into contact with a nose," can be reasonably represented in terms of the primitive type *propel,* which underlies an action in which an intentional or natural/mechanical actor applies a force to an object, with the possibility of a physical state change to it and/or another object.[4] The verb "punch," in this sense of the word, designates a human hand as the object to which the force is applied, and clearly indicates that the hand came into *contact* with another object. (There are other possibilities: the verb "swing at" or "throw at" are neutral about contact.)

Working on the representation of (1) from the bottom up, I need representations for the entities "Olivia," "Muhammed," "fist," and "nose." In ERKS formalism, these would respectively be:.

HUM0:
(person gender (fem) persname (Olivia))

HUM1:
(person gender (masc) persname (Muhammed))

BP0:
(bpart bptype (grasper))

BP1:
(bpart bptype (proboscis))

based on the ERKS types *person* and *b(ody)part*. The symbols HUM0, etc., name the meaning structures (which I will also loosely call *concepts* or *conceptualizations*). This allows them to be reused, as I will show. The (not entirely serious) choice of "grasper" and "proboscis" for the *bptype* fields of BP1 and BP2 was made to emphasize that the representation should not contain words, but only indicators of function or form that are true of many entities simultaneously. Monkeys, men, and robots, for example, all have functional grasping parts. (A special case where words need to be stored in an ERKS form occurs with "names," which are presumably unique labels for an entity.)

In BP0 and BP1, note that fields such as *bptype* amount to a downward extension of the ISA-hierarchy of Diagram 2.1. The primitive type is being associated with an ISA-subset whose elements are mutually exclusive, and which together account for all the real-world entities in the parent type. The point of having *bptype* around, of course, is that many of the inferences associated with eyes, noses, hands, etc., are conveniently associated with the superset class, where they need to be stored only once.

With this said, I can propose a simple representation for (1a) as follows:

EVNT0:
(propel actor HUM0 object BP0 to (physcont part BP1))

(Forms such as EVNT0 are called "partially atomized," since they contain some labeled role-fillers representing meaning structures which potentially occur in more than one place in the representation.) In the role-frame of a *propel*, the (actor) path is expected to be animate and the (obj) path is filled with a physical object. The filler of the (to) path in a propel-concept is required to be a primitive type expressing a relationship of *physical configuration* (e.g., location, orientation, or contact) between two objects.

Of the nuance assertions, the first two, (1b) and (1c), clearly function to modify or comment on the event expressed in the kernel assertion. Assertion (1b) allows us to distinguish (1) from something like "Olivia tapped Muhammed on the nose." (It is interesting that the prepositions "in" and "on" seem correlated with the expected degree of forcefulness of the associated *propel* events.) For the moment, I'll simply incorporate (1b) and (1c) into the representation as follows:

EVNT0:
(propel actor HUM0 obj BP0 to (physcont part BP1)
  time (PAST) quantity (FORCEFUL))

The assertion "hand was in form of a fist," (1d), is an example of an *attributional* concept, one in which an intrinsic state or attribute of an object (such as color, weight, extent, etc.) is described. The attribute *partform* (i.e., "form of a part") is used to express the state of an object that is "malleable" in some sense; that is, it can take on several forms. A version of an attributional concept expressing (1d) is

STATE0:
(s-attr actor BP0 attr (partform val (fist)))

The primitive type *s-attr* is used in STATE0 to encode a *stative attributional* assertion about the object in the (actor) path, along the attribute dimension in the (attr) path. The (attr val) filler specifies the particular "value" of the attribute for this object. (I will have more to say about this below.) In STATE0, the filler "fist" is *not* an English word, but represents a selection from the contrast-set for the *partform* role, when expressed in conjunction with a particular object that is an intrinsic part of another, in this case a hand. (Other choices might include "flat," "cupped," "pointing," etc.) Note that this nuance allows us to distinguish verbs such as "slap" and "poke" from "punch."

Assertions (1e) and (1f) are typical examples of *physical configurational* concepts. Configurational concepts express a relationship between two or more entities. In this case, the relation is "physically part of;" that is, one object is attached to another in such an integrated way that a severe negative change in the physical state of health (for animate entities) or usability (for artifactual objects) is likely to occur if the two are separated. An ERKS representation for (1e) is as follows:

STATE1:
(p-config con1 BP0 con2 HUM0 confrel (partof))

Here, the *confrel* slot contains the particular conf(igurational) rel(ation-ship) encoded by the form, viz., "partof." This nuance allows us to distinguish (1) from such statements as "Olivia hit Muhammed with a rock."

Example (1f) is the same type of configurational as the above. Example (1g) is a *composition* of physical configurationals. I will have more to say about these when I consider relations among conceptualizations.

Once the MIFP has been encoded in this way, I can form "the" representation of sentence (1) in the following ERKS structure:

(3)
Olivia punched Muhammed in the nose
(ms kernel EVNT0 nuance1 STATE0 nuance2 STATE1 nuance3 . . .)

This is a form based on the special *m(eaning) s(tructure)* primitive, which is used in setting up dictionary entries for words in the analyzer and generator. Note that the organization allows a search process, looking, for example, for a word sense to express a concept, to make increasingly

.fine-grained discriminations. First, one would look at the kernel form, then at (nuance1), (nuance2), etc. One can easily order the nuances by counting up the number of word senses that the associated form distinguishes from one another.

Exercise II

Make up an ERKS meaning structure for each of the examples of Exercise I.

To make meaning structures such as (3) easier to understand, I will mostly use a "collapsed" form based on the kernel structure. The collapsed form for (3) is

(4)
(propel actor HUM0
　　obj (bpart bptype (hand) partform (fist) partof HUM0)
　　to (physcont part (bpart bptype (nose) partof HUM1)))

Here the stative *partof* and *partform* conceptualizations have been "summarized" by making the associated *confrel* and *con2* fillers into a role-filler pair associated with the respective *con1* filler. For example, the filler

(bpart bptype (nose) partof HUM1)

is a shorthand for "the nose which is part of Muhammed," i.e., (1f). The role *partof* doesn't belong to the role-frame of *bpart*. This is just a convenient way of reducing structures like (3) to an economical form.[5]

2.6　Building a Model Corpus

The distinctions that a representation designer wishes to have appear in the language behavior of the system are the key to the richness of the required representation scheme. In the previous section, I contrasted the meanings of such verbs as "slap," "punch," "tap," and "poke" to motivate the nuances chosen. Clearly, this is necessary if one wants the language-processing interface to understand *something* about the differences among these kinds of events.

A systematic way to approach this task is to accumulate a *model corpus*. This is a collection of sentences or sentence fragments that, taken as a whole, samples as large a fragment as possible of the knowledge content of the domain of interest. The corpus obviously cannot contain *everything* that might be said about the domain. It's enough to include sentences that are representative of entire classes of inputs (varying, for example, in the entities mentioned).

The designer will normally want all or a large part of the corpus to be understandable/generatable by the language-processing interface. The process by which one sets down a corpus for a domain is the analogue of the knowledge-extraction process undertaken by designers of expert systems of the more usual variety (for instance, Haye83; Weis84). In language-processing systems it is quite possible for the expert informant and the system designer to be the *same* person. The reason for this, and the motivation for the model corpus, is simply the observation that if some item of knowledge is important to us, we can normally say it. Indeed, speakers of a language can usually find a number of ways of expressing the same idea. In a functioning system, the model corpus grows continually as its designers gain experience, although, one hopes, at a slower and slower rate as time goes on. A good corpus is the key to domain coverage.

It's useful to build up the model corpus in a *bottom-up* manner. By this I mean that the sentences that are composed describe knowledge items of increasing complexity. Here, I'm defining complexity in terms of the level and subtree relations among primitive types as indicated by the ISA–hierarchy and by the role-frames of the types. Then, *representative* sentences from one layer can be used as units at the next higher level. At each level, a number of near and exact paraphrases of each knowledge item should be formed and the distinctive nuances noted.

Working in a bottom-up manner, one first writes down descriptive sentences concerning the entities that appear in the knowledge domain. Next one writes sentences that describe attributes of these entities. Considering these stative assertions, one then makes up sentences describing the entities in action. The actions would be expected to affect one or more of the selected states. Similarly, a given action may have a number of enabling state conditions that need to be in force before the action can occur. (I have in mind here a simple analysis of cause/effect relations among acts and states, which I will get to later.) Finally, composite relations among the acts and states beyond simple cause and effect need to be expressed in (typically complex) sentences. For a particular domain, the corpus will range in size from a minimum of several hundred sentences.

When a reasonable corpus has been collected, the primitive decomposition process can begin. The entities, actions, etc., described in the model corpus are divided into a number of classes on the basis of *conceptual similarity*. The notion of similarity is very difficult to pin down exactly. The overall idea is to look for classes of words that seem to be related by similarities among the *inferences* and *implications* they allow one to draw. Often, for reasons of economy, the representation designer follows a "cut-and-try" process, not creating two primitive classes from a single prior one until some detail of language behavior or inference forces the issue. The initial subdivision of the domain, however, can be guided by some simple rules of thumb.

For example, when considering a primitivization of a collection of entities, these are some useful rules:

1. If animate entities are being classified, is there any systematic difference in the characteristic *intentions* among classes of actors? Are there "heroes" and "villains," are the actors "altruistic" or "greedy," "passive" or "active"?
2. If artifactual (i.e., man-made) objects are being contrasted, are there systematic distinctions in the way these objects are *used* by actors, that is, a distinction by *function?*
3. If locations are being examined, are there important differences in the *activities* that characteristically happen there?

For each of the commonsense types shown in Diagram 2.1, a useful distinction (usually in form or function) exists which allows one to group entities together. It's often useful to express the distinction in an ERKS structure called the *discriminator,* and to store the discriminator as the first fact or rule about the new class. The discriminator can then be inherited by the class's ISA–subset.

For example, I might discriminate intentional actors from artifacts by noting that "actors have goals," or, to put it another way "actors want things." In a world full of interacting people, distinctions based upon likely goals are almost certain to be useful. In particular, knowledge of such goals will very likely be strong *predictors* of what the actors are likely to do in given circumstances. Note that discriminators automatically provide an orthogonal inference about two classes: for example, I can say that "an artifact *cannot* want things."

The process of subdivision continues until the distinctions apparent in the model corpus have all been expressed in an ERKS structure, each attached to a primitive type. The corpus has thus been effectively *annotated,* i.e., marked by which sentences contributed to which distinction. It will turn out that characterizing the corpus, including its nuances and near-paraphrases, in this way *guarantees* that any sentence expressing one or more of the distinctions can be understood or generated by the language interface. Thus, the reasons for the system's misunderstanding or not understanding an input can be directly traced to a distinction that was not made, or that was incorrectly made, in the corpus.

2.7 A Simple Corpus

To make these ideas more concrete, let's examine a simple corpus of related sentences built up from a *single* primitive type. This illustrates several corpus-design principles of general utility. The corpus is given in Figure 2.1, in which the sentences all describe *movement* events. The underlying primitive actional is called *ptrans,* standing for p(hysical)

Figure 2.1
A ptrans Corpus

---

1) Olivia went to Hartford

2) a car went to Hartford

3) Olivia left Hartford

4) Olivia went into Hartford

5) Olivia drove to Hartford

6) Olivia took a book to Hartford

7) Olivia sent Muhammed to Hartford

8) Olivia sent a book to Hartford

9) Olivia sent Muhammed to Hartford with a book by car

---

trans(fer) of location of a movable object by an intentional actor, perhaps by some interconnecting path.

The bottom-up design methodology tells me that I should try to represent the entities mentioned first. Thus, I have my two people from before, a car, a book, and a city:

HUM0: "Olivia"
(person persname (Olivia) gender (fem))

HUM1: "Muhammed"
(person gender (masc) persname (Muhammed))

VEH0: "car"
(veh vtype (car))

MCONT0: "book"
(mcontainer mconttype (book))

POL0: "Hartford"
(polity poltype (munic) polname (Hartford))

Here are occurrences of three new primitive types for entities, *veh,* standing for vehicles (self-propelled artifacts) of various kinds; *mcontainer,* representing physical containers of mental information (ideas), such as books, clocks, street signs, and blackboards; and *polities,* self-contained political units such as municipalities, states, provinces and nations.

I hope it's clear that I am not inventing a primitive type per word seen! The motivation for the vehicle type, for example, is the simple observation that there are many man-made objects in the world whose *function* is to transport goods and people from place to place. Many of these objects use specially designed paths, called "roads," "tracks," "canals," or "air routes." (These are classed under a primitive type called *link*.) Similarly, there are many objects whose main function is to act as repositories for information, which is available to higher animate actors on demand. The information they contain is the most important thing about them for normal purposes—more important, for example, than physical differences such as exist between wrist watches and Big Ben. Thus I have chosen to focus on this aspect of objects of this sort as the ERKS discriminator for the type.

Before discussing the representation of *ptrans* events, I will describe the required role-frame of roles that define the type, which is shown in Figure 2.2. The role names are self-explanatory, except perhaps for *inst* or *mode*. The *inst* role is intended to specify the *means* or inst(rumentality) by which the action of movement is accomplished. The instrumentality is normally a supporting action(s) co-occurring with the main action. Thus, (inst) is filled with a simple or complex action, i.e., by a structure of type *episode* or one of its subset types.

The *mode* role is intended to store the *modality* stated for the event in the sentence: whether it is asserted to have occurred, to not have occurred, to be only potential, to be not possible, etc. Modal specifications are typically associated with words such as "not," "can," "cannot," "might," and the like. The difficult problems caused by modal words cannot be addressed adequately in an introductory book like this. I will simply insert a tag into the ERKS form to indicate that such a word was seen. Examples of both (inst) and (mode) fillers occur in the corpus.

Each role in Figure 2.2 is shown with a *constraint* expression, involving predicates on one or more of the other primitive entity types. The types used include *simple animate,* which underlies self-moving entities such as animals; *higher animate,* for such entities as persons and groups of persons; *forces,* either natural (such as "the wind") or mechanical ("jet engine"); *geo(logical/graphical) feat(ures),* such as mountains or rivers; *episodes,* simple or complex actions; and *p-configs,* physical relationship configurations. The constraint "movable" is meant to express such complex ideas as "should not be part of or physically attached to something," "not completely immobile" (as are *geofeat* entities), or (very difficult to determine!) "not too big to be moved by the current actor." Very often the constraints on role fillers may involve arbitrary computation (by a reasoning system, for example), in addition to surface-semantic information.

I've taken Sentence 1 from Figure 2.1 as the *base sentence* in the

Figure 2.2
Role-Frame of ptrans

Role	Description	Constraint
actor	animate initiator of the event	simple animate, higher animate or natural/mechanical force
obj	the object moved	object must be "movable," thus for example, not a geo(graphical) feat(ure)
to	location-predicate about destination relation	one of the p(hysical) conf(igurationals)
from	location-predicate about initial location	see (to)
via	path along which motion took place	type link
inst	instrumentality of motion	type episode
time	relative time specification	type times
mode	modality of the event (asserted, negated, potential, etc.)	type modes

corpus because it is extremely simple. An MIFP for this sentence might go as follows:

> It is asserted to be the case that Olivia transported herself to the general area (i.e., to at least the proximity) of the polity named Hartford, coming from some *unspecified place* by an *unspecified means,* at a time in the past of *now.*

An ERKS form for this expression is as follows:

EVNT1:
(ptrans time (times time1 (:past))
      mode (modes mode1 (:t))
      actor HUM0
      obj HUM0
      to (prox part POL0)
      from (nil)

via (nil)
inst (nil))

In EVNT1, we see that the (actor) and (obj) fillers are the same, viz., "Olivia." We have been given a filler for (to), but not for (from), (via) or (inst). Thus, the latter have been filled with the "empty" filler (nil). (Because of the standard default for ERKS forms, they could just as well have been left out of the representation altogether.) The time slot has been filled with a distinguished filler (:past), indicating the relative time occurrence of EVNT1 with respect to *now*. (For problems with representing time, see Alle81 and McDe82.) Here I will simply tag the ERKS form with an indication of the time relation that was seen. Thus, I need to allow for the occurrence of other relative-time specifiers such as perfective ("has gone") and progressive ("was going") by providing more time-role names for the *times* type. Similarly, the distinguished filler (:t) has been included to indicate that the speaker of the utterance is asserting that EVNT1 actually occurred.

How can I get more sentences for our corpus, starting with the base form, Sentence 1? One thing to do is to *deform* the structure by introducing new fillers for the slots, or by providing fillers for *empty* slots in the structure. Many instances of the former kinds of deformation do not lead to interestingly different sentences. "Muhammed went to Peoria" is not significantly different from Sentence 1 for representation purposes. But if I say "the car went to Hartford," Sentence 2, I get a new structure that is different from (1) in that *the intentional actor has not been named,* i.e., the filler of (actor) is (nil).

Interesting things happen when one starts filling empty slots in structures such as EVNT1. If one chooses to focus on where Olivia came *from,* he might get Sentence 3. Here, the filler of the (from) slot is (prox part POL0) and the (to) slot is empty. Similarly, if one changes the predicate relation mentioned in the (to) slot, he might get Sentence 4, "Olivia went into Hartford," where the filler becomes (inside part POL0). (The *inside* type denotes a containment relationship.)

A particularly rich source of examples arises when we start to fill the (inst) slot in structures such as EVNT1. For example, in Sentence 5, "Olivia drove to Hartford," I have implicitly added to the MIFP of (1) a clause such as "by Olivia's driving a car." That is, I've specified an action, with a car and Olivia as participants, which is in support of the movement action (which I'm taking to be the kernel of both Sentences 1 and 5). Note that I could have gotten almost the same effect with the sentences "Olivia went to Hartford by car," or "Olivia was taken to Hartford by car." The only distinction here is that Olivia is not explicitly named as the intentional actor of the *ptrans,* that is, the driver, as she is in Sentence 5. In these cases, (actor) would be filled with (nil).

A simple representation for "driving car" would add the nuance that "car propelled itself" in the (inst) slot of EVNT1:

EVNT2:
(propel actor VEH0 obj VEH0)

with the same time/modal information as EVNT1. Actually, the representation of such highly structured, complex events as "driving" is better handled using the primitive type *goal-episode*. I will defer discussion of this until Section 2.10.

Another nuance that might be considered is "Olivia was inside the car," which can be expressed as:

STATE0:
(p-config confrel (inside)
   con1 HUM0 con2 VEH0)

Now consider what happens when I deform the (obj) role in EVNT0. I might get something such as Sentence 6, "Olivia took a book to Hartford." Here, I can realize the (obj) role with MCONT0, the mental-container representing the book.

However, an MIFP for Sentence 6 is really something more like "Olivia transported *a book and herself* to Hartford." Looking at the paraphrase in this way brings up what is known as the *group-object/coordinated action* dilemma. The dilemma arises from the need to choose between a representation in which "Olivia and book" are considered to be a group-object as the filler in an event; or whether *two separate, coordinated events,* "Olivia took book" *and* "Olivia took herself" are to be preferred.

My solution to this dilemma is derived from the basic requirement of *representational continuity*. Small changes in meaning should not lead to large changes in the meaning structure. The sentence "Olivia went to Hartford and Muhammed went to New York" describes two separate events that are mentioned together for some unspecified reason. In terms of ERKS representation, the form of this would be

REL0:
(coord con1 (ptrans actor HUM0
            obj HUM0
            to (prox part POL0))

      con2 (ptrans actor HUM1
            obj HUM1
            to (prox part POL1)))

(HUM1 and POL1 are "Muhammed" and "New York," respectively.) This is an instance of a *coord*, the first of the primitive types expressing a relation between *episodes* rather than entities, a "coordination" of events. The sentence "Olivia went to Hartford, and Muhammed did too," also seems to describe separate events.

The change in meaning between this and "Olivia and Muhammed went to Hartford," or "Olivia went to Hartford with Muhammed" (in which Muhammed's intentionality is being suppressed for some reason) seems to be too small to justify a change in representation to something like:

EVNT3:
(ptrans actor HUM0
    obj (group con1 HUM0 con2 HUM1)
    to (prox part POL0))

in which the primitive type *group* is being used to indicate that a set of entities is to be considered as a unit for some purpose. Consideration of such coordinate constructions as "Olivia ran down the hall and jumped out the window," also gives support to the coordinated-actions approach to coordinate constructions. In this book, I shall prefer representations such as REL0 to EVNT2 when there is a question.

Now consider Sentence 7, "Olivia sent Muhammed to Hartford." Here, the MIFP is something like "Olivia did some unspecified action, which caused Muhammed to transport himself to Hartford." This is another example of a *con(ceptual) rel(ationship)* between events, represented as

REL1:
(cause con1 (episode actor HUM0)
    con2 (ptrans actor HUM1 obj HUM1 to (prox part POL0)))

In *cause* concepts, (con1) is taken to be the antecedent event, (con2) the consequent. Sentence 8 has an almost identical representation, except that the "book," MCONT0, is being transported, and we don't know the actor of the *ptrans:*

REL2:
(cause con1 (episode actor HUM0)
    con2 (ptrans actor (nil) obj MCONT0 to (prox part POL0)))

Finally, Sentence 9, "Olivia sent Muhammed to Hartford with a book by car," mentions the *actor* and *inst* of the imbedded *coord:*

REL3:
(cause con1 (episode actor HUM0)
    con2 (coord con1
                (ptrans actor HUM1 obj MCONT0 to (prox part POL0)
                    inst (propel actor VEH0 obj VEH0))
                con2
                (ptrans actor HUM1 obj HUM1 to (prox part POL0)
                    inst (propel actor VEH0 obj VEH0))))

One can continue this process of elaborating on fillers in simple concepts, and of composing concepts using *conrels,* until one has distinct and reasonable representations for all the words the language interface must deal with. For example, one can easily do "run," "walk," "take the train" (distinctions in (inst)); "drive up I-95" (filling (via) with an entity of type *link*); "arrive" and "depart" (distinctions on whether the action is "complete"); "ride a horse" and "ride the subway" (conveyances), and so forth.

Exercise III

Develop MIFPs and ERKS forms for the following (mostly) *ptrans/propel* sentences. Consult Appendix I for ideas about representations for entities, etc.:

1. Olivia left off a watch.
2. The plane crashed into a mountain.
3. The plane crashed.
4. The plane flew over the city.
5. The car crossed the river.
6. The road crossed the river.
7. The drugs went to the city by truck.
8. Ronald visited the city.
9. The ship docked.
10. Ronald climbed the mountain.

2.8 Primitive Actionals and Statives

In this section, I will talk about a variety of sentence representations based upon the primitive *actional* and *stative* types of ERKS to illustrate the kinds of things one can do with the representational system. I want to stress that there is no single "correct" representation for any sentence. The only requirement is that the set of representations be internally consistent, change form slowly with small changes in meaning, and completely cover the knowledge domain in an economical, orthogonal manner.

An actional type, as its name indicates, is used to express a basic element of classes of events in the world. Since actionals describe events, they tend to have a fixed, usually short, duration. Stative types are used to describe attributes of entities, relationships among entities, or changes in these attributes and relationships. Statives and actionals are very closely linked in ERKS: actions have the effect of changing one or more states, and certain states need to be in force before actions can take place. Obviously, actions that don't change the state of the world are as useless to a representation as a state that doesn't effect the kinds of events that entities can participate in.

The first example is yet another *ptrans:*

(5)
The DC-10 took off.
(ptrans actor (person)
        obj (veh vtype (airplane) vname (DC-10))
        from (topof part (link linktype (runway)))
        to (inside part (link linktype (air-corridor))))

The MIFP of (5) is "an (unmentioned) person physically transferred an airplane vehicle from the surface of an (unmentioned) runway into an (unmentioned) air-corridor type link." Note how the surface semantics of "take off" allows one to fill in the person controlling the plane. (I could actually have added the role "pilot".) The words also allow one to put in two *links,* the runway, and the controlled airspace that commercial planes must fly in. Before event (5) happened, the following *p-config* was true:

The plane was on the runway
(p-config confrel (topof)
        con1 (veh vtype (airplane) vname (DC-10))
        con2 (link linktype (runway)))

After the takeoff, a new relationship has been established:

The plane is in the air corridor
(p-config confrel (inside)
        con1 (veh vtype (airplane) vname (DC-10))
        con2 (link linktype (air-corridor)))

The cluster of locational relationships involving the object *ptransed* is the basic set of inferences surrounding this ERKS type. There are also characteristic inferences about the locations of the people and objects carried by the plane.

The ERKS type *atrans* underlies events in which possession, ownership, or control of objects is transferred between animate entities. An abstract transfer of this kind represents the meaning of

(6)
Olivia handed Muhammed a pen.
(atrans actor HUM0
        obj INST0
        to (poss part HUM1)
        inst (ptrans actor HUM0
                obj INST0
                from (physcont val BP0)
                to (physcont val BP1)))

INST0: (inst insttype (pen))

BP0: (bpart bptype (hand) partof HUM0)
BP1: (bpart bptype (hand) partof HUM1)

Here a certain kind of *inst* (instrument, an object, usually graspable, with a definite function) is going from the possession of one person to that of another.[6] Note that the transfer is instrumented by a *ptrans* event in which the object goes from contact with the hand of the first person into contact with the second's.

The main resultative inference from (6) is:

(7)
Muhammed has the pen.
(a-config confrel (poss)
    con1 HUM1
    con2 INST0)

an abstract configuration of possession between Muhammed and the pen.

Events in which an actor takes a substance into the body are handled by the ERKS type *ingest*. For example,

(8)
Olivia inhaled smoke.
(ingest actor HUM0
    obj (pobj pobjtype (smoke)) from (inside part (bpart bptype (nose)
                                                    part of HUM0))
    to (inside part (bpart bptype (lungs) partof HUM0)))

The *to* and *from* roles are customarily filled with locational predications on the entry point and destination of the object *ingested,* here, an unstructured physical object, smoke. Acts of ingestion have the same locational inferences as *ptrans*. For certain kinds of objects, viz., those of type *ingobj* (ingestible object), one may also conclude:

(9)
(s-change actor (ingobj) toward (exist) mode (:neg))

that is, the object is consumed (ceases to exist).

An important class of actions has to do with *mental acts* of perception and communication. Such actions are handled by the primitive type *mtrans* (mental transfer). An animate actor perceives events or states of the world by transferring information from a sensory body part:

(10)
Olivia saw Muhammed leave.
(mtrans actor HUM0
        from (bpart bptype (eyes) partof HUM0)
        to (cp partof HUM0)

```
mobj (ptrans actor HUM1
            obj HUM1
            from (inside part (nil))))
```

The information, described by a conceptualization in the *mobj* role, is transferred to a "mental location," the "conscious processor" *(cp)* of the actor of the *mtrans*.

The *cp* is thought of as containing one "thought" at a time. Thus, we can say:

(11)
Olivia thought about Muhammed's leaving.
```
(a-config confrel (inside)
        con1 (ptrans actor HUM1
                    obj HUM1
                    from (inside))
        con2 (cp partof HUM0))
```

I'm here positing the abstract analog of the physical locational relationship, to "position" the idea of Muhammed's leaving in the mental location *cp*.

The mental location *ltm* (long-term memory) is another source of information:

(12)
Olivia remembered that Muhammed left.
```
(mtrans actor HUM0
     from (ltm partof HUM0)
     to (cp partof HUM0)
     mobj (ptrans actor HUM1
                 obj HUM1
                 from (inside)))
```

Communication events also occur between animate actors:

(13)
Olivia told Muhammed to leave.
```
(mtrans actor HUM0
     from (cp partof HUM0)
     to (cp partof HUM1)
     inst (speak actor HUM0)
     mobj (s-goal actor HUM0
                 mobj (ptrans actor HUM1
                             obj HUM1
                             from (inside))))
```

Here, "tell to leave" has been paraphrased as "it is actor's goal that another person engage in a certain *ptrans*." The instrumental action *speak* is used to distinguish this event from "write a letter," or other mode of communication.

The type *s-goal* is the very important *goal stative,* which asserts a relationship between a higher animate entity and a desired action or state of the world. Goal statives are extremely useful predictors of actions (see, for example, Wile78; Dyer82). For example, if I hear:

(14)
Olivia wanted (to eat) a hamburger.
(s-goal actor HUM0
      mobj (ingest actor HUM0
               obj (ingobj ingtype (hamburger))
               from (bpart bptype (mouth))
               to (bpart bptype (stomach)))))

I can start to speculate about whether Olivia will walk to the refrigerator, to the supermarket, or McDonald's.

Exercise IV

Develop ERKS structures for the following sentences:

1. Somoza recalled that he had recalled the troops from Honduras.
2. Olivia drinks.
3. Olivia handed Muhammed a wrench.
4. The sign said "Come to Jamaica."
5. Olivia returned $100 to Walter.
6. Ronald asked for $200,000,000 from the American people.
7. Reuben saw Jesse in the street.
8. George received a tank from GM.
9. 17 inches of snow fell on the mountain.
10. Ronald asked Walter for a dollar.
11. Ronald took an aspirin.
12. Walter watched Ronald on TV.
13. George went to three drugstores.
14. Walter fell off the chair.
15. The addict injected the heroin.

Attributional statives often take values along a *scale.* The attribute *health* of animate entities, for example, can have values describing "in top condition," "in reasonable shape," "ok," "mildly ill," "seriously sick," and "dead." Historically, the range of scale values has been restricted to $[-10, +10]$. Thus, one might do "Olivia was sick" as:

(15)
(s-attr actor HUM0
      attr (health val (−5)))

Here the *val* role labels the scale value. The exact choice of which numbers to use doesn't really matter. The relative ordering of the states described by the adjectives does.

Stative configurationals can also lie along a scale. One can distinguish "Olivia loathes going to New York" from "Olivia loves to go to New York" by filling the (confrel val) path in:

(16)
(a-config confrel (affinity val (nil))
            con1 HUM0
            con2 (ptrans actor HUM0
                        obj HUM0
                        to (prox part POL0)))

with (say) −7 or +7, respectively. In both (15) and (16), the representation technique is the same: gather a group of words that seem to be descriptive of the same underlying attribute or relation, and arrange them on a scale in order of "intensity."

Exercise V

Develop ERKS structures for the following sentences:

1. Olivia was furious with Muhammed.
2. The temperature of the oven fell 100 degrees.
3. The pie turned brown in the oven.
4. Olivia complained about the temperature in the room.
5. Othello's arm was broken.
6. The ship broke up and sank.
7. New York is 53 miles from Princeton.
8. Olivia ordered a well-done steak.
9. The tree reached to the ceiling.
10. The baby cried unhappily.

2.9 Conceptual Relationships

Abstract configurationals define non-physical relationships among entities. The primitive type *conrel* (conceptual relationship) is the superset of types that express relationships among actions or states.[7] The main types of *conrels* are: (a) temporal, (b) causal and (c) logical.

The following expresses a combined temporal and causal relationship:

(17)
Olivia borrowed a pen from Muhammed
(coord con1 ATR0
        con2 (s-goal actor HUM0
                     mobj ATR1))

ATR0:
(atrans actor HUM0
        obj INST0
        from (poss part HUM1)
        to (poss part HUM0))

ATR1:
(atrans actor HUM0
        obj INST0
        from (poss part HUM0)
        to (poss part HUM1))

REL0:
(after con1 ATR1 con2 ATR0)

HUM0: "Olivia"
HUM1: "Muhammed"
INST0: (inst insttype (pen))

The paraphrase of (17) is "there was a coordination of two events: an
atrans of a certain instrument from Muhammed to Olivia, and Olivia's
goal of *atransing* the pen back. The latter *atrans* is temporally in the
future of the former." The conrel *coord* is the weakest of the causals: it
merely states that there was *some* causal relation between two (co-
occurring) events. This kind of *conrel* is most often associated with uses
of the conjunction "and." For example, in

(18)
Olivia and Muhammed walked down the street
(coord con1 (ptrans actor HUM0
                    obj HUM0
                    via LINK0)
        con2 (ptrans actor HUM1
                    obj HUM1
                    via LINK0))

LINK0: (link linktype (street))

one has a coordination of movement actions by intentional actors.
    The conrel *after* in (19) just expresses a temporal relation between two
events, without any implied causal relationship:

(19)

Olivia left before Muhammed walked down the street
(after con1 (ptrans actor HUM1
                obj HUM1
                via LINK0)
        con2 (ptrans actor HUM0
                obj HUM0
                from (inside)))

Conventionally, the (con1) filler is taken to have occurred after the (con2) filler.

A stronger causal link can be seen in

(20)

Olivia murdered Muhammed
(cause con1 (episode actor HUM0)
        con2 (s-change actor HUM1
                        toward (health val (-10)))))

The paraphrase of (20) is "Olivia did something which caused a terminal state-change in Muhammed's health." "Murder," thus, is not an event, but a causal pattern. Note, also, that there is an *after* conrel among the inferences from (20): causes must always precede their effects.

A kind of "negative causal" is expressed in

(21)

Olivia prevented Muhammed from leaving the room
(disenable con1 (episode actor HUM0)
        con2 (ptrans actor HUM1
                obj HUM1
                from (inside part (struc structype (room))))))

Here one is saying that something Olivia did inhibited a *ptrans* on the part of Muhammed.

A case where there are events which causally "support" one another is

(22)

Olivia bought a book from Muhammed for $15
(dual con1 (atrans actor HUM0
                obj (mcontainer mconttype (book))
                from (poss part HUM1)
                to (poss part HUM0))
    con2 (atrans actor HUM0
                obj (money montype (US-currency)
                        amount (unit utype (dollar)
                        umag (num numval (15)))

```
from (poss part HUM0)
to (poss part HUM1)))
```

Here, one has an *atrans* of money and a book in opposite directions, and the *dual* causal expresses the idea that the events are mutually causative of each other.

The *rut* primitive is a causal relation connecting a sequence of actions <episode1>, <episode2>, etc., with a specific condition <stative1>, a stative conceptualization. Its meaning is analogous to the DO-UNTIL construction in ordinary programming languages: the <episodei> are to be executed (or instantiated) until the condition, often expressing a threshold value of some short, becomes true. *Rut* links are often expressed in English in compound sentences connected by "until." Consider, for example, "Beat the egg whites until they're stiff." As often happens, however, the causal relationship may be absorbed into a single word, as for example in

(23)
Olivia filled the tank with gas.
```
(rut threshold
     (s-attr actor CONTAINER0 attr (capacity val (0)))
     con1
     (ptrans actor HUM0 obj INGOBJ0
             to (inside part CONTAINER0)))
```

CONTAINER0:
(container ref (def) contype (tank))

INGOBJ0:
(ingobj ingtype (gasoline))

Here, "fill" is paraphrased as "put gas inside until tank has no more capacity" and subsumes the surface realization of the causal relation. Further conceptualizations to be executed as controlled by the threshold concept would be included with the role names *con2, con3*, etc.

A "logical" type of *conrel* is expressed in

(24)
Olivia or Muhammed left
```
(disj con1 (ptrans actor HUM0
                   obj HUM0
                   from LOC0)
      con2 (ptrans actor HUM1
                   obj HUM1
                   from LOC0))
```

LOC0: (inside part (nil))

Here, the conrel *disj* (disjunction) is used to represent the speaker's claim that one or the other of the events occurred. (The conjunction "or" in English usually expresses the logical "exclusive or.")

Rules, statements linking episodes in the world, have the property that the assertion of one, called the *antecedent,* allows one to conclude that the other, the *consequent,* is true, too. Thus, rules allow us to add and retract statements as we learn more things. If the consequent is necessarily true, we have a *valid* inference rule:

(25)
All men are mortal
(implies con1 (a-config confrel (member)
                    con1 ?entity
                    con2 (team teamtype (humanity)))
         con2 (s-change actor ?entity
                    toward (health val(−10))
                    mode (modes mode2 (:can))))

?entity: (entity)

This says that if a particular membership relation is true of an entity, then a potential change in the entity's health can be assumed, as well. Conventionally, the *con1* role in a rule designates the antecedent, and *con2* role designates the consequent.

In (25), I'm treating "mankind" as a certain type of *team.* A *team* is a primitive higher-animate type consisting of a collection of entities that are not distinct, but which are thought of as acting together. I'm also using the prefix "?" to indicate that the filler named "?entity" is universally quantified. (Alternatively, one could imbed the entire meaning structure in a *forall* relation.) What this means is that rules are typically used within formal reasoning systems such as the First-Order Predicate Calculus. I'll defer further discussion of this until Chapter 9.

If the causal relationship is only contingent, one can use the *cancause* connective:

(26)
Smoking can kill you
(cancause
  con1 (rut con1 (ingest actor ?person
                  obj POBJ0
                  to (lungs part ?person)
                  from (bpart bptype (mouth) partof ?person)
                  inst (ptrans actor ?person
                        obj POBJ0
                        from (inst insttype (cigarette))))

```
con2 (s-change actor ?person
            toward (health val (−10))))
```

POBJ0: (pobj pobjtype (smoke))

Here, the paraphrase is "repeated inhalation of smoke from a cigarette can lead to a terminal change in health." The relationship is not necessarily true, but only contingently so. There are many ways to become dead. Additional roles can be added to the *cancause* to express "degrees of belief" about relationships such as (26).

A final "catch-all" connective is *plausible,* which is useful for expressing rules of the "other things being equal" or "in default assume" variety. For example,

(27)
If it's noon, the sun is shining
```
(plausible
    con1 (episode abstime (timdur durtype (oclock)
                                  durmag (num numval (12))))
    con2 (s-attr actor (hbody hbodytype (star) hbodyname (Sun))
            attr (visible)
            mode (modes mode1 (:t))))
```

The paraphrase is roughly "if there's something happening at noon, then it's plausible that (rather whimsically) the heavenly body known as the Sun will be visible." I have chosen to attach the time specification to some unknown event; an attribution about the *tim(e) dur(ation)* would probably do as well.

Exercise VI

Represent:

1. Olivia got high from inhaling the smoke.
2. Ronald grew corn with fertilizer.
3. Olivia and Muhammed walked up the steps.
4. Ronald took an aspirin for his headache.
5. The Treasury sold $200,000,000 in bonds.
6. Walter returned the car to Jesse.
7. If you drop the glass, it will break.
8. Drinking causes headaches.
9. Turn the volume on the TV up.
10. I may or may not go.

2.10 A Representational Case Study: CADHELP

In the past few sections, I have been looking at ERKS structures built by single sentences. Let's approach the representation problem from the opposite direction: from the standpoint of a *knowledge structure* devised for an application domain, and the kinds of language that describe it. Along the way, I will summarize the representation ideas that have been discussed.

2.10.1 The CADHELP Microworld

The case study is the self-explaining CAD system CADHELP (Cull82a), developed at the University of Connecticut in 1979–1981. CADHELP produced coordinated textual and graphical descriptions of the operation of a simple computer-aided design system, which include common pitfalls and ways of recovering from mistakes. In Chapter 7 I will describe how the explainer generated natural language text from the system's knowledge base. Here I will describe the knowledge base.

CADHELP operated in the familiar task domain of logic circuit design. It was given the minimal set of functions required to create a schematic representing a design incorporating SSI/MSI components. The graphical features provided by the system included the ability to select, place, and orient components, and to make connections between devices. One could edit a design by adding, deleting, and moving components and by adding, deleting, or redrawing interconnections. The system provided a technique for creating connections with right-angle line segments, as well as a mechanism for commenting on the design by associating text with a particular device or a special comment symbol.

The main channel between the user and CADHELP was a 20 x 20-inch data tablet and its associated penlike stylus, plus a light pen sensitive to the graphic display itself. The surface of the tablet was divided into a drawing area, a master command block, and 64 permanently allocated 1-inch square command blocks. Touching the tip of the stylus to the tablet communicated information to the system. Additionally, the tip of the stylus contained a switch, which was turned on if the stylus was pressed sufficiently hard. Pressing the stylus on the master command block aborted an ongoing command. Exiting the command this way, or normal terminations, returned the user to the system's toplevel, where another command could be selected. The drawing area was used for a variety of input functions, such as making interconnections and moving graphical objects on the screen. The command blocks on the tablet were used to select and control the execution of the graphical features.

The commands that were implemented and known to the explanation subsystem included:

1. SELECT: This is CADHELP's toplevel. Any command can be initiated by touching the stylus to the command block labeled with its name.

2. CATALOG: This allows the user to peruse CADHELP's database of logic devices (called the "warehouse").
3. CREATE: Select a device and position it in the design area on the display.
4. CONNECT: Draw a connection between devices containing right-angle segments. This feature uses a simple extension of the graphical operation called "rubber-banding," in which a line segment appears to stretch away from an origin in response to stylus movements.
5. DELETE: Remove a device from the design.
6. DISCONNECT: Delete an interconnection.
7. EDIT: Arbitrarily add and delete line segments, without having the system check for logical coherence in the signal paths until the command is exited.
8. MOVE: Move an existing symbol.
9. ROTATE: Orient a device symbol left, right, up or down.
10. ANNOTATE: Associate text with a component or comment symbol.
11. READ: Read text created by an ANNOTATE.
12. EXPLAIN: Generate an explanation of the operation of one of the prior commands. The explanation consists of text coordinated with an animated display.

2.10.2 A Typical Command

Despite the apparent simplicity of these features, a fair amount of detail about the operation of the features needed to be represented to the explainer. In a CREATE operation, for example, the user would first look through the system's device-template database, using the CATALOG feature. To CATALOG, the user touched the stylus to the drawing area of the tablet. The CAD tool responded by drawing a device in a dedicated area of the display, the catalog area. If the user now moved the stylus *horizontally,* a new device would appear of the same class as the prior one, but of a different type (e.g., a three-input vs. two-input NAND gate). To view a member of a different class (e.g., a counter vs. gate), a *vertical* movement of the stylus would be made.

When the device the user wanted to create finally appeared in the catalog area, he told the tool of the choice by pressing the stylus on the block labeled MARK1. (Pressing with some force was necessary to activate the stylus switch that means "attend to this command.") The tool then made the device being displayed "movable." (A new instance of the device type was also created.) Now the user positioned the device in the design. To enable the user to locate the device with the stylus, the system then drew a cursor which moved as the user moved the stylus. The user moved the stylus, and thus the cursor, in the direction of the device in the catalog area. When the device and cursor overlapped, the device began to move as the cursor moved. (This operation is known technically as "dragging.") By moving the stylus appropriately, the user could position the device. When the device reached the desired spot, the user would inform the system of his decision by pressing MARK1 once more.

2.10.3 Knowledge Representation Issues

This description of a typical graphical feature possibly needing to be explained by CADHELP will introduce the fascinating representational issues that come up in even such a simple system. As usual, I will work on these issues from the bottom up.

In looking at the operations, one sees first that a number of entities must be represented. There are two animate entities, the user and the system:

*USER: (person eprole (*user))
*SYS: (person eprole (*system))

The role named *eprole* stands for "episodic role," the character played by the two participants in a feature-episode. The "*" means that these entities are unique. Their functions do not vary from one feature invocation to another.

There are several mental containers: the command blocks, the drawing area, and the various areas of the display. For example, the Master Command Block is

*MCB:
(mcontainer mconttype (command-block)
    mcontname (MASTER))

I conceive of these containers as being "on" the tablet or display:

(p-config confrel (topof)
    con1 *MCB
    con2 (struc structype (*tablet)))

There are also several instruments:

"the stylus"
*STYLUS:
(inst insttype (stylus))

The instruments have several important functional parts:

"the tip of the stylus"
*TIP:
(sensor sensortype (tip))

```
(p-config confrel (partof)
      con1 *TIP
      con2 *STYLUS)
```

Here, I need a new ERKS type, *sensor*. Think of this as a specialization of "bodypart" for components whose function is passing information from the world on to the animate entity's control center, the *cp*. Also on the screen or in the warehouse are the graphical objects:

```
"a 3-input NAND"
(device devicetype (NAND)
      fan-in (3))
```

```
"the device has an input port"
(p-config confrel (partof)
      con1 (device-port porttype (input))
      con2 (device))
```

```
"signal path"
(link linktype (signal-path)
      end1 (device-port)
      end2 (device-port))
```

These kinds of objects are in the ISA-subset of *gobjs,* the domain-specific class of graphical objects. Graphical objects have some attributes:

```
"the gobj is being monitored by the system"
(s-attr actor (gobj)
      attr (active))
```

```
"the gobj is not displayed"
(s-change actor (gobj)
      attr (visible)
      mode (:neg))
```

```
"the system makes the gobj movable"
(cause con1 (episode actor *SYS)
      con2 (s-change actor (gobj)
                  toward (movable)))
```

Finally, the design itself, an "information structure:"

```
"a device is in the design"
(a-config confrel (inside)
      con1 (device)
      con2 (infostruc inftype (*design)))
```

In considering the actions in this microworld, one can see the need for the *ptrans* ("the system moves the cursor"), *mtrans* ("the system gets a hit from the light pen"), and *propel* ("the user touches the drawing area with the stylus") actionals from the core ERKS system. We also need the specialized actions *draw* and *clone:*

"the user draws a line"
(draw actor *USER obj (link lnktype (signal-path)))

"the system makes a copy of a device"
(clone actor *SYS obj (device))

The "draw" primitive has as its result a connection configuration's coming into existence:

(p-config confrel (signal-connection)
          con1 (link lnktype (signal-path))
          con2 (device-port)
          con3 (device-port))

Here, I have generalized *p-config* to allow configurations involving three entities. The *clone* primitive brings a new device into the world:

(s-change actor (device)
          toward (exist))

All of this is straightforward enough. The really new representational complexity is caused by the intricate, causally patterned nature of graphical operations such as the CREATE command discussed in Section 2.10.2. These kinds of knowledge are typically modeled by *goalepisodes,* causally interconnected chains of "primitive" actions all carried out in service of a goal. The goal of a CREATE, for example, is

"user wishes to add a device to the design"
(s-goal actor *USER
        mobj (a-config confrel (inside)
                    con1 (device)
                    con2 *DESIGN))

Historically, goalepisodes of the kind needed here were called *situational scripts* (Scha77). (Another type of goalepisode is the *named plan* of [Wile80].) Scripts are relatively rigid, temporally/causally ordered agglomerations of knowledge about stereotyped situations. Many of the entities in scripts are *script variables,* that is, placeholders bound to different real entities in different uses (or *instantiations)* of the script.

In CADHELP, the structures modeling the graphical features were called *feature scripts.* The units of each feature script were causal links tying together an action with one or more stative assertions. An interconnection of causal links such that the resultant states of one became the enabling states of the next were called *causal chains.* The collection of

Diagram 2.2
The Feature Script $point

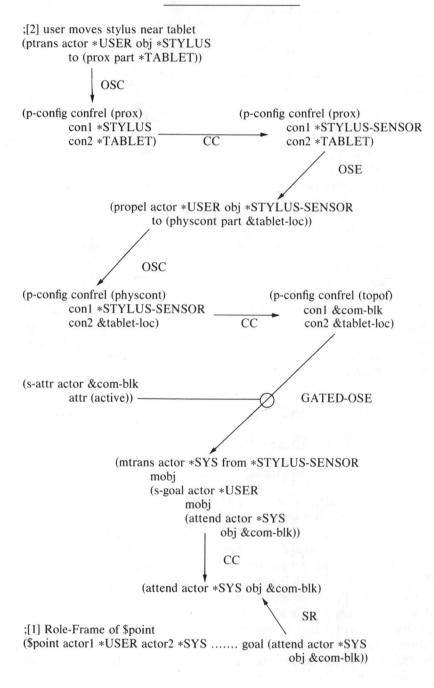

;[2] user moves stylus near tablet
(ptrans actor *USER obj *STYLUS
      to (prox part *TABLET))

    | OSC

(p-config confrel (prox)   (p-config confrel (prox)
    con1 *STYLUS   con1 *STYLUS-SENSOR
    con2 *TABLET)   CC   con2 *TABLET)

                                  OSE

    (propel actor *USER obj *STYLUS-SENSOR
       to (physcont part &tablet-loc))

          OSC

(p-config confrel (physcont)   (p-config confrel (topof)
    con1 *STYLUS-SENSOR   con1 &com-blk
    con2 &tablet-loc)   CC   con2 &tablet-loc)

(s-attr actor &com-blk
    attr (active))   ⊘   GATED-OSE

    (mtrans actor *SYS from *STYLUS-SENSOR
       mobj
       (s-goal actor *USER
           mobj
          (attend actor *SYS
             obj &com-blk))

              CC

    (attend actor *SYS obj &com-blk)

                 SR

;[1] Role-Frame of $point
($point actor1 *USER actor2 *SYS .... goal (attend actor *SYS
                                   obj &com-blk))

causal chains together with the goal they are executed in service of constituted the feature script.

Diagram 2.2 is a fragment of the feature script "point at a command block," *$point*. (The prefix "$" indicates that we have a knowledge structure of type *script*.) Its role-frame, together with the goal of the user, is expressed at [1]. The desired action, the *mobj* of the goal, is connected to the causal chain by the *sr* (scriptal result) link. The causal chain itself begins at [2]. The *ptrans* event is the "one shot cause" of the "proximity" stative that obtains between stylus and tablet. One-shot causals such as *osc* indicate that the antecedent need be only momentarily "true" for the consequent to become true. "Continuous" causals, on the other hand, indicate that the enabling condition must be continuously present for the associated action to take place. For example, "gas in tank" continuously enables "engine runs" in a car. The proximity of the stylus is *causally coupled* to a proximity configuration between the stylus sensor (the tip) and the tablet. The *cc* causal is used whenever the designer chooses not to spell out the details of a causal chain linking two events, perhaps because he doesn't understand the causality completely. Here, the events that have been "elided" are that the user is grasping the light pen correctly (he doesn't have it upside down, for example) and that he moves it toward the tablet, tip forward. The nearness of the tip to the tablet is the one-shot enabling condition for the user's touching the tip to the tablet at a variable location called *&tablet-loc*. (The prefix "&" indicates a script variable.) This *propel* event in turn is the one-shot cause for the *physcont* relation between tip and tablet location. That relation, in turn, is causally connected to the stative expressing that a (variable) *&com-blk* (command block) is at the location touched. The missing conditions are that the user aimed the tip at a command block, rather than, say, the drawing area. The "topof" relationship enables the *mtrans* event, "system gets a hit from the stylus." This takes place, however, only if the "gating" event, "command block active," is simultaneously true. Enabling statives with ancillary conditions are called "gated causals." Finally, the system *attends* to the command block touched, because of the (missing) rule in a system like CADHELP: "do what the user wants, if possible."

2.11 Summary

This ends the introduction to representation design for language-processing systems. I have sketched out some general design techniques, and given a number of suggestive examples of their use. It should be clear that the process isn't algorithmic; it depends critically on the designer's creativity in coming up with special purpose primitives. Nevertheless, the use of the bottom-up design method, the derivation of the MIFP, and the careful evolution of a model corpus allow a systematic approach to representation for applications. These applications can, as I suggested with the CADHELP case study, include some quite technical task domains.

Notes

1. The same meaning representation can be realized in sentences from many different natural languages. Thus, the representational system can function as an *interlingua,* a canonical, intermediate language for a Machine Translation system. Cf., e.g., Carb81.

2. Diagram 2.1 is a simplified version of the actual type hierarchy supplied with the NLP Toolkit.

3. These techniques are similar to those used by some semanticists and psycholinguists to evolve "semantic fields," systematic expositions of the nuanced distinctions among words of related meaning (e.g., Mill76).

4. Most of the primitive actionals and statives I will introduce are from Conceptual Dependency (Scha73a). Similar notions have been proposed elsewhere, e.g, in (Norm75) and (Mill76).

5. The dictionary definitions supplied with the NLP Toolkit all use the collapsed form of word senses. This will change, sometime.

6. Yes, the entity *inst* has the same name as the role *inst* in episodes. The context should keep them from being confused.

7. Most of the *conrels* in ERKS have been taken from Commonsense Algorithms (Rieg76) and Preference Semantics (Wilk75).

3

Software Tools for Representation Design

3.0 Introduction

Since this book is intended as a practical introduction to one important class of NLP techniques, it's important to understand, as early as possible, the concrete realizations of ideas about representation and processing. Chapter 2 introduced ERKS forms for meaning representation in terms of symbolic expressions in the programming language Lisp. This chapter will discuss some key data structures and program fragments written in that language. Taken together, these programs comprise a set of *software tools* for assisting a designer during the evolution of a language processing interface.[1]

First I present some simple Lisp functions for moving around in the ISA–hierarchy shown in Diagram 2.1, repeated as Diagram 3.1. Then I discuss a collection of creation, updating, and access functions useful for manipulating ERKS forms. My intention throughout has been to promote *clarity* and *consistency* of exposition. The functions and data structures are not the most elegant or efficient possible, but since the tools are used continually in the rest of the book, it's important that the reader gain at least an understanding of their input/output behavior, and why their functionality is necessary.

3.1 Navigating in an ISA–Hierarchy

Each header from an ERKS meaning structure is either a constant (such as a name) or one of the primitive types from the ISA–hierarchy. As a simple introduction to Lisp symbolic computing techniques, consider the problem of determining whether a primitive type is connected to another in this ISA–hierarchy. For example, we may wish to know whether a type is below another in the hierarchy, in the sense of being found in its dependent subtree.

As a practical matter, one must decide on a data structure to represent the hierarchy, and a set of operators to answer various questions about relations among types in the hierarchy. Since the primitive types have unique names, the most straightforward (although not the only) approach to a usable data structure is to associate the pointer information with the type names.

Diagram 3.1
A Tangled ISA–Hierarchy for ERKS

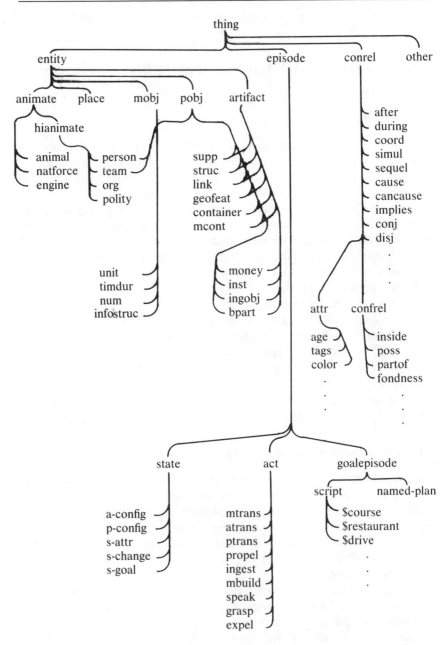

Note: Links are bi-directional as implemented

In Lisp, this is naturally done through the *property list* of the atomic name. Examination of Diagram 3.1 shows that a given type may have several parents (for instance, *person*) and/or several children (for instance, *attr*). Thus, for a given type, one can place the names of the parents in a list, and associate this list with the property named "superset," as indicated in Figure 3.1. Similarly, the children are associated with the property called "subset." The complete hierarchy can then be built up by a series of calls on the Lisp primitive function *putprop*, as shown. (Actually, only a subset of these calls is needed, as I will show in Section 3.2.)

Figure 3.1 also contains the Lisp definitions of some simple functions for working with the ISA–hierarchy, expressed in the Lisp dialect called Franz Lisp (Fode80). This dialect is widely used on DEC VAX-class minicomputers, other minicomputers such as the Pyramid 90x, and workstations such as the Sun 2. Franz is also reasonably compatible with other "standard" Lisps such as MacLisp and UciLisp. Since these are the first real program fragments to be presented in this book, it's important that the reader understand what they do and the documentation standard I will use for function definitions.

Probably the simplest useful question one can ask in an ISA–hierarchy is whether a given primitive type appears in a collection of other types. If we view the Lisp "list" data type as a representation for a "set," this question is simply answered by use of the built-in Lisp function *memq*. I have provided, however, a separate definition *is-among-p* to make subsequent functions more readable. In this book, an atomic name ending in "-p" will always stand for a predicate, a function that returns nil if the test it encodes fails for the given arguments, non-nil otherwise. By definition, a predicate should have no side effects.

The definition of *is-among-p* appears at [1] in Figure 3.1. Comment lines for functions will begin with the ";" character. Documentation for the function includes a description of its arguments and the value returned. Thus we see that *is-among-p* takes an atomic symbol (bound to *typ*) as its first argument, and a list of atoms, *typs*, as its second argument. (Type-checking could be a standard prologue in functions such as these.) The function simply uses *memq* to check on the presence of the type. This function returns the tail of the list beginning with the first (and presumably only) occurrence of the type in the list, if there is one, else nil. Thus, *is-among-p* returns the input type (using *car*) as its result if the type exists, else nil.[2]

At [2] is the definition of the function *is-linked-p,* which checks to see whether a path consisting of only subset or superset pointers exists between typ1 and typ2. If the two types are identical, the predicate is trivially true. For the general case, the function traces only superset pointers, first between typ1 upward toward typ2, then the reverse, using

Figure 3.1
ISA–Hierarchy Representation and Predicates

```
; Primitive type:
;    attr
;    property name    value
;    superset   (conrel)
;    subset   (color age ...)
(putprop 'attr '(conrel) 'superset)
(putprop 'attr '(age tags color) 'subset)


;[1]
;IS-AMONG-P: is a primitive type among a given list of types?
; Args: typ, the type (an atom)
;      typs, a list (really set) of atomic types
; Returns: typ, else nil
(def is-among-p (lambda (typ typs)
 (car (memq typ typs))))


;[2]
;IS-LINKED-P: is there a path between two types
; consisting of only subset or superset pointers?
;NOTE: a type is assumed to be linked to itself
;   Args: typ1 and typ2, ERKS primitive types
;   Returns: t if inputs are the same, else what is-above-p returns (q.v.)
(def is-linked-p (lambda (typ1 typ2)
   (or (eq typ1 typ2)
      (is-above-p typ1 typ2)
      (is-above-p typ2 typ1))))


;[3]
;ISABOVE-P: is typ1 above typ2 in hierarchy?
;      This chases superset pointers starting at typ2
;      in a depth first manner
; Args: typ1 and typ2, ERKS types
; Returns: typ1, else nil
(def is-above-p (lambda (typ1 typ2)
 (or (is-among-p typ1 (get typ2 'superset))
    (is-above1 typ1 (get typ2 'superset)))))

;IS-ABOVE1: helper function for is-above-p
(def is-above1 (lambda (typ typs)
 (cond ((null typs) nil)
      ((is-above-p typ (car typs)))
      ((is-above1 typ (cdr typs))))))
```

Figure 3.2
A Sample Type Declaration

```
(def-ERKS-type ptrans
    superset (act)
    intrinsic-slots
    ((actor couldbe-animate-p)
     (obj ptransobj-p)
     (to couldbe-locrel-p)
     (from couldbe-locrel-p)
     (via couldbe-link-p)
     (inst couldbe-episode-p)
     (time times-p)
     (mode modes-p))
    extrinsic-slots
    ((rel couldbe-episode-p))
    )
```

---

the function *is-above-p*. As shown at [3], this function first looks to see whether the first type exists in the immediate superset of the second, then calls a helper function *is-above1*. The helper simply makes a recursive call to *is-above-p* with its first argument and the car of the second. If this fails, *is-above1* calls itself recursively with its first argument and the cdr of its second. (An iterative version of *is-above-p* is also possible, and probably more efficient.)

Exercise I (Easy)

Write a function *show-subtree,* which takes as its argument a type name and prints out its dependent subtree of types in a breadth-first manner. What problems are caused by the multiple ISA–inheritance links?

3.2   Defining ERKS Types

The primitive types are the basis of the symbolic structures used by the kinds of NLP systems of interest in this book. Thus, it is extremely important that the different modules of the system share a consistent view of the types and their attributes. The usual way to accomplish this is by providing two standard tools to system implementors: (a) a set of *data-type defining* and *documenting* functions; and (b) a collection of *instantiating, updating,* and *accessing* functions that operate on the data types thus defined. The purpose of these functions is similar in spirit to the "record package macros" discussed in Char80.

The *def-ERKS-type* record function is provided for defining the attributes of a new primitive type. Figure 3.2 shows the call to the function needed to define the primitive type *ptrans*, which was discussed in Chapter 2 in connection with the sample corpus of Figure 2.1. This type is the ERKS primitive expressing an action involving movement of a physical object from one location to another by an animate actor.

Since the function is actually a *macro* form, its argument list can be of arbitrary length and the arguments are passed without being evaluated. (Actually, Lisp simply supplies the entire run-time expression as the binding of the macro's single argument.) The macro, using the argument list, creates and returns a Lisp s-expression, which is then evaluated to produce the desired type-defining side-effects. (See Chapter 3 of Char80 for a discussion of the typical uses of Lisp macros.)

The sample type-defining call in Figure 3.2 shows the name of the new type as the first argument to the macro, followed by the atom "superset" and a list of the primitive types immediately above this one in the ISA–hierarchy (see Diagram 3.1). We see from the figure that the type *act* is the only immediate parent of *ptrans*.

Next, the call contains an attribute named "intrinsic-slots," followed by an association list of slot (or role) names and predicates (called *constraints*), then an attribute called "extrinsic-slots" with an analogous association list. The intrinsic roles of a type are the "built-in" roles that are essential to the meaning of the type. The constraints associated with the roles are predicate functions, labeled, as mentioned earlier, with the "-p" suffix. These can be applied to proposed fillers to check them for consistency with the type's requirements. Most constraint expressions look for one or a combination of other primitive types of the representation system being designed. Thus, for example, the call in Figure 3.2 specifies that the *actor* (intentional initiator) of a ptrans-structure should belong to the class of (i.e., "could be") animate entities. (See Diagram 3.1 for a specification of these entities.)

The extrinsic roles of a type are those not essential to its meaning, but which a given utterance may "add on" in the manner of a parenthetical comment. In Figure 3.2, the role name *rel* (standing for "relative" clause or conceptualization) is given as the only extrinsic role of a ptrans-structure. This extrinsic role would be used for sentences such as "Going to LA, which always annoys me, was especially irritating during the Olympics." Here, the representation for the dependent subclause "which always annoys me" would be attached to the ptrans-structure underlying the "going" concept, using the role name *rel*.

The *def-ERKS-type* function is a *record macro*. It defines a number of data structures and operations for each type that is declared. First, it must associate the superset, intrinsic, and extrinsic roles with the new type. (There are a number of ways to implement this association. The simplest, and the one used here, is via the property list of the atom naming the type.) Next, the function uses the superset attribute to connect the new type into the ISA–hierarchy (again using property-list structures). Thus, the complete set of *def-ERKS-type* specifications builds the ISA–hierarchy for the representational system being developed.

Next, it defines two functions to test for occurrences of the class: a predicate to test for an exact instance of the type, and a predicate to test for a possible instance. "Exact" simply means that the candidate structure has the type as the toplevel header. "Possible" means that the candidate structure is either an exact instance, or is directly connected to the class by a path in the ISA–hierarchy. For the ERKS type *ptrans* the functions are *ptrans-p* and *couldbe-ptrans-p,* respectively.

Thus, referring to Diagram 3.1, one can see that a candidate structure based on an *episode* is a possible instance of a *ptrans,* since a path exists between them (through the type *act*) in the hierarchy. A structure based on a *person,* however, cannot be an occurrence of a *ptrans,* since no strictly upward or downward path connects them.

Finally, the record macro creates a function *ptrans-f,* which returns a new ERKS structure of type *ptrans.* This function uses a prototype role-frame, stored on the property list of the type, of the allowed roles of the type, with their associated constraints.

The point of these structures and functions is to provide a minimal set of type-defining and testing functions which an implementor can (and should!) use when adding a new type. Similarly, the record macro provides a single source of *documentation* for the new type. One simple way to provide this documentation is through comments included in the permanent record (file) containing the defining macro call for the type. Another easy way, one that is visible in the run-time Lisp system in which the type-defining calls are actually carried out, is to provide a "comments" property (perhaps an English string) with the type definition.

The Franz Lisp definition of the *def-ERKS-type* macro is shown at [1] in Figure 3.3. This function consists of a "prolog," starting at [1a], in which the new names "ptrans-p," "couldbe-ptrans-p," and "ptrans-f" are created using the Franz function *concat,* which creates a Lisp atomic symbol from a list of atoms given as its arguments. Then, beginning at [1b], the type defining expression is constructed by use of the well-known Lisp quasi-quote facility (see Wile84, Chapter 14; Fode81, Chapter 3, for a description of this facility). The form to be returned is based upon the Lisp *prog* special form, which gives the effects of Algol- or C-style block structure.

At [1c], the expression places the attribute-value pairs on the property list of the type, using the function *dfps* (a multiple *defprop),* which is defined at [2]. At [1d], the new type is connected into the hierarchy by adding its name to the subsets of other types mentioned as its supersets. The helper function *consprop* is defined at [3].

Figure 3.3
The def-ERKS-type Macro

```
;[1]
;DEF-ERKS-TYPE: define attributes and functions for an ERKS
; primitive type
;   Args: arg, the actual call to the macro (see, e. g., Figure 3.2)
;   Returns: a body of LISP expressions to be evaluated
;   Side-Effects: things are added to the property list of the type
;     and various functions come into existence
 (def def-ERKS-type (macro (arg)
     ;[1a]
     ;Extract the type from the argument, form the testing predicates and
     ;     the frame builder
     (let* ((type (cadr arg))
           (predfn (concat type '-p))
           (couldbefn (concat 'couldbe- predfn))
           (instancefn (concat type '-f)))


;[1b]
;Set up the defining expression using the backquote/comma
;     substitution macro. This form will be returned, after
;     the substitutions take place, and then evaluated.
'(prog ( )
;[1c]
;Put the various attributes on the property list of the type
(dfps , @ (cdr arg))


;[1d]
;Connect new type into the ISA-Hierarchy
(do ((typs (get ',type 'superset)(cdr typs)))
    ((null typs)( ))
    (consprop (car typs) ',type 'subset))


;[1e]
;Define the functions
;(1) Check that an ERKS structure is an instance of the type
(def ,predfn (lambda (arg)
  (ERKS-type-p arg '(,type))))
;(2) Check that an ERKS structure could be an instance of the type
(def ,couldbefn (lambda (arg)
  (couldbe-ERKS-type-p arg '(,type))))
;(3) Define a function to return an instance of an ERKS
; structure based on the type
(def ,instancefn (macro (arg)
  (make-ERKS-structure arg)))
;(4) Mark each function as being associated with this type
(putprop predfn type 'predfn-for)
```

```
(putprop couldbefn type 'couldbefn-for)
(putprop instancefn type 'builderfn-for)


;[1f]
;Define a prototype structure for the type (to be used by
; the instantiating function)
(define-ERKS-structure ',type))
)))


;Various Helper Functions


;[2]
;DFPS: define multiple property list entries for an atom
; Args: the cadr of arg is the name of
;  the atom, the cddr is a list of pairs of property names and
;  values
; Returns: the atom whose property list was updated
(def dfps (macro (arg)
  '(dfp1 ',(cadr arg) ',(cddr arg))))

(def dfp1 (lambda (nam plst)
(cond ((null plst) nam)
      (t (putprop nam (cadr plst)(car plst))
         (dfp1 nam (cddr plst)))))


;[3]
;CONSPROP: add a new item to a property value on an atom
; Args: nam, the atom whose property list is to be modified
; val, the new value
; attr, the attribute
; Returns: the atom which was modified
; Side-Effect: the item becomes the first value in the attribute list
; associated with the property name on the symbol's property list
(def consprop (lambda (nam val attr)
    (putprop nam (cons val (get nam attr)) attr)
    nam))


;[4]
;ERKS-TYPE-P: check an ERKS structure to see if it is based on one
; of a list of types
; Args: con, an ERKS structure representing a conceptualization
; typs, a list of ERKS primitive types
; NOTE: con is either itself an ERKS (list) structure, or an atom
; bound to a list structure
; Returns: the ERKS type of con, if it exists among the typs, else nil
(def ERKS-type-p (lambda (con typs)
    (is-among-p (type-of con) typs)))
```

(continued on next page)

Figure 3.3 (*Continued*)

```
;[4a]
;TYPE-OF: get the ERKS primitive type from a structure, or an atom
; bound to the structure
(def type-of (lambda (con)
   (car (atom-eval con))))
```

```
;[4b]
;ATOM-EVAL: if form is an atom, eval it; else just return it
;NOTE: atoms are assumed to be bound to something; we should check for this!!
(def atom-eval (lambda (form)
        (cond ((atom form)(eval form))
              (form))))
```

```
;[5]
;COULDBE-ERKS-TYPE-P: see if an ERKS structure could be an instance
; (in the hierarchical sense) of one of a list of types
; Args: con, an ERKS concept (or a list bound to a concept)
; typs, a list of types
; Returns: non-nil if concept could be an instance of one of the
; types
(def couldbe-ERKS-type-p (lambda (con typs)
     (is-linked-p (type-of con) typs)))
```

At [1e], calls to the Franz special form for function-definition, *def,* are constructed to define the new functions *ptrans-p, couldbe-ptrans-p* and *ptrans-f.* Note that *ptrans-p* is defined in terms of *ERKS-type-p,* which is shown at [4]. This function extracts the type from a structure (using the basic function *type-of,* [4a]) and passes it to the function *is-among-p,* which was defined in Figure 3.1.

It is often convenient to bind ERKS forms (list structures) to atoms, and the data-type functions need to be sensitive to this. The function *atom-eval* shown at [4b] converts an atomic ERKS input into the list form, for these cases.

Exercise II (Easy)

1. I have been implicitly assuming that the *def-ERKS-type* call for a given type will occur only once. Are any problems likely to arise with the given definition if a user wants to redefine a type? (Hint: look at the function *consprop* in Figure 3.3.) Make the record macro "complain" when a type gets redefined, using the Franz built-in output function *msg* (q.v.), and fix any problems that arise during the redefinition.

2. Suppose an atom passed to *atom-eval* is unbound, i.e., has not been assigned a value. How would you fix the function to allow for this case? (Hint: look at the definitions of the Franz functions *errset* and *boundp.*)

The function *ptrans-f* defined by the *def-ERKS-type* call is responsible for creating instances of structures based on this type. It uses the role-frame defined for the type, and thus is called the *ptrans frame function*. The call to the frame function that would create my initial example of an ERKS structure, (2.1), in Chapter 2 is shown at [1] in Figure 3.4. Note the imbedded calls to the frame functions for *person, inst, inside,* and *polity*.

Every instance of an ERKS type should be created by a call of this sort. The point of doing things this way is that the frame function can guarantee that the structure returned is legal, including the imbedded examples of other types (which are created by their own calls to the associated frame functions). The function does this by checking that each role name provided to it in the argument list is among the allowed roles of the frame, and that the proposed fillers meet the constraints pronounced in the type declaration. As a software engineering measure, quoted forms such as

'(ptrans actor (person))

are *never* used to create ERKS structures, since the needed checking then doesn't take place. As a result, ERKS forms created in different parts of the running system are essentially guaranteed to drift out of consistency with one another.

The function *ptrans-f* was defined at [1e] and [1f] of Figure 3.3 in terms of the helper functions *define-ERKS-structure* and *make-ERKS-structure*. Definitions for these functions are given at [2] and [3] of Figure 3.4, respectively. The function *define-ERKS-structure* simply combines the intrinsic and extrinsic role information and stores it on the "role-frame" property of the type name.

When a new form is to be created, the macro *make-ERKS-structure* uses the role-frame and constraint information to make a legal instance of the form (including legal subforms), according to the specifications provided in the call to the toplevel frame function. The heart of the function is the do-loop at [3a], which checks that the current role name has been declared for the type; that the filler, if a frame function, returns a value that is accepted by the constraint function announced for the role; that the filler otherwise conforms to the constraint or is a member of the declared contrast set for the role. (That *ptrans-f* is the frame builder for this type was set up by the code at [1e] in Figure 3.3, when the type was declared.)

The function *add-pair* (shown at [4]) adds a role-filler pair to a form, returning the pointer to the form as its result. The function *error* (not shown) prints an error indicator to the user, and pauses to let the user examine the state of the system.

It is often convenient to associate a *name* with each of the fillers in an ERKS structure, to make changes in the structure simple (by rebinding

Figure 3.4
The Functions define-ERKS-structure and make-ERKS-structure

```
;[1]
;Use of the frame functions to create the structure of Example (2.1)
;      from Chapter 2
(ptrans-f actor (person-f persname (Marie) gender (fem))
        obj (inst-f insttype (wrench))
        to (inside-f part (polity-f polname (Peoria) poltype (munic))))


;[2]
;DEFINE-ERKS-STRUCTURE: set up the prototype role frame of roles and
;      constraints
; Args: typ, the new ERKS type
; Rtns: the typ
; Side-Effects: puts the role-frame on the property list of the type
(def define-ERKS-structure (lambda (typ)
 (putprop typ (append (get typ 'intrinsic-slots)
                      (get typ 'extrinsic-slots)) 'role-frame)
   ))


;[3]
;MAKE-ERKS-STRUCTURE: make a new instance of the type
; Args: specs, the specifications for the new form (including imbedded
;      calls to other frame functions)
; Rtns: a pointer to the new structure if no error, else indicator "err"
(def make-ERKS-structure (macro (specs)
      ;car of input is toplevel frame function
 (let* ((frfun (car specs))
      ;primitive type associated with this function (See Fig. 3.3)
      (type (get frfun 'builderfn-for))
      ;roleframe for this type
      (roleframe (get type 'role-frame))
      ;result structure is based on type
      (rescon '(,type))
      ;error indication
      (bad! ( )))


;[3a]
;Iterate through the specifications, checking that role name is
;legal, and filler conforms to constraints
(do ((pairs (cdr specs)(cddr pairs))
     ;current role name
     (role ( ))
     ;current filler
     (filler ( ))
     ;current constraint
     (constraint ( )))
```

```
;Stop when we run out of role-filler pairs, or something bad
;happens
((or (null pairs) bad!))


;Bogus role name?
;NOTE: role frame has form ((actor animate-p)(obj ...))
(cond ((null (assoc (setq role (car pairs)) roleframe))
        (error "Unknown role name" role "in" type)
        (setq bad! 'err))

;Is proposed filler to be generated by another
; frame function?
;NOTE: filler will be a list, whose car is a frame-function
;NOTE: (car nil) = (cdr nil) = nil
    ((get (car (setq filler (cadr pairs))) 'builderfn-for)
      ;Evaluate imbedded frame function to get filler
    (cond ((eq (setq filler (eval filler)) 'err)
            ;Error will have been signaled during evaluation
            ; of imbedded function
            (setq bad! 'err))
          ;does filler conform to constraint?
          ((null (apply
                  (setq constraint
                        (cadr (assoc role roleframe)))
                  (list filler)))
          (error "Filler" filler "doesn't fit"
          constraint "in" type)
          (setq bad! 'err))
          ;[3b]
          ;add role and filler
          ((setq rescon (add-pair rescon role filler)))))

;Is constraint a function call?
    ((atom constraint)
      (cond ((null (apply constraint (list filler)))
              (error "Filler" filler "doesn't fit"
              constraint "in" type)
              (setq bad! 'err))
            ;add role and filler
            ((setq rescon (add-pair rescon role filler)))))

;Constraint is a contrast set; is filler a member?
    ((memq filler constraint)
      ;add role and filler
      (setq rescon (add-pair rescon role filler)))
    ((error filler "not in contrast set" constraint "in" type)
    (setq bad! 'err)))
    ) ;end of do
```

(continued on next page)

Figure 3.4 (*Continued*)

```
;[3c]
;return error indication, else result
(or bad! rescon)
)))

;[4]
;ADD-PAIR: extend an ERKS structure with a new role/filler pair
; Args: form, an ERKS form, role, a role name, filler, another ERKS form
; Rtns: the extended form
(def add-pair (lambda (form role filler)
     (append form (list role filler))
))
```

---

the name) and to store special information with the filler (on the property list of the name). ERKS structures in which all the fillers (as well as the toplevel structure) are named are called *atomized forms,* since each filler is associated with a Lisp atom. The atomized version of Example (2.1) is shown in Figure 3.5, together with the changes in *make-ERKS-form* and *add-pair* needed to produce these forms. As shown, one need merely bind a newly generated name to the ERKS substructure. (The built-in function *newsym* generates a stream of symbols with "leader" given by the argument, and "tag" an increasing sequence of numbers.) Note that *add-pair* is given an atomized filler at [3b] in Figure 3.4, since the call to the imbedded frame function returned the name of an atomized ERKS structure. Thus, it needs to notice this and not create an unnecessary name.

3.3   Access and Updating Machinery

Once the primitive types and their instantiators are in place, we need functions to *find* substructures imbedded in instances of the type; and to *change* such substructures. Let's assume, for convenience, that we are dealing with completely atomized structures.

Recall that fillers in ERKS forms are uniquely specified by a role path, a list of role names to be followed into a structure to locate a filler. The function *grf* (for get-role-filler) shown at [1] in Figure 3.6 follows role paths into ERKS forms, returning the symbol it finds at the end, if there is one. The function is very simply written recursively, by pursuing successive path components in fillers associated with prior path components. Note the use of *atom-eval* to convert a named ERKS form to a list

Figure 3.5
Atomized Version of Example (2.1)

---

c0:
(ptrans actor c1 obj c2 to c3)

c1:
(person persname c4 gender c5)

c2:
(inst insttype c6)

c3:
(inside part c7)

c4:
(Marie)

c5:
(fem)

c6:
(wrench)

c7:
(polity polname c8 poltype c9)

c8:
(Peoria)

c9:
(munic)

```
;ADD-PAIR: for atomized forms
(def add-pair (lambda (form role filler)
     (append form (list role
;if filler already has a name, use it
     (cond ((atom filler) filler)
          ;otherwise, make a name up
          ((set (new-conatom) filler)))))))
```

```
;at [3c] in Figure 3.4, use
(or bad! (and (setq bad! (new-conatom))
          (set bad! rescon)
          bad!))
```

```
;NEW-CONATOM: generate a new atom to place in a concept
(def new-conatom(lambda ()(newsym 'c)))
```

Figure 3.6
The Functions get-role-filler and set-role-filler

```
;[1]
;Access function G(et) R(ole) F(iller):
; Args: path, a role path into form, an ERKS form
; Rtns: filler at end of path, else ( )
(def grf (lambda (path form)
        ;if no path, answer is current form
       (cond ((null path) form)
             ;is first component of path a role name in current form?
            ((null (memq (car path)(atom-eval form))) nil)
              ;pursue the rest of the path starting with the filler of
              ;the first-named role
            ((grf (cdr path)(cadr (memq (car path)(atom-eval form))))))))
))


;[2]
;Updating function S(et) R(ole) F(iller):
; Args: path, a role path, expected to exist up to next to last component
; in form, an ERKS form; filler, the filler to be placed at the end
; of the path
; Rtn: form
(def srf (lambda (path form filler)
;current filler of path
(let ((curr (grf path form)))
        ;just rebind it
       (cond (curr (set curr (atom-eval form))
              form)
             ;if path up to next-to-last component doesn't exist, fail
            ((null (setq curr (grf (rcdr path) form)))
             (error "Path" path "doesn't exist in" form)
             nil)
            ((add-pair curr (rcar path) filler)
             form))
)))
```

---

of roles and atomic fillers. Note also that the null path ( ) corresponds to the current toplevel name, as required.

The corresponding updating function *srf* (for set-role-filler) is shown at [2]. It is only slightly more complicated than *grf*. This is because it may have to call *add-pair* to add the last role in the path to the structure found at the end of the path less its last role, if this was not already present. Otherwise the modification simply consists of rebinding the preexisting name. Note that *srf* demands that the structure contain a filler at the next-to-last path. Otherwise we would be effectively adding a filler to a null type. Here, an ambiguity would arise as to which type was meant, since role names are occasionally repeated among the primitive types. The functions *rcar* and *rcdr* (for right *car* and *cdr,* respectively) are the analogues of these functions for the righthand sides of lists. They are easily implemented using *reverse.*

To illustrate the use of these functions, consider how the ERKS form for Example (2.1) might be built up:

(2.1)
```
(ptrans actor (person gender (fem) persname (Marie))
      obj (inst insttype (wrench))
      to (inside part (polity polname (Peoria) poltype (munic))))

      ;make an empty ptrans concept
      (setq foo (make-ERKS-structure (ptrans-f)))
      ;make a partially specified person
      (setq baz (make-ERKS-structure (person-f persname (Marie)
                                             gender (fem))))

      ;insert the person into the ptrans
      (srf '(actor) foo baz)
      ;compose the (obj) filler and insert it
      (srf '(obj) foo (make-ERKS-structure (inst-f insttype (wrench))))
      ;etc.
```

As another illustration, consider how *make-ERKS-structure* might be extended to allow for *equivalent* substructures, that is, sets of paths with identical fillers. For this, I provide the function (shown at [1] in Figure 3.7) with a second argument containing a list of sublists, each one of which is a set of equivalent paths. The equivalences are simply placed on the "equivs" property of the resulting symbol. Then, the function calls *map-equivs* (shown at [3]) to enforce the required equivalences. The function *srf* would have to assure that all the equivalent paths got an updated structure if any one of them did. The code to do this is shown at [2]. (The helper function *bagassoc* is the analogue of *assoc* for cases where we want to retrieve a sublist any member of which matches the key, instead of just the first. That is, the sublists are treated as "bags" of keys, rather than key-data associations. Function *delete* is the built-in Franz function that removes a specified structure from the toplevel of a list. Both of these functions have simple recursive definitions.)

I can use the equivalence feature to build Example (2.1) in such a way that the (actor) and (obj) paths always get the same fillers:

Figure 3.7
Enforcing Equivalences

```
;[1]
;MAKE-ERKS-STRUCTURE
;NOTE: for equivalences, we assume that the filler of the
; FIRST path in each equivalence set will be specified
; in the first argument
(def make-ERKS-structure (lambda (specs equivs)
      (let* ...
      ;name of result added to let* prologue
      (resname (new-conatom))
      ....
      ;body as before
      ;[3c]
      (cond ((null bad!)
              (set resname rescon)
              (map-equivs resname equivs)
              (putprop resname equivs 'equivs)))
      (or bad! resname)
)))


;[2]
;SRF
;Notice if path is among equivalence set; remap these equivalences
(def srf (lambda (path form filler)
;current filler of path
(let ((curr (grf path form))
      ;equivalence set path is in
      (eqs (bagassoc path (get form 'equivs))))

      ;if filler already exists, just rebind it
      (cond (curr
              (set curr (atom-eval form))
              ;if equivs, remap with path as first argument
              (and eqs
                  (map-equivs form (list (cons path (delete path eqs)))))
              form)

              ;if path up to next-to-last component doesn't exist, fail
              ((null (setq curr (grf (rcdr path) form)))
                (error "Path" path "doesn't exist in" form)
                nil)
              ((add-pair curr (rcar path) filler)
                ;if equivs, remap with path as first argument
                (and eqs
                    (map-equivs form (list (cons path (delete path eqs)))))
                form))
```

```
;[3]
;MAP-EQUIVS: enforce equivalence sets, taking first path in each sublist
; as the one to be copied from
(def map-equivs (lambda (con equivs)
        (mapc '(lambda (eqlst)
                    (mapc '(lambda(x)
                            (srf x con (grf (car eqlst) con)))
                        (cdr eqlst)))
            equivs)))
```

```
;make an empty ptrans concept, with the desired equivalences
(setq foo (eval (make-ERKS-structure (ptrans-f actor (nil))
                                    (((actor)(obj))))))
;foo has identical fillers:
foo:
(ptrans actor c55 obj c55)
;which are initially empty
c55:
(nil)
;insert a person into the (obj) path:
(srf '(obj) foo (make-ERKS-structure (person-f persname (Marie))))
;and both paths change:
foo:
(ptrans actor c55 obj c55)
c55:
(person persname c56)
```

Exercise III (Easy)

Write two functions, *grv* (get-role-value) and *srv* (set-role-value), that respectively return the evaluated form at the end of a given path, or set the atom at the end of the path to be the atomized form of the third argument. For example, after the above operations on the concept labeled "foo:"

```
(grv '(obj persname) 'foo) = (Marie)
(srv '(obj persname) 'foo '(Ronald))
followed by
(grv '(obj persname) 'foo) = (Ronald)
```

Exercise IV (More Difficult)

Write a function *xpn* (expand) that displays an atomized form with all the filler atoms removed.
For example,

```
(xpn 'foo) = (ptrans actor (person persname (Ronald))
                    obj (person persname (Ronald)))
```

How would you display repeated subforms, e.g., c55 in the original form?

3.4   The def-wordsense Record Macro

The dictionaries that the analysis and generation programs to be described use are based upon *wordsenses,* associations between a word and an ERKS structure representing one of its distinct meanings. Wordsenses represent an essential part of the permanent knowledge the overall system has about language. Thus the structuring of, and access to, this knowledge is a vital design concern.

A wordsense database can be systematically maintained by the *def-wordsense* record macro, a simplified definition for which is shown in Figure 3.8. The wordsenses are expected to be unique symbols whose property lists will hold the wordsense data. The first argument in the call to *def-wordsense* is that symbol, and the rest of the argument is a property list structure that will be associated with the symbol through a call to *dfps*.

Three of these properties are concerned with the "surface form" of the wordsense, i.e., the English words that are associated with the sense. The first is the "surface form" itself, which is the root form of the word. The other two are defined for irregular verbs: the "pastform" and the "partform," the irregular past and participial forms, respectively. One thing that *def-wordsense* must do is to link the irregular forms to the root form, so that the basic wordsense data can be used. This is accomplished by the code at [3]. If the past or perfect forms exist, the function makes a call to *add-syns* to define them in terms of the root word and a *morphological fragment.* "Given," for example, would be defined as a synonym for the phrase "perf$ give," where "perf$" is the lexeme representing the perfective (participial) fragment.[3] How these fragments are used will be discussed in the next chapter.

A slight difficulty is caused by the fact that the "surface-form" is a list. The reason for this is that we want to allow phrasal wordsenses. We use the Franz function *concatl* to create a symbol to define the synonyms in terms of. (This is bound to the variable *surfptr* at [1].) If the list contains a single word, as in the example for "understand," the surface pointer is the word (the root form). If it is a list, the symbol is the concatenation of the words in the phrase. For example, the symbol for "kick the bucket" would be "kickthebucket." The surface pointer symbol is the one that the analyzer dictionary entry is actually written for, as we shall see in the next chapter. Phrasal wordsenses are defined in terms of this symbol by the call to *add-phrases* at [2].

The "ws-structure" property defines the meaning structure, through the frame functions, corresponding to the root word. The properties "constraints" and "equivs" give the constraint expressions and equivalent subconceptualizations for the sense, respectively. These data are

Figure 3.8
The def-wordsense Record Macro

```
;DEF-WORDSENSE: define a sense of a word, including
; 1. sense name
; 2. surface-form (a list, to allow for phrases)
; 3. pastform and partform, the past and participial forms, if
; these are irregular
; 4. ws-structure, the ERKS-structure corresponding to the word sense
; This is defined using the frame functions to fill in
; whatever roles must be there; therefore, it is a
; template in the SOT-search sense
; 5. equivalences, equivalent subroles
; 6. focus, a path to the default focus (subcon to be said first
; by generator).


;EXAMPLE:
;(def-wordsense wsUNDERSTAND1
      ; surface-form (understand)
      ; partform (understood)
      ;Paraphrase: someone can decide on a mental-mapping relation between
      ; something in the world (e.g., something told to the person)
      ; and a knowledge structure "possessed by" the actor
      ; ws-structure
      ; (mbuild-f time (times-f time1 (:pres))
                  ; mode (modes-f mode1 (:t))
                  ; actor (( ))
                  ; mobj (a-config-f confrel (mental-map)
                              ; con1 (infostruc-f possby (()) somerel (( )))
                              ; con2 (( ))
                              ; time (times-f time1 (:pres))
                              ; mode (modes-f mode1 (:t))))
      ; equivs (((actor)(mobj con1 possby)))
      ; focus (actor)
      ; )
      (def def-wordsense (macro (arg)
            (let* ((tag (cadr arg))
                  (surfform (cadr (memq 'surface-form (cdr arg))))
                  ;[1]
                  ;define a symbol to stand for the root word or phrase
                  (surfptr (concatl surfform))
                  ; grab any irregular forms
                  (pastform (cadr (memq 'pastform (cdr arg))))
                  (partform (cadr (memq 'partform (cdr arg)))))
            ;if tag already used, complain
            (cond ((get tag 'ws-structure)
                  (msg ERR-MSG nl "Wordsense" tag "already exists")
                  (pause 'def-wordsense)))
```

Figure 3.8 (*Continued*)

```
;[2]
;if the surface form is a phrase, call add-phrases to
;define the synonym
(cond
        ((greaterp (length surfform) 1)
           (add-phrases '((,surfptr , @ surfform)))))
;[3]
;set up irregular form correspondences
(cond
        (pastform
           (add-syns '((,pastform (past$ ,surfptr))))))
(cond
        (partform
           (add-syns '((,partform (perf$ ,surfptr))))))
        '(dfps ,tag , @ (cddr arg))
)))


;ADD-SYNS: set up a correspondence between a word/phrase and a
; synonym
;Arg: an association list of the form (word synonym), where
; synonym may be a phrase
;Rtns: t
(def add-syns (lambda (arg)
        (cond ((null arg) t)
                 ((putprop (caar arg)(cadar arg) 'root-syn)
                  (add-syns (cdr arg))))
))
```

stored on the property list of the wordsense symbol. The wordsenses are used as data by the dictionary managers for the conceptual analyzer and generator, which we will describe in succeeding chapters.

Exercise V (Easy)

Extend the *def-wordsense* macro to handle the following cases of irregular forms: (a) words such as "run," for which the root form and the participial form are the same; (b) words such as "hit," in which the root, simple past, and participial form are all the same; and (c) irregular plurals, such as "children" (what about "sheep"?). (Hint: define morphological fragments analogous to past$ and perf$.)

3.5 Summary

This chapter has defined a set of useful data-type managing functions for ERKS types and the ISA–hierarchy defined on them. Since the ERKS types can be thought of as a kind of record, we need functions to test for instances of them, to create legal instance forms, to access their various fields, and to update those fields. The testing and creation functions are defined automatically by the record-type macro *def-ERKS-type*. The type-defining call also links the type into the ISA–hierarchy. A collection of functions was introduced that allow a user to move around in the hierarchy and to ask questions about properties that can be inherited by the types. Functions for accessing and updating parts of ERKS forms were also discussed. Finally, I defined the *def-wordsense* macro, which creates the basic data structure required by the dictionaries used by the analyzer and generator: the word sense, an association between a surface form (a word or phrase) and its underlying meaning structure. The reason for managing all this through records is to automate the process of function and data definition, thus drastically reducing the chances for errors.

Notes

1. The functions and data structures presented in this chapter are slightly simplified forms of the actual programs included with Version 1.10 of the NLP Toolkit. Minor discrepancies will doubtless appear as future versions of the Toolkit are developed.

2. I'm relying on the Franz implementation feature that makes (car nil) = (cdr nil) = nil, to allow *is-among-p* to work even when the input type isn't in the list. In some Lisps, taking the car of any atom is an error.

3. The operation in which an inflected form is reduced to a root word plus a fragment is called "root stripping." When the fragment comes before the root form in the input stream, we have an instance of "affix hopping." (In English, most of the important fragments are in fact suffixes; i.e., they "follow" the root form.)

4

Surface-Semantic Conceptual Analysis

4.0   Introduction: Lexicon-Driven Analysis

This chapter is an introduction to the model of language analysis I
describe in this book: *conceptual analysis,* the mapping of natural
language sentences into a semantic representation. I will discuss the analyzer
as a tool, in terms of some simple examples. (In Chapter 5, we'll see how the
tool can be used to solve a variety of difficult problems.) What I'll be trying
to communicate as we go along is a way of thinking about language-
processing problems, to which a tool of this sort is well suited.

The program is technically a *surface-semantic conceptual analyzer.* Its
job is to convert a surface form, a string encoding an English sentence or
sentence fragment, into a well-formed meaning representation at the level
of the surface semantic categories of ERKS. This semantic structure can
then be passed off to a variety of reasoning and inference processes for
deeper "understanding." The analyzer itself should not build anything
into the representation that the words of the sentence do not explicitly
mention or directly imply, in the sense of the Maximal Inference-Free
Paraphrase.

The mapping from words into meaning representation is driven by
whatever morphological, syntactic, semantic, contextual, etc., cues are
available. In contrast to other well-known models of analysis, conceptual
analysis does not first process the input syntactically, then assign a
semantic reading to the syntactic structure (such as in Wood70; Gins78;
Marc80). Nor does it conduct a simultaneous syntactic and semantic
analysis (such as in Wino72; Brow75). (Such analyzers are often called
"parsers.")

The conceptual analysis approach centers, rather, upon the *lexicon* as
the locus of processing. Thus there is no explicit grammar in the analyzer
to be presented (and none in the generator, either). By this, I don't mean
to imply that the analyzer does not use syntactic features such as word
order and noun-group constituency: it does, constantly! We shall see,
however, that such features are used *by the words themselves* as they
cooperate to form fragments of meaning.

It's not that people who take this approach haven't noticed that certain
patterns of processing occur over and over again across many different
words. The generalization called "intransitive," for example, is certainly

real enough. We haven't made these generalizations explicit because, in the company of many semanticists and psycholinguists (for instance, Mill76), we have really been mostly concerned with the relationships between individual words and what they *mean*. Thus, "intransitive" is viewed as a pattern reflective of an underlying conceptual fact: certain words build meaning structures which subsume conceptual "objects."

Thus, defining a word begins to look like a process of *design:* we add new processing information as new constructions involving the word are introduced. More important, we restructure old definitions as new senses of the words come to mind. Designing word definitions so that the intricate process of meaning disambiguation can be supported turns out to be a problem very naturally posed within the lexicon itself.

It is true that an explicit grammar is an economical encoding of control information and would make certain tasks easier. A purely grammatical model, however, is too top-down in nature to be able to cope robustly with real language users. Ungrammatical inputs occur constantly in real language use. We wanted a process that would produce at least fragments of meaning for really deviant sentences, rather than simply failing to produce anything at all. We also wanted a psychologically plausible model of analysis; certainly people don't first decide whether an input is grammatical, then try to decide what it means.

It must be emphasized that language understanding is an intensely *predictive* process. As a new sentence in a conversation starts, for example, people seem to operate in a bottom-up manner, piecing together fragments of meaning from the first few words until their conceptual *expectations* can come into play to drive the understanding process in a more top-down manner. These expectations can come from the words themselves, or from the conversational context of preceding exchanges.

As an engineering matter, the interface designer needs a model of analysis that can operate smoothly across the entire spectrum of expectations. The analyzer should operate "left to right," a word or phrase at a time. "Understanding" of the sentence by the complete system (i. e., the analyzer and the deep-memory modules) should be complete at the end of the sentence, or shortly thereafter. This means that units of meaning should be made available to the memory system as soon as they are available (e. g., at noun-group or clausal boundaries). We also wish to resolve ambiguities in word meaning as soon as possible; that is, to disambiguate "on the fly." Therefore, the interface between analyzer and memory is crucial.

4.1 A Simple Model of Sentence Structure

For introductory purposes, I will use a very simple model of English sentence structure as consisting of *a verb kernel plus constituents*. This model assumes that a sentence is built around a core consisting of the main verb, its auxiliaries, and possibly some modal words or adverbs. The core may be "contiguous," as in declarative and imperative sentences, or it may be "distributed," as in question forms. The core is surrounded by constituents, functional units of meaning usually based on noun groups or imbedded (e. g., infinitive- or progressive-form) verbs.

The model of a declarative sentence posits an indefinite number of constituents *preceding* and *following* the kernel, as follows:

<const><const>...<verb kernel><const><const>...<const>

For example, the sentence

(1)
Olivia was not punching Muhammed in the nose

has the single constituent "Olivia" preceding the kernel phrase "was not punching," and the two constituents "Muhammed" and "in the nose" following. In many grammatical treatments of sentence structure, constituents are called (or associated with) cases (e. g., Fill72). I use the term "constituent" to emphasize the conceptual contribution of these functional units to the meaning of the sentence.

In traditional grammatical terms, the kernel phrase in (1) contains an indication of tensing ("was"), aspect ("-ing"), and mode ("not"), all modifying the *root form* "punch." In more conceptual terms, the tensing information is a linguistic device usually used to communicate the time relation between the event the sentence describes and "now." Similarly, the *progressive* aspect indicates that the event was co-occurring with another, unnamed event in the past. The modals serve to indicate whether the speaker is communicating that the event really occurred (the simple declarative), did not occur (as in this example), is simply potential ("can"), etc. I will treat forms of "be," "have" and "do" used as auxiliaries, morphological endings such as "-ed" and "-ing," and modal words as *function lexemes*. These lexical units do not themselves have an ERKS representation, but serve to modify the meaning structure built by another word (the verb root).

The phrase "in the nose" is called a "prepositional constituent," since it is *marked* or *governed* by the preposition "in." Note that the constituents immediately preceding and following the kernel of (1) are *unmarked;* that is, no function word such as a preposition is needed to indicate the relationship of the constituent to the meaning of the sentence as a whole. Traditionally, the constituents preceding and following the verb in an active-voice, simple declarative sentence have been called the *syntactic subject* and *object,* respectively. Since I want to relate the *position* of a constituent in a sentence to the way in which it contributes to the overall meaning, I will say that the preceding and following constituents are in the *actor-spot* and *obj-spot,* respectively, with respect to the verb kernel. These terms are used because the constituents often end up in the conceptual *actor* and *obj* roles in the underlying ERKS meaning structure.

In the passive form

(2)

Muhammed was not being punched in the nose by Olivia

the constituents "Olivia" and "Muhammed" appear in the same conceptual role as in (1), as hitter and hittee, respectively. That is, except for the shift in *sentential focus* (roughly, the constituent that is expressed first), (1) and (2) are paraphrases of each other. Thus, we see that the actor-spot constituent is systematically governed by the preposition "by" in the passive voice, and the obj-spot constituent is found in the syntactic subject spot.

Some verbs can take two unmarked following constituents. For example, we might have "Olivia gave Muhammed a book." I will call the immediately following constituent (the grammatical indirect object) a *recip-spot* constituent, since the concept built often goes into the conceptual recipient role in the ERKS structure. In this case, the second constituent is the obj-spot constituent. In other surface forms, the obj-spot constituent can appear in the syntactic object (first following constituent) position in the active voice (e. g., "Olivia gave a book to Muhammed") and in the syntactic subject ("A book was given") or object ("Muhammed was given a book") position in the passive.

Constituents governed by prepositions are said to be in the *prep-spot* with respect to the verb. Prep-spot constituents (or "prepconsts," for short) normally have a preferred position in a sentence. For example, "Olivia punched in the nose Muhammed" sounds a little odd, if only because of the noun-noun pair "nose Muhammed." The sentence "In the nose Olivia punched Muhammed" is presumably a form created by a focus shift to "the nose" by the speaker, who wants to talk about it for some reason. Each English verb has a characteristic set of prepconsts, together with one or a few preferred orderings.

Many verbs (especially *mtrans* and *s-goal* words) take *imbedded sentences* or, to put it in more meaning-related terms, *dependent conceptualizations.* For example, we might have

(3)

Olivia wanted to punch Muhammed in the nose.

Here, the dependent conceptualization is the infinitive form "to punch Muhammed in the nose." With respect to the syntax/semantics of "want," this constituent appears *positionally* in the prep-spot, governed by preposition "to," and *semantically* is required to be an instance of the

ERKS type *episode*. It is important to note that *the positional/semantic specifications of "punch" do not change* when the verb is used in an imbedded sentence. That word still wants an *animate* actor (not explicitly mentioned in (3)) in the act-spot, a *physobj* in the obj-spot, and a *bpart* in a prepconst associated with "in."

A similar observation can be made about gerund forms such as:

(4)
Olivia considered punching Muhammed in the nose.

Thus it appears that the information necessary to built up complete meaning structures for at least simple sentences such as (1–4) amounts to specifying two different kinds of information. First, there is the *preferred positioning* of the characteristic constituents of a verb with respect to the verb kernel. Second, there is the *preferred surface semantics* associated with each constituent. This idea is the key to the style of analysis I will next present.

4.2   Production Systems, Requests, and Processing Overview

The basic source of expectations for a surface semantic analyzer comes from the words themselves. Certain words can predict that other meaning units are likely to occur in the sentence environment because of the semantic requirements of the meaning structure(s) they build. For example, if we have a sentence containing "eat," there are high-level predictions for an animate eater and an ingestible object, both to be found in characteristic places in the sentence. What we need is a way of associating these predictions with the words in the system's dictionary, from which they can be summoned when the word is actually seen in the input stream.

A flexible and attractive means for accomplishing this is to organize the analyzer as a *production system* (e. g., Newe72; Rych76). In a production system, the units of processing are individual *productions,* or test-action pairs. The productions are maintained in a special memory called *production memory.* The test parts of the productions monitor a *working memory* of facts or hypotheses, usually describing the current state of the understanding or problem-solving process. The control of the system resides with a very simple *interpreter.* This repeatedly selects the subset of productions whose test conditions match the current state of working memory (the so-called "conflict set" [Haye79]). Then, by a process of *conflict resolution,* the interpreter selects one production out of the conflict set, and "fires" it, i. e., executes its "actions." Typical actions add and delete forms from the working memory. The cycle of conflict-set formation, conflict resolution, and production firing continues until no productions are applicable to the working memory, at which point the problem posed to the system has hopefully been "solved."

Models of this sort are attractive for problem-solving processes, including language understanding, for several reasons. First, many kinds of knowledge can be conveniently thought of as being organized in small, weakly interacting "packages." Rules of thumb about a given situation are a common example of packaged knowledge of this type. You may not quite know why a given behavior is "good" in a given circumstance, but you do know that it has worked before. Packaged knowledge also has the possibility of incremental growth. One hopes to be able to add new rules to the collection without upsetting preexisting rules. (In actuality, interesting, unexpected interactions nearly always happen, as the system evolves.)

In a language analyzer, the packages come with the language's words, phrases, and morphological fragments. Stored with the words in the program's dictionary are two different kinds of information: (a) associations between the word and meaning structures corresponding to the individual wordsenses, and (b) predictions about lexical, conceptual, and contextual entities that will be seen in the environment surrounding the word when it is actually used in a sentence.

Expectations associated with a word definition are encoded in a special type of production rule called a *request* (Ries75). Associated with a meaning structure built by a word is a set of expectations embodied in requests indicating how the structure's characteristic roles are to be filled. The special feature of requests considered as productions is that, in addition to modifying working memory, they can also *add and delete productions (requests)* from the production memory. Requests are *activated* when the associated word definition is loaded, i. e., placed in a short-term memory of requests to be *considered*.

In the algorithm to be presented, the request consideration process repeatedly selects a request and evaluates its test part. If the test returns "non-nil," the request is said to have "fired," its actions part is evaluated, and it is removed from the request memory. (That is, there is no explicit calculation of the conflict set of requests.) Requests can check semantic, lexical, or contextual features of the run-time environment, and create or interconnect conceptual structures. Moreover, they can cause other requests to be activated or deleted.

To motivate this, let's consider an overview of the conceptual analysis of the sentence

(5)
Olivia ate an apple.

For the moment, I will ignore the details of how morphology and noun groups such as "an apple" are handled. Figure 4.1 contains a simple dictionary definition for "Olivia," built on top of the wordsense

Figure 4.1
Dictionary Definition (Simplified) for ''Olivia''

```
(def-wordsense wsOLIVIA1
 surface-form (Olivia)
 ws-structure (person-f gender (fem) persname (Olivia)))

(adictdef Olivia
 pos noun
 topreq
 ((test t)
  (actions
   (add-word-con wsOLIVIA1))))
```

---

wsOLIVIA1, as shown. Here, *adictdef* (analyzer dictionary definition) is a record macro for managing the analyzer's dictionary. It operates, much like *def-wordsense* and other macros discussed in Chapter 3, by placing information on the property list of the symbol, and updating various global databases (e. g., for lexical and phrasal synonyms, irregular forms, etc.). In (5), ''Olivia'' has p(art)-o(f)-s(peech) ''noun.'' This information is used by the analyzer to decide whether or not to be in ''noun group'' mode, as described below.

The property *topreq,* which stands for ''top request,'' is associated with a list structure having two sublists, the first containing the keyword ''test,'' the second containing the keyword ''actions.'' The test part of the request is the *cadr* of the sublist having the ''test'' keyword, viz., the built-in symbol *t*. This always evaluates to non-nil, so the actions part of the request, the list of forms in the *cdr* of the ''actions'' sublist, is always executed one after the other the first time the request is considered. The single action shown calls the function *add-word-con* to add an atomized ERKS structure derived from the associated wordsense (which defines a named person as shown) to the short-term memory of available concepts called the C-LIST. The word ''apple'' would access a definition similar to that of ''Olivia,'' except that the structure added to the C-LIST would be based upon the primitive *ingobj*, or ingestible object. Ordering of concepts on the C-LIST is defined by the order in which the corresponding words are seen in the input sentence. Thus, in (5) the concept for ''Olivia'' *precedes* the ones for ''ate,'' ''an'' and ''apple'' in the C-LIST.

Exercise I (Easy)

Using the wordsense wsOLIVIA1 of Figure 4.1, the functions of Chapter 3, and the global C-LIST, write a version of *add-word-con* that adds an instance of ''Olivia'' to the working memory, i.e., at the righthand side of the C-LIST.

Neither of these words activates any further requests. As Figure 4.2 shows, however, the word "eat" does. Here, "eat" first adds an instance of the wordsense ERKS form to the C-LIST, then calls the function *activate* to add two new requests to request memory. (I will often speak of the words as "doing things." As we shall see, the production system control is actually *interpreting* the requests and explicitly calling the Lisp evaluator when a predicate needs to be checked or a side-effect needs to be propagated.)

The function : = in the test part of "eat" is the analyzer's *run-time binding operator*. It is the analogue for our production system interpreter of the Lisp function *setq,* which binds symbols to values. As it is evaluated, this function propagates the actual name of the concept, say c567, returned by *add-word-con* for this instance of "eat" into the body of the request. All instances of the placeholder symbol "topcon" will be replaced by that name. (Actually, since the name will become an argument to Lisp functions, what is propagated is the quoted form 'c567.) The binding operator : = always returns non-nil when used in this way. Therefore, we get the effect of (test t) in the test part of the definitions of "Olivia" and "apple" with a slightly shorter definition.

The function *activate* (which is yet another s-expression rewriting macro) expects a list of s-expressions from which it can create requests to place in the request memory. The requests thus obtained from the dictionary definition are said to be in a *cluster,* and are activated as a single *pool.* Thus, certain global actions (such as deletion) can be applied to all the members of the pool simultaneously. Having pools of requests is a way of treating related predictions together. For example, a request pool might encode mutually exclusive possibilities for a conceptual form a word is looking for.

The s-expressions supplied to *activate* can either be literal data structures embodying requests in their test/action format (as in Figure 4.1), or calls to parameterized *request-generating macros,* which return request bodies containing the actual values of the parameters. The latter case produces easier-to-read definitions, so it is the one I have illustrated in Figure 4.2. (I'll get to the details later.)

The first request generator, named *actspot-req,* embodies a test which seeks a *person* (using the predicate *couldbe-person-p*) to fill the *actor* slot in the concept built by "eat." The place where the request looks for conceptual actor is in the syntactic actor-spot. As our constituent sentence model assumes, the actor-spot is among the C-LIST items preceding the concept for "eat" in the active voice, and in a prepositional phrase marked by "by" in the passive. The second request generator, named *objspot-req,* seeks an ingestible object to fill the conceptual *obj* slot in the *ingest* structure. The desired C-LIST location is the obj-spot: following that structure if the voice is active, preceding it if passive. Both request generators are targetted on initially empty slots in the wordsense

Figure 4.2
Definition (Simplified) of the Word ''Eat''

```
(def-wordsense wsEAT1
 surface-form (eat)
 ws-structure
 (ingest actor (nil)
        object (nil)
        from (bpart-f bptype (mouth) partof (nil)
        to (bpart-f bptype (stomach) partof (nil))
        time (times-f timel (:pres))
        mode (modes-f model (:t)))
 equivs
 (((actor)(from partof)(to partof)))
 )
(adictdef eat
 pos v
 topreq
 ((test := topcon (add-word-con wsEAT1)))
  (actions
   (activate
    (actspot-req topcon (actor) couldbe-person-p)
    (objspot-req topcon (obj) couldbe-ingobj-p)))))
```

for ''eat.'' They are attempting to fill a ''gap'' in a conceptual structure, and thus are called ''gap requests,'' or ''gapreqs'' for short.

The definition shown in Figure 4.2, as simple as it is, can handle the following corpus of sentences involving ''eat:''

(6a) Olivia ate an apple.
(6b) An apple was eaten by Olivia.
(6c) Olivia ate.
(6d) An apple was eaten.
(6e) Eat!

In (6c) and (6d), the expectations for ''ingestible'' and ''person,'' respectively, have not been fulfilled. In (6e), neither request ever fires.

The analyzer, proceeding left-to-right through Sentence (6a), first activates and fires the request for ''Olivia,'' adding the associated structure to the C-LIST. Next, the top request for ''eat'' adds the *ingest,* and queues up a pool containing the two requests. The *actspot-req* fires immediately, since ''Olivia'' is already available and the voice is active. (I will describe how voice is handled during the discussion of the copula ''to be,'' below.) The concept is inserted into the *ingest* as the filler of the path (actor), and the ''Olivia'' concept disappears from the C-LIST. (We say it is "no longer available.") In this case, the *objspot-req* is a *prediction,* and does not fire when first considered. Next, ignoring the determiner "an," the topreq for "apple" fires, and the *ingobj* gets placed on the C-LIST. Now the second request for "eat" fires, and the "apple" concept becomes the (obj) filler in the *ingest.* Since there are neither active requests nor more words to activate requests from, the process terminates, leaving a well-formed conceptual structure as its result.

The foregoing, in overview, is how the analyzer's basically bottom-up request consideration process proceeds. The request consideration regime as presented so far is given in a flow chart in Diagram 4.1. In summary, each word results in the activation of a topreq pool (a pool containing a single request) when it is "read" from the input stream. Consideration of a topreq always results in the addition of a conceptual structure to the C-LIST. It may also result in the activation of further pools of requests, e. g., gapreq pools that search in the C-LIST for entities having the desired positional and semantic properties, which get inserted into the parent concept. Any request is at liberty to activate more requests, so the topreq can be thought of as being the root of a spreading tree of requests. When no more requests fire in a consideration cycle, a new topreq pool is created from the next word. This continues until we run out of words and the request pools are "quiescent." At this point, if the sentence made sense in surface semantic terms, there should be a single ERKS structure left corresponding to its meaning.

4.3 Request Pool Consideration

Every call to the function *activate* results in the creation of a pool of related requests, which are considered together by the production system monitor. As in any production system, the *timing* of the consideration process is extremely important. We want the pools to be looked at in such a way that they have the maximum chance of building a well-formed conceptual structure. On the other hand, we want the control algorithm to be as simple as possible. One reason for this is simply efficiency. More important, however, whenever an idea about processing goes into the control algorithm rather than into the requests themselves, *that knowledge is lost.* In principle, there is no way for the system to be "aware" of the knowledge: it has been "buried" in the code rather than in the data the system manipulates.

The request consideration regime to be discussed is based upon the following very simple heuristics: first, once created, the requests remain in existence until either they fire, delete themselves, or are deleted by another request. This is because they are predictions about where certain kinds of entities will be seen. (This can cause problems: requests persisting beyond when they could possibly be applicable can fire when

Diagram 4.1
Request Consideration Flow Chart (Overview)

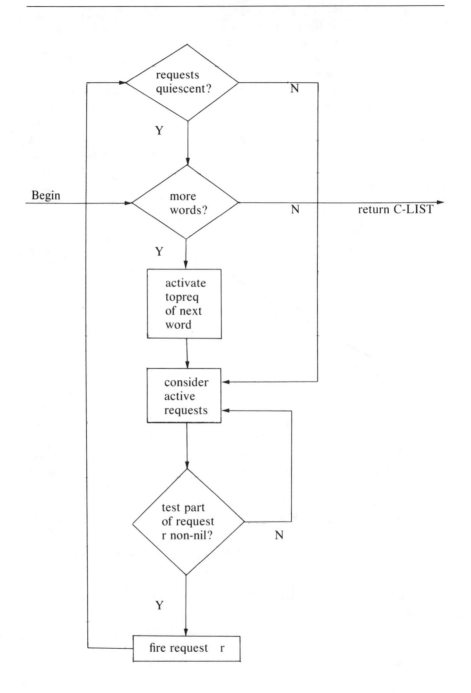

they shouldn't, with possibly disastrous side-effects. Ways of minimizing this problem will be discussed later.)

Next, during any given cycle of consideration, the system will continue to look at the test parts of all relevant requests until none fire (in which case, we say the pools are "quiescent.") At quiescence, the system reads the next lexical unit (fragment, word, or phrase), activates its topreq, and starts considering requests anew. Finally, if a request from a given pool fires, the current round of consideration stops if the actions part of the request causes something "interesting" to happen. This avoids the expense of accumulating the conflict set and resolving conflicts by restarting after the first request with interesting side effects. Interesting events include the appearance of a new concept on the C-LIST (which a prior request may be waiting for), a meaning disambiguation event, the creation of a new pool, the insertion of one concept into another, etc.

4.3.1 Analysis Environment

Use of these heuristics is conditioned by a notion of the *current analysis environment*. The model of sentence structure is based on a verb kernel with surrounding constituents, and there are slightly different processing requirements for each.

In ordinary, *structure-driven* mode, all existing request pools are considered in order of *recency*. One processing idea here is that the older requests have been considered several times without firing, hence are less likely to go off than the newer ones. More important, in languages like English that have few inflected forms, words that should go together conceptually tend to be near one another. Thus, processing request pools most-recent-first lets the nearest words have the first shot at a C-LIST item. The reason this mode is called "structure driven" is that the requests are normally concerned with finding C-LIST concepts to insert in other conceptual structures (i.e., the requests are gapreqs). The requirements of the structures for fillers, embodied in gapreqs, thus drive the consideration process.

In *position-driven* mode (Gers79), a constituent is being assembled. Constituents are usually expressed by noun groups, so this style of processing is also called "noun-grouping." The reason for the term "position-driven" is that it is the position of a subconstituent in the noun group with respect to the *head noun* that determines its contribution to the meaning of the constituent. For example, the noun group "iron tire" means something completely different from "tire iron." The first presumably means a "tire made of iron" ("tire" being the head noun), while the second means "an implement used to manipulate a tire." In position-driven mode, only the pools created by the words in the current noun group are considered. The reason for this is clear: we want the constituent to assemble itself completely before allowing a request from a word external to the noun group to get access to it. In the sentence "I gave John the tire iron," for example, the gapreq of "give" would be equally happy with a concept corresponding to "tire" or "tire iron." Thus we must delay consideration of the requests of "give" until the noun group is assembled.

While noun-grouping, all pools accumulated so far (the "ng-pools") in the noun group are considered in order of recency. A new pool activated in the current cycle (the "latest pool") is given exactly one chance to fire. The reason for this is that the pool may contain a request for an entity *preceding* the concept on the C-LIST. This entity, if it exists at all, should already be present, and so we give the request a chance to pick it up. After a single scan of the ng-pools and the latest pool, if there is one, the system reads the next word, and continues.

When a word is read that cannot possibly be in the current noun group, the system enters *end-of-noun-group* ("end-NG") mode and begins trying to assemble the noun-group constituent. The ng-pools are scanned in order of recency, and re-scanned when a request action does something interesting.

Determining when to enter and leave noun-grouping mode can be extremely difficult. Often, detailed consideration of syntactic relations, such as person and number agreement, is necessary. Consider, for example, the relations among "that, "block" and "supports" in the following sentences:

(7a) I know that the block supports the pyramid
(7b) I know that block supports the pyramid
(7c) I know that supports the pyramid
(7d) I know that blocks support the pyramid
(7e) I know that blocks support for the pyramid.

In (7a–c), we see "that" functioning as a connective for the imbedded concept, a determiner, and a demonstrative pronoun, respectively. In (7d), the number disagreement is what tells us that "that" cannot be in the noun group with "blocks." In (7e), finally, we must resolve the ambiguous word "blocks" as a tensed main verb rather than as a plural noun. My elementary treatment of noun-grouping will ignore all these problems. I will assume that proper nouns, determiners (including numbers), modifier words (such as adjectives) and pronouns can start noun groups, and that tensed forms and function words such as prepositions and conjunctions end them. This will be sufficient to handle a number of interesting cases.

Exercise II (Difficult)

Determine a set of sufficient conditions that will allow "that" to determine what its part-of-speech is. What should its actions be in the various cases illustrated by Examples (7a)—(7e)?

When the ng-pools are quiescent, we hope that a single concept is all that is left on the C-LIST. If this is so, a special request will fire, which is activated whenever the system enters noun-grouping mode, and which picks the constituent up and sends it off to any available memory process (for referent search, for example). This special request is one of a class called *shipreqs,* since its job is to ship the completed result to inference processes that may be able to come to a "deeper" understanding of it. Shipreqs also exist to send off clause-level C-LIST items.

Paired with the noun-group shipreq is a *diagnostic* request (or diagreq). If something other than a single C-LIST item remains after the ng-pools become quiescent, the system needs to diagnose what happened. Many special heuristics can be applied to solve problems of this sort, but in general, access to reasoning processes capable of connecting conceptual items on the basis of general or domain-specific knowledge will be needed. Problems are particularly caused by noun-noun pairs, simply because it is impossible to anticipate all the possible relations between nouns that might be mentioned in a surface-semantic dictionary defini-tion. For example, "ski jump cab" would presumably not go together unless the dictionary designer remembered that large ski jumps have elevators, whose compartments can be called "cabs." (This is an example from a recent winter Olympics.) In cases such as this, the surface semantic portion of the understander must be able to pass off the noun-group fragments to the reasoning part of the system. The diagreqs are the machinery provided for this purpose.

4.3.2 Request Types

The request pool consideration process is also affected by the *type* of pool being considered. (With the single exception discussed below, pools are considered to be uniform in type.) Each pool type has a consideration *discipline,* which details how the individual requests are to be handled. For topreqs, the discipline is very simple, since there is only one request that always fires. In a gapreq pool, *all* requests are considered (in the order in which they appear, textually speaking, in the dictionary), and any that wish to are allowed to fire. Shipreqs and diagreqs are normally treated like gapreqs. They appear in a single pool, and if the diagreq fires, the result of diagnosis is picked up by the shipreq for communication to memory.

Specialized side-effects are associated with the function *kill,* which takes as arguments one of the keywords "self" and "rest-of-pool." When this function is executed as a request action, it causes the request it is part of, or the other requests in its pool, to be removed from consideration. Thus, any request can decide it is no longer relevant, or that the other requests in its pool are not.

A use of the *kill* operator can be seen with pools of the *o(ne)-s(hot) gapreq* variety. These are gapreqs that have a consideration discipline that allows them to be looked at exactly once. An os-gapreq either fires at that time or its pool is removed from the active pool list. This kind of gapreq is normally used when a word has an expectation for a preceding concept in the C-LIST. For example, a name-word such as "Teddy" could contain an expectation for a title-word, such as "Senator." If a title-concept exists in a given sentence, it will already be in the C-LIST, where the os-gapreq can see it.

In addition to these there are several other types of request pool. I will defer discussion of their consideration discipline until I have explained what they do.

4.4   Requests in More Detail

We're now in a position to look at the requests themselves, in more detail. In the rest of this chapter, I will describe the machinery needed to handle the sentence

(8)
Muhammed was punched in the nose by Olivia.

This will culminate in a detailed trace of the analyzer actually running on the sentence in Section 4.6.

In Section 4.2, I gave a definition of the word "Olivia" in terms of a specific wordsense, wsOLIVIA1. Clearly, this approach is wasteful of space, since we would have to repeat the process of providing wordsenses and definitions for all the hundreds of personal names we know. What one should look for in such cases is a useful *abstraction*, an entity or episode that subsumes many different instances of other concepts. A good abstraction here is the concept of a "named person." What is needed is some means for defining the characteristics of a named person for once and for all, and then instantiating it many times, one for each name the system is to know about.

What are the surface semantic characteristics of a named person? First is the characteristic set of names: personal name, middle name, and family name(s). (The order of the names depends on the cultural group to which the person belongs.) Given the personal name, one can often make a judgment about the gender of the person involved. (Of course, the "first name" may just be an initial, as in "T. Robert Jones.") Many surnames are symbols for which no dictionary definition will exist; they will simply appear to be "unknown" to the analyzer. (Usually, they will have an initial capital.) Sometimes, the last name may look like a first name: "John Paul." The middle name may be spelled out, or it may be an initial. There may be a preceding "title" word: "President Lyndon Johnson."

A complete request cluster for handling all these possibilities can be

Figure 4.3
The def-named-person Macro

```
;A macro form for creating a named person:
(def def-named-person (macro (arg)
   (let* ((name (cadr arg))
          (gender (cddr arg)))
      '(adictdef ,name
             pos n
             topreq
             ((test (:= topcon (add-con (person-f persname (,name)
                                                   gender ,gender)
                                          ()())))
             (actions
             (activate
             ;treat following unknown as a surname
             (gapreq
              (test (:= unkcon (if-ngavail topcon (g)
                             (and (foll g topcon)
                                   ;unknown is a special type for
                                   ;words not in the dictionary
                                   (semfeature g 'unknown-p)))))
             (actions
                (fill-gap '(surname) topcon unkcon)))))))
  )))

(def-named-person Olivia fem)
(def-named-person Muhammed masc)
```

---

written, but it would be too complicated for my present purposes. A dictionary definition for "named person," which is sufficient to handle noun groups containing a known personal name and unknown surname, can be created through the use of the dictionary macro *def-named-person,* as shown in Figure 4.3. The figure also shows the function calls needed to define "Olivia" and "Muhammed," as needed by our example.

As the figure indicates, the function creates a call to the *adictdef* dictionary macro, overwriting the placeholders "gender" and "name" with the actual parameters given in the call. The definition becomes effective when the form returned by the macro is evaluated. The test part of the topreq contains a call to the function *add-con*. This function, which is called by *add-word-con* in ordinary dictionary entries based on wordsenses, takes three arguments. The first is an ERKS frame to be evaluated for an instance of a concept. The second argument (empty here) is an association list of paths into the first argument and fillers (ERKS frames) to be placed at the end of the paths The third (also empty) is a collection of equivalences to be enforced in the concept. After all this is done, the first argument is placed at the end of the C-LIST and it is made available for the requests to look at.

The actions part of the topreq activates a gapreq targetted on the *surname* field in the named-person concept. Here, finally, is the basic form of a request: a function, *if-ngavail*, that searches the C-LIST for concepts satisfying a predicate. This function collects the available C-LIST items surrounding the first argument (called the "pivot") that are in its noun-group, and *applies* the remainder of its argument (after making it into a lambda-expression) to each of these items in turn. The first item for which the predicate returns non-nil is returned by *if-ngavail* as its result, which is then propagated via placeholder "unkcon."

Let's look at the symbolic computing activity required to make all this work. The Franz Lisp definition of *if-ngavail* is shown in Figure 4.4. This function calls *getngp* to collect the noun-group expanse of the C-LIST that the pivot appears in, then uses *test-avail,* a simple recursive function, to apply the lambda expression formed to each of those items in turn. (All the argument "(g)" signifies is the formal variable in the lambda expression.)

The only real complication here is that the predicate should be applied to the C-LIST items in order of nearness to the pivot. That is, it should pick up the nearest available concept that satisfies the condition. As shown in the definition, *getngp* collects the items following and preceding the pivot at [1] and [2], respectively, in order of nearness, using the fact that the C-LIST grows from left to right. (The markers "begin-ng" and "end-ng" are placed on the C-LIST by the system on transitions into and out of noun-grouping mode, respectively. These markers are not available and thus are not seen by the requests.) Then, at [3], *getngp* calls *interleave,* to merge these two lists so that *test-avail* first sees the immediately following concept, then the immediately preceding one, then the next following, then the next preceding, etc.

Exercise III (Easy)

Write a definition of the function *interleave,* which takes two lists, say (1 2 3) and (4 5 6) and interleaves them into (1 4 2 5 3 6). What should the function do when the lists are of different length?

The predicate specified in Figure 4.3 has a *positional* part and a *semantic* part, connected by the logical operator *and*. The positional specification is that the C-LIST item FOLLow the pivot. The semantic feature is that it be "unknown." Words that are not in the system's dictionary are treated as instances of the special ERKS type *unknown*. Thus, "SHRDLU" would become:

(unknown lexval (SHRDLU))

Figure 4.4
The Function if-ngavail

```
;IF-NGAVAIL: examine noun-goup expanse of C-LIST surrounding pivot,
;      the cadr of arg, using predicate, the cddr of the arg
;Returns: first C-LIST item which the predicate accepts
;typical run-time form: (if-ngavail 'c155 (g)(and (prec g 'c155)
;                                      (semfeature g 'person-p)))
(def if-ngavail (macro (arg)
      ;need extra eval because pivot is quoted
   (let* ((pivot (eval (cadr arg)))
            ;create a lambda expression
            (l-body (cons 'lambda (cddr arg)))
            (cons (getngp pivot)))
      '(test-avail ',cons ',l-body)
      )))


;TEST-AVAIL: return first C-LIST item conforming to a lambda expression
(def test-avail (lambda (lst l-body)
   (cond ((null lst) nil)
         ((apply l-body (list (car lst)))(car lst))
         ((test-avail (cdr lst) l-body)))
                  ))


;GETNGP: grab noun group C-LIST items surrounding pivot, organized
;      nearest following, then nearest preceding, then next-nearest
;      following, etc.
;NOTE: don't include pivot
(def getngp (lambda (pivot)
  (prog (head tail)
      ;[1]
      ;get available concepts following pivot
      ;NOTE: C-LIST (stored in global :c-list) grows left-to-right
      (do ((cs (cdr (member pivot :c-list))(cdr cs)))
          ((or (equal (eval (car cs)) '(end-ng))
               (null cs))
           ())
          ;if concept is available, keep it
          (cond ((available (car cs))
                 (setq tail (append1 tail (car cs)))))
      )
      ;[2]
      ;get available concepts preceding pivot
      (do ((cs (cdr (member pivot (reverse :c-list)))(cdr cs)))
          ((or (equal (eval (car cs)) '(beg-ng))
            (null cs))
           ())
          (cond ((available (car cs))
                 (setq head (append1 head (car cs)))))
      )
```

Figure 4.4 (*Continued*)

```
;[3]
;head and tail are organized by nearest-to-pivot first
;return interleaved list
(return (interleave tail head))
)))
```

The function *semfeature* checks on semantic features of a C-LIST item by applying the predicate or lambda expression supplied to it, much like *test-avail.* (Complications arise when the concept given to the function is ambiguous, as we will see in the next chapter.) Typically, the predicate is a combination of the basic surface semantic predicates supplied with the ERKS types. Thus, the function *semfeature* is at the heart of the surface semantic analysis scheme!

If the noun group does contain an unknown word, its name will be propagated into the actions part of the request, and made the subject of a *fill-gap* operation. This function, a version of which is shown in Figure 4.5, inserts one concept into another at a specified path, making the "eaten" one unavailable. Note that *srf* is used to do the actual insertion, and that *link-con-to-filler* uses the property lists of the conatoms to record the details of the insertion. The need to do bookkeeping of this kind is a major reason why the analyzer uses atomized forms. Note also that *fill-gap* notices when an "unknown" is being inserted: it just copies the (lexval) filler and throws the "unknown" form away.

Figure 4.6 contains the request cluster needed for "punch." After adding an instance of the ERKS form for wsPUNCH1, the definition activates three requests. The first (specified at [1]) searches the clause surrounding the toplevel concept for an instance of a person appearing "in-act-spot" with respect to the toplevel. (For the moment, the "clause" is simply all the items on the C-LIST. Conjunctions and other constructions can subdivide the C-LIST into parts, as described in the next chapter.) The function *if-clavail* works in a manner analogous to *if-ngavail,* and so will not be discussed further here. It's worth pointing out, however, that the request shown at [1] is a low-level form such as *actspot-req,* the actor-spot request generator, could have created. Its definition as a macro is given in Figure 4.7. Note the use of the quasi-quote's splicing macro to add the arbitrary actions to the actions part of the request.

The request given at [2] in Figure 4.6 searches for a objspot constituent that is a person, to be the possessor of the bodypart with which the hand

Figure 4.5
The Function fill-gap (Simplified)

```
;FILL-GAP is called when one concept wants to gobble another
;Returns: gobbling concept
(def fill-gap (lambda (path con filler)
  ;[1]
  ;if filler is an unknown, real filler is in (lexval) path
  (cond
   ((unknown-p filler)
    (make-unavail filler)
    (setq filler (grf '(lexval) filler)))
    ;make filler unavailable
   ((make-unavail filler)))

;use srf to insert the filler
(srf path con filler)

;mark con as having gobbled filler, and filler as having been
;eaten by con
(link-con-to-filler con filler path)
con))

;LINK-CON-TO-FILLER: remember that one concept "ate" another
;       Put path and filler name on "ate" property of con
;       Put con on "ateby" property of filler
;Returns: con
(def link-con-to-filler (lambda (con filler path)
    ;mark con as having gobbled filler; include path to eaten con
    (appendprp con (list filler path) 'ate)
    ;mark filler as having eaten con
    (putprop filler con 'ateby)
    con))

;Modification of fill-gap to account for prepconsts:
;[1]
  (cond
    ;if filler is an unknown, real filler is in (lexval) path
   ((unknown-p filler)
    (make-unavail filler)
    (setq filler (grf '(lexval) filler)))
    ;if filler is a prepconst, real filler is in (mynom) path
   ((prepconst-p filler)
    (make-unavail filler)
    (setq filler (grf '(mynom) filler))))
```

Figure 4.6
The Definition of ''punch''

```
(def-wordsense wsPUNCH1
 surface-form (punch)
 ws-structure
 (propel-f actor (nil)
      obj (bpart-f bptype (hand) partof (nil))
      to (physcont val (bpart-f bptype (nil) partof (nil))))
 equivs
 (((actor)(obj partof)))
 )

(adictdef punch
 pos v
 topreq
 ((test (: = topcon (add-word-con wsPUNCH1)))
  (actions
   (activate

    ;[1]
    ;pick up the actor
    (gapreq
     (test (: = actorcon (if-clavail topcon (g)
                           (and (in-act-spot g topcon)
                                (semfeature g 'couldbe-person-p)))))
      (actions
       (fill-gap '(actor) topcon actorcon)))

    ;[2]
    ;pick up the possessor of the bodypart
    (gapreq
     (test (: = bpartowner (if-clavail topcon (g)
                            (and (in-obj-spot g topcon)
                                 (semfeature g 'couldbe-person-p)))))
      (actions
       (fill-gap '(to val partof) topcon bpartowner))))

    ;[3]
    ;pick up the bodypart; don't lose the possessor of the bodypart
    (gapreq
     (test (: = bpartcon (if-clavail topcon (g)
                          (and (prepconst g '(in on upside))
                               (semfeature g 'couldbe-bpart-p)))))
      (actions
       (fill-gap '(to val) topcon
            (merge-con bpartcon (grf '(to val) topcon)))))

)))
```

Figure 4.7
The actspot-req Request Generator

```
;ACTSPOT-REQ: the actor-spot request generator
;Typical call: (actspot-req 'c496 (actor) person-p
;                                    <arbitrary actions>)
(def actspot-req (macro (arg)
 (let ((pivot (cadr arg))
       (path (caddr arg))
       (pred (cadddr arg))
       (actions (cddddr arg)))

    "((gapreq
       (test (:= actorcon (if-clavail ,pivot (g)
                                  (and (in-act-spot g ,pivot)
                                       (semfeature g ',pred)))))
         (actions
          (fill-gap ',path ,pivot actorcon)
          ,@actions)))
    )))
```

---

comes into contact. This request is generated in a manner analogous to the macro form of Figure 4.7.

Finally, the request at [3] searches the C-LIST for a prepconst based on "in," "on" or "upside," and containing a *bpart,* to be the "target" of the *propel.* The phrase "in the nose" satisfies this requirement. It has the conceptual form:

(9)
(prepconst prep (in) mynom (person gender (masc)
                                  persname (Muhammed)))

The presence of prepconsts requires the modification of *fill-gap* at [1] in Figure 4.5, as shown.

There's an interesting timing problem here. If the sentence to be analyzed is "Olivia punched Muhammed upside the head," the objspot filler, "Muhammed," will be picked up and inserted in the path (to val partof). Then the prepconst will be picked up and inserted in the (to val) path, thereby *overwriting* the "Muhammed" concept. I avoid this problem by merging the existing (to val) filler with the prepconst subform at [4]. The function *merge-con* creates a new concept that is a merger of two prior ones, in the sense that it contains all the non-empty fillers from both of them.

Figure 4.8
Simple Version of "in"

```
(adictdef in
 pos prep
 topreq
  ((test (: = topcon (add-con (prepconst-f prep (in))()())))
   (actions
    (activate
     (gapreq
      (test (: = nomcon (if-prepclavail topcon (g)
                                        (semfeature g 'couldbe-entity-p))))
      (actions
         (fill-gap '(mynom) topcon nomcon))))
   )))
```

Exercise IV (Moderately Difficult)

Write a version of *merge-con.* Fail if the two input concepts are of different types, or conflict in a given role.

It needs to be emphasized that this problem arises because I'm using the short form of the conceptual structure for "punch," rather than the full meaning structure, as discussed in Chapter 2.

The conceptual structure (9) was built by the phrase "in the nose." What actually happens is that "in" captures its constituent, as shown in Figure 4.8. The function *if-prepclavail* accepts only the constituent immediately following the preposition, unless the sentence is a question or subclause form. In these cases, it will take the (conceptual form of) a wh-word (e.g., "who" or "what") if no following constituent is available. This is intended to handle cases such as "Who did John give the book to?"

Definitions for the determiner "the" and bodypart "nose" are shown in Figure 4.9. In the definition for "the," the part of speech "adj" indicates that the determiner is a modifier word, like an adjective, and thus can start a noun group. Thus, "Popeye the sailor man" will be treated as two noun groups, as will appositive forms such as "George Washington, first President of the United States." The topreq places a marker on the C-LIST and activates a request. The request looks for a following entity and fills its (ref) role with the filler (def), that is, it marks the entity as having been definitely referenced. After the shipreq operation at end-of-NG, the (ref) role can be examined by memory processes to see whether a referent search is needed to identify the constituent. A phrase such as "the man" or "that man" should initiate such a search,

Figure 4.9
Definitions for "the nose"

```
(adictdef the
 pos adj
 topreq
 ((test (: = topcon (add-con '(def)()()))
  (actions
   (activate
    (gapreq
     (test (: = nomcon (if-ngavail topcon (g)
                               (and (foll g topcon)
                                    (semfeature g 'couldbe-entity-p)))))
      (actions
       (fill-gap '(ref) nomcon topcon))))
    )))

(def-wordsense wsNOSE1
 surface-form (nose)
 ws-structure
 (bpart-f bptype (nose) partof (person-f))
 )

(adictdef nose
 pos noun
 topreq
 ((test (: = topcon (add-word-con wsNOSE1)))
  (actions
   ()))
```

whereas "a man" or "some man" should not. Since this request will be the first activated (except for the noun-group shipreq) in a given noun group, it will be the last to be considered, and thus will mark the assembled noun group constituent. That is, the system will prefer to place the reference specifier with the concept built by the head noun.

Strictly speaking, this will not always be correct. For example, in "the Shah of Iran's car," it is presumably "the Shah" that is being referenced, not "Iran" or "the car." Depending on how one treats the possessive form, either concept may get the (ref) role. A better solution for cases like this involving descriptions of *unique* entities is to make "the Shah of Iran" a phrasal synonym for the well-known person.

Even so, this simple definition of "the" has several problems. First, if the noun group ends up being fragmented, the determiner will modify the nearest following entity, not the entity corresponding to the head noun. What the request should do is to wait until the noun-group diagnosis routines have worked on the fragments, then modify the result.

Exercise V (Moderately difficult)

Modify the definition of "the" to wait until a single noun-group result has emerged. (Hint: use the function *getngp.*)

A second problem with "the" has to do with the longevity of requests. If for some reason the request doesn't fire at the end of its noun group, it will hang around forever being uselessly considered. It won't be able to modify another noun-group constituent, since *if-ngavail* will give it only concepts from its own noun group. Nevertheless, one needs some means of removing a request when it can no longer be applicable. An arrangement that accomplishes this is shown in Figure 4.10. I have added a request that checks the analysis environment, using the function *envmnt*. The idea is that if the system returns to default (i.e., structure-driven) mode, then it must have exited from noun-grouping. Therefore, the requests of "the" can no longer be applicable, and the function call (kill rest-of-pool) will get rid of them. Since the requests are considered in the order in which they were activated, the request looking for an entity will always get a chance to fire before the request-killing request.

The definition of "nose" is typical for entities. All it does is place the entity on the C-LIST and exit. (The call to : = doesn't do anything useful. I just want to write topreqs in a standard form.) The case frame for entities is normally completely filled in: there are no gaps needing to be filled, and thus no gapreqs.

Exercise VI (Easy)

Modify the definition of "nose" to handle "nose of John," that is, to pick up the entity whose bodypart has been specified.

4.5 Morphological Fragments and "to be"

Only two more things need to be explained before I turn to the analysis of Sentence 8: the treatment of morphological fragments and the copula "to be." As we will see, certain fragments cooperate with "be" to implement aspectives and voicing.

My approach to morphology is to break a word into an ending followed by the root form. (This operation is sometimes called "root stripping.") For example, "punched" would become "pastperf\$ punch," where "pastperf\$" is the morphological fragment that indicates either the simple past or the perfective form of the verb. The reason that the fragment is made to precede the root form (affix hopping) is that decisions can be made about voicing before the root-form requests are activated.

Root stripping is very easy for irregular forms: one simply provides fields in the wordsense definition that declare the forms to the analyzer. For example, the perfective/participial form "given" would be associated with the field "partform" in the wordsenses for "give:"

Figure 4.10
Extended Definition of "the"

```
(adictdef the
 pos adj
 topreq
 ((test (: = topcon (add-con '(def)()())))
  (actions
   (activate
   (gapreq
   (test (: = nomcon (if-ngavail topcon (g)
                              (and (foll g topcon)
                                   (semfeature g 'couldbe-entity-p)))))
  (actions
   (kill rest-of-pool)
   (fill-gap '(ref) nomcon topcon)))
  ;if we return to default mode, kill sibling requests
  (gapreq
     (test (eq (envmnt) 'default))
     (actions
       (kill rest-of-pool))))
 )))
```

```
(def-wordsense wsGIVE1
     surface-form (give)
     pastform (gave)
     partform (given)
     ws-structure
     ....
     )
```

For regular verbs, the program must isolate the ending, then see if what's left of the lexeme corresponds to a known word. A very simple set of Lisp functions for root-stripping forms such as "punched" is shown in Figure 4.11. I use *explode* to break a symbol into a list of its characters, and exploit the fact that *def-wordsense* places a root word's topreq on a property of that name, to see whether a symbol is indeed a known word. (The function *add-syns* defines single word synonyms of a root word by placing the root form on the "root-syn" property of the synonym.)

Exercise VII (Difficult)

Write a root-stripping package that can handle suffix phenomena such as "doubling" (e.g., "stripping") and "elision" (e.g., "smiled"). A useful utility to have is *symbol-slice,* which given a symbol and two indices, returns a symbol consisting of the characters between the indices. For example, (symbol-slice 'foobaz 1 4) returns "ooba."

Figure 4.11
Simple Root Stripper for "-ed"

```
;FIND-ED: see if lexeme ends in "ed" and what's leftover is a
;      known word
;Returns: list of "pastperf$" and root, else nil
(def find-ed (lambda (lex)
 (let* ((chars (explode lex))
      (ending '(,(cadr (reverse chars)) ,(car (reverse chars))))
      (rest (implode (setdiff chars ending))))
      (cond
        ((and (equal ending '(e d))
            (is-knownword rest))
        '(pastperf$ ,rest)))
      )))

;IS-KNOWNWORD: is symbol a known word
(def is-knownword (lambda (sym)
 (or (is-rootform sym)(has-synonym sym))))

;IS-ROOTFORM: is symbol a root form?
(def is-rootform (lambda (sym)
 (get sym 'topreq)))

;HAS-SYNONYM: is symbol a synonym for a root form?
(def has-synonym (lambda (sym)
 (get sym 'rootform)))
```

Exercise VIII (Difficult)

Extend root-stripping to *prefix* forms, e.g., turn "unnecessary" into "not necessary."

Now we need to consider the handling of that troublesome word "be." By itself, "be" means almost nothing. Its major uses are as indicators of function for constituents. In particular, forms of "be" can be used to indicate the progressive aspect, as in "John was running," or the passive voice, as in "John was hit." As an introduction to "be," I consider these similar cases in Figure 4.12. First, the figure records the corpus of sentences the definition is intended to handle. This documentation is useful as the complexity of the definition grows. Then it shows a call to *add-syns* to define phrasal equivalents of the tensed forms of "be." The topreq first places a pivot on the C-LIST (so the location of "be" in the sentence can be remembered). The initial version of the definition won't use the pivot. Then "be" calls *next-word* to pick up the next lexical unit

Figure 4.12
Simple Definition of "to be"

```
;Corpus of "to be"
;      1. Olivia was running down the street
;      2. Olivia was punched by Muhammed

(add-syns '((is are am (pres$ be))(was were (past$ be))(been (perf$ be))))

(adictdef be
 pos v
 topreq
 ((test (:= topcon (make-unavail (add-con '(be)()()))))
  (actions

   ;pick up next lexical unit
   (:= nextlex (next-word))

      ;[1]
      ;if the next word is the progressive fragment, throw it away,
      ;and set up to modify the "time" of a following concept
   (cond ((eq nextlex 'prog$)
          ;announce the good news
          (msg ROUTINE-MSG
               nl "BE: gobbling prog$")
          ;get rid of fragment
          (skip-item)
          ;now grab following concept
          (activate
          (gapreq
             (test (:= follcon (if-clavail topcon (gek)
                             (and (foll gek topcon)
                                  (semfeature gek 'couldbe-episode-p)))))
             (actions
               (addmode follcon (make-cd '(:t)))
               (addtime follcon (make-cd '(:prog)))))))

      ;[2]
      ;if perfect mark is seen or perfform of next-word is same as
      ;root form (e.g., "the IRS is run by thieves"), then the
      ;  passive voice is ok. Put a marker on the C-LIST
      ;  which in-act-spot and in-obj-spot will see...
   ((or (eq (get nextlex 'partform) nextlex)
        (memq nextlex '(pastperf$ perf$)))
    ;announce the good news
    (msg ROUTINE-MSG
         nl "BE: gobbling perf$")
    ;passive shift is ok
```

Figure 4.12 (*Continued*)

```
        (make-unavail (add-con '(pass-ok) nil nil))
        ;discard perfective fragment
        (cond ((memq nextlex '(perf$ pastperf$))
               (skip-item)))
        ;now grab following concept
        (activate
        (gapreq
          (test (: = follcon (if-clavail topcon (gek)
                             (and(foll gek topcon)
                                 (semfeature gek 'couldbe-episode-p)))))
          (actions
          (addmode follcon (make-cd '(:t)))))))))
))))
```

from the sentence, without actually activating its requests. Note that the lexeme could actually correspond to a phrase.

It then tests for the presence of the progressive fragment (at [1]) and the perfective (at [2]) in sequence. If the sentence has the progressive, "be" calls *skip-item* to remove the next lexeme from the sentence. Then it activates a request to pick up the following concept, using *couldbe-episode-p,* and to mark that concept as "progressive" and "asserted" with the calls to *addtime* and *addmode,* respectively. (These functions implement the details of the *time* and *mode* roles in concepts.)

The handling of the perfective is only a little more complicated. First, "be" may have a verb whose perfective form is the same as the root form. For example, "the IRS is run by thieves." The first clause of the *or* construction at [2] handles this case. Second, the input stream may explicitly contain the perfective fragment (if the verb has an irregular form, e.g., "given,"), or a fragment that can either be the past or perfective (e.g., for regular transitive verbs). The second clause of the *or* handles this case. If there is an explicit fragment, "be" discards it and places a marker on the C-LIST that the passive shift is allowed ("OK") for this verb. The functions *in-act-spot* and *in-obj-spot* search for this marker, as the function definitions I am finally able to give in Figure 4.13 indicate. The reason "be" places the marker on the C-LIST rather than raising a flag is that the system may get a multiclause sentence where the first clause is passive and the second is active, e.g., "John was hit and slapped Mary." If a single flag is used, the verb "slapped" will seem to have the passive voice. The function *mypassok* looks at the passive-ok marker nearest to the concept created by the verb.

Figure 4.13
The Functions in-act-spot and in-obj-spot

```
;IN-ACT-SPOT: test whether con is in the syntactic-actor spot with
;      respect to verbcon (normally a topcon created by a verb)
(def in-act-spot (lambda (con verbcon)
      ;if active voice, in-act-spot is preceding verbcon
      (cond ((and (null (mypassok verbcon))
                        ;don't accept a prepconst
                        (null (prepconst-p con)))
            (prec con verbcon))

            ;if passive, it's in a by-phrase
            ((prepconst con '(by)))

            (t ()))
))
```

```
;IN-OBJ-SPOT: is con in the syntactic object spot with respect to verbcon,
;      which is normally a topcon created by a verb-form
(def in-obj-spot (lambda (con verbcon)
      ;don't accept a prepconst
  (cond ((prepconst-p con)())

            ;if passive shift is allowed, in-obj-spot is preceding verbcon
            ((mypassok verbcon)
            (prec con verbcon))

            ;if active, it's following
            ((foll con verbcon)))
))
```

4.6   A Processing Example

This section presents an example of the analyzer running on our sample sentence:

   Muhammed was punched in the nose by Olivia

Below is a transcript, slightly edited for readability, from a "script" session with the analyzer, which is a Franz Lisp program running under 4.2BSD Unix. The analyzer is a major part of the NLP Toolkit. The version that was used for this transcript was modified slightly from the distribution version to deal with the simplified definitions presented in this chapter.

Comments are interspersed with the program's outputs. It is hoped that the sample run will communicate a feeling for the simplicity of the analyzer's control and the complexity of the request interactions.

The program starts with all output messages enabled, and with pauses at strategic points. The toplevel function *xchange* manages one conversational exchange. The generator (see Chapter 6) is called to express a concept, then the analyzer is called to process an input sentence in the context of concept expressed. Here, a default message is printed. Output lines beginning with "*" are places where the program has paused to let the user examine the current state of the system.

```
(xchange)
Please enter request:
Sentence:
Muhammed was punched in the nose by Olivia

Entering ng mode
*get-item

New word is Muhammed

Considering topreq pool: ap1 (ar2) Muhammed

Executed ar2
Available: (c73)
*consider-req
(plist 'ap1)
(parnt Muhammed type topreq parent-pool ap1 requests (ar2) *topcon
c73)

(plist 'ar2)
(body
 ((test (:= 'c73 (add-con (person-f persname (Muhammed) gender
                                               (masc))
                      nil nil)))
 (actions
  (activate
  (gapreq
   (test (:= unkcon (if-ngavail 'c73 (g)
                           (and (foll g 'c73)
                                   (semfeature g 'unknown-p)))))
  (actions
   (fill-gap '(surname) 'c73 unkcon)))))))

(xpn c73)
(person persname (Muhammed) gender (masc))
```

The analyzer starts by echoing the sentence. It enters noun group mode because "Muhammed" has part-of-speech "noun." The dictionary definition is activated as topreq pool ap1, with single request ar2. The request fires and places the concept c73 on the C-LIST. Then the system enters a pause inside the function *consider-req,* which examines a single request. I have used the Franz function *plist* to show the property list structures associated with ap1 and ar2. We see that "Muhammed" is the parent-word of the pool ap1, that it is a topreq pool, and that the topcon created for it is c73. The actual request for ar2 is stored on the "body" property of the symbol. ("ap," "ar" and "c" are stems for *newsym* symbol chains for pools, requests, and atomized ERKS forms, respectively.) Note how the quoted form 'c73 has been substituted for the token "topcon" in ar1. I used the function *xpn* to display the new C-LIST item. This function converts atomized forms to more-or-less readable flat-list forms.

    Leaving ng mode
    *get-item

    New word is past$

    Considering gapreq pool: ap2 (ar3) Muhammed

    Considering shipreq pool: ap0 (ar0 ar1) NGP

    Shipping noun group result: c73

    Executed ar1
    Available: (c73)
    *consider-req

The morphological fragment past$, which was created by a root-stripping operation on the word "was," forces the system into end-of-noun-group mode. The system looks at the ng-pools in reverse order of their activation. Thus, the surname gapfiller for "Muhammed" (pool ap2) is considered before the shipreq/diagreq pool ap0. (Pool ap0 was activated at the beginning of the noun group. Its details are not germane here.) There is a single result for the noun group, viz. c73, and the shipreq ar1 sends it off. (Of course, there's no memory module to receive this result, so the shipreq operation is useless.) The "Muhammed" concept is still available, however.

    Considering gapreq pool: ap2 (ar3) Muhammed

    Considering topreq pool: ap3 (ar4) past$

    Executed ar4
    Available: (c73)
    *consider-req

Considering gapreq pool: ap4 (ar5) past$

Considering gapreq pool: ap2 (ar3) Muhammed
*get-item

New word is be

Considering gapreq pool: ap4 (ar5) past$

Considering gapreq pool: ap2 (ar3) Muhammed

Considering topreq pool: ap5 (ar6) be

BE: gobbling perf$

Executed ar6
Available: (c73)
*consider-req

(next-word)
punch

The topreq pool for the past-fragment places a pivot on the C-LIST and begins looking for a following concept whose *time* is to be modified. Notice how the *surname* request of "Muhammed" hangs around after the noun group is exited. One needs to add a request to the *def-named-person* macro that is analogous to the request we added to the definition of "the" in Figure 4.10. Finally, the topreq of "be," Figure 4.12, gets in, notices the past-or-perfective fragment that was stripped off of "punch," and declares that the passive shift is OK. Note that the function *next-word* now indicates that "punch" is the next word in the sentence: the fragment has been discarded.

Considering gapreq pool: ap6 (ar7) be

Considering gapreq pool: ap4 (ar5) past$

Considering gapreq pool: ap2 (ar3) Muhammed
*get-item

New word is punch

Considering gapreq pool: ap6 (ar7) be

Considering gapreq pool: ap4 (ar5) past$

Considering gapreq pool: ap2 (ar3) Muhammed

Considering topreq pool: ap7 (ar8) punch

Executed ar8
Available: (c80 c73)
*consider-req

```
(xpn c80)
(propel actor c81 obj (bpart bptype (hand) partof c81)
      to (physcont val (bpart partof (person)))
      time (times time1 (:pres)) mode (modes mode1 (:t)))

(xpn c81)
(person)
```

Considering gapreq pool: ap8 (ar9 ar10 ar11) punch

Executed ar11
Available: (c80)
*consider-req

```
(plist 'ar11)
(body
  ((test (: = 'c73 (if-clavail 'c80 (g)
                       (and (in-obj-spot g 'c80)
                              (semfeature g 'couldbe-person-p)))))
   (actions
     (fill-gap '(to val partof) 'c80 'c73))))

(xpn c80)
(propel actor c81 obj (bpart bptype (hand) partof c81)
        to (physcont val (bpart partof (person persname (Muhammed)
                                              gender (masc))))
        time (times time1 (:pres)) mode (modes mode1 (:t))))
```

Now both "be" and "past" are looking for a concept to modify. Pool ar8, from "punch," will provide them with one. One of the gapreqs of "punch," ar11, sees "Muhammed" in the obj-spot (preceding, because of the passive), and inserts the concept into c80 at the (to val part) path.

Considering gapreq pool: ap8 (ar9 ar10) punch

Considering gapreq pool: ap6 (ar7) be

Executed ar7
Available: (c80)
*consider-req

Considering gapreq pool: ap8 (ar9 ar10) punch

Considering gapreq pool: ap4 (ar5) past$

Executed ar5
Available: (c80)
*consider-req

(xpn c80)

(propel actor c81 obj (bpart bptype (hand) partof c81)
    to (physcont val (bpart partof (person persname (Muhammed)
                                            gender (masc))))
    time (times time1 (:past)) mode (modes mode1 (:t))))

The gapreq of "be" confirms that the "punch" concept is asserted. The gapreq of past$ marks the tensing of c80 as "simple past."

Considering gapreq pool: ap8 (ar9 ar10) punch

Considering gapreq pool: ap2 (ar3) Muhammed
*get-item

New word is in

Considering gapreq pool: ap8 (ar9 ar10) punch

Considering gapreq pool: ap2 (ar3) Muhammed

Considering topreq pool: ap9 (ar12) in

Executed ar12
Available: (c93 c80)
*consider-req

(xpn c93)
(prepconst prep (in)))

Considering gapreq pool: ap10 (ar13) in

"In" places an empty prepconst on the C-LIST, and activates a request, ar13, to find its constituent (see Figure 4.8).

Considering gapreq pool: ap8 (ar9 ar10) punch

Considering gapreq pool: ap2 (ar3) Muhammed

Entering ng mode
*get-item

New word is the

Considering topreq pool: ap12 (ar16) the

Executed ar16
Available: (c96 c93 c80)
*consider-req

(xpn c96)
(def)
*get-item

New word is nose

Considering topreq pool: ap14 (ar19) nose

Executed ar19
Available: (c97 c96 c93 c80)
*consider-req

(xpn c97)
(bpart bptype (nose) partof (person))

Leaving ng mode
*get-item

New word is by

Considering gapreq pool: ap13 (ar17 ar18) the

Executed ar17

Available: (c97 c93 c80)
*consider-req

(xpn c97)
(bpart ref (def) bptype (nose) partof (person))

Considering shipreq pool: ap11 (ar14 ar15) NGP

shipping noun group result: c97

Executed ar15
Available: (c97 c93 c80)
*consider-req

The analyzer accumulates the ng-pools for "the nose." When "by" is seen, it enters end-ng mode. Working backward through the ng-pools, "the" modifies "nose," and the shipreq sends the completed concept off. Now the program enters structure-driven mode, "in" captures its constituent (ar13), and a gapreq of "punch" picks up the completed prepconst (ar10). Notice how "Muhammed" and "the nose" get merged properly.

Considering gapreq pool: ap10 (ar13) in

Executed ar13
Available: (c93 c80)
*consider-req

(xpn c93)
(prepconst mynom (bpart ref (def) bptype (nose) partof (person))
        prep (in)))

Considering gapreq pool: ap8 (ar9 ar10) punch

Executed ar10
Available: (c80)
*consider-req

```
(plist 'ar10)
(body
  ((test (: = 'c93 (if-clavail 'c80 (g)
                              (and (prepconst g '(in on upside))
                                   (semfeature g 'couldbe-bpart-p)))))
   (actions
    (make-unavail 'c93)
    (fill-gap '(to val) 'c80
      (merge-pp (grf '(to val) 'c80) (grf '(mynom) 'c93))))))
```

(xpn c80)
(propel actor c81 obj (bpart bptype (hand) partof c81)
  to (physcont val (bpart partof (person persname (Muhammed) gender
                                                                (masc))
                        ref (def)
                        bptype (nose)))
  time (times time1 (:past)) mode (modes mode1 (:t)))

Considering gapreq pool: ap8 (ar9) punch

Considering gapreq pool: ap2 (ar3) Muhammed

Considering topreq pool: ap15 (ar20) by

Executed ar20
Available: (c102 c80)
*consider-req

(xpn c102)
(prepconst prep (by) mynom (nil)))

Considering gapreq pool: ap16 (ar21) by

Considering gapreq pool: ap8 (ar9) punch

Considering gapreq pool: ap2 (ar3) Muhammed

Entering ng mode
*get-item

New word is Olivia

Considering topreq pool: ap18 (ar24) Olivia

Executed ar24
Available: (c106 c102 c80)
*consider-req

(xpn c106)
(person persname (Olivia) gender (fem)))

Leaving ng mode
*get-item

New word is pr

Considering gapreq pool: ap19 (ar25) Olivia

Considering shipreq pool: ap17 (ar22 ar23) NGP

shipping noun group result: c106

Executed ar23
Available: (c106 c102 c80)
*consider-req

Considering gapreq pool: ap19 (ar25) Olivia

Considering gapreq pool: ap16 (ar21) by

Executed ar21
Available: (c102 c80)
*consider-req

(xpn c102)
(prepconst prep (by) mynom (person persname (Olivia) gender (fem))))

The prepconst c102 for "by Olivia" gets assembled in the same fashion as "in the nose," and the final gapreq of "punch" picks it up:

Considering gapreq pool: ap19 (ar25) Olivia

Considering gapreq pool: ap8 (ar9) punch

Executed ar9
Available: (c80)
*consider-req

(plist 'ar9)
(body
  ((test (: = 'c102 (if-clavail 'c80 (g)
                        (and (in-act-spot g 'c80)
                             (semfeature g 'couldbe-person-p)))))
   (actions
     (fill-gap '(actor) 'c80 'c102))))

(xpn c80)
(propel actor c106 obj (bpart bptype (hand) partof c106)
  to (physcont val (bpart partof (person persname (Muhammed) gender
                                              (masc))

```
              ref (def)
              bptype (nose)))
      time (times time1 (:past)) mode (modes model (:t)))
```

(xpn c106)
(person persname (Olivia) gender (fem))

The two surname requests from "Olivia" and "Muhammed" get (use-lessly) considered, then the topreq for "period" (the symbol "pr," which is added to every sentence which doesn't have terminal punctuation) adds a "clausepoint" concept. After one more cycle of request consideration, the process terminates.

Considering gapreq pool: ap19 (ar25) Muhammed

Considering gapreq pool: ap2 (ar3) Olivia

Considering topreq pool: ap20 (ar26) pr

Executed ar26
Available: (c110 c80)
*consider-req

(xpn c110)
(clp)

Considering gapreq pool: ap19 (ar25) Olivia

Considering gapreq pool: ap2 (ar3) Olivia

Sentence:
(Muhammed was punched in the nose by Olivia pr)
result: (c80)
(exit)

4.7 Summary

This chapter presented a model of conceptual analysis as a mapping from a surface form into a surface-semantic conceptual structure, on the basis of word-order, syntactic, morphological, and shallow semantic informa-tion. The key concept is that of the *request,* a special kind of production whose test samples the state of a very simple working memory of concepts; and whose actions can create and interconnect concepts, and add or delete other requests. A request typically encodes, in a restricted, well-defined programming language, a prediction about a concept or constituent that will be seen at some point during analysis. The way one approaches analysis, i.e., the writing of dictionary definitions, was illustrated in this paradigm by a series of simple, but very important, cases.

5

Problems in Conceptual Analysis

5.0 Introduction

Language analysis presents a vast array of fascinating and very difficult problems, and the Conceptual Information Processing approach has provided solutions to many beyond the scope of this book. This chapter will discuss a small number of interesting and critical analysis problems to illustrate the kinds of things one can do with the analysis tool. The problem areas to be considered are

1. the analysis of tri-constituent forms and imbedded sentences. Tri-constituent sentences contain indirect objects; imbedded sentences contain subclauses, e.g., infinitives.
2. a more complete analysis of prepositions and the copula "to be." Here we will see our first example of wordsense ambiguity.
3. a more general approach to word-meaning ambiguity, including the handling of pronouns.
4. coordinate constructions and a definition of "and."
5. question forms, and "to be," revisited.
6. use of expectations provided by memory: ellipsis expansion as a diagnostic process.

5.1 Tri-Constituent Forms and Imbedded Sentences

5.1.1 Handling Indirect Objects

Tri-constituent forms are sentences that contain three non-prepconst constituents.[1] For example,

(1)
Olivia gave Muhammed a book.

The constituents are "Olivia," in the actspot, "Muhammed" in the recip-spot, and "a book," in the objspot. Note that (1) has a number of forms that are equivalent if the focus shift is ignored:

(1a) Olivia gave a book to Muhammed.
(1b) A book was given to Muhammed by Olivia.
(1c) Muhammed was given a book by Olivia.

Figure 5.1
Definition of "give"

```
;Corpus for "give"
;     1. Olivia gave a book to Muhammed
;     2. Olivia gave Muhammed a book
;     3. Muhammed was given a book by Olivia
;     4. A book was given to Muhammed by Olivia

(def-wordsense wsGIVE1
 surface-form (give)
 pastform (gave)
 partform (given)
 ws-structure
 (atrans-f actor (person-f)
          obj (entity-f)
          from (poss-f part (person-f))
          to (poss-f part (person-f))
          time (times-f) mode (modes-f))
 equivs
 (((actor)(from part)))
 constraints
 (((obj) atransobj-p))
 )


;ATRANSOBJ-P: is the object atransable?
;Returns: obj, else nil
(def atransobj-p (obj)
 (and (is-among-p (type-of obj)
                 '(money mcontainer struc veh container supp ingobj))
      obj))

(adictdef give
 pos v
 topreq
 ((test (:= topcon (add-word-con wsGIVE1)))
  (actions

   ;pick up the actor
   ;this will always be in act-spot, so we can use the short form
   (activate
    (actspot-req topcon (actor) couldbe-person-p))

   ;pick up object atransed
   ;this will either be in-obj-spot, or simply following the kernel
   (activate
    (gapreq
```

```
(test (: = objcon (if-clavail topcon (foo)
                  (and (or (in-obj-spot foo topcon)
                           (foll foo topcon))
                       (semfeature foo 'atransobj-p)))))
   (actions
    (fill-gap '(obj) topcon objcon))))

;pick up the recipient
;this will either be in-obj-spot, or in a to-prepconst
(activate
  (gapreq
   (test (: = recipcon (if-clavail topcon (baz)
                       (and (or (in-obj-spot baz topcon)
                                (prepconst baz '(to)))
                            (semfeature baz 'couldbe-person-p)))))
   (actions
    (fill-gap '(to) topcon recipcon))))
)))
```

All the forms of (1) can be handled by a simple extension of the request-writing techniques discussed in the last chapter. The requests, of course, are associated with the verb "give," as illustrated in Figure 5.1.

The definition of "give" is based on the wordsense wsGIVE1, and should by now have a familiar form. This sense of "give" is an *atrans,* an abstract transfer of ownership or possession of an object between two persons. Henceforth, I shall follow the practice of placing requests targetted at different gaps in separate pools, so that I can use (kill rest-of-pool) as needed. The technique used to take care of all the cases is based on the observation that the recipient must be higher animate, while the object atrans-ed must be a member of some other class. The function *atransobj-p* gives a listing of the ERKS types that could, on surface-semantic grounds, be considered atrans-able. (In the most general case, we would need a call to the memory/reasoning system to establish this.)

Thus, both the conceptual object and recipient can be searched for in-obj-spot, since the surface-semantic tests are mutually exclusive (or "orthogonal"). To the (obj) filler gapreq I add a positional specifier that says the conceptual object may simply be following (as in 1a). To the (to part) filler gapreq I add a specifier that says the recipient may appear in a to-prepconst. The orthogonality of the surface semantics of the recipient and object can be exploited in the same way for many other tri-constituent verbs, such as "send," "get," "lend," "buy," "sell," etc.

5.1.2 Infinitives and Gerunds

Many imbedded sentences contain infinitive or gerund forms:

(2) Olivia wanted to punch Muhammed in the nose.

(3) Olivia likes punching Muhammed in the nose.

(4) Ronald's punching Olivia in the nose pleased Muhammed.

Sentence (2) contains an infinitive, a verb governed by the preposition "to." Sentences (3) and (4) contain gerunds, imbedded progressive forms. In (4), the conceptual actor of the imbedded verb is realized by a possessive constituent.

To handle infinitive forms, one must first allow "to" to capture episodes as well as entities (cf. Figure 5.2). Then, one can write a definition of "want," as shown. The prepspot-req will pick up an infinitive form as soon as it becomes available. Note that the definition of "punch" (Figure 4.6) *need not be modified at all*. It can still find its constituents in the usual places: in-act-spot, etc. Thus, the definition can handle

(5) Olivia wanted Ronald to punch Muhammed.

(6) Olivia wanted Muhammed to be punched by Ronald.

In both sentences, "Ronald" is in the act-spot of "punch," as usual, and "Muhammed" is in the obj-spot. Note: I am *not* handling sentences such as:

(7) John wanted Mary.

with this definition of "want." Sentence (7) can be paraphrased as "John sexually desires Mary," and is better treated as a separate wordsense.

For Sentence (2), where the conceptual *actor* of "punch" is not provided, we can infer that it is the same as the *actor* of the toplevel concept ("want"). I take care of this by checking (at [1]) to see if the (mobj actor) filler is empty at the clausepoint, using *emptycon,* and copying the (actor) filler if it is. (I have to wait for the clausepoint to be sure that the *actor* has been seen at the time the imbedded episode is picked up: "to punch Muhammed in the nose was desired by Olivia.")

Verbs such as "like" will accept either a gerund, as in Sentence (3), or an infinitive, as in "John likes to punch Ronald." It can identify that a progressive has been seen by examining a concept using *progressive-p,* as shown in Figure 5.3. The function exploits the fact that the prog$ fragment places its aspective marker in the *time2* role of the *time* filler of a concept. The definition of "like" uses the function in a straightforward manner, as shown. Again, I'm not handling sentences such as "John likes candy" with wsLIKE1. This is a different wordsense. (I will discuss multiple wordsenses in Section 5.3.)

Semantically, the gerund form given in Sentence (3) differs from the

Figure 5.2
Infinitives

```
(adictdef to
  pos prep
  topreq
  ((test (: = topcon (add-con (prepconst-f prep (to))()()())))
   (actions
    (activate
     (gapreq
      (test (: = prepcon (if-prepclavail topcon (f)
                                     (or (semfeature f 'couldbe-entity-p)
                                     ;take acts/states, too
                                         (semfeature f 'couldbe-episode-p)))))
       (actions
         (fill-gap '(mynom) topcon prepcon))))
  )))

(def-wordsense wsWANT1
  surface-form (want)
  ws-structure
  (s-goal-f actor (person)
         mobj (episode-f)
         time (times-f) mode (modes-f))
)

(adictdef want
  pos v
  topreq
  ((test (: = topcon (add-word-con wsWANT1)))
   (actions

    ;actor
    (activate
     (actspot-req topcon (actor) couldbe-person-p))

    ;imbedded sentence?
    (activate
       (prepspot-req topcon (mobj) (to) couldbe-episode-p
            (activate
             ;[1]
             ;imbedded actor mentioned?
             (clpspot-req topcon
                  (cond ((emptycon '(mobj actor) topcon)
                         (fill-gap '(mobj actor) topcon
                               (grf '(actor) topcon)))))))))
  )))
```

Figure 5.3
Gerund/Infinitive Forms

```
;PROGRESSIVE-P: is concept a progressive form?
;Returns: arg, else nil
(def progressive-p (lambda (arg)
 (and (eq (type-of (grf '(time time2) arg)) ':prog)
      arg)))

(def-wordsense wsLIKE1
  surface-form (like)
  ws-structure
  (a-config-f confrel (affinity-f val (5))
          con1 (person-f)
          con2 (entity-f))
 )

(def-word like
  pos v
  topreq
  ((test (: = topcon (add-word-con wsLIKE1)))
   (actions
    (activate
     (actspot-req topcon (con1) couldbe-person-p))
    (activate
     (gapreq
     (test (: = epcon (if-clavail topcon (foo)
                       ;if it's a gerund, it's in-obj-spot
                       (or (and (in-obj-spot foo topcon)
                                (semfeature foo 'progressive-p))
                       ;or an infinitive
                       (and (prepconst foo '(to))
                                (semfeature foo 'couldbe-episode-p))))))
      (actions
       (fill-gap '(con2) topcon epcon)))))
  )))
```

---

gerund form of Sentence (2) only in that the conceptual actor has been mentioned. That is, if the verb form is progressive, we may have a possessive form appearing in-act-spot, as in (3), or in-obj-spot, as in:

(8) Olivia likes Ronald's being punched.

(9) Ronald's having been punched was pleasing to Olivia.

Before I talk about gerund forms such as (4), I need to describe how the possessive construction is handled. Assume that a possessive form such

Figure 5.4
A Simplistic Version of the Quasi-Preposition "fo"

```
(adictdef fo
  pos adj
  topreq
  ((test (: = topcon (add-con (prepconst-f prep (fo))()()))
   (actions
    (activate
     (gapreq
      (test (: = mycon (if-ngavail topcon (foo)
                              (and (prec foo topcon)
                                   (semfeature foo 'couldbe-entity-p)))))
     (actions
      (fill-gap '(mynom) topcon mycon)
      (activate
       (gapreq
        (test (: = posscon (if-ngavail topcon (baz)
                                (and (foll baz topcon)
                                     (semfeature baz 'couldbe-entity-p)))))
       (actions
        ;[1]
        (fill-gap '(poss) posscon topcon)))))))))
  )))
```

as "Ronald's" has been root-stripped into the phrase "Ronald fo." (Contracted forms such as "it's" can be handled through *add-syns*.) A version of a definition for the quasi-preposition "fo" ("of" spelled backwards) is shown in Figure 5.4. Note how the part of speech "adj" causes the system to remain in noun-group mode while the fo-constituent is assembled. The first gapreq picks up the preceding concept and places it in (mynom). It then activates a gapreq (which will fire at end-ng) to find a following entity to be "possessed."

This definition presents two problems. First, the constituent of "fo" may be a full-fledged noun group in its own right. In "President Ronald Reagan's limousine," the definition given would get only the unknown "Reagan." This is just another example of the need for more noun-group syntax in the analyzer. The second problem is deeper. The possessive relation in English (and in many other languages, as well) encompasses a host of *conceptual relations* among entities and episodes, in addition to simple possession. Contrast "John's hat" with "car's bumper," "Syria's army," and "Melvin's murder." Instead of the *fill-gap* at [1] in Figure 5.4, I should be making a call to the reasoning/memory system to supply a relationship between the "possesser" and "possessed" concepts. Deter-

Figure·5.5
The Functions in-act-spot and in-obj-spot, Revisited

```
;IN-ACT-SPOT: test whether con is in the syntactic-actor spot with
;      respect to verbcon (normally a topcon created by a verb)
(def in-act-spot (lambda (con verbcon)

        ;if active voice, in-act-spot is preceding verbcon
  (cond ((and (null (mypassok verbcon))
                ;don't accept a prepconst
                (null (prepconst-p con)))
        (prec con verbcon))

        ;[1]
        ;if a progressive form, take a preceding possessive constituent
        ((progressive-p verbcon)
         (and (prec con verbcon)
              (prepconst con '(fo))))

        ;if passive, it's in a by-phrase
        ((prepconst con '(by)))

        (t ()))
  ))
```

```
;IN-OBJ-SPOT: is con in the syntactic object spot with respect to verbcon,
;      which is normally a topcon created by a verb-form
(def in-obj-spot (lambda (con verbcon)
        ;don't accept a prepconst
  (cond ((prepconst-p con)())

        ;if passive shift is allowed, in-obj-spot is preceding verbcon
        ((mypassok verbcon)
         (prec con verbcon))

        ;[2]
        ;if passive, and a progressive form, accept preceding possessive
        ((and (mypassok verbcon)(progressive-p verbcon)
              (prec con verbcon)(prepconst con '(fo))))

        ;if active, it's following
        ((foll con verbcon)))

  ))
```

---

mining such relations is well beyond the power of simple surface semantics.

Accepting the definition of "fo" for illustrative purposes, however, we can handle Sentence (4) by simply modifying the functions *in-act-spot* and *in-obj-spot,* as indicated at [1] and [2], respectively, in Figure 5.5. We just look for a preceding prepositional constituent based on "fo," making it the actspot constituent in the active voice, the objspot constituent in the passive. Thus, the requests written for verbs such as "punch" do not need to know about the gerund form at all.

5.1.3 Relative Clauses

Another source of imbedded sentences comes from relative clauses, such as

(10) Olivia, who likes Muhammed, punched Ronald.

The key to the analysis of Sentence (10) is the word "who." (The commas also give information about clause placement, which I will ignore.) Clearly, both "who" and "Olivia" refer to the same real-world entity, i.e., they are *co-referents*. The word "who" is a "washed-out" version of the concept underlying "Olivia." In surface-semantic terms, one would like "who" to be able to do many of the things "Olivia" can. A simple definition of "who" capable of handling (10) and several other cases is given in Figure 5.6.

The topreq adds a "higher animate" concept to the C-LIST. The rather odd-looking test part is intended to pick up an immediately preceding *entity* or *episode,* or return an indicator ("empty") that there was no "significant" concept on the C-LIST at the time. The latter condition indicates that the sentence is a question form, and the function *add-f* (for "add-flag") is used to make this known to the rest of the requests. If something was on the C-LIST, then a subclause is starting, and the call to *add-f* is used to indicate that as well.

If the preceding concept is higher animate, then I've got a co-referent for "who." Since the co-referent will generally carry more information than "who," I use *copy-con* to make a copy of it, and call *fill-gap* with the empty path to overwrite the topcon with the copy. Next, I activate a request to wait for the copy to disappear (perhaps because it is in-act-spot with respect to a following verb). When it does, I pick up the concept that grabbed it, using the function *eater-of* (which knows about the property list structure established by *fill-gap*). Finally, I attach that concept to the co-referent concept using the *rel* role (which stands for "relative clause concept"). The resulting concept for (10) is:

(10) Olivia, who likes Muhammed, punched Ronald.
(propel actor "Olivia"

Figure 5.6
A Version of "who"

```
;Corpus of "who"
;      1. who is on the roof (question form)
;      2. I know who is on the roof (imbedded sentence)
;      3. Olivia, who is on the roof, is sexy

(adictdef who
  pos noun
  topreq
  ((test (: = topcon (add-con (hianimate-f ref (:q))()()))))
   (actions
    (activate
     (gapreq
      (test (: = preccon (cond
                           ((if-clavail topcon (g)
                            (and (prec g topcon)
                                 (or (semfeature g 'couldbe-entity-p)
                                     (semfeature g 'couldbe-episode-p)))))
                           (t 'empty))))
      (actions
       (cond
         ;if C-LIST is empty, it's a question form
         ((eq preccon 'empty)
          (add-f 'ques))
         ;otherwise, we're in subclause mode
         ((add-f 'subcl)
          ;if the preceding concept is higher animate, make a
          ;copy of it for the subclause to work with, and wait
          ;for the copy to disappear
          (cond
           ((couldbe-hianimate-p preccon)
            (fill-gap () topcon (copy-con preccon))
            (activate
             (gapreq
              (test (null (available topcon)))
              (actions
               (: = eater (eater-of topcon))
               ;form a "relative-clause" concept
               (fill-gap '(rel) preccon eater)))))))
        ))))))

;EATER-OF: returns concept name for concept into which fill-gap
;       inserted argument
(def eater-of (lambda (arg) (get arg 'ateby)))
```

---

obj (bpart bptype (hand) partof ''Olivia'')
to (physcont val (bpart partof (person gender (masc)

        persname (Ronald)))))

''Olivia''
(person gender (fem)
   persname (Olivia)
   rel (a-config confrel (affinity val (5))
         con1 (person gender (fem) persname (Olivia))
         con2 (person gender (masc) persname (Muhammed))))

This definition of ''who,'' while elegant, certainly doesn't handle all the cases. In particular, the use of ''who'' as a prepositional constituent isn't covered.

Exercise I (Moderately Difficult)

Fix the definition of Figure 5.6 so that sentences such as "To whom are you referring?" work properly. Does the current definition do "I know to whom you are referring" correctly?

5.2 Prepositions and "to be," Revisited

The discussion of prepositions in Chapter 4 treated them as pure function words: they indicate where in the overall conceptual frame their constituents go, but have no meaning themselves. A similar comment was made concerning ''be:'' it functions as an indicator of things like the passive shift, and that's all. This is much too simplistic. This section will present an approach to the meaning of prepositions, and how other words, such as the copulative verb, can take advantage of these meanings.

The basic motivation is provided by sentences such as these:

(11) Olivia was in the house.
(12) Olivia was in the army.
(13) Olivia graduated in 1984.

It seems clear that prepositional phrases such as ''in the house,'' ''in the army'' and ''in 1984'' *do* mean something in isolation. For example, ''in the house'' contributes a meaning fragment that says something like ''if someone [an event, for example] is looking for a particular kind of locational relationship, this phrase can build one.'' In addition to their function-word status, that is, certain prepositions, when accompanied by certain kinds of concepts, do define a fragmentary meaning structure.

To understand this, consider the extended definition of the preposition ''in'' in Figure 5.7. In addition to the original request to pick up a noun-group concept (Figure 4.8), the request cluster now contains sepa-

Figure 5.7
"in," Revisited

```
(adictdef in
 pos prep
 topreq
  ((test (:= topcon (add-con (prepconst-f prep (in)
                                        mynom (nil)
                                        canbuild (nil)) ()()))))
   (actions
    ;STRATEGY: look for special cases, then take any old nominal
    (activate
     ;in a place
     (gapreq
      (test (:= placecon (if-prepclavail topcon (g)
                                   (semfeature g 'couldbe-place-p))))
       (actions
          (kill rest-of-pool)
          (fill-gap '(mynom) topcon placecon)
          ;canbuild a p-config fragment
          (fill-gap '(canbuild) topcon
              (make-structure (pconfig-f confrel (inside-f))))
          (fill-gap '(canbuild con2) topcon placecon)))

     ;in April
     (gapreq
       (test (:= durcon (if-prepclavail topcon (g)
                                      (semfeature g 'couldbe-timdur-p))))
        (actions
          (kill rest-of-pool)
          (fill-gap '(mynom) topcon durcon)
          (fill-gap '(canbuild) topcon durcon)))

     ;in the army, build an a-config fragment
     (gapreq
       (test (:= orgcon (if-prepclavail topcon (g)
                                      (semfeature g 'couldbe-org-p))))
        (actions
          (kill rest-of-pool)
          (fill-gap '(mynom) topcon orgcon)
          (fill-gap '(canbuild) topcon
              (make-ERKS-structure (a-config-f confrel (member-f))))
          (fill-gap '(canbuild con2) topcon orgcon)))

     ;in <nominal>
     (gapreq
       (test (:= nomcon (if-prepclavail topcon (g)
                                      (semfeature g 'couldbe-entity-p))))
        (actions
          (kill rest-of-pool)
          (fill-gap '(mynom) topcon nomcon)))
          ))))
```

rate gapreqs checking for *place, timdur* (time-duration), and *org*. If one of these is found, an appropriate meaning fragment is constructed and inserted into the *canbuild* slot of the *prepconst*. Thus, "in the house" would become:

(prepconst prep (in) mynom "the house"
        canbuild (p-config confrel (inside) con2 "the house"))

"the house"
(struc structype (building) ref (def))

How are such structures used? One important way is with "to be." A request cluster for "be" that handles Sentences (11) and (12) is given in Figure 5.8. (I have left out the tests from the definition of Figure 4.12 for the morphological fragments. The requests of Figure 5.8 would be activated if those tests failed.)

The first new thing in the definition is that two wordsenses are supplied to *add-word-con* instead of the usual one. This is our first example of an *ambiguous word:* "be" can mean "be somewhere," which is wsPCONFIG, or it can mean "be in relation to," which is wsACONFIG. When *add-word-con* gets more than one argument, it adds a special structure called a *vel* (Latin "non-exclusive or") to the C-LIST, to represent the possible word meanings. The particular concept created by the given definition is:

(vel v1 (p-config) v2 (a-config))

The first two actions extract the subconcepts corresponding to the two wordsenses and propagate them.

Exercise II (Easy)

Assume the actions-form being evaluated is bound to a variable called *actions*. Write a definition of the run-time binding operator $:=$ that works the way I said it should: if its second argument returns non-nil, the operator should replace all instances of its first argument, a placeholder, with the quoted form of what was returned. That is, for placeholder "foo" and result "c55," "foo" gets replaced by "'c55." (Hint: look at the definition of the Franz function *subst.*)

Next, modify your function to notice when its first argument is a *list* of placeholders, and arrange that each placeholder gets replaced by the corresponding member of the list returned by the second argument. How would the definition of Figure 5.8 change if $:=$ had this capability?

After propagating the *vel* possibilities, "be" activates a pair of requests to see if one of the senses has indeed been seen. These are our first examples of *disambiguating requests*. If the system got Sentence (11), the

Figure 5.8
"to be," Revisited

```
;Generic p-config
(def-wordsense wsPCONFIG
 ws-structure
 (p-config-f)
 )

;Generic a-config
(def-wordsense wsACONFIG
 ws-structure
 (a-config-f)
 )

;Corpus for "be"
;      1. Olivia was running down the street
;      2. Olivia was punched by Muhammed
;      3. Olivia was in the house
;      4. Olivia was in the army

(adictdef be
 pos v
 topreq
 ((test (: = topcon (add-word-con wsPCONFIG wsACONFIG)))
  (actions

    ;Olivia is in the house
    (: = pconfcon (grf '(v1) topcon))

    ;Olivia is in the army
    (: = aconfcon (grf '(v2) topcon))

    (activate
    ;[1]
    ;if we see a prepconst with a p-config in the canbuild slot
    ;"be" means "be somewhere"
    (gapreq
     (test (: = loccon (if-clavail topcon (f)
                          (and (foll f topcon)
                               (prepconst-p f)
                               (semfeature (grf '(canbuild) f)
                                           'p-config-p)
                          f))))
      (actions
      (p-assert topcon pconfcon)
      (make-unavail loccon)
      (fill-gap '(confrel) pconfcon (grf '(confrel) loccon))
      (fill-gap '(con2) pconfcon (grf '(con2) loccon))
```

```
;pick up other entity in p-config
(activate
    (actspot-req pconfcon (con1) couldbe-pobj-p))))

;[2]
;if we see a prepconst which canbuild an a-config
;"be" means "have abstract relation to something"
(gapreq
  (test (: = relcon (if-clavail topcon (f)
                        (and (foll f topcon)
                             (prepconst-p f)
                             (semfeature (grf '(canbuild) f)
                                         'a-config-p)
                             f))))
  (actions
      (p-assert topcon aconfcon)
      (make-unavail relcon)
      (fill-gap '(confrel) aconfcon (grf '(confrel) relcon))
      (fill-gap '(con2) aconfcon (grf '(con2) relcon))
      ;pick up other entity in a-config
      (activate
          (actspot-req aconfcon (con1) couldbe-entity-p))))
))))
```

---

phrase "in the house" would satisfy the test part of the request at [1]. (The last form in the *and* construction returns the constituent itself. This is necessary because *if-clavail* returns whatever the predicate returns, and "be" expects the whole prepconst.) The resulting actions first throw away the other request; call the function *p-assert* ("positively assert") to arrange that the ambiguous concept is replaced by (or "compressed down to") the *p-config;* copy the appropriate information from the prepconst; and activate a request to pick up the *con1* filler. The *a-config* request at [2] works analogously.

This request cluster very economically solves the problems caused by sentences like (11) and (12). Note that a large number of prepositions can take "physical location" as their meaning, e.g., "on," "near," "under," etc. One would need a request for each one, or at least some way of deriving the necessary *confrel* for each. By allowing the prepositions to build their meaning fragments according to the surface semantics of the associated noun group, we get a cooperative solution to the problem.

5.3 Word Meaning Disambiguation

The selection of the intended meanings of words in context is a key problem for any language analyzer.[2] The best-known case of the meaning selection problem is *wordsense disambiguation,* the process of choosing the correct underlying representation for a word having several senses. Consider the word "sense" itself:

(14a) Most words have more than one sense.
(14b) Sight is our most important sense.
(14c) Some people have no sense at all.

"Sense" is a well-behaved word in that it has only a relatively few alternative meanings. Other words have dozens of possible readings. For example, "give" and "take" have been metaphorically extended to so many situations that they are essentially meaningless in isolation. Their disambiguation requires access to substantial amounts of context. A wordsense disambiguation scheme, therefore, will require a model of context consisting of both the meanings of surrounding words and higher-level expectations.

Choosing the referent of a *definite noun phrase* is another example of the word-meaning selection problem. A definite noun phrase consists of a proper name, a pronoun, or a construction introduced by the definite article or certain other modifiers:

(15a) John kicked the ball.
(15b) The Celtics extended their streak.
(15c) He threw John out.

The problem is finding the real-world referent of phrases such as "John," "the Celtics," "the ball," "their streak," and "he." Note that the choice of referent may interact with the wordsense disambiguation process. For example, the memory/reasoning subsystem's ability to identify a real ball in John's vicinity reinforces the selection of "round toy" as the intended meaning of "ball" in (15a). Sentence (15b) illustrates that a referent may be found in the current clause unit (i.e., by identifying "Celtics" with "their"). Reflexive pronouns such as "himself" explicitly call for this type of search process. Finally, the identification of "he" as a bartender in (15c) would yield a different meaning to the sentence than if "he" were a third baseman.

Another example of the word-meaning selection problem occurs in *ellipsed inputs.* These are sentence fragments (typically noun phrases) presented without an accompanying proposition during a conversational interaction. For example, in

(16a) Q. Where did you go on New Year's Eve?
       A. 3 parties

(16b) Q. Who was eligible for Federal matching funds in the
           1980 presidential election?
       A. 3 parties

reference to the *conceptual form* of the immediately preceding question is needed to select the intended sense of "parties."

One source of knowledge that can be used to solve these kinds of problems is *rules of syntax*. The intended reading of "visiting" in the following example cannot be determined without examining the conceptual context:

(17) Visiting relatives can be a nuisance.

If I change the syntactic form of (17) slightly, however, the meaning is clear:

(18a) Visiting relatives is a nuisance.
(18b) Visiting relatives are a nuisance.

In (18a), the singular form of the copula selects the "I-visit-relatives" meaning of "visiting," while the plural form in (18b) selects the "relatives-visit-me" meaning. Syntactic phenomena of this type have been extensively studied (e.g., Hobb76; Hobb78; Nash78). I'll primarily be concerned here with more powerful knowledge sources that use "semantic," "conceptual," and "pragmatic" features.

Surface semantics can be used to exploit the constraints placed by certain words on other words in a sentence. Here the conceptual type of a word meaning can set up expectations about, or *selectional restrictions* (Katz63) on, the senses of surrounding words. If a word has multiple senses and one sense is based on a predicted type, then this should be the intended sense. The word "ball," for example, has at least two meanings, "spherical toy" and "formal dance." Suppose we have the sentences:

(19a) John kicked the colorful ball.
(19b) John attended the colorful ball.

In (19a), one selects the "toy" sense of "ball" because of the selectional restrictions imposed by "kick:" a *propel* concept requires a physical object as the thing propelled. In (19b), "attend" selects the "formal dance" sense of "ball," since one of its meanings is "act in a role in a goalepisode." Example 19 illustrates a process of *staged disambiguation*. Once the verb has selected one of the meanings of "ball," the intended meaning of "colorful" becomes clear: we are talking about physical color in (19a) and ambience in (19b).

For this selection process to proceed, an analyzer needs a means for making the alternative meaning structures of a word explicitly accessible. This is the motivation for the *vel* construction introduced in the Section 5.2. A definition for "ball" using a *vel* is given in Figure 5.9. When the topreq fires, the C-LIST acquires an ambiguous concept:

```
(vel v1 (inst insttype (ball) instform (spherical))
     v2 (goalepisode getype ($formal-dance)))
```

Figure 5.9
Definition of "ball"

```
(def-wordsense wsBALL1
  surface-form (ball)
  ws-structure
  (inst-f insttype (ball) instform (spherical))
  )

(def-wordsense wsBALL2
  surface-form (ball)
  ws-structure
  (goalepisode-f getype ($formal-dance))
  )

(adictdef ball
  pos noun
  topreq
  ((test (: = topcon (add-word-con wsBALL1 wsBALL2)))
   (actions ()))))
```

Note that "ball" does not activate requests which try to disambiguate the *vel*. Nominal words normally rely on requests of other words to compress the ambiguous structure down to a single meaning.

Verb words, on the other hand, often do activate disambiguating requests, called "velreqs." Figure 5.10 contains a partial definition for the word "take," which covers four of its senses:

(20a) I took $10000 from Foo Bank. (atrans)
(20b) I took a pill. (ingest)
(20c) I took a pill from the medicine cabinet. (ptrans)
(20d) I took a train to Bermuda. (ptrans)

The velreq cluster, starting at [1], attempts to find surrounding constituents which will allow a decision to be made. The first velreq looks for an atrans-able entity in-obj-spot, which is neither a vehicle nor a drug. If it finds it, it *asserts* that the *atrans* sense of "take" may be the preferred reading. I say "may be" because the consideration process for velreqs gives *all* the requests a chance to perform a disambiguation. When each request has had a chance to fire, the system packages up the result: a single concept if the word has been completely disambiguated, or another *vel,* if only a partial disambiguation is possible. In the "colorful ball" example, for instance, when the system begins grouping the concepts associated with the noun phrase, the velreqs associated with "colorful"

Figure 5.10
Definition of "take"

```
;Corpus for "take:"
;       1. I took $10000 from Foo Bank
;       2. I took a pill
;       2a. I took a pill from the medicine cabinet
;       3. I took a train to Bermuda

(def-wordsense wsTAKE1
  surface-form (take)
  pastform (took)
  partform (taken)
  ws-structure
  (atrans-f actor (person-f)
          obj (entity-f)
          to (poss-f part (person-f))
          from (poss-f part (person-f)))
  equivs
  (((actor)(to part)))
  )

(def-wordsense wsTAKE2
  surface-form (take)
  ws-structure
  (ingest-f actor (person-f)
          obj (ingobj-f)
          to (inside-f part (bpart-f bptype (stomach) partof (person-f)))
          from (inside-f part (bpart-f bptype (mouth) partof (person-f))))
  equivs
  (((actor)(to partof)(from partof)))
  )

(def-wordsense wsTAKE3
  surface-form (take)
  ws-structure
  (ptrans-f actor (person-f)
          obj (entity-f)
          to (nil)
          from (nil))
  )

(adictdef take
  pos v
  topreq
  ((test (:= topcon (add-word-con wsTAKE1 wsTAKE2 wsTAKE3)))
   (actions

    ;take atransobj from someone
    (:= atrcon (grf '(v1) topcon)
```

Figure 5.10 (*Continued*)

```
;ingest something
(: = ingcon (grf '(v2) topcon))

;ptrans something
(: = ptrcon (grf '(v3) topcon))

(activate

 ;[1]
 ;atransobj in-obj-spot selects atrans, but
 ;don't take vehs and drugs
 ;NOTE: This requires a memory probe, in general
 (velreq
  (test (: = objcon (if-clavail topcon (g)
                         (and (in-obj-spot g topcon)
                              (semfeature g 'atransnotvehdrug-p)))))
   (actions
    (assert topcon atrcon)
    (fill-gap '(obj) atrcon objcon)
    ;get recipient
    (activate
      (actspot-req atrcon (actor) couldbe-hianimate-p))
    ;get donor
    (activate
      (prepspot-req atrcon (from part) couldbe-hianimate-p))
   ))

 ;drug in-obj-spot selects ingest, unless a from-phrase is seen
 (velreq
 (test (: = drugcon (if-clavail topcon (g)
                         (and (in-obj-spot g topcon)
                              (semfeature g 'drug-p)))))
   (actions
    ;can't be a ptrans
    (deassert topcon ptrcon)
    (activate
      ;[2]
      ;if from-phrase with p-config is seen, it's an atrans
      ;with a ptrans as instrument
      (velreq
       (test (: = fromcon (if-clavail topcon (g)
                              (and (prepconst g '(from))
                                   (p-config-p (grf '(canbuild) g))
                                   g))))
         (actions
          (make-unavail fromcon)
          (assert topcon atrcon)
```

```
     (fill-gap '(obj) atrcon drugcon)
     (fill-gap '(inst) atrcon (make-structure (ptrans-f)))
     (fill-gap '(inst from) atrcon (grf '(canbuild) fromcon))
     (fill-gap '(inst obj) atrcon drugcon)
     ;get actor
     (activate
      (actspot-req atrcon (actor) couldbe-hianimate-p))))


     ;if we reach clp, it's an ingest
     (velreq
      (test (: = clpcon (if-clavail topcon (h)
                              (and (foll h topcon)
                                  (semfeature h 'clp-p)))))
      (actions
       (assert topcon ingcon)
       (fill-gap '(obj) ingcon drugcon)
       ;get actor
       (activate
        (actspot-req ingcon (actor) couldbe-hianimate-p))))
     )))


;veh in-obj-spot selects ptrans
(velreq
 (test (: = vehcon (if-clavail topcon (g)(and (in-obj-spot g topcon)
                                        (semfeature g 'veh-p)))))
 (actions
  (assert topcon ptrcon)
  ;retrieve the ptrans-goalepisode of the veh
  ;NOTE: this requires a memory call, in general
  (fill-gap '(inst) ptrcon (get-goalepisode vehcon))
  (fill-gap '(inst veh) ptrcon vehcon)
  ;get actor
  (activate
     (actspot-req ptrcon (actor) couldbe-hianimate-p))


  ;get location
  (activate
    (gapreq
     (test (: = placecon (if-clavail topcon (g)
                          (and (prepconst-p g)
                               (p-config-p (grf '(canbuild) g))
                               g))))
     (actions
      (make-unavail placecon)
      (fill-gap '(to) ptrcon (grf '(canbuild) placecon)))))))


))))
```

will each select a sense of "ball." The vels associated with "colorful" and "ball" will be replaced by a single *vel* representing the ambiguous concept "toy with several colors" and "formal dance with high level of ambience."

Note that what this requires is a means for saving and restoring the state of the analysis process just before a velreq is considered and just after it fires. Since the state of the working memory is completely described by the C-LIST, it suffices to remember the state of the C-LIST as a velreq pool starts, then remember the revisions to the C-LIST (i.e., the compressed *vel* subconcepts) caused by a request's firing. Before each request is considered, the analyzer restores the C-LIST to the saved state. The simplicity of the production system model makes the management of processes such as staged disambiguation very simple.

Returning to the "take" example of Figure 5.10, one can see that the presence of an *ingobj* of the drug variety will allow the decision for an *ingest* to be made, unless there is also a from-phrase with a locational constituent. In the latter case, "take" is an *atrans,* with a *ptrans* as instrument. Certainly, the *ptrans* sense of "take" is inappropriate, thus the call to *deassert* to remove it from the *vel.* The test for the other two cases is made by the velreq cluster at [2]. If "take" finds a locational from-phrase (by examining the *canbuild* role of the *prepconst,* as usual), it asserts the *atrans* and constructs a *ptrans* concept to act as instrument, as shown. On the other hand, if the system reaches a clausepoint without finding such a phrase, "take" asserts the *ingest.* Finally, "take" tests for a vehicle in-obj-spot. If "take" finds it, it can assert the *ptrans* sense, wsTAKE3, and make an instance of the goalepisode in which the vehicle is a role to be the instrument of the *ptrans.* (The function *get-goalepisode* is really a memory call, in general.) Other senses of "take" can be handled in a more-or-less straightforward manner by extending the definition of Figure 5.10.

5.3.1 Pronominal Reference

Pronouns can also be handled by the *vel* mechanism, but the knowledge source used is not surface semantics but *semantic discourse context.* A pronoun may be thought of as an ambiguous concept consisting of all the co-referent concepts previously seen that "match up" with it in semantic terms. For example, in

(21)
John knew the aspirin might upset his stomach.
He took it anyway.

the possible referents of "it" are "aspirin" and "stomach." In this case, "it" must resolve to "aspirin" because of the semantic requirements of (one sense of) "take." Note that if the second sentence of (21) were "He coated it by drinking milk," the referent would shift to "stomach." That is, no purely syntactic process can guarantee that the correct anaphoric reference will be located.

A simple definition of the pronoun "it" is given in Figure 5.11. The definition calls the function *find-referents* to get the possible referents for "it." This function applies the predicate supplied to certain members of a global variable *nlpcontext*. In the simplest case, this global holds the concept names for all the "substantive" concepts the analyzer has formed. The "substantive" concepts include the noun-group constituents and clause and sentence-level concepts. (This version ignores "expletive" versions of "it," as in "it's raining," and episode referents of "it," as in "I went to LA today. It was a pain.")

Exercise III (Very Hard, if Done Right!)

Modify the noun-group shipreq pool I discussed in Section 4.4 to update the NLP context global. How far back to look in the NLP context during referent search is problematical. The function shown in Figure 5.11 must be considered as only the beginning of a complete solution for this problem!

When the list of possible referents is returned to "it," its topcon is overwritten either with a single concept, if there was only one possible referent, or with a *vel* of the possible referents, if there are more than one. For example (21), the resulting concept would be

    (vel v1 (bpart bptype (stomach) partof "John")
         v2 (ingobj ingtype (aspirin)))

(The possessive pronoun "his" would already have been resolved to "John" by a similar process of referent search.)

Now "take" is in a position to disambiguate itself *and* the ambiguous "it" concept. The *ingest* sense of "take" selects the *ingobj* sense of "it," and the *vel* gets compressed properly.

Exercise IV (Not Too Difficult)

Write a definition to handle *reflexive pronouns* such as "himself" and "itself." What are the rules about where the co-referent of a reflexive can be? What do these rules imply about the structure of the semantic discourse context (bound to the global *nlpcontext*)?

Figure 5.11
Definition of "it"

```
(adictdef it
  pos pron
  topreq
  ((test (: = topcon (add-con (entity-f ref (def))()()))))
   (actions
    (: = refcons (find-referents arg 'it-p))
    ;if single referent, just overwrite
    (cond ((eq (length refcons) 1)
           (fill-gap () topcon (car refcons)))
          ((greaterp (length refcons) 1)
           (fill-gap () topcon (make-vel refcons))))
   )))

;FIND-REFERENTS: get context atoms which match under predicate supplied
;Returns: matching referents in order of nearness to arg in NLP context
(def find-referents (lambda (arg pred)
  (find-ref1 pred (get-discourse-context arg) nil))))

(def find-ref1 (lambda (fn lst res)
     ;return result in order of temporal nearness to arg
  (cond ((null lst) res)
        ((apply fn (car lst))
         (setq res (cons (car lst) res))
         (find-ref1 fn (cdr lst) res))
        ((find-ref1 fn (cdr lst) res)))))

;GET-DISCOURSE-CONTEXT: get analyzer subcons in context of arg given
;Note: this will be all atoms in the global *nlpcontext* to the past
;      of arg; this global grows left to right, like the C-LIST
(def get-discourse-context (lambda (arg)
  (cdr (memq arg (reverse *nlpcontext*)))))

;IT-P: can arg be a referent of "it"?
;Returns: arg, else nil
(def it-p (lambda (arg)
          (and (couldbe-entity-p arg)
               (null (intersec (grv '(gender) arg '(masc fem))))
               arg)))
```

The *vel* mechanism can also use the internal knowledge sources of the expert reasoning system it is working with, provided that system is able to package its knowledge in a velreq cluster. See (Cull84) for more details.

5.4 Coordinate Constructions

Coordinate constructions come in a variety of forms. Consider, for example, the following small corpus for "and":

(22a) John walked and cried.
(22b) John talked to Mary and Sue ran away.
(22c) John walked and Mary cried.
(22d) John and Mary walked down the street.
(22e) John went to New York and New Haven.

What we are getting in each case is a coordination of events at the conceptual level. The analysis problem is in forming the appropriate *coord* concept. A definition of "and" that is sufficient to handle (22a–e) is shown in Figure 5.12. The definition is based on a new kind of request, called a "peekreq." The peekreq is allowed to look at the C-LIST on every request consideration cycle, before the other requests get in. Peekreqs normally don't modify the C-LIST, but simply "peek" at what's there. (With the introduction of the peekreq, the model of the analyzer's control is now complete: see Diagram 5.1 for a flow chart.)

Note that the toplevel request for "and" is a peekreq: I want the request to be considered immediately so that the concept immediately preceding "and" can be picked up before another gapreq makes it unavailable. The function *availprec* gets the concept immediately preceding its argument on the C-LIST. The peekreq also places an empty *coord* concept on the C-LIST. The presence of the *coord* marks a clausepoint, i.e., it divides the C-LIST into two parts that are expected to correspond to full concepts. "And" may have to infer one of these concepts, as we see below.

Having picked up the preceding concept, the definition activates another peekreq to get the immediately following concept. Once "and" has found it, it waits to see what happens to the preceding and following concepts by the time of the next clausepoint. At the clausepoint, it gets the result of any *vel* compression steps that may have been applied to the two concepts, sees which of them have become unavailable, and looks at various cases.

If both are episodes and are still available (Sentence 22a), "and" places them in its *coord,* at [1]. If both are still available and "and" has either two entities or an entity and an episode, there's nothing it can do, the sentence is garbled, and it throws away the *coord* at [2].

At [3], "and" handles sentences such as (22b), where both preceding and following concepts are typically entities (here, "Mary" and "Sue").

Figure 5.12
A Simple Definition of "and"

```
;Corpus for "and"
;      1. John ran and (Bill) jumped
;      2. John and Bill ran
;      3. John hit Mary and Bill
;      4. John went to Hartford and New Haven

(adictdef and
   pos conj      ;end ng
   peekreq       ;try this right now, before prec "entity" disappears
     ;add a coord for the result; NOTE: this creates a clp right here!!
   ((test (:= topcon (add-con (make-cd (coord-f)) ()())))
    (actions

     ;get immediately preceding con
     (:= preccon (availprec topcon))


     (cond
       ;if no preceding con, give up
       ;"and I ran down the street"
       ((null preccon)
        (make-unavail topcon))

       ;get immediately foll con
       (t
        (activate
          (peekreq
           (test (:= follcon (availfoll topcon)))
           ;now wait for next clp to form coord
           (actions
             (activate
             (clpspot-req topcon


               ;if prec con was a vel at the time of the peekreq, it
               ;should have been disambiguated by now
               (:= realpre (cond ((isvel preccon)
                                   (get-velresult preccon))
                                  (preccon)))


               ;if foll con was a vel at the time of the above req, it
               ;should have been disambiguated by now
               (:= realfoll (cond ((isvel follcon)
                                    (get-velresult follcon))
                                   (follcon)))


               (:= andcons (list realpre realfoll))
```

```
;available ones
(: = availcons (available andcons))
;unavailable ones
(: = unavailcons (setdiff andcons availcons))

(cond
;handle various cases:
;[1]
; Both concepts were episodes, and are still
; available. Stuff the coord with them.
; For example, ''John walked and cried''
((and (null unavailcons)
      (couldbe-episode-p realpre)
      (couldbe-episode-p realfoll))
 (fill-gap '(con1) topcon realpre)
 (fill-gap '(con2) topcon realfoll)
 ;if (con2 actor) is empty, copy (con1 actor)
 (cond
    ((emptycon '(con2 actor) topcon)
    (fill-gap '(con2 actor) topcon (grf '(con1 actor) topcon)))))

;[2]
; Both still available: give up, let memory level
;        diagnostics do the job
; Here, we have something strange, such as ''Mary walked and Bill''
;        or an ellipsed form such as ''Mary and Bill''
((null unavailcons)
(make-unavail topcon))

;[3]
;   Both are gone: stuff the coord with the
;        cons that ate them
;For example, ''John hit Mary and Sue ran down the street''
((null availcons)
(fill-gap '(con1) topcon (eater-of realpre))
(fill-gap '(con2) topcon (eater-of realfoll)))

;[4]
; The available entity is an episode, and the unavailable
; one is an entity. Stuff the coord with the episode and
; the eater of the entity
; For example, ''John walked and Mary sang''
((and (couldbe-episode-p (car availcons))
      (couldbe-entity-p (car unavailcons)))
 (fill-gap '(con1) topcon (car availcons))
 (fill-gap '(con2) topcon (eater-of (car unavailcons))))

;[5]
; Both are entities, and one is available but the other
; isn't. Make a copy of the eater of the unavailable
```

Figure 5.12 (*Continued*)

```
        ; concept, and insert the available concept at the same
        ; place as the one that disappeared
        ; For example, "John and Mary were sad," or "John flew to
        ; Bermuda and the Bahamas"
        ((and (eq (length unavailcons) 1)
              (couldbe-entity-p realpre)
              (couldbe-entity-p realfoll))
         (prog (newcon eater path)
               (setq eater (eater-of (car unavailcons)))
               (setq newcon (copy-con eater))
               (setq path (get-path (car unavailcons) eater))
               (fill-gap path newcon (car availcons))
               (fill-gap '(con1) topcon eater)
               (fill-gap '(con2) topcon newcon)))

    ;[6]
     ; Pack it in...
     (t (make-unavail topcon)))
  )))))))))

;EATER-OF: get concept which "ate" con
;     Uses property list structure maintained by fill-gap (cf. Fig. 4.5)
(def eater-of (lambda (con)(get con 'ateby)))

;GET-PATH: get path in con that subcon occupies
;     Uses property list structure maintained by fill-gap (cf. Fig. 4.5)
(def get-path (lambda (subcon con)
  (cadr (assoc subcon (get con 'ate)))))
```

Both entities have been inserted into other concepts. The request uses the function *eater-of* to obtain the concept that captured the entities. (See the definition of *fill-gap*, Figure 4.5.)

Sentences like (22c) are handled by the code at [4]. One concept is an episode and the other is an (unavailable) entity, so "and" just places the episode and the "eater of" the entity into the *coord*. Finally, at [5], "and" handles cases like (22d) and (22e) in which both concepts are entities but only one is still available. The idea is to make a copy of the concept that captured the unavailable concept, and insert the available entity into the copy at the end of the same path as the unavailable one. Then "and" inserts the two episodes into the *coord*.

This definition of "and" is by no means complete, but it is easily generalized.

Diagram 5.1
Request Consideration Flow Chart, Revisited

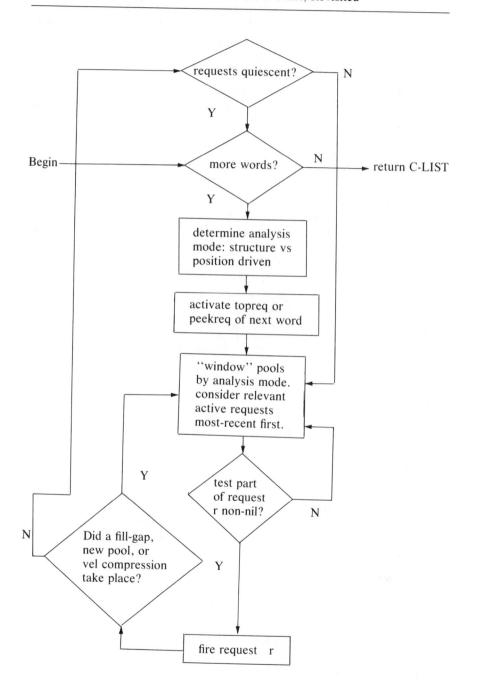

Exercise V (Tricky!)

Does the current definition of "and" handle clauses with imbedded sentences properly? For example, "John told Mary to run and she cried" or "John told Mary to run and hide." What extensions, if any, are needed?

Exercise VI (Moderately Difficult)

Modify the definition of "and" to handle multiple "and" constituents. For example, "John, Mary and Bill ran down the street." (Hint: what would a definition of "comma" look like?)

5.5   Ellipsis Expansion

A final illustration of conceptual analysis techniques is an approach to the problem of *ellipsis expansion,* the imbedding of a fragmentary form in a full concept that represents the intended meaning. The expansion process cannot proceed without a source of *expectations* about the conceptual form the input is expected to take. The system needs some machinery to manage the use of such expectations.

Let's consider a simple model of a *conversational exchange,* i.e., an output generated by the language-processing system to its user, followed by the analysis of the user's response. In a question-asking exchange, for example, the system might be interested in finding out where a certain person is:

(23) Where is John at?
c0:
(p-config confrel (prox)
        con1 (person gender (masc) persname (John))
        con2 (locale ref (:q)))

(defprop c0 (con2) qfocus)

The system uses the generator (as described in the next chapter) to express the question embodied in concept c0. The property list of c0 contains a pointer to the subform that is the subject of the question; this is the concept "focused on" by the question, hence the property name "qfocus." Then it calls the analyzer to parse the response, which might be

(24) Bermuda

c55:
(polity poltype (nation) polname (Bermuda))

This ellipsed form must be handled in the context of the question that was asked.

Here we need the notion of an *exchange frame,* a data structure that contains the context created by a system utterance followed by a user reply. Such a structure is easily created by a record-package macro, and might have a slot-filler form such as

```
(fr3 gen-con (c0)
    to-user (where is John at)
    from-user (Bermuda)
    analyzer-con (c55)
    nlpcontext ((c0 c42 c52)(c55))
    prior-frs (fr0 fr1 fr2)
    ...
)
```

The exchange frame's name is fr3. At the point at which the analyzer finishes with the ellipsed user utterance, the frame contains three important sources of context. The first is the NLP context, which has now been generalized from the description given in Section 5.3. Instead of being stored on a global, the record of the processing carried out by the language-processing interface for this exchange is stored in the *nlpcontext* field of the frame. Note that there are separate sublists for what the generator produced (i. e., the concepts that were expressed as noun groups, viz., "where" and "John," and full concepts, viz., c0 itself) and the analyzer's noun-grouping and clausepoint results (here, simply "Bermuda," c55).

The second source of contextual information is the conceptual form of the question, stored in the *gen-con* field of the frame. Finally, there is a pointer to previous exchange frames stored with the *prior-frs* field of the frame. Using this, the analyzer can search into the indefinite past of the conversation.

How can we use this context to handle the ellipsed form (24)? One way is by associating a diagreq cluster with the definition of "period," as shown in Figure 5.13. When "period" is read, a clausepoint is added to the C-LIST and a *lastreq* is activated to look for the corresponding clause-level concept. A lastreq is the opposite of a peekreq: it gets considered only after all the other pools in the system have become quiescent. Once the pools settle down, one can use *availprec* to grab the preceding concept, and call *diagnose-clause* to look at the result in the context of the available expectations. The function *get-exps* merely returns the generator's input concept for this simple case. The simple form of the function *diagnose-clause* shown in Figure 5.13 accepts the concept produced by the analyzer as a valid result if its ERKS type is compatible with one of the expectations. (The function *rem-nil* removes all occurrences of *nil* from a list. If anything remains, there must have been a matching expectation.)

If the result concept is an entity, and one of the expectations is a

Figure 5.13
Ellipsis Expansion in the Context of a Question

```
(adictdef pr
  pos foo ;period doesn't belong to a noun group
  topreq
  ((test (: = topcon (add-con (clp-f)()()))))
   (actions
    (activate
     (lastreq
      (test (: = clpcon (availprec topcon)))
      (actions
       (: = realcon (diagnose-clause clpcon))
       (send-concept-to-memory realcon))))
   )))

;DIAGNOSE-CLAUSE: compare clause level result with expectations
;     Use these to expand ellipsed results...
(def diagnose-clause (lambda (clpcon)
  (let* ((fr (get-current-fr))
         (exps (get-exps fr))
         (typ (type-of clpcon))
         (couldbefn (get-couldbefn typ))
         (qform ())
         (subcon ())
         (result ()))

    (cond
      ;[1]
      ;if clpcon and one of exps agree in type, good...
      ((car (rem-nil (mapcar '(lambda(x)(apply couldbefn x))
                            exps)))
       (setq result clpcon))

      ;[2]
      ;if clpcon is an entity, and one of exps is a question form
      ;compare qfocussed subcon to clpcon
      ((and (couldbe-entity-p clpcon)
            (setq qform (get-qform exps)))
       (setq subcon (grf (get-qfocus qform) qform))
       (cond
         ((eq typ (type-of subcon))
          (setq result (copy-con qform))
          (fill-gap (get-qfocus qform) result clpcon))))

      .....other heuristics

      ;just return clpcon
      (t (setq result clpcon)))
```

result)))

;GET-EXPS: retrieve expectation concepts from an exchange frame
(def get-exps (lambda(fr)
  ;the only source of expectations is the concept the generator expressed
  ;use the record package macro to retrieve it.
  (xfr-gen-con fr)))

;GET-QFOCUS: return the path to the question focus in a concept
(def get-qfocus (lambda (con)(get con 'qfocus)))

Figure 5.14
A Concluding Example: Ronald drank a Diet Coke

Maximal Inference-Free Paraphrase:

1. A person named Ronald ingested a certain substance from the mouth
to the stomach.

2. This event happened in the indefinite past of "now," and is now
over.

3. Both the mouth and the stomach are body-parts of Ronald.

4. The substance is an ingestible object with physical phase
"liquid," and with the name "Diet Coke"

5. The liquid is a product of an organization named "Coca Cola, Inc."

6. The liquid is meant to be ingested by people who want to reduce their
weight.

Query: What about "from the can"? What about "grasping container,"
     "moving it to mouth," etc.? What is Coke's intention,
     as opposed to the dieter? What about "diet coke" in general,
     as opposed to the particular coke Ronald drank?
     LATER...

ERKS forms (from the bottom up):

Entities:

HUM0: (person persname (Ronald) gender (masc))
BPART0: (bpart bptype (mouth))

Figure 5.14 (*Continued*)

BPART1: (bpart bptype (stomach))
ING0: (ingobj ingtype (soda) ingname ("Diet Coke") phase (liquid))
ORG0: (org orgname ("Coca Cola, Inc.") orgocc ($soda-maker))

Action (the "kernel assertion"):

EVNT0: (ingest actor HUM0 obj ING0 from (inside part BPART0)
              to (inside part BPART1)
              time (times time1 (:past))
              mode (modes mode1 (:t) mode3 (:perf)))

Nuances:

STATE0: (p-config confrel (partof) con1 BPART0 con2 HUM0)
STATE1: (p-config confrel (partof) con1 BPART1 con2 HUM0)
STATE2: (a-config confrel (product-of) con1 ING0 con2 ORG0)

"if someone wants to reduce their weight, they drink diet coke"
REL0:
(cancause
  con1
  (s-goal actor "someone" mobj (s-change toward (weight val "less")
                                          leaving (weight val "original")))
  con2
  (ingest actor "someone" obj "diet coke" from "mouth" to "stomach"))

The complete meaning structure:

(ms kernel EVNT0
    nuance1 STATE0
    nuance2 STATE1
    nuance3 STATE2
    nuance4 REL0)

The "compressed" form, as produced by the analyzer:

(ingest actor HUM0
    obj (ingobj ingtype (soda) product-of ORG0 rel REL0)
    from (inside part (mouth) partof HUM0)
    to (inside part (stomach) partof HUM0)
    time "past"
    mode "asserted and perfect")

NB: the complete structure is recoverable from the compressed form!!!

Figure 5.15
Wordsenses and Dictionary Entries for:
Ronald drank Diet Coke from the bottle.

```
; "Diet Coke"
; NOTE: "Ronald" is done with "named-person" cluster, a la Chapter 4.
(def-wordsense wsDIETCOKE1
  surface-form (Diet Coke)
  ;NOTE: this is the compressed form of the meaning structure; see Figure 5.14
  ws-structure
  (ingobj-f ingtype (soda) ingname ("Diet Coke") phase (liquid)
        product-of (org-f orgname ("Coca Cola")
                  orgocc ($soda-maker)))
  )

;define a typical container
(def-wordsense wsBOTTLE1
  surface-form (bottle)
  ws-structure
  (container-f conttype (bottle))
  )

(def-wordsense wsDRINK1
  surface-form (drink)
  pastform (drank)
  partform (drunk)
  ; default sentential focus
  focus (actor)
  ;NOTE: this is the compressed form of the meaning structure; see Figure 5.14
  ws-structure
  (ingest-f actor (nil)
        obj (ingobj-f ingtype (nil) phase (liquid))
        from (inside-f part (bpart-f bptype (mouth) partof (nil)))
        to (inside-f part (bpart-f bptype (stomach) partof (nil)))
        ;NOTE: I paraphrase "drink from a bottle" as "ingest by
        ; ptransing the liquid from the bottle"
        inst
        (ptrans-f actor (nil)
          obj (nil)
          from (inside part (container-f)))
        ; since I want the generator to use this as well, set the actual
        ; time/mode
        ; in the APE definition below
        time (times-f)
        mode (modes-f)
        )
  equivs
  (((actor)(from part partof))
   ((actor)(to part partof))
```

Figure 5.15 (*Continued*)

```
 ((actor)(inst actor))
 ((obj)(inst obj)))
 constraints
 (((actor) couldbe-animate-p)
 ((obj) liquid-p))
 )

(adictdef drink
 pos v
 topreq
 ((test (: = topcon (add-word-con wsDRINK1)))
 (actions
  ;set time and mode (defaulting to pres/t); frags and modals will
  ; modify this if present
  (addtime topcon (make-special-structure '(:pres)))
  (addmode topcon (make-special-structure '(:t)))
  (activate

  ;grab an actor
  (gapreq
   (test (: = actorcon (if-clavail topcon (g)
                          ; NOTE!!
                          (and (in-act-spot g topcon)
                               (semfeature g 'couldbe-animate-p)))))
   (actions
    (fill-gap '(actor) topcon actorcon)))

  ;grab an ingestible
  (gapreq
   (test (: = objcon (if-clavail topcon (g)
                       (and (in-obj-spot g topcon)
                            (semfeature g 'couldbe-ingobj-p)))))
   (actions
    (fill-gap '(obj) topcon objcon)))

  ; grab a container
  (gapreq
   (test (: = contcon (if-clavail topcon (g)
                        (and (prepconst g '(from outof))
                             (semfeature g 'couldbe-container-p)))))
   (actions
    (fill-gap '(inst from part) topcon contcon)))

  ))))

; BOTTLE: a classic container
(adictdef bottle
```

```
pos noun
topreq
((test (: = topcon (add-word-con wsBOTTLE1)))
 (actions
 ; "Beer bottle" LATER
 ())))

; FROM: a typical preposition (simplified)
(adictdef from
 pos prep
 topreq
 ((test (: = topcon (add-con (prepconst-f prep (from) mynom (())
                                    canbuild (())) ()())))
  (actions
   (activate
   (gapreq
              ; look "in prep spot:" immediately following unless
              ; it's a q-form ("Where is John going to") or subclause
              ; ("I know where John is going to"), in which case we
              ; may want to grab a q-con
   (test (: = nomcon (if-prepclavail topcon (g)
                             ;accept entities or nominalized concepts
                             ; (I stopped John from *running away*)
                                    (semfeature g 'nomconcept-p))))
   (actions
       (kill rest-of-pool)
       ; "my nominal"
       (fill-gap '(mynom) topcon nomcon)))
       ))))
```

question-form (as will be the case if the system asks a question during an exchange), the code at [2] checks the type of the analyzer result against that of the concept imbedded in the question form that has the *question focus*. Here the type of "where" is compatible with that of "Bermuda," and one can thus heuristically conclude that the answer validly matches the question expectation.

If one wishes to supply a full concept as the analyzer's output, it is a simple matter to make a copy of the matching expectation (using *make-ERKS-structure*) and insert the ellipsed concept into it at the end of the path specifying the question focus.

5.6 A Concluding Example

To sum up many of these ideas, this section is an extended example of the conceptual analysis of the verb "to drink," as exemplified by the sentence

Figure 5.16
Definition of "drink" Using Request-Generating Macros

```
(adictdef drink
  pos v
  topreq
  ((test (:= topcon (add-word-con wsDRINK1)))
   (actions
     ;set time and mode (defaulting to pres/t); frags and modals will
     ; modify this if present
     (addtime topcon (make-special-structure '(:pres)))
     (addmode topcon (make-special-structure '(:t))

     ; RULE: each gap gets its own request cluster (so "kill" operations
     ; don't cream the wrong requests)
     (activate
                 ; get constraint from wordsense
      (actspot-req topcon (actor) wsDRINK1))

     (activate
      (objspot-req topcon (obj) wsDRINK1
        ;get rid of sibling request
          (kill rest-of-pool))
     ; at clausepoint, default to "repeatedly drinks alcohol"
     (clpspot-req topcon
                 ;get rid of sibling request
                 (kill rest-of-pool)
                 (fill-gap '(obj ingtype) topcon (make-special-structure '(alcohol)))
                 ;make rut concept: what's the threshold? dead?
                 (:= rutcon (make-ERKS-structure (rut-f con1 (nil))))
                 (fill-gap '(con1) rutcon (copy-con topcon))
                 ;overwrite
                 (fill-gap () topcon rutcon)))

     (activate
      (prepspot-req topcon (inst from part) (from outof) couldbe-container-p))
     )))
```

---

(25) Ronald drank a Diet Coke.

The kernel of the meaning structure that this sentence builds is based on an *ingest*. A version of an MIFP for (25) is given in Figure 5.14. A new idea here is the description of "Diet Coke" (generically) as a liquid people drink if they are interested in reducing their weight.

An analyzer definition in fully written-out form for the *ingest* sense of

Figure 5.17
A Vel Example for "drunk"

```
;Senses of "drunk"
;     1. soda was drunk
;     2. ronald was drunk

; first, a wordsense for the stative sense of "drunk"
; MIFP: actor is in a physical state of intoxication
(def-wordsense wsDRUNK1
  surface-form (drunk)
  focus (actor)
  ws-structure
  (s-attr-f actor (nil)
        attr (phystate-f statetype (intoxication) stateval (5))
        time (times-f)
        mode (modes-f))
  constraints
  ((actor couldbe-pobj-p))
  )

; DRINK: as before, but with no partform
(def-wordsense wsDRINK1
  ;want to allow for phrasal surface forms; thus the list forms
  surface-form (drink)
  pastform (drank)
  ; default sentential focus
  focus (actor)
  ;NOTE: this is the compressed form of the meaning structure; see ../ERKS/
  ; MIFP
  ws-structure
  (ingest-f actor (nil)
        obj (ingobj-f ingtype (nil) phase (liquid))
        from (inside-f part (bpart-f bptype (mouth) partof (nil)))
        to (inside-f part (bpart-f bptype (stomach) partof (nil)))
        ;NOTE: we paraphrase "drink from a bottle" as "ingest by
        ; ptransing the liquid from the bottle"
        inst
        (ptrans-f actor (nil)
                obj (nil)
                from (inside part (container-f)))
        ; since we want GEN to use this as well, set the actual time/mode
        ; in the APE definition below
        time (times-f)
        mode (modes-f)
            )
  equivs
  (((actor)(from part partof))
   ((actor)(to part partof))
```

Figure 5.17 (*Continued*)

```
((actor)(inst actor))
((obj)(inst obj)))
constraints
(((actor) couldbe-animate-p)
((obj) liquid-p))
)

;get the affix into the input stream where "be" can see it
(add-syns '((drunk (perf$ drunktag))))

; DRUNKTAG: the pointer to the request cluster underlying the lexeme drunk...
(adictdef drunktag
  pos v ;just "verb" forms for now
  topreq
  ((test (: = topcon (add-word-con wsDRINK1 wsDRUNK1)))
   (actions
    ; first propagate the vel subcons
    (: = ingcon (grf '(v1) topcon))
    (: = physcon (grf '(v2) topcon))
    ; assert 'em
    (addtime ingcon (make-special-structure '(:pres)))
    (addtime physcon (make-special-structure '(:pres)))
    (addmode ingcon (make-special-structure '(:t)))
    (addmode physcon (make-special-structure '(:t)))

    ;NOTE: disambiguation can be done on nature of entity preceding/in-obj-spot,
    ;        animate vs. ingobj
    (activate
     ;yes, matilda, there is a velprecspot-req request generator...
     (velreq
      (test (: = objcon (if-clavail topcon (g)
                          (and (prec g topcon)
                               (semfeature g 'couldbe-animate-p)))))
      (actions
       ; assert says "remember that this request noticed a valid disambiguating
       ; event." Thus, we can have "staged" disambiguation, where a
       ; 5-ways ambiguous concept can become 3-ways ambiguous, then
       ; completely compressed...
       (assert topcon physcon)
       (fill-gap '(actor) physcon objcon)))

     (velreq
      (test (: = objcon (if-clavail topcon (g)
                          (and (in-obj-spot g topcon)
                               (semfeature g 'liquid-p)))))
      (actions
       (assert topcon ingcon)
```

```
(fill-gap '(obj) ingcon objcon)
;get an actor
(activate
 (actspot-req ingcon (actor) couldbe-animate-p))))
))))
```

"drink" is shown in Figure 5.15. The kernel of the MIFP has been augmented to handle the *ptrans* instrumental that can be seen in

(26) Ronald drank Diet Coke from the bottle.

The same definition is given again in Figure 5.16, in terms of the appropriate request generators. Note that a clausepoint request has been added that redoes:

(27) Ronald drinks.

as "Ronald repeatedly ingests alcohol," if we don't get an object.

Exercise VII (Easy)

We should really default to "repeatedly drinks alcohol" only if we have the so-called "timeless present," as in (25). Fix the cluster of Figure 5.16 to check for this.

Figure 5.17 is an initial attempt to deal with the fact that "drunk" can be a stative word as well as the participial form of "drink." Thus, I've given the word "drunk" its own wordsense and special APE definition (using the surface pointer "drunktag"). Now "drink" is no longer directly associated with "drunk." When "drunk" is seen, both senses get placed on the C-LIST in a *vel,* and the surface semantics of the constituent in-obj-spot is used to make the discrimination.

As a final illustration, Figure 5.18 shows arrangements for dealing with the adjectival uses of "drunk." The corpus is now:

(28)
Soda was drunk.
Ronald was drunk.
Diet Coke was drunk by the drunk man.
A tab was drunk.
A tab was pulled.

Here, "tab" has been made ambiguous, even though one would expect the "soda" sense of the word to be capitalized.

The only tricky thing about the new definition of "drunk" is that it can't be expanded into "perf$ drunktag," as before. The reason is that

Figure 5.18
A Further Vel Example for "drunk"

```
;       1. soda was drunk
;       2. ronald was drunk
;       3. dietcoke was drunk by the drunk man
;       4. a tab was drunk
;       5. a tab was pulled

; first, a wordsense for the stative sense of "drunk"
; MIFP: actor is in a physical state of intoxication
(def-wordsense wsDRUNK1
  surface-form (drunk)
  focus (actor)
  ws-structure
  (s-attr-f actor (nil)
          attr (phystate-f statetype (intoxication) stateval (5))
          time (times-f)
          mode (modes-f))
  constraints
  ((actor couldbe-pobj-p))
  )


; DRUNK: unfortunately, the perfective affix we defined for "drunk" in
;       Figure 5.17 stops noun-grouping, so
;       "drunk man" doesn't go together right. KLUDGE this thru the
;       "root-or-partform" trick
(adictdef drunk
  pos adj        ; leave noun-grouper on
  root-or-partform t        ; this is a participal form
  topreq
  ((test (:= topcon (add-word-con wsDRINK1 wsDRUNK1)))
   (actions
    ; first propagate the vel subcons
    (:= ingcon (grf '(v1) topcon))
    (:= physcon (grf '(v2) topcon))
    ; assert 'em
    (addtime ingcon (make-special-structure '(:pres)))
    (addtime physcon (make-special-structure '(:pres)))
    (addmode ingcon (make-special-structure '(:t)))
    (addmode physcon (make-special-structure '(:t)))

    ;NOTE: disambiguation can be done on nature of a nearby entity
    ; animate vs. ingobj
    (activate
     ;ronald was drunk
     (velprecspot-req topcon physcon (actor) couldbe-animate-p)
     ;dietcoke was drunk
     (velobjspot-req topcon ingcon (obj) liquid-p
```

```
      (activate
        (actspot-req ingcon (actor) couldbe-animate-p)))

  ; also, if current noun group contains an animate, we can squash
  ; the vel, add a rel-clause
  (velreq
   (test (: = entcon (if-ngavail topcon (g)
                    (and (foll g topcon)
                         (semfeature g 'couldbe-animate-p)))))
   (actions
    (assert topcon ingcon)
    (fill-gap '(rel) entcon ingcon)
    (fill-gap '(rel actor) entcon ingcon)))

   ))))

; TAB: the fastener
(def-wordsense wsFASTENER1
  surface-form (tab)
  ws-structure
  (fastener-f fstype (throwaway-tab))
  )

; TAB: the fastener vs. the soda
; NOTE: typically, entities don't look around to compress themselves, since
; they can figure in so many real world situations...
(adictdef tab
  pos noun        ; is there a verb form
  topreq
                  ; use the dietcoke ws
  ((test (: = topcon (add-word-con wsDIETCOKE1 wsFASTENER1)))
   (actions
    ; propagate the subcons
    (: = sodacon (grf '(v1) topcon))
    (: = fastenercon (grf '(v2) topcon))
    ;change the name
    (srf '(ingname) sodacon (make-special-structure '(Tab)))
    )))
```

---

the perfective/participial fragment stops the noun-grouper in the middle of a phrase such as "the drunk man." Thus, I've now made "drunk" an adjective. The problem with so-doing is that "be" now has no way of telling that "be drunk" might be a legitimate passive. I've used the "root-or-partform" property improperly to tell "be" that this is a participial form. (See discussion of irregular forms in Exercise 3.5.) We are now really at the limit of what the analyzer's simple-minded approach to noun-grouping can accomplish.

5.7　Summary

This chapter has explained how the conceptual analysis tool can be used to handle some very difficult problems in surface semantic analysis. I also presented a unified view of wordsense disambiguation, pronoun reference and definite noun-phrase resolution. The analyzer as described has definite problems with sophisticated noun-group syntax, and in particular with ambiguous noun/verb words such as "fear" and "mail." Yet this is by no means the end of the things this approach can handle. The reader who has followed to this point is now equipped to develop his own solutions to the language phenomena of interest, at least at the surface-semantic level.

Notes

1. Such sentences are also called "tri-valent" or "ditransitive." I use this terminology to emphasize the contribution of the constituents to the overall sentence meaning.

2. The material in this section is based on the M.S. thesis of M. J. Pazzani, "Word Meaning Selection in Multimodule Language Processing Systems," Department of Electrical Engineering and Computer Science TR-CS-80-12A, University of Connecticut, 1980. See also (Cull84).

6

Generating Natural Language from a
Conceptual Base

6.0 Introduction

This chapter deals with the inverse of the analysis process considered in the last two chapters, viz., *conceptual generation*. In the most general terms, generation is the mapping from a *knowledge structure,* an interconnected assemblage of primitive ERKS forms representing a substantial component of domain knowledge, into a series of sentences in a natural language. As indicated in Diagram 6.1, this process can be usefully thought of as being composed of two distinct subprocesses. The first is a mechanism for *summarizing* the knowledge structure, i.e., selecting key pieces of it for expression. Knowledge structures, e.g., *goalepisodes,* often contain more detail than we want to express; we rely on the hearer's inferencing abilities to fill in what we left out. A simple example of a knowledge structure summarization process will be discussed in Chapter 7 in connection with the CADHELP system.

The remainder of this chapter will consist of a description of a possible realization of the second subprocess: a concept-at-a-time generator, which is responsible for converting an ERKS form into a single sentence. The summarizer supplies a stream of conceptualizations to the generator. The concept supplied to the generator must be well formed; it will arrange that the English produced is grammatical.

First some comments concerning the general nature of the process to be modeled. The system begins with a concept to be expressed, and possibly an indication of a sub-concept to be "said" first. It is told nothing about the words or syntactic constructions to be used. This is in contrast with other models of generation (for instance Simm72; Swar77] in which the program's input is a syntactic phrase structure of some sort, including some or all of the words to be used.

Another observation is that the generation process need not in any way be the processing inverse of the analysis process, as for example, some purely grammatical approaches would claim. The system to be described starts (as people usually seem to) with a complete, well-formed "thought" to be "said." Thus, the generation process is *top-down,* in a way that analysis never can be. As we have seen, analysis has a very

Diagram 6.1
Generator Subsystem

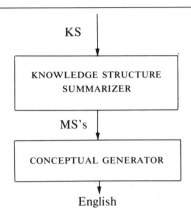

strong bottom-up flavor of recognition, as the listener attempts to match the fragments of meaning from the words that are being heard against his conceptual expectations. A corollary of these two ideas is that literally *everything* (words, syntax, focus, connectives, etc.) a generator of this kind chooses to express the idea it is given will be motivated by *conceptual features* of the given concept, its conversational context, or the goal-following activities of the overall system. In many cases, therefore, the generator algorithm to be described will not be able to "say" the most fluent-sounding thing, because a conceptual reason for choosing the fluent construction is not apparent. This is the price one pays for a radical conceptual-level approach.

6.1 Overview of the Generation Process

The generator I will describe has data and control structures that are reminiscent of the analysis module discussed earlier. Its primary data structure is a short-term memory, called the C-LIST, consisting of concepts intermingled with words and morphological fragments. The basic control structure of the generator accesses the C-LIST in an iterative process of *looking up* word(s) to express the meaning of a concept that is currently the focus of attention (at the "front" or "top" of the C-LIST); and of *inserting* leftover subconcepts in appropriate places around the chosen word(s) on the C-LIST.[1] The subconcepts may be accompanied by "function" words, such as prepositions or conjunctions, that serve to mark the conceptual case in the parent concept from which the subconcept came. From time to time during the basic iteration,

Diagram 6.2
Conceptual Generator Flow Chart (Overview)

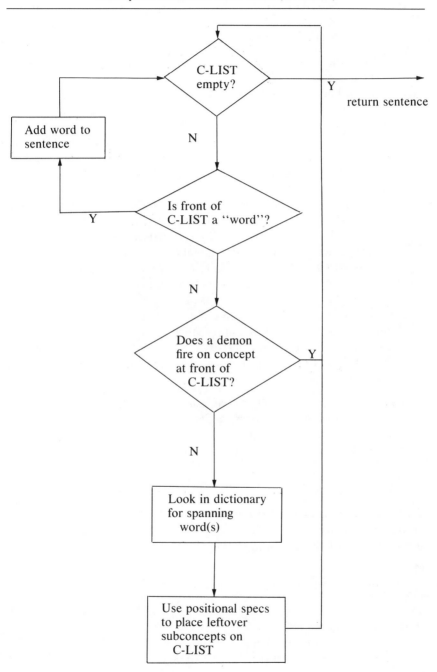

"demon" subprocesses may intervene to prescribe a more economical means of expressing a concept than a dictionary entry may allow.

Initially, the C-LIST contains a single ERKS form to be expressed. The overall generation cycle can be described by the following rules (see also the flow chart of Diagram 6.2):

1. If the front of the C-LIST is empty, there is nothing to generate; return.
2. If a word or fragment is on the front of the C-LIST, then "say" the word by saving it on a special list to be returned, after some post-processing, as the generator's result.
3. If a concept is at the front of the C-LIST, see if any of the "demon" processes want to do anything to it. (The demons, called *sketchifiers,* are described in Section 6.4.) If a demon fires, go to Rule 1 and start over.
4. When none of the demons fires, remove the concept from the front of the C-LIST and try to find a word in the dictionary to express the concept. The dictionary entries are based on *wordsenses,* associations between words and conceptual forms. The conceptual form of an entry that matches a C-LIST item is a *template* for the item: a pattern containing roles and fillers that must be present in the item if the dictionary entry is to be used.
5. If the current concept is completely "spanned" by an entry, i.e., the template is "equal" to the entry, then replace it on the C-LIST by the word(s) of the entry. Otherwise, insert the fillers not matched into the C-LIST, using the positional constraints stored with the wordsense found.

It is worth noting that Rule 3, above, usually embodies a decision *not* to say something that the dictionary would normally want to say. Thus, the model of generation I'm presenting can be thought of as an "exhaustive" algorithm (Rules 1,2,4 and 5) being *restrained* by rules of type 3.

6.2 Dictionary Entries

To illustrate how the generator works, let's consider the dictionary entries needed to generate the example sentence we looked at before, from a concept, say c55, produced by the analyzer:

(1)
Olivia punched Muhammed in the nose

c55:
(propel actor c27
        obj (bpart bptype (hand) partof c27)
        to (physcont val (bpart bytype (nose)

```
            partof (person persname (Muhammed) gender (masc))))
      time (times time1 (:past))
      mode (modes mode1 (:t)))
```

c27:
(person gender (fem) persname (Olivia))

(Note: this is a partially expanded form for readability. Actually the generator, like the analyzer, works with completely atomized forms.)

The first thing to note is that the generator uses many of the same wordsenses as the analyzer did to arrive at c55 in the first place. Thus, for example, the generator definition for "punch" is based on wsPUNCH1 as shown in Figure 6.1. This wordsense is exactly as was shown in Figure 4.6, except for the additional field *focus*. This field is specified to give the generator a sentential focus, a subconcept to "say first" if the concept supplied doesn't contain one. The wordsense provides the generator with the template to match C-LIST items against (stored on the "ws-structure" property) and the word to use (stored on "surface-form") if the entry is selected.

The function *gdictdef* adds the additional information necessary to make the wordsense wsPUNCH1 available to the generator. This function, the analogue of *adictdef* for the analyzer, supplies the specification of syntax for sequencing words. These specifications are sensitive to the "focus" property provided with the input concept, and all use the positioning predicates *pr* (precedes) and *fo* (follows). The dictionary definition for main verbs such as "punch" contains pairs consisting of a path to a focused-on subconcept, and a set of positional specifications for leftover fillers. At [1] in Figure 6.1, for example, are the specifications to be used when the *(actor)* path is to be the sentential focus. (In the case of c55, the system will default to this path.) The specification is an association list (alist) consisting of a path into the C-LIST item, and a set of predicates for placing the filler found at the end of the path on the C-LIST. At [2], for instance, is the alist for the *(actor)* filler:

```
((actor)
(pr)(pr (to val partof)) (pr (to val)))
```

What this says to do is: if the *(actor)* path in the C-LIST item matching the template is nonempty, then position it on the C-LIST *preceding* the word ("punch") spanning the item, *preceding* the filler of the *(to val partof)* path, and *preceding* the filler of the *(to val,* path). Similarly, the filler of *(to val partof)* is to *follow* the word "punch," *follow* the filler of *(actor)*, and *precede* the filler of *(to val)*. The specification for the *(to val)* filler is:

```
((to val)
(fo)(fo (actor))(fo (to val partof))(fo in))
```

Figure 6.1
Generator Definition for "punch"

```
; This is EXACTLY the same wordsense as the analyzer used; see
;      Figure 4.6
(def-wordsense wsPUNCH1
  surface-form (punch)
  ws-structure
  (propel-f actor (nil)
         obj (bpart-f bptype (hand) partof (nil))
         to (physcont val (bpart-f bptype (nil) partof (nil))))
  equivs
  (((actor)(obj partof)))
  ;default focus for the generator
  focus
  (actor)
  )

(gdictdef wsPUNCH1
  ;[1]
  ;syntax for the active voice
  (actor)
   ;[2]
   ;(actor) placement for (actor) focus (active voice)
  (((actor)
    ;the realization of the (actor) is
    ; to precede "punch" on the C-LIST
    (pr)
    ; to precede the realization of the (to val partof) filler
    (pr (to val partof))
    ; and to precede the filler of (to val)
    (pr (to val)))
   ; (to val partof) placement in active voice
   ((to val partof)
    ; following "punch"
    (fo)
    ; following the (actor)
    (fo (actor))
    ; and preceding the (to val) filler
    (pr (to val)))
   ; (to val) placement
   ((to val)
    ;following "punch"
    (fo)
    ; following (actor)
    (fo (actor))
    ; following (to val partof)
    (fo (to val partof))
    ; and following the function word "in"
```

```
(fo in)))

;[3]
;syntax for the passive voice
(to val partof)
(((to val partof)
 (pr)(pr (actor))(pr (to val))
 ((to val)
 (fo)(fo (to val partof))(pr (actor))(fo in))
 ((actor)
 (fo)(fo (to val partof))(fo (to val))(fo by)))
 )
```

This says the *(to val)* filler is to follow the word, the *(actor)* filler, and the *(to val partof)* filler. It is also to follow the *function word* "in," which is simply inserted as a lexical entry on the C-LIST. Thus, the entry specifies the standard ordering of constituents for the active voice of the verb "punch."

Exercise I (Easy)

1. How could the positional specification format be extended to allow for more than one standard ordering of constituents? For example, tri-constituent verbs have two standard realizations in the active voice: one with the indirect object ("Olivia gave Muhammed a book") and one with a to-prepconst ("Olivia gave a book to Muhammed").

2. How might the generator select one or another of the standard orderings provided by the above, if more than one is available? (Hint: see the documentation for the Franz function *rand,* a random number generator.)

3. Does the dictionary format described above allow for function "words" that are really phrases? For example, could one insert "out of" as a function word in "Olivia threw Muhammed out of the window"?

The second association of focus and specification in a dictionary entry is assumed by the generator to correspond to the passive voice. At [3] in Figure 6.1, we see that the passive voice goes with the sentential focus on the *(to val partof)* filler. If c55 were expressed using the passive, the dictionary would specify an ordering of constituents on the C-LIST as follows:

(to val partof) "punch" "in" (to val) "by" (actor)

To handle "Olivia" and "Muhammed," one has the generator's analog of the analyzer's *def-named-person* (Figure 4.3), viz., wsNAMED-PERSON1, as shown in Figure 6.2. The motivation is exactly the same:

Figure 6.2
Generator Definition for "named-person"

```
(def-wordsense wsNAMED-PERSON1
  ;"word" is the empty lexeme
  surface-form (nil)
  ws-structure
  (person-f persname (nil) surname (nil))
    )

(gdictdef wsNAMED-PERSON1
  ()
  (((persname)
   (pr)(pr (surname)))
   ((surname)
   (fo)(fo (persname))))

  sempreds
  (or (filledp '(persname))(filledp '(surname)))
    )
```

---

to be able to generate all the thousands of names there are with a single, concise definition.

Figure 6.2 contains several new things. First, the word in the wordsense is "nil," the "empty" lexeme. It will have no direct realization in the sentence, but merely serves as a pivot to position the naming information. In the call to *gdictdef,* the empty path () indicates that there is no focus, as is typical of nominal concepts. The syntactic predicates position the *persname* filler preceding the empty lexeme, the *surname* filler following.

Also shown are some "semantic predicates" (sempreds), arbitrary Lisp code (without, however, side-effects!) that makes special checks on the given item. These checks test for conditions that are hard to encode using simply the structural information in the template. (Any matching process, for NLP or anything else, needs a structured way to "escape to Lisp" to look for things that are difficult to represent.) The predicates here use *filledp* to demand that at least one of the name slots in the input be filled. (Entries without such a sempred would allow the realization of unnamed persons, such as "a man" or "he.")

Exercise II (Easy)

Write a dictionary definition for the word "because," as in "I went to the store because I wanted some milk." How would you distinguish this from a sentence using the word "so;" for example, "I needed some milk so I went to the store"?

The dictionary entry for "nose" is contained in the following function call:

(gdictdef wsNOSE1)

Since there are no imbedded concepts to be expressed (at least in the simple cases), one merely needs to declare the wordsense defined earlier (cf. Figure 4.9) to the generator.

Exercise III (Not Too Hard)

Transitive verbs have the standard SVO (subject-verb-object) pattern of constituent realization in the active voice. Consider what the *gdictdef* entry for such verbs would look like.

1. What is the characteristic pattern of positional specifications? What parts of the specification vary?

2. By analogy with the analyzer's request-generating macros, could one supply a SVO macro that would allow the entry for a transitive verb to be given in a concise form? How would *gdictdef* know it was looking at such a form? (Hint: see the documentation for the Franz function *getd.)* Could the passive specification also be handled by SVO?

6.3   Morphology and the Verb Kernel

The generator's dictionary lookup routines are responsible for selecting the word or words that span as much of the current concept as possible. Sometimes information in the concept does not map into a complete word, but is expressed by morphological changes in a root form, or by the addition of auxiliary items. Examples are the "'s" fragment indicating possession, and the "to" that signals the infinitive form in the phrase "to graduate is my heart's desire."

When the concept sent to the dictionary contains temporal or modal information, a surface verb kernel must be built to express the *time* and *mode* slots of the concept, and the verb form must be made to agree in person and number with the focus of the sentence. Temporal and modal information is like sentential focus information in that it is not an integral part of the meaning of the concept, but expresses auxiliary information. The *time* information expresses the temporal relationship of the action or state to the time of the speech act ("now"), and possibly to the time of some other event. (Our scheme for representing time is based loosely on the theory discussed in Bruc72.) Modal information expresses the ability, intent, obligation, etc., of the speaker and/or hearer to participate in the expressed action or state.

This information can be extraordinarily difficult to represent fully. For example, the complex concept expressed by the modal "should," in "You should take CS 110 next semester," refers to the belief of the speaker concerning what events it would be in the best interests of the listener to enter into. As another example, consider the temporal relationship expressed in, "In September, I was to have been going for three months." Here, the kernel phrase "was to have been going" says that, at some past time, the action of "going" was in the future, and ongoing with some unnamed event. I make no claim to have representation machinery for all these cases. The following paragraphs simply describe a summary representation used for time and modal concepts, which is sufficient to allow the generator to express this information with the appropriate words.

I will examine two related situations having to do with inflected forms and the generation of the verb kernel of the sentence: the addition of morphological fragments to words, and the generation of auxiliary verbs and modal words. (The former process is the inverse of root-stripping during analysis; cf. Section 4.5.) The first discussion describes two special cases of morphological change, formation of the possessive and the plural. Then, the process of building the verb kernel will be described in two stages: first, subject-verb agreement and modals; then tensing. Finally, the changes to the verb kernel that occur during the generation of questions is briefly discussed. These processes are all extremely intricate, and only a partial, but reasonably complete, solution to the problems will be presented.

6.3.1 Plural and Possessive Morphology

As the lookup/insertion process proceeds, a special *case* role may be placed in an ERKS structure on the C-LIST, to mark the form a word should take. The generator determines the filler of this role by the "function" of the word in a sentence (e.g., as expressing a "possessor" concept, or as the syntactic object of an action.) The *case* slot can be filled with one of following atoms, which represent the standard surface cases of English: subj(ective), obj(ective), nom(inalized), refl(exive), and poss(essive).[2] The variation in surface form that results can be seen in the first person pronoun forms: I, me, mine, myself, and my, respectively.

The *case* filler "plural" can also be used to represent the plural form of a concept. This situation occurs, for example, when the *typmem* (typical member) of a *group* is being expressed. For example, the word "oranges," whose underlying representation is paraphrased "a group of indefinite size with typical member orange," can be generated as "orange + plural fragment." In English, only the cases "plural" and "poss" cause morphological changes in words other than pronouns.

There are at least two ways such changes to words can be managed in this type of generator. One way is to have dictionary entries to represent the generic "possessive" and "plural," and have these map into the fragments "':'s" and "':s", respectively. Then, just before the utterance is presented to the user, the generator can apply a post-processor to find these fragments and make them into suffixes of the word immediately preceding the fragment. Note that such a post-processor would also be useful for such tasks as capitalizing the first word of the sentence, enforcing "a/an" agreement with the following word, or putting "?" on the end of a question sentence.

Exercise IV (Not Too Hard)

Write a function *post-proc* which takes as input a list representing the output sentence, possibly with interspersed fragments, and converts this into a list containing the appropriate inflected forms. (Hint: see the documentation for the Franz functions *explode* and *concat.*) Be sure to handle irregular forms, e.g., (child :s) should become (children). (Hint: think of the fragments as *executable procedures.*)

What additional information would be needed to create final punctuation for questions or imperatives?

A problem with this method is that the syntactic predicates for *every* word that could possibly be pluralized and/or possessivized would need to include ordering information specifying the placement of the fragment. A more economical method, which is, in fact, used by the Toolkit's generator, is to check the *case* slot after the dictionary lookup, and add "s" or "'s" to the word found to span a concept if the slot is filled with "poss" or "plural." The function called to add "s" to form the plural is made aware of irregular forms, such as "men" for "man" + "s", by including the field "pluralform" in the *def-wordsense* declaration for the word. (The same method is also used by the morphology routines that add "ed" to form the past tense or the participle form, using the fields "pastform" or "partform," respectively.)

6.3.2 Subject-Verb Agreement and Modals

The other process that involves morphological changes to words (and a good deal more besides) occurs when the concept sent to the dictionary contains temporal or modal information. Tensing, aspect, modal expression, subject-verb agreement and, as we shall see later, question formation interact in complex ways at that time.

Perhaps the most straightforward procedure is subject-verb agreement. In the conceptual-mapping style of the generator, subject-verb agreement can be enforced by examining *conceptual* features of the focused-upon subconcept to determine whether it is in the first person, second person, plural, etc. For the generator, first person singular, designated ":1pers," is assigned to any concept whose *convrole* (conversational role) is filled with *(*self),* or whose *eprole* (episodic role) is *(*sys).* (That is, the reasoning system using the generator expresses itself as "I," or "the system.") By convention, second person, ":2pers," is assigned to plural concepts and concepts whose *convrole* is the *(*other)*. The default is third person, ":3pers."

This information is used to signal a morphological change in the root form of the verb for third person when the tensing is present, e.g., the addition of "s:"

I run slowly.
He runs slowly.
Do you run slowly?
Does he run slowly?
He has been running slowly.
You have been running slowly.

This information is also necessary for selecting the correct forms of the verb "be." Examples of these are shown below.

I am here.
You are there.
He is nowhere.
The grapes are on the table.

The encoding of the information contained in the *time/mode* roles of a concept expressed in ERKS is straightforward; its translation into English is somewhat less so. Let's first look at the modal information. The *mode* slot contains three kinds of information, each of which fills its own slot. Submode role *mode1* contains *(:t)* (for "true" or "asserted") or *(:neg)* (for "false" or "deasserted"). "Not" is the realization of the latter modality in a sentence expressing a negated concept, and is positioned by the verb-kernel routines immediately following the first word in the verb kernel (i.e., in English we say, "John had not gone," not "John not had gone"). If the concept is negated, and there is no modal concept such as "can" or "might," the operation of *do-support* must be carried out. This is the addition of a tensed form of "do" that agrees with the subject in person and number. In the case of simple negation, this produces sentences such as "John does not go." Do-support is not needed if a modal concept is present to carry the tense, such as in "John can not go."

Exercise V (Not Too Hard)

Modify the function *post-proc* of Exercise IV to convert kernel phrases such as "can not" into forms such as "cannot" and the contracted form "can't." (Note: see the Franz documentation on the "read table" to disable the standard meaning of "'" in Lisp.)

Information for the modal concepts such as "can" and "might" is contained in the second modal slot, *mode2*. Its contents represent the "true" modals: "can/could" (:ablty), "should" (:urge), "may" (:prmssn), "might" (:pntnt), "must" (:oblig), and "will" (:intnt). (The fragments listed in parentheses following the modal words are the fillers the generator expects in the *mode2* slot and are a shorthand for "ability," "urge," "permission," "potential," "obligatory," and "intent," respectively.) These fillers are translated into their corresponding surface forms (with "could" being generated in the presence of past tense).

The *mode3* role is reserved for the special *(:nom)* filler, which indicates that the concept is nominalized (and hence is tenseless). "Lunch" and "World War II" are examples of nominalized concepts. An exception to this is the case of a nominalized verb where the *time2* role (which designates aspect) contains *(:prog)* (progressive). In this case, a gerund form is produced; this is how, for example, the word "running" is produced in the sentence "Jason's running is improving."

6.3.3 Tensing

The final part of the generation of the verb kernel involves the interpretation of the relative time information. The *time* role in a verb concept also has three imbedded slots, *time1*, *time2* and *time3*. In the current implementation (Version 1.10), *time1* can be either ":past," ":pres" or ":futr" tense. The *time2* slot is filled with the aspect, which says whether the action is complete or ongoing with respect to the time in the *time1* slot. The aspect is indicated with either ":prog" or ":perf," for progressive or perfective, respectively. The *time3* role is reserved for the special fillers ":ts" (transition-start) and ":tf" (transition-finish), which serve to indicate that a state-change or action has just been initiated or ended, respectively (cf. Rescher & Urquhart's "realization operator" in Resc71). The transition fillers are realized in such sentences as "I started to go" and "I arrived."

Some examples of tensing and aspect follow.

:past	—I went
:past, :perf	—I had gone
:past, :prog	—I was going
:pres	—I go
:pres, :perf	—I have gone
:pres, :prog	—I am going
:futr	—I will go
:futr, :perf	—I will have gone
:futr, :prog	—I will be going

Two final issues are related to the method for expressing the information in the *time* slot. One concerns the expression of the appropriate form of the verb "be" in cases such as statives ("I am sick") or passives ("Muhammed was hit"). In the first case, the phrase stored with the attributional concept in the dictionary is ''be sick.'' The lookup routines notice this and cause the ''be'' to be replaced with the correct form, using the temporal and subject information as described in the paragraph on subject-verb agreement. For passives, the correct form of ''be'' is *added* to the verb kernel in the correct place. Note that the generator ''knows'' it is being asked to express a passive construction, because the sentential focus path selects the *second* set of syntactic predicates from the dictionary definition. (See Section 6.2.)

The second issue has to do with cases where *no tense* is to be expressed (e.g., ''to go'' as in ''Jason wants to go home''). The *time1* filler will contain '':infize'' (for infinitive) in these cases. (Currently, this arises as a result of the operation of the infinitive ''demon,'' discussed in Section 6.4.1.) In this case, the word ''to'' is added to the root form that was found by the dictionary lookup. (The extensions needed to allow the generator to express modal or aspective information in infinitives such as ''I want not to go'' and ''I want to have gone before he arrives'' are beyond the scope of this discussion.)

6.3.4 Subject-Auxiliary Inversion

A final phenomenon that influences the form of the verb kernel is the change in focus that occurs when a question is asked. If the concept being generated is a question that is inquiring about the filler of the *mode* role, the first auxiliary in the kernel must be moved to the front of the clause (''fronted'') to produce the question form (and do-support must be performed if no auxiliary exists). This produces sentences such as:

Was John going? (Move tense auxiliary)
Did John go?   (Move ''do'' obtained from do-support)
Can John go?   (Move modal auxiliary ''can'')

Since the auxiliary needs to be fronted, the verb kernel must be split (e.g., ''did have to go'' becomes ''did'' and ''have to go'' in the sentence ''Did John have to go?''). This is accomplished in the verb-kernel routines by returning the first auxiliary as a word to be *inserted* into the C-LIST in the ordinary way, not as a part of the phrase that is the verb kernel. The positional specification for the auxiliary to be fronted is formed by specifying that it precede the realization of the concept that is the sentential focus. In general, the auxiliary that is moved may be a modal, a form of *do* generated by do-support, or the auxiliary of a progressive or stative concept (e.g., ''Is the ball on the table?'').

Sometimes only a subpart of the full conceptualization is being questioned. For example, in ''Who ran to Boston?,'' the identity of the *actor* is desired. Note that here the normal sentential focus, the *actor* role, is the subconcept being questioned (the so-called ''qfocus''). In the process of generating these ''fill-in-the-blanks'' questions (Lehn78), if the sentential focus and qfocus are different, then an auxiliary must be fronted along with the wh-phrase expressing the questioned subconcept.[3] Consider, for example, the question "Where did John run to?" In this sentence, by the time the dictionary is told to look up the case frame that will match the word "run," the qfocus part of the concept has already been expressed by "where." (Query: why doesn't "to" get fronted, as well?) The verb-kernel routines notice this and arrange that *did* is returned from the lookup routine with syntax specifying that it is to be placed before the filler of the *actor* role, the default sentential focus for "run."

These considerations should make it clear that the interaction among tense, aspect, modals, negations, questions, and focus is intricate. We have seen that relatively straightforward extensions to the basic lookup and insert process described in the last section will serve to handle most of the phenomena covered by focus, temporal, and modal information in an ERKS form. By far the more serious question for an intelligent system is, where did this information come from in the first place? (I will comment on this further in Chapter 7; see, also, Appe85.)

6.4 "Advanced" English Syntax

In this section I will discuss the data and processing constructs needed to handle a somewhat more complicated example than Sentence 1:

(2)
Olivia wished to hit Muhammed's nose with her hand

c49:
(s-goal actor c27
      mobj (propel actor c27
              obj (bpart bptype (hand) partof c27)
              to (physcont val (bpart bptype (nose)
                                partof c35))
              time (times time1 (:past))
              mode (modes mode1 (:t)))
      time (times time1 (:past))
      mode (modes mode1 (:t)))

c27: (person gender (fem) persname (Olivia))
c35: (person gender (masc) persname (Muhammed))

This is a typical imbedded-sentence construction, in which the imbedded clause is a (loose) paraphrase of (1). As usual, concept c49 could have come either from the memory/reasoning system or the analyzer.

First, we need definitions for "wish," "hit," "her" and "hand." "Hit" and "hand" look like "punch" and "nose," respectively. (The

Figure 6.3
Generator Definition of "wish"

```
(def-wordsense wsWISH1
 surface-form (wish)
 ws-structure
 (s-goal-f actor (nil) mobj (nil))
 focus
 (actor)
 constraints
 (((actor) couldbe-hianimate-p)
  ((mobj) couldbe-episode-p))
 )

(gdictdef wsWISH1
 ;never mind the passive form
 ()
 (((actor)
   (pr)(pr (mobj)))
  ((mobj)
   (fo)(fo (actor))(fo that)))
 )
```

definition of "her" will be deferred until Section 6.4.3.) A definition for "wish" is shown in Figure 6.3. Note that the function word "that" is used to set off the *mobj* concept, which is then placed on the C-LIST to be completely expressed.

6.4.1   The Infinitive Construction

An important feature of (2), which is not covered by the definition of "wish" given in Figure 6.3, is the infinitive construction used to express the imbedded conceptualization. Note that this allows a concise expression of c49, which is literally something like "Olivia wanted it to be the case that she punch Muhammed in the nose."

Conventions for producing "advanced" syntactic constructions such as this are implemented in this generation scheme by a set of rules, called *sketchifiers,* that operate when certain semantic features are present in the item at the front of the C-LIST. These rules "notice" certain kinds of redundancies in concepts and their surrounding context and then arrange a "sketchy" expression of the concept, leaving the redundant information to be inferred. Sketchifying rules may change the form of the utterance by marking redundant concepts as not to be "said," by adding function words to the C-LIST, or by modifying the concept so that certain concise syntactic constructions (e.g., infinitive or progressive forms) can be used.

In concept c49, the redundant information is this: the *actor* of the imbedded *mobj* is the same entity as the toplevel *actor*. The "infinitive" sketchifier, a simple version of which is shown in Figure 6.4, is responsible for spotting redundancies of this kind. The function *defdemon* declares a sketchifier to the generator subsystem. The rule has a test part (which, as usual, is to have no side effects) and an actions part. The test part checks that the concept at the front of the C-LIST, obtained by a call to *front-clist,* is a "mental" action or state, i.e., one that contains a conceptualization that is at a "mental location" *(cp* or *ltm)* of an actor. If the actor "possessing" the concept is the same as the actor of the imbedded concept, then the infinitive can be used. (Actually, this is true only for certain "mental act" words, as we see below.)

The actions of the sketchifier first arrange that the imbedded *actor* concept is not re-expressed, through the call to the function *dont-say.* Then, at [1], the sketchifier modifies the *mobj* concept so that the verb kernel routines described in the last section will use an infinitive form. It then (at [2]) places the modified concept inside a C-LIST "frame" and pushes the frame back onto the C-LIST. A C-LIST frame is a list structure consisting of a word or phrase, the concept the word(s) express, and the location of the concept in its parent concept. We can see that the current frame has no word (the concept hasn't been looked up yet) and that it occupies the (mobj) path in its parent. Finally, the rule marks the (mobj) concept as not needing to be "said."

Sketchifier rules of this type are an extremely powerful and economical means of producing complex syntactic phenomena by examining conceptual features of concepts to be expressed. For example, simple extensions of the rule given will allow expression of sentences such as

(3) I wanted John to go

where it just sketchifies the tensing information present in the imbedded concept. Likewise, one can easily block the use of the infinitive in cases where the imbedded concept contains a modal other than :t and :neg:

(4) I wish that I could go

Exercise VI (Not Too Difficult)

Modify the sketchifier of Figure 6.4 so that it handles cases (3, 4) correctly.

A slightly more complex test is needed to handle imbedded passives, such as

(5) John wanted to be kissed

Sketchifying rules can become extremely complicated as they are asked to handle the full range of constructions required by a fluent

Figure 6.4
Simple Version of the Infinitive Sketchifier

```
; Infinitive Sketchifier (Simplified)
; If the topcon is an mtrans, mbuild or an s-goal, and the top actor is the
; same as the sub actor, squash the sub actor and use the infinitive form

(defdemon #inf
   ((test (and (mental-concept-p (front-clist))
           (eq (grf '(actor) (front-clist))
               (grf '(mobj actor) (front-clist)))))
   (actions
    (let ((parentcon (front-clist)))
        ;mark the subcon actor as not needing to be said
        (dont-say '(mobj actor) parentcon)
        ; [1]
        ;arrange that the mobj gets the infinitive form
        (set-infinitive (grf '(mobj) parentcon))
        ;push mobj back onto the C-LIST for later expression
        (msg N "inf: pushing infized imbedded sent")
        ; [2]
        (push-clist '(nil ,(grf '(mobj) parentcon) ,(list parentcon 'mobj)))
        ;mark the mobj as not needing to be said (it will be said later)
        (dont-say '(mobj) parentcon)
   ))))

;MENTAL-CONCEPT-P: is the argument a mental actional or stative?
(def mental-concept-p (lambda (arg)
  (memq (type-of arg) '(s-goal mbuild mtrans))))

;DONT-SAY: mark subcon of concept as not to be expressed
;     Accumulate paths into con not having to be said
(def dont-say (lambda (path con)(appendprp con path 'dont-say)))

;SET-INFINITIVE: make verb-kernel routines use the infinitive form
;Note: this is done by resetting the time1 filler; the time2, time3
;     fillers will continue to get expressed
;     For example, "to have punched"
(def set-infinitive (lambda (con)
   (srf '(time time1) con (make-special-structure '(:infize)))))

;C-LIST manipulators:
;Note: the C-LIST is maintained in two globals, :front-of-clist
;     and :rest-of-clist

;FRONT-CLIST: return current front of clist
(def front-clist (lambda () :front-of-clist))

;PUSH-CLIST: push a C-LIST frame onto the (rest of the) C-LIST
(def push-clist (lambda (frame)
  (setq :rest-of-clist (cons frame :rest-of-clist))))

;REPL-FRONT-CLIST: reset the front-of-clist global
(def repl-front-clist (lambda (frame)
  (setq :front-of-clist frame)))
```

generator system. For example, some mental act words use progressive constructions to express imbedded conceptualizations:

(6) I saw John running down the street

Some words change the form of the infinitive complement slightly when the imbedded actor is different from the toplevel actor:

(7) I planned for John to go

In certain cases, other verbs don't allow any sketchification at all:

(8) I believed that John would go

(For some reason, the infinitive form sounds all right if the toplevel form is passivized: "John is believed to be going home.") As an engineering matter, there simply is no substitute for the accumulation of a corpus for words such as mental act verbs, which illustrates all the things one wants a generator to be able to say.

6.4.2   The Possessive Sketchifier

I now turn to the two possessive constructions in Sentence (2): "Muhammed's nose" and "her hand." First, recall that the concept that stands for

(9)
Muhammed's nose
(bpart bptype (nose) partof (person persname (Muhammed)
                                      gender (masc)))

is really a shorthand form of

(10)
A nose such that it is physically part of Muhammed
(bpart bptype (nose)
       rel (p-config confrel (partof)
                con1 "nose"
                con2 "Muhammed"))

The full-blown concept above is a typical example of the *rel* clause construction that expresses a relationship between an entity and a modifying conceptualization (cf. Section 5.1.3). (This construction in turn is shorthand for the complete form of the meaning structure, as discussed in Chapter 2.)

In English, the possessive form is regularly used to express "physically part of" relationships, as well as many other relations. One can consider of a form such as (9) to be a sketchified, more concise form of (10). A version of the "possessive" sketchifier that handles instances of this relationship is shown in Figure 6.5. One can see that the sketchifier checks for a non-empty *(partof)* filler in the item at the front of the

Figure 6.5
The "partof" Possessive Sketchifier

```
; (Physically Partof) Possessive Sketchifier
; If a concept has an imbedded (partof) role, extract the
; subcon, give it the possessive case...

(defdemon #poss-sketchifier
  ((test (filled '(partof) (front-clist)))
   (actions
    (let* ((parentcon (front-clist))
           (subcon (grf '(partof) parentcon)))
      ;don't say the partof subcon in the parentcon
      (dont-say '(partof) parentcon)
      ;don't express the (ref) role of the parent:
      ;    "a man's car"
      (dont-say '(ref) parentcon)
      ;[1]
      ;push parent back onto C-LIST
      (push-clist '(nil ,parentcon nil))
      (srf '(case) subcon (make-special-structure '(poss)))
      (repl-front-clist '(nil ,subcon (partof ,parentcon)))
      ))))
```

C-LIST. If it finds one, it marks the parent as containing a subconcept that needn't be said. It also marks the parent's *(ref)* filler as not needing expression. (That is, we don't say "the the boy's dog.") The determiner in a noun group containing a possessive refers to the "possessor" constituent rather than the "possessed." For example, in "the man's car," it is "the man," not "the car." If we absolutely must place a determiner on the "possessed" concept, we will say something such as "a car of the man." The current scheme can't handle this case.

Next (at [1]) the sketchifier pushes the parent concept back onto the C-LIST. Then, it puts a (case) filler containing the possessive marker "poss," onto the *(partof)* subcon, and calls *repl-front-clist* (cf. Figure 6.4) to put the subcon at the front of the C-LIST. Recall that in Section 6.3.1 a process was described that would add "'s" onto the surface form found to express the concept matched by the dictionary lookup, if that concept had *case* "poss." Consider again Figure 6.2, which shows the wordsense definition for named persons. Unfortunately, the process described in Section 6.3.1, if applied to this wordsense, will generate the phrase "nil's Muhammed"! Remember that the empty lexeme "nil" is used as the surface form only to provide a pivot for positioning the various fillers of

Figure 6.6
"named person," Revisited

```
(gdictdef wsNAMED-PERSON1

  <see Figure 6.2 for base definition>

  ;arbitrary actions field
  ;here, make the surface form possessive, if someone wants you to
  actions
  ; the global :pcon (parent concept) stores the concept the
  ; generator is currently trying to express
  (cond ((possessor-p :pcon)
          ; clear the case slot since its expression will be handled here
          (srf '(case) :pcon (make-special-structure '(nil)))
          (form-possessive (cond ((filled '(surname) :pcon)
                                    '(surname))
                                  ('(persname)))
            :pcon)))
)
```

---

the surface roles of named concepts. It is certainly not intended to carry the possessive marker.

There are two alternatives at this point. One is for the possessive demon not to mark the case of the (partof) filler as possessive, and instead to push a morphological fragment standing for "possessive", i.e., "'s", onto the C-LIST (which would then be added to the word it follows during post-processing). This would correctly handle a case such as "John Doe's tie," but our postprocessor would have to be expanded to handle a case such as "me" + ":'s" is "my". (Also, after reading about the entity reference demon at the end of this section, think about how "mine" could be generated from, for example, "my car." Might this extra element on the C-LIST affect the process?)

The other way to proceed is to upgrade the dictionary definition for named persons so that it notices the possessive case and modifies the *persname,* unless the *surname* is filled. The dictionary definition creation function, *gdictdef,* permits another field, the *actions* field (see Figure 6.6). The "actions" field in a dictionary definition specifies arbitrary code to be run *after* the match of the input item to the definition has been accepted. (That is, after the structural match has succeeded and the "sempred" actions have returned non-nil.) In the case at hand, the actions expression checks for a "possessive" marker in the input item. If one is found, it clears the case slot (to prevent "nil's" from being generated) and calls the function *form-possessive* to possessivize the surname, if it exists, or the personal name. Thus, one would get "Muhammed Ali's," or "Muhammed's," respectively. This use of the actions field illustrates a technique whereby the sketchifiers and dictionary lookup routines can cooperate: the sketchifiers identifying the need for a special form, the lookup functions handling its realization.

Exercise VII (Moderately Difficult)

1. Write a version of the "partof" sketchifier for an entity's "clothes;" for example, "John's pants" or "sports car's tonneau." What is the characteristic relationship the sketchifier needs to notice? Do the actions of the "partof" sketchifier need to be changed at all?

2. What other relationships between entities could analogs of these sketchifiers be written for? Could a single, giant rule be written for these cases?

3. An alternative realization for "X's Y" is "Y of X." What would have to change in the actions of the partof sketchifier to allow this form? How could the sketchifier choose one or the other? (Hint: see Exercise I, this chapter.)

6.4.3   The Entity-Reference Sketchifier

The second possessive form in (2), "her hand," follows a processing path similar to "Muhammed's nose" but with one important difference. Since "Olivia" is being generated for the *second* time, we need to arrange for the use of a pronoun, if appropriate. It should be clear that a pronoun, such as "she," is just a sketchified form of another concept, here "Olivia."

The sketchifier whose main job is identifying when pronouns are needed is called "entref" (for entity-reference). A much simplified version of it is shown in Figure 6.7. The test part first checks to see if the *(ref)* filler is already set. (This avoids the possibility of an infinite loop, when other sketchifiers are pushing and popping the C-LIST.) Then it makes sure the item is an entity. When the rule fires, it first checks the NLP context to see if the current concept is being re-expressed. The function *is-in-nlpcontext* (not shown) examines the generator part of the "nlpcontext" field of the current exchange frame (cf. Section 5.5) for a concept that merges properly with the item. If there is one, the *(ref)* role of the item gets filled such that the dictionary will find a pronoun of matching gender and number.

Of course, this is much too simplistic. We need to be careful of cases where confusion might result because there is more than one possible referent:

(11) Mary sent a card to Elaine. She read it.

"She" is presumably "Elaine," but there is a chance for confusion

Figure 6.7
The Entity-Reference Sketchifier

```
; Entity Reference Sketchifier (Simplified)
; Determine whether entity is being re-expressed. If so
; use a pronoun. Otherwise, see if it is unique. Else, mark
; it with indefinite reference

(defdemon #entref
  ((test (and (empty '(ref) (front-clist))
              (couldbe-entity-p (front-clist))))
   (actions
    (let ((parentcon (front-clist)))

          (cond
          ;if concept is being re-expressed, use a pronoun
          ((is-in-nlpcontext parentcon)
           (srf '(ref) parentcon (make-special-structure '(pron))))
          ;if concept is "unique," definite reference
          ((uniq-p parentcon)
           (srf '(ref) parentcon (make-special-structure '(def))))
          ;else indef
          (t (srf '(ref) parentcon (make-special-structure '(indef)))))
          ))))

;UNIQ-P: does concept represent a unique entity in the world?
(def uniq-p (lambda (con)
  ;for now, is it named?
  (named-p con)))

;NAMED-P: does concept have one of its name fields (stored with
;         "surfslots" property of the type) filled?
(def named-p (lambda (con)
  (let* ((type (type-of con))
         (surfslots (get type 'surfslots)))

          (car (rem-nil (mapcar '(lambda(x)(filled (list x) con))
                                surfslots)))
          )))

; wsHER-POSS: the possessive form of the female personal pronoun
(def-wordsense wsHER-POSS
  surface-form (her)
  ws-structure
  (person-f gender (fem) case (poss))
  )

(gdictdef wsHER-POSS)
```

---

because "Mary" was the sentential focus of the first sentence. Reflexive pronouns also cause problems:

(12) John hurt himself jumping out the window.

Exercise VIII (Difficult!)

How can the NLP context be used to handle the problems caused by (11) and (12)? (Hint: see discussion about the "prior-frs" field of the exchange frame in Section 5.5.) Watch out for sentences such as "John wants Mary to like himself," which is no good, versus "John wants to like himself," which is all right.

Deciding on a pronominal realization for reappearances of entities is a special case of the "entity reference" problem, deciding what determiner, if any, to assign to an entity to be expressed. Note that the sketchifier has this problem even if the entity is a new one. This is an *extremely* difficult problem that I will ignore almost entirely here, saying only that proper names are definitely "definite." Figure 6.7 gives some code for discovering this fact from the ERKS type of the entity.

In the case of "her hand" in (2), there is an interesting interaction among the "possessive" and "entity-reference" sketchifiers and the dictionary. The possessive sketchifier first notices the "her" concept in the bodypart concept, and marks it with *case* (poss). Then the entref sketchifier decides that a pronoun is needed. The matching dictionary definition is wsHER-POSS, as shown in Figure 6.7. Notice that here we also need to remove the case filler "poss." This is because the surface form "her" spans the meaning of case "possessive," and we want to prevent the morphology routines from adding "'s" to this upon seeing the case filler.[4] (There is also an "objective" sense of "her," as in "John told her to go.")

Exercise IX (Not Difficult)

Unlike the case of named persons (where it was necessary to prevent the empty lexeme from receiving the possessive morphology) for the definition of "her," the surface form is all right as is. Thus, it is annoying to have to obliterate the case filler. Suggest a test that can be applied before the invocation of the function that forms the possessive to prevent the addition of the "'s". (Hint: recall how "pluralform" was used to handle the irregular plural form.)

6.5 A Processing Example

This section will show the machinery described in the last two sections in action. The generator will be working with a concept that will eventually be expressed as Sentence (2):

Olivia wished to hit Muhammed's nose with her hand

As in the case of the analyzer, the example below is output, slightly edited for readability, from a "script" session with the generator.[5] Comments are interspersed with the program's outputs.

The program starts with all its output messages enabled, and with pauses at strategic points. Lines beginning with "*" are pauses where the user can examine the state of the system. The generator toplevel function is *g*, which is called with the concept c78.

```
(xpn 'c78)
(s-goal actor c90
        mobj (propel actor c90 obj (bpart bptype (hand) partof c90)
            to (physcont val (bpart partof
                                (person persname (Muhammed)
                                       gender (masc))
                              bptype (nose)))
          time (times time1 (:past)) mode (modes mode1 (:t)))
          time (times time1 (:past)) mode (modes mode1 (:t)))

c90: (person persname (Olivia) gender (fem))

(g 'c78)

GEN:top of c-list
(s-goal actor (person persname (Olivia) gender (fem))
        mobj (propel actor c505 obj (bpart bptype (hand) partof c505)
            to (physcont val (bpart partof (person persname (Muhammed)
                                                   gender (masc))
                              bptype (nose)))
          time (times time1(:past))mode (modes mode1(:t)))
          time (times time1(:past))mode (modes mode1(:t)))

*#act-rule
*#s-attr
*#imp
*#locale
*#abstime
*#qfocus
*#inf
inf: pushing infized embedded seat
*#sayrel
*#act-rule
*#locale
*#abstime
*#sayrel
```

Here we see the various sketchifier rules "tasting" the concept at the front of the C-LIST. *#inf* is the infinitive sketchifier presented in Figure 6.4. The message indicates that the imbedded concept has been placed back on the C-LIST.

DICT to match:
(s-goal actor (person persname (Olivia) gender (fem))
       mobj (propel actor c505 obj (bpart bptype (hand) partof c505)
     .....)

DICT result: Dw78 (wished)

Now the generator goes to the dictionary, which matches the concept to entry Dw78 (the internal form of wsWISH1). The verb-kernel routines return the past form of "wish," as shown.

GEN: using
(wished)

*gentop

inserting (nil c505 (c504 actor)) at:
((pr c504) (pr (c504 mobj)))

GEN: clist:
c505
(person persname (Olivia) gender (fem))

(wished)

c508
(propel actor (person persname (Olivia) gender (fem) ref (def))
      obj (bpart bptype (hand) partof c505)
      to (physcont val (bpart partof (person persname (Muhammed)
                               gender (masc))
                     bptype (nose)))
    time (times time1 (:infize)) mode (modes mode1 (:t)))

Here we see the insertion process defined by the definition of "wish," Dw78 (cf. Figure 6.3). The *actor* concept is placed on the C-LIST preceding "wished" and the *mobj* concept. The latter is not inserted because the "inf" sketchifier marked it as "don't say." The C-LIST now contains the *actor* concept, the lexical item "wished," and the *propel* concept, which was pushed by the sketchifier. Note that the (time time1) slot of the latter has been marked with ":infize," which will trigger an infinitival realization in the verb-kernel routines when this concept finally gets to the front of the C-LIST.

GEN: top of c-list
(person persname (Olivia) gender (fem))

*#act-rule

```
*#pp-rule
*#entref
entref: def-izing unique entity c505
entref: updating nlp context with c505
*#poss
(xpn c505)
(person persname (Olivia) gender (fem) ref (def)))
*#poss1
*#poss2
*#adjectival
*# sayre1
*#act-rule
*#pp-rule
*#adjectival
*#sayre1
```

DICT to match: (person persname (Olivia) gender (fem) ref (def))

DICT result: Dw80 (nil)

GEN: using
(nil)

*gentop

The "Olivia" concept reaches the front of the C-LIST. The sketchifier "entref," which is responsible for noticing repeated occurrences of entities (so a pronoun can be used), marks it as being definitely referenced. This is because the person has a proper name. The concept also goes into the shared NLP Context where the analyzer or generator can see it if necessary. Then the system goes to the dictionary, which returns the definition for "named-person," Dw80 (cf. Figure 6.6).

inserting ((Olivia) (Olivia) (c505 persname)) at:
((pr c505) (pr (c505 surname)))

GEN: clist:
(Olivia)

(nil)

(wished)

```
c508
(propel actor (person persname (Olivia) gender (fem) ref (def))
   .....)
```

utterance is (Olivia)
utterance is (Olivia)
utterance is (Olivia wished)

The surface-slot filler (Olivia) is positioned preceding the empty lexeme (nil) on the C-LIST. The system pops "Olivia," the empty lexeme and "wished" off the C-LIST, and throws the empty lexeme away.

GEN: top of c-list
(propel actor (person persname (Olivia) gender (fem) ref (def))
        obj (bpart bptype (hand) partof c505)
        to (physcont val (bpart partof (person persname (Muhammed)
                                        gender (masc))
                bptype (nose)))
        time (times time1 (:infize)) mode (modes mode1 (:t)))

*#act-rule
*#s-attr
*#imp
*#locale
*#abstime
*#qfocus
*#inf
*#sayre1

DICT to match:
(propel actor (person persname (Olivia) gender (fem) ref (def))
  ....)

DICT result: Dw79 (to hit)

GEN:using
(to hit)

*gentop

inserting (nil c509 (c508 obj)) at:
((fo c508) (fo (c508 actor)) (fo (c508 to val)) (fo (funcword with)))

inserting (nil c512 (c508 to val)) at:
((fo c508) (fo (c508 actor)) (pr (c508 obj)))

GEN: clist:
(to hit)

c512
(bpart partof (person persname (Muhammed) gender (masc))
bptype(nose))

(with)

c509
(bpart bptype (hand) partof (person persname (Olivia) gender (fem)))

utterance is (Olivia wished to hit)

The infinitivized *propel* concept reaches the front of the C-LIST. The dictionary returns "to hit" as its realization. The insertion routines position the fillers "Muhammed's nose" and "Olivia's hand," as shown. "To hit" gets popped off.

GEN: top of c-list
(bpart partof (person persname (Muhammed) gender(masc))
bptype(nose))

*#act-rule
*#pp-rule
*#entref
entref: def-izing possessor concept c512
entref updating nlp context with c512
*#poss

(xpn c512)
(bpart partof (person persname (Muhammed) gender (masc))
      bptype (nose) ref (def))

*#poss1
poss/partof rule forming possessive of
(person persname (Muhammed) gender (masc))

*#poss2
*#adjectival
*#sayrel
*#act-rule
*#pp-rule
*#entref
entref def-izing unique entity c513
entref updating nlp context with c513
*#poss

(xpn c513)
(person persname (Muhammed) gender (masc) case (poss) ref(def))

*#poss1
*#poss2
*#adjectival
*#sayrel
*#act-rule
*#pp-rule
*#adjectival
*#sayrel

DICT to match:
(person persname (Muhammed) gender (masc) case (poss) ref(def))

DICT result: Dw80 (nil)

GEN: using
(nil)

*gentop

inserting ((Muhammed's)(Muhammed's)(c513 persname)) at:
((pr c513)(pr(c513 surname)))

GEN :clist:
(Muhammed's)

(nil)

c512
(bpart bptype (nose) ref (def))

(with)

c509
(bpart bptype (hand) partof (person persname (Olivia) gender (fem)))

utterance is (Olivia wished to hit Muhammed's)
utterance is (Olivia wished to hit Muhammed's)

Here we see a typical entref/possessive interaction. First entref marks "nose" as being "definite" because it is part of a "definite" possessor, "Muhammed." Then, the possessive demon, #poss1, extracts the possessor subconcept and pushes "nose" back onto the C-LIST. Next, entref marks "Muhammed" as "definite," and the actions field of the "named-person" definition (Figure 6.6) forms "Muhammed's," as shown. The system pops off "Muhammed's" and the empty lexeme.

GEN: top of c-list
(bpart bptype (nose) ref(def))

*#act-rule
*#pp-rule
*#entref

entref updating nlp context with c512
*#poss

(xpn c512)
(bpart bptype (nose) ref (def))

*#poss1
*#poss2
*#adjectival
*#sayrel
*#act-rule

*#pp-rule
*#adjectival
*#sayrel

DICT to match: (bpart bptype (nose) ref (indef))

DICT result: Dw82 (nose)

GEN: using
(nose)

*gentop

GEN: clist:
(nose)

(with)

c509
(bpart bptype (hand) partof (person persname (Olivia) gender (fem)))

utterance is (Olivia wished to hit Muhammed's nose)
utterance is (Olivia wished to hit Muhammed's nose with)

GEN: top of c-list
(bpart bptype (hand) partof (person persname (Olivia) gender (fem)))

*#act-rule
*#pp-rule
*#entref

entref: def-izing possessor concept c509
entref updating nlp context with c509

*#poss

(xpn c509)
(bpart bptype (hand) partof (person persname (Olivia) gender (fem))
ref(def))

*#poss1

poss/partof rule forming possessive of
(person persname (Olivia) gender (fem))

*#poss2
*#adjectival
*#sayrel
*#act-rule
*#pp-rule
*#entref

entref pron-izing unique entity c505

entref updating nlp context with c505
*#poss

(xpn c505)
(person persname (Olivia) gender (fem) ref (pron) case (poss))

*#poss1
*#poss2
*#adjectival
*#sayrel
*#act-rule
*#pp-rule
*#adjectival
*#sayrel

DICT to match:
(person persname (Olivia) gender (fem) ref (pron) case (poss))

DICT result: Dw83 (her)

GEN: using
(her)

*gentop

"The nose" gets sent off to the dictionary, but is realized as "nose," because the (ref) slot was marked (by the possessive demon) as "don't say." The words "nose with" get popped off the C-LIST, and the entref and possessive demons work on "Olivia's hand" in a manner analogous to "Muhammed's nose." When entref gets in again to examine "Olivia," it sees that she is being expressed for the second time, and arranges for a pronoun realization. The dictionary returns the possessive form of "her," Dw83.

GEN: clist:
(her)

c509
(bpart bptype (hand) ref (def))

utterance is (Olivia wished to hit Muhammed's nose with her)

GEN: top of c-list
(bpart bptype (hand) ref (def))

*#act-rule
*#pp-rule
*#entref

entref updating nlp context with c509

*#poss

(xpn c509)
(bpart bptype (hand) ref (indef))

*#poss1
*#poss2
*#adjectival
*#sayrel
*#act-rule
*#pp-rule
*#adjectival
*#sayrel

DICT to match: (bpart bptype (hand) ref (indef))

DICT result: Dw81 (hand)

GEN: using
(hand)

*gentop

GEN: clist:
(hand)

utterance is (Olivia wished to hit Muhammed's nose with her hand)

Result:
(Olivia wished to hit Muhammed's nose with her hand)

6.6 Summary

In this chapter, an algorithm was described for performing conceptual generation, the mapping of an ERKS form into an English sentence in three distinct subprocesses. First, an iterative process of dictionary look-up of words spans the concept currently at the focus of attention in the generator's short-term memory. Each word thus found replaces the concept, and any left-over imbedded concepts are inserted into the short-term memory, according to the instructions stored in the dictionary entry, together with any needed function words (e.g., prepositions). Second, before each dictionary access step, a collection of test-action pairs called sketchifiers examines the current concept at the focus for redundant subconcepts, for which a distinct summarizing syntactic construction (such as an infinitive or coordinate) is available. These processes modify the focus, possibly rearranging the short-term memory so that the special syntactic form can be used. Finally, certain well-behaved discourse phenomena such as pronoun generation are handled by quasi-sketchifiers that look at a data structure called the NLP Context, which is shared between analyzer and generator. The NLP Context is maintained on the basis of a "conversational exchange," a discourse unit based on one item generated by the system, followed by the response from the user.

Certain adaptations of the module described here for use in the ACE system are discussed in Chapter 10.7.

Notes

1. The elegant lookup-then-insert iteration to be described was originally developed by Mallory Selfridge, working with the author in the Intelligent Systems Design group at the University of Connecticut.

2. The distinguished *case, time* and *mode* fillers to be presented in this section are the conventional ones shared by the analyzer and generator in Version 1.10 of the NLP Toolkit.

3. Wh-phrases are phrases initiated by wh-words such as "who," "what," "when," etc., which ask questions about entities. The details of wh-phrase movement in questions are covered in Section 10.7, in connection with the qfocus "demon."

4. If all of this is starting to sound like random hackery, please note that we are here dealing with some of the most intricate problems in the realization of concepts. Accept my assurance that the generation scheme sketched out here can deal with nearly all of this without strain, and that hard words such as possessive pronouns can be handled without complicating the easier cases unnecessarily!

5. As with the analyzer transcript from Chapter 4, this one was created by a version of the generator that had been modified slightly from the distribution program in the NLP Toolkit, to allow the simplified versions of the sketchifiers, etc., described in this chapter to work as advertised.

Part II
Building a Conversationalist

7

Summarizing Knowledge Bases

7.0 Introduction: What to Say versus How to Say It

"Friendly" computer interfaces require analyzing and generating programs whose language behavior mimics that of human beings. For a generation program to model human performance, it must be capable of more than mere translation of some input representation of a sentence into English. Such a program must be able to determine *what to say* in order to communicate with a user in a natural fashion. Part of this naturalness comes from knowing what *not* to say. If a body of knowledge, represented in its entirety in a program's memory system, is to be communicated, only part of it need actually be said. Some of it can be inferred by the listener or is not important to the communication. To build programs that can make the distinction between useful and useless information, it is essential that the designer try to understand the techniques people use when choosing what to say. This chapter presents a particularly simple model for making distinctions of these sorts, based upon a notion of explanations as summaries.

Language generation tasks can be organized hierarchically according to their complexity. Generation of a single sentence with minimal surrounding context can be achieved by the generation program described in Chapter 6. For example, Sentence (7.1) is understandable without any additional information, even if the person Jacob is not known.

(7.1) My friend Jacob was looking for his shoes yesterday.

The next level of complexity in generation can be found in the production of paragraph length text. Here the individual sentences must be connected using conventions that tie the sentences together to form a unit. For example, the sentences given below represent a cohesive unit.

(7.2) My friend Jacob went to buy some cooking apples today.
(7.3) Some of the apples he bought were bad.
(7.4) I told him to take the bad ones back.

This chapter is adapted from the Master's thesis of Marie Bienkowski, "Generating Natural Language Explanations," Department of EE&CS CS-TR-83-1, University of Connecticut, Storrs, January 1983.

These sentences illustrate some common phenomena occurring in paragraph-length text. Note the different ways of referring to the apples. They are first introduced as "some cooking apples." Next, in Sentence (7.3) the apples are referred to as "the apples he bought," which ignores what type of apples they are, and informs us that the apples were in fact obtained. A new item, the group of bad apples, is introduced in (7.3) as a subset of all the apples bought. Finally, in Sentence (7.4) no explicit mention of the apples bought is made; they are implicit in the mention of those that were bad in "the bad ones." It is also interesting to observe what has been left out in each sentence—for example, the mention of the store where Jacob went and bought the apples. This omission might not have occurred if the intent of the story were to tell someone that some particular market sells bad fruit. This example illustrates that in more complex generation tasks, what to say and how to say it are functions of what has been said before, what the listener can be expected to infer, and what the intent of the conversation is. Giving an overview of some simple techniques to handle phenomena of these sorts is the main business of this chapter.

From a knowledge-engineering viewpoint, generation of language in a mixed-initiative conversation is an extremely difficult task for computer programs. Mixed-initiative conversation, where either participant can select the topic of discussion, has complications well beyond that of generation of single sentences or paragraph-length text. One obvious problem is having to analyze the input from the other participant for meaning. Not only does the computer as a conversationalist have to understand what a speaker is saying, it must know how to use that understanding to determine what the speaker knows about a subject. In a text generation task a program can expect that the user has understood what he has already been told, plus what he has inferred from what he has been told. In a conversational system, however, the problem of deciding what to say is more complex, since more information about what the user knows is available. For example, an appropriate answer to

(7.5) Who has been eating the eclairs?

might be the ellipsed response

(7.6) John has.

Sentences (7.5) and (7.6) illustrate that deciding how much can be deleted safely from an utterance in a conversation depends upon the preceding context (i.e., what the user and program say) and how much the program can assume the user knows about the topic of discussion. We will have more to say about mixed-initiative conversations in Chapters 9 and 10.

7.1 Explanations as Summaries

In a multi-sentence generation task, decisions regarding what to say occur throughout the generation process, from the time it is decided that something is to be selected from memory for expression until it is actually expressed in the words of the language. For this reason, it is most informative to study language generation by examining problems in both subprocesses. A useful vehicle for this exploration is the study of explanations, for several reasons. First, explanations can be given as descriptive paragraphs, and an implementation can be produced without the distracting details associated with conversational interaction. Such a system can be expanded to accept input from the user regarding the ongoing explanation. This limited conversational ability can be used to clarify or reexplain any unclear ideas.

Second, restricting the task to explanation defines exactly what the system and user can be expected to know; i.e., the system can be expected to know a lot; and the user not too much. This leads to a specification of the pragmatic information and world knowledge such a program should have regarding the contents of the user's head. Third, if the domain to be explained is well defined, a situational context can be established and used by the program to assist in generating natural-sounding output. The situational context refers to the physical situation experienced by the user, and includes things such as the tools commonly used for a task and actions associated with those tools (which may need to be explained initially, but then become part of the context). An example of this use of situational information in explanations is the use of specialized terms. For example, a recipe in a beginning cook book would state:

Butter and flour a 9-inch cake pan:
rub butter on the pan, sprinkle flour on it, and shake out any excess flour.

After this short explanation, the verbs *butter* and *flour* can be used without further explanation.

An important subprocess often used by explanations involves the *summarization* of a knowledge structure. As we saw in Chapter 2, a knowledge structure is an intricately interconnected assemblage of actionals, supporting statives, etc., encoding the content of a domain, which is subject to causal laws or social rules. For example, the operation of a car's ignition system can be represented by a sequence of events, each one enabling or causing another. The representation of how to tune up a car is more complicated, since the behavior of the mechanic must be represented, as well as the result of that behavior on the car. More complex still is representing how to open a checking account. Ideas about money, and a bank's holding onto your money, then paying it out to certain other people and institutions must be captured.

There are many reasons for representing the domain knowledge in its entirety, and for representing it in an abstract form. The best reason is that the same knowledge may be used for a number of tasks: language generation, story understanding, planning, question answering, etc. If the system generating explanations knows more than it should say, a selector mechanism is needed to embody a method of examining a piece of knowledge and selecting from it those concepts to be expressed. The selection process is an important type of *summarization*.

The selector/summarizer uses rules that are dependent upon several things. One is the domain being explained. For example, the naive mechanic must be told explicitly every step in timing a car, but the person new to the banking world is helped along by persons operating in their functions in the bank and need not be told all the details. Another factor influencing the selector rules is the intent of the explanation, why the listener wants to know. If the listener is actually going to attempt a tune-up, more detail will be given (including precautions: "Don't get too near the fan when the car's running"). A third factor used in the rules is general knowledge of how to conduct an explanation. These include guidelines such as to define a potentially unfamiliar term and to say things in the order in which they occur.

7.2 Explanations in CADHELP

Systems that frequently need explaining are computer programs designed to assist a user in accomplishing a specific task. It is desirable to choose a system whose behavior offers sufficiently challenging problems in generation of English, yet is not so complicated that the knowledge an expert has of the system is too complex to represent. A computer-aided design (CAD) domain has both these features: an explainable, finite set of commands that such a system can perform, and a definite physical environment experienced by the user—graphics screen, terminal, input devices—that can be represented and used for situational context. It is also relatively easy during the design process to model the overt actions of the user and the system in terms of simple actions.

Three types of explanations can be built into a CAD system. One is the simple explanation of how to use a command. This is performed at the request of the user and describes in varying levels of detail how the command is actually performed. Another kind of explanation is prompting text that guides the user through a complicated feature by reminding him of his expected behavior or by notifying him of the occurrence of events of interest. A third type is a HELP facility, which rescues the user who has made a mistake and attempts to describe to him what went wrong.

In most CAD systems, the explanations and prompts, if any, are simply stored text. This becomes tedious for experienced users and makes the programming of a HELP facility cumbersome. If the text is not canned but generated from some stored representation, the explanations given can become more and more terse as the user gains experience. In addition, if the system knows how the feature is supposed to be executed, when errors occur they can be pinpointed in a flexible manner. An additional benefit of having the system actually know how the features operate is to have the explanation of a feature occur in a modality other than language; for example, as graphical animation to assist in the explanations.

Considerations such as these led to the design of CADHELP, a self-explaining CAD system for simple SSI and MSI logic circuits. The explanatory part of CADHELP can express how each feature is to be performed (e.g., adding a gate to the design or connecting two gates). Each command the CAD system can execute is described in a knowledge structure called a *feature script*.[1] Each feature script is a detailed description of the expected behavior of the user and the response of the system to that behavior during the execution of a particular command. These feature scripts are detailed enough to be used both as the input for generation of English (Cull81b) and the production of graphical animation (Neim82).

It is important to remember that the CADHELP explanation mechanism described below is really no more than a first step toward an intelligent, general-purpose explaining facility. The data-driven style it uses is much too limited to allow the flexibility that real explanations, especially those with mixed initiative, require. As a summarizer, however, this model may represent a useful subroutine to the more general facility.

The CADHELP system is divided into two basic parts, the CAD tool itself, which performs graphical operations concerned with the design, and the explanation mechanism, which is responsible for providing natural language and graphical output to the user (see Diagram 7.1). The function of the explanation mechanism is to explain how a particular feature works, and to assist in the execution of a feature by generating prompts to guide the user. The CAD features that were implemented are summarized in Figure 7.1.

To illustrate CADHELP's language behavior, I will examine the CREATE command. CREATE is used to select a device from CADHELP's database of devices, called the "warehouse," and position it on the screen. Thus, CREATE adds new devices to the design. First, the user peruses the warehouse, looking for the device to be created. The

Diagram 7.1
Block Diagram of CADHELP

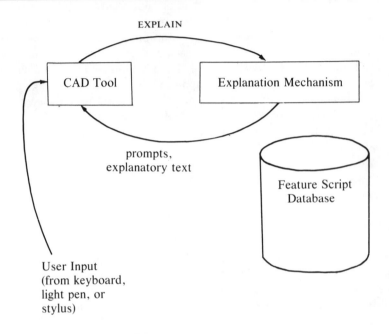

perusal process is implemented by a feature called CATALOG. To catalog, the user touches the stylus on the drawing area of the tablet. The CAD tool responds by drawing a device in a dedicated area of the display, the catalog area. If the user now moves the stylus horizontally in the drawing area, a new device will appear that is of the same class as the device currently being displayed, but of a different type (e.g., 2-input vs. 3-input NAND gates). To view a member of a different class (e.g., a counter vs. an OR gate), a vertical movement of the stylus is made.

When the device the user wants to create finally appears in the catalog area, he informs the CAD tool of his choice by pressing the stylus on the command block labeled MARK1. Pressing with some force is necessary to activate the switch in the stylus that means "attend to this command." The tool then makes the device being displayed movable. Now the user must position the device in the design. To enable the user to locate the device with the stylus, the system draws a cursor that moves on the screen as the user moves the stylus on the drawing area. The user moves the stylus, and thus the cursor, in the direction of the device to be added. When the device and the cursor overlap, the device also begins to move as the stylus moves. By moving the stylus appropriately, the user

Figure 7.1
CADHELP Command Summary

SELECT
This is CADHELP's top level. Any command can be initiated by touching the stylus to the Command Block labeled with its name.

CATALOG
allows the user to peruse CADHELP's database of logic devices.

CREATE
select a device and position it in the design area.

CONNECT
draw a connection between devices containing right-angle segments. This feature uses a simple extension of the graphical operation called *rubber-banding,* in which a line segment appears to stretch away from an origin in response to stylus movements.

DELETE
delete a device from the design.

DISCONNECT
delete an interconnection.

DRAG
move an existing symbol.

ROTATE
orient a device symbol left, right, up or down.

ANNOTATE
associate text with particular device or comment symbol.

READ
read text associated with a logic component or comment symbol.

---

positions the device. When the device has reached the desired spot, the user informs the system of his decision by pressing the MARK1 command block.

CADHELP uses the explanation mechanism to describe features such as CREATE both when the user SELECTs the command EXPLAIN and through prompts during normal operation of a feature. After choosing to execute EXPLAIN, the user is asked to press the command block that is labeled with the name of the feature to be described. He is also asked to select the level of explanation desired by touching one of the blocks labeled SUMMARY, NORMAL, or ERRORS.

In a summary level of explanation, the intent of the command is given. The intent of a command is the result that execution of that command will produce. For example, the intent or goal for CREATE is *To add a device to the design, use the CREATE command.*

The normal mode of explanation provides the user with a step-by-step description of his expected behavior and the response of the CAD tool to that behavior. In addition, system features and components that have not been mentioned in other explanations are described (such as the catalog area in the output shown below). For example, the first time the user requests a NORMAL explanation of the CREATE command, CADHELP responds with:

To add a device to the design,
use the CREATE command.

Move the stylus to the tablet.
Touch the stylus on the drawing area.
A device that is in the catalog area will become visible.
The catalog area is in the lower right hand corner of
the screen.

Repeat the following until the device in the catalog area
is of equal type to the device that you want to add to the
design.
    Move the stylus horizontally.
    A new type of device will become visible.

Repeat the following until the device in the catalog area
is of equal class to the device you want to add to the
design.
    Move the stylus vertically.
    A new class of device will become visible.

Move the stylus to the command block that is labeled MARK1.
Press the stylus on the command block labeled MARK1.

A prompt will become visible.
A cursor will become visible.
The cursor is in the lower right hand corner of the screen.

Move the stylus to the tablet.
Touch the stylus on the lower right hand corner of the
drawing area.

Repeat the following until the cursor is
over the device in the catalog area.

Move the stylus to a new location.
The cursor will move to a new location.
The new location will correspond to the location of
the stylus in the drawing area.

Repeat the following until the device is at a screen
location that you want that the system record.
Move the stylus to a new location.
The device will move to a new location.

Move the stylus to the MARK1 command block.
Press on MARK1.
The device will be added to the design.

An ERRORS explanation is like a NORMAL one, except that the explanation mechanism also describes what can go wrong during the execution of the feature. For example, while the user is moving the cursor toward the device in CREATE, he may move the stylus outside of the drawing area. The Explanation Mechanism will explain this potential error as follows:

.

.

.

Repeat the following until the cursor is
over the device in the catalog area.
Move the stylus to a new location.
The cursor will move to a new location.
The new location will correspond to the location of
the stylus in the drawing area.
If you move the stylus out of the drawing area
the location of the stylus on the tablet will not
correspond to a location on the screen.
The cursor will not move.

.

.

.

The actual use of the graphical features during design is accompanied in CADHELP by prompts that are intended to lead the user step by step through the operation. The prompts are very much like the NORMAL mode of explanation illustrated above. Unlike the prompts provided with existing CAD systems, however, these are not canned; they are generated from the knowledge structure each time they are expressed. Thus, the system is verbose with a new user but becomes more and more laconic as it gets out of the way of the experienced designer.

For example, the first time the user operates the CREATE command, the explanation mechanism provides the CAD Tool with a sequence of prompts that is nearly identical to the NORMAL explanation shown above, minus the first sentence, which expresses the intent concept. The only difference is that the EXPLAIN command produces the future tense in expressing the actions of the CAD tool, whereas the prompting mechanism uses the present tense, since the system's actions are occurring in real time. If the user operates CREATE a second time, CADHELP generates a more abbreviated prompt sequence:

Move the stylus to the tablet.

To see the warehouse move the stylus horizontally and move the stylus vertically.

To tell the system to add the device to the design press the stylus on MARK1.

Move the stylus to the lower right hand corner of the drawing area.

To move the cursor move the stylus.
To move the device move the stylus.

To tell the system to record the screen location press on MARK1.

The third time CREATE is used, CADHELP generates the following simple prompt sequence:

Move the stylus horizontally and move the stylus vertically.
Press on MARK1.
Move the cursor with the stylus.
Move the device with the stylus.
Press on MARK1.

Thus CADHELP's explanations become more brief as the user gains experience.

7.3 Representational Overview

To generate language and graphical animation for CADHELP features as complicated as CREATE, a complex representation of the command, as an expert sees it, is needed. As we saw in Section 2.10, each command in CADHELP is represented as a separate *feature script* stored in the system's permanent database. A feature script is composed of the ERKS representations of the physical and mental actions and states of the user and the system, causally linked together. The links used in feature scripts are listed in Figure 7.2.

Figure 7.2
Causal Links Used in Feature Scripts

OSE:
a state one shot enables an event; it must be present once for the event to occur.

OSC:
an event one shot causes some states; it need not continue to be performed in order for the states to still exist.

CC:
one state is causally coupled to another; the two are causally connected but the exact nature of the causality is not specified.

INITIATE:
an event (usually a perception of some state in the world) initiates another event (usually a mental event).

REASON:
a mental event is the reason for another (usually physical) event.

IR:
this blurs the distinction between an REASON and an INITIATE link, when this information is not useful.

RUT:
repeat links until threshold (satisfaction condition) becomes true.

TRNPT:
indicates a turning point in the script, a set of mutually exclusive paths which can be followed.

SR:
performing the acts comprising a script leads to some important states.

GRC:
the overall goal of the script (a state) is linked by this to the action that caused it.

ANTAG:
an antagonism between two states exists.

In addition to the primitive ERKS forms and the interconnecting links, certain "primitive" imbedded scripts were used (see Figure 7.3). These occurred in two cases. First, if several feature scripts shared common actions and states (perhaps differing only in the entities manipulated), these common concepts could be represented once and used by all feature

Figure 7.3
Imbedded Scripts Used in Feature Scripts

Non-Expandable Imbedded Scripts:

$prompt
the system executes this to cause a prompt to appear on the screen.

$clone
used to make a copy of a device or other graphic object.

$draw
the system makes a line or device visible on the graphics display with this script.

$undraw
the system makes a line or device invisible on the graphics display with this script.

$makemap
the system forms a correspondence between two objects, for example, between the position of the stylus and a cursor on the screen.

$cadfeat
this script is used to refer to any other CADHELP feature, without necessarily specifying which.

Expandable Imbedded Scripts:

$press
used to inform the system of a user intention by the user pressing the stylus on a command block.

$move
used to move a graphical object on the screen by moving the stylus along the corresponding points in the drawing area.

$viewrhs
used to view the contents of the warehouse by moving the stylus in the drawing area.

---

scripts. This made the feature scripts more concise and allowed easier development of new scripts. For example, one common sequence is that of pressing the stylus on a command block on the tablet, and this is represented as the *$press* imbedded script. (The "$" indicates that the associated type is a script, one of the subtypes of the ERKS primitive goalepisode.) Hence, any feature script needing to express this feature could refer to *$press*. Since several command blocks could be pressed with the stylus, the *$press* script uses a script variable, &cmdblk, to represent the command block to be pressed, and any feature script using it will instantiate &cmdblk with the actual occurrence of a command block, for example *MARK1. The notation *MARK1 is a convenient shorthand for the complicated concept representing the MARK1 command block on the data tablet. It is expanded when encountered in any concept to its full form.

The imbedded script representation is usually used for those actions performed by the user. Similar imbedded scripts represent those actions performed by the system. These scripts, however, are not expandable into a causal chain of actions and states. This shortening is done for several reasons. First, the view of the CAD features modeled in CADHELP is the expert user's view, and the expert user is aware that the system performs complicated actions in the form of code, but is not aware of the exact details. The expert user is aware only of the consequences of those actions, and this is represented explicitly. Second, the graphical animation expert using the representation did not need to know the details either. If this expert knew the desired result, it used its own code to depict that result on the graphics display. A third point concerns whether or not to simply make these scripts primitive actions in the system. This was not done because of a wish to emphasize the complex nature of the action, and also to leave open the possibility that in an extension of the system, these scripts might become expandable.

7.4 Concept Selection

CADHELP's database, then, contains feature scripts, one for each command CADHELP knows. By the nature of the representation design process, *all* of the concepts in the feature scripts are expressible by the generator. The resulting output would be tedious to read because of all the unnecessary detail present. HELPCON is the interface program between the database and generator that alleviates this problem.

Recall the generator's sketchifying rules, discussed in Chapter 6. These are decision rules that decide, based on the semantic features of the concept being expressed, what linguistic form to use to communicate the idea in the most economical fashion. HELPCON contains analogous rules that examine higher-level knowledge structures, the feature scripts, to select concepts to be sent to the generator. An entire feature script is input to HELPCON, and it is responsible for traversing the links of the feature script and selecting concepts for expression by the generator. The traversal of the script provides the main control for HELPCON, and at each link HELPCON applies a particular rule that decides whether or not to express the link and the concepts it connects. There is one rule per causal link type (see Figure 7.2), making HELPCON data-driven and easily extensible.

HELPCON's rules use several types of information to decide whether to express a concept or not. One is the type of link. A rule that fires because a certain link is present may do nothing more than suppress expression of the link and the concepts that it connects. For example, CC is a rule that looks at causal couplings of states. In this domain, causal coupling can be inferred by the user. For example, if the stylus is in a new location, the tip of the stylus, which is part of the stylus, is in a new location also. In domains where the causal coupling of states may be less transparent, the CC rule could be reformulated to explain the coupling the first time it was encountered. Later, we would expect the user to be able to infer it.

Other link types that merely suppress the link and its concepts are IR, REASON, and INITIATE. Since HELPCON is concerned only with the overt physical actions of the user, any mental actions or states are ignored in the explanation. Links connecting mental actions and states, whether those actions were by the system or the user, would be important if CADHELP were programmed to attempt to describe in detail user mistakes, or teach the user how to design, or even to debug feature scripts. For example, something like

> I thought that the prompt would cause (initiate) you to decide to delete a particular device and that would be the reason you would move the stylus.

could be generated to explain why the system had waited for the stylus to be moved, when the user wasn't expecting to have to move it.

Two rules corresponding to links used in the CADHELP feature scripts are responsible for selecting important user actions and for focusing upon important states. These are OSE and OSC, respectively. The OSC rule operates upon one-shot-causal relationships, where an action causes a state. The action may be performed by the system or the user, and if it is performed by the system, it and the resulting state are ignored. If the action is performed by the user and it is an overt physical action (i.e., not a mental event), then OSC decides that this is something the user should be told. The state one-shot-caused by the action is not expressed, since the user is assumed to be able to infer the consequences of his actions. In a more complicated HELP situation, an explainer may want to tell the user the consequences of his actions, especially if they are in error.

The OSE link mainly serves to call attention to states the system expects the user will notice. In CADHELP, these are events such as prompts appearing, objects blinking or devices appearing on the graphics display. Since the script describes the expected behavior of the user, these important states are represented as the object of user *mtrans* (mental transfer) events. OSE will select a state to be expressed if it sees that the state one-shot-enables the user to *mtrans* that state. HELPCON selects the state, rather than the user *mtrans* of the state, to avoid constructs such as

You will see a prompt appear on the screen.

The representation of these *mtrans* actions explicitly is useful in pinpointing important events to be animated by the animator, and could prove useful in explaining how to detect potential errors. Consider, for example,

If you do not see the prompt appear,
press the ON/OFF button or turn up the
intensity of the graphics device.

Another set of rules HELPCON uses aids in the traversal of the feature script. TRNPT is one of these. Feature scripts are organized temporally, but are not necessarily linear. At certain points in a script, there may be mutually exclusive paths that can be followed. For example, in CADHELP, the user can lengthen a connection or shorten a connection during the CONNECT command, but not both simultaneously. TRNPT is responsible for assuring that, when one of these turning points is reached, each path is traversed in turn. The user is assumed to know about the exclusiveness of the different paths, and no introduction like: "Do one of the following" is used.

An important property of parts of a feature script is that they can be repeated any number of times until some termination condition is reached. The associated ERKS primitive is called *rut*, for Repeat Until Threshold. This is useful for expressing segments of a script that are performed by the user over and over until some desired state of the design is reached. For example, drawing a connection between two devices can be thought of as the process of drawing connected horizontal and vertical segments until the connection is complete. *Rut* episodes may be imbedded. For example, each segment of a connection is the "sum" of many small movements in a straight line. A *rut* episode is defined by a satisfaction condition, which expresses the state that will cause the *rut* to terminate, as well as a set of causally linked states and actions that are to be repeated. *Rut* episodes are handled by expressing the satisfaction condition imbedded in the construct "Repeat the following until," then subjecting the actions and states to be repeated to the HELPCON process.

Another property of feature scripts is that they can share large portions of standardized actions using imbedded scripts, such as moving a device using the stylus. The rule SR (Scriptal Result) is responsible for deciding what to do with these scripts. The feature scripts used by CADHELP are represented so that the actual expansion of the imbedded script is not inserted when it is called, but a pointer to an instantiated version is established. A reference to the script is inserted in the main path of the outer feature script, along with values for some script variables. This reference is causally linked to one or more states via SR. These states are the important conditions that are true in the world after the imbedded script is executed.

The first time a reference to an imbedded script appears, HELPCON's SR rule expands it, i.e., places all the actions and states making up that script into the mainstream of processing, where they are traversed. In addition, SR is sensitive to the number of times it has expanded an imbedded script, so when it reaches subsequent references, it will queue for expression the *intent conceptualization* of the script, then the *main concept* of the script. The intent of the script is its goal concept, the desired state of affairs the associated episode achieves. For example, one uses the *$press* script to inform the system of some event in the design process. The main concept of the script is the (usually) single action that summarizes what the user is to do. In the CADHELP microworld, it is usually summarized best by one verb and one instrument, e.g., "Press the stylus on the tablet," or "Move the device with the stylus." Like SR, several of HELPCON's other rules are sensitive to previous explanations, namely OSE, OSC, and RUT.

HELPCON's rules use several other kinds of information. We made a general assumption that the user would always remember what he was told, and that what he remembered was correct. Such assumptions are, of course, problematic in mixed-initiative explaining. Knowledge of the types of links that can connect concepts, as well as the nature of the concepts in the script, was also used. In addition, keeping track of what had been said concerning scripts and their imbedded entities in prior explanations aided in making subsequent explanations brief and to the point.

The foregoing description of how HELPCON summarizes during explanation of feature scripts has been general and imprecise. To clarify the process, a small segment of a feature script going through HELPCON's pruning is shown in Section 7.5.

7.5   An Example

The script to be examined by HELPCON is the imbedded script *$move*. This script is called from a main script such as *$connect* by the following two concepts, linked by an SR:

```
($move actor *user      ; the call to the move script,
       drag-obj *cursor  ; where the object to be
       obj *stylus       ; moved is the cursor.
       to &new-dev-srloc ; it is to be moved until it
       loc &newcurs-srloc ; overlaps the device the user
```

```
         sat-cond (p-config con1 *cursor          ; has chosen to create.
                   con2 &desr-cr-dev
                   confrel (overlaps)
                   mode (nil)
                   time (nil)))
       —— SR ——
   (p-config con1 *cursor          ; the important result after
             con2 &desr-cr-dev          ; doing the script
             confrel(overlaps) mode(nil))
```

The script variables for *$move* are listed below. The call as shown above will instantiate these with the appropriate fillers. Notice that the stylus is not a script variable, since moving the stylus is the only way a graphical object can be moved in the CAD tool.

Variables to be bound:

&drag-obj: the object that is to be moved, in this case, the cursor.

&sat-cond: the satisfaction condition for the repeat until threshold

&loc: the location that is going to be changing, in this case, the location of the cursor.

&toloc: the location to which the moved object is going, used to decide if the RUT is finished.

The main concept and the intent of the script are also accessible to SR, in case it chooses a less verbose expression for the script. In this example, the script *$move* will be expanded, but the intent and main concept for *$move* are shown below in their uninstantiated form. The main concept for *$move:* "Move some object with the stylus"

```
(ptrans actor *user
        obj &drag-obj
        to (nil) from (nil)
        via (nil) mode (nil) time (nil)
        inst (ptrans actor *user
                     obj *stylus
                     to (nil) from (nil)
                     via (nil) inst (nil)
                     mode (nil) time (nil)))
```

The intent concept for *$move:* "To move some object, use the stylus"

```
(cause precon (s-goal actor *user
                      mode (nil) time (nil)
                      goal (ptrans actor *user
                                   obj &drag-obj
```

```
                         to (nil) from (nil)
                         mode (nil) inst (nil)
                         focus (actor) via (nil)
                         time (nil)))
      postcon (ptrans actor *user
                    obj *stylus
                    to (nil) from (nil) mode(nil)
                    inst (nil) focus (actor) via (nil)
                    time (nil)))
```

What follows is the actual expansion of *$move*, assuming it was called as above. The script is instantiated (by substituting actual CAD system entities for each of the script variables), and each link will cause the appropriate rule in HELPCON to fire. The comments indicate what is happening to the immediately preceding and following concepts at each step.

The user maps the location of the device (where he wants to move the cursor to) to a location called &endpnt, which is the desired ending point.

```
      ($makemap actor *user
               con1 &new-dev-srloc con2 &endpnt
               maprel(corresp))
               —— SR ——
```

The SR rule suppresses expression of the immediately preceding and following concepts, since they are performed by the system. Note that the script requires this level of detail so that the graphical animator can mimic what the user is doing.

The result of the mapping is an abstract configuration, i.e., the user knows that the &new-dev-srloc is the desired ending location of the cursor.

```
      (a-config con1 &new-dev-srloc con2 &endpnt
               confrel(corresp))
               —— OSE ——
```

The OSE rule suppresses any user mental action.

The following enables the user to decide where he is going to move the stylus:

```
      (mbuild actor *user mobj &dltaloc)
               —— REASON ——
```

The REASON rule throws away the *mbuild* and the *mknow*, but the animator has now presumably picked out a destination point and knows it. The decision above is the reason he knows where the stylus is going to be moved.

```
      (mknow actor *user mobj &dltaloc)
               —— RUT ——
```

This link begins the RUT. The RUT rule expresses the satisfaction condition of the RUT, prefaced by the introduction ("Do the following until the cursor is over the device you want to add to the design"). The RUT points to all the following concepts, which are imbedded in the RUT:

```
(rut sat-cond (p-config con1 *cursor
               con2 &desr-cr-dev
               confrel(overlaps) mode(nil))
         —— INITIATE ——
```

The rule above allows HELPCON to ignore mental events that initiate user actions.

The fact that the user knows where to move the stylus initiates the action of moving the stylus. This is also the first action of the RUT:

```
(ptrans actor *user obj *stylus
         to &dltaloc from &sty-daloc
         via (nil) inst (nil) mode (nil) time (nil))
         —— OSC ——
```

The OSC rule notices that the user has performed some physical action resulting in some state, so it causes the action to be expressed ("Move the stylus to a new location"), but ignores the state resulting from the action.

The movement of the stylus has caused the location of the stylus to change:

```
(s-change actor *stylus
         mode (nil) time (nil)
         attr (loc val &newsty-daloc dir (to)))
         —— OSE ——
```

The OSE rule sees that the state is enabling a system action, not a user one, so it deems the state and the action unimportant, and neither is expressed.

The change enables the system to notice the change in location of the stylus:

```
(mtrans actor *sys
         mobj (s-change actor *stylus
                  mode (nil) time (nil)
                  attr (loc val &newsty-daloc dir (to)))
         from (nil) to (*cp* part *sys)
         mode (nil) time (nil) inst (nil))
         —— INITIATE ——
```

The INITIATE rule suppresses both the system perception and the mental action it initiated.

The perception event on the part of the system initiates a "realization" on its part that the user has the goal of moving the cursor:

```
(mbuild actor *sys mode (nil) time (nil)
      mobj (s-goal actor *user mode (nil) time (nil)
            goal ($draw actor *sys obj *cursor
                  loc &newcurs-srloc
                  mode (nil) time (nil)))
      —— REASON ——
```

The REASON rule suppresses the system's reason and actions. The system's realization is the reason the system attempts to form a correspondence between the location of the stylus, on the tablet, and a location for the cursor, on the screen.

```
($makemap actor *sys
          con1 &sty-daloc con2 &newcurs-srloc
          maprel (corresp)
          mode (nil) time (nil))
      —— SR ——
```

The SR rule discards the result of the imbedded non-expandable script. The result of the makemap script is an abstract configuration between the location of the stylus on the tablet and a point on the graphics display.

```
(a-config con1 &sty-daloc con2 &newcurs-srloc
          confrel (corresp)
          mode (nil) time (nil))
      —— OSE ——
```

OSE will suppress any system actions. Knowing the point on the graphics display enables the system to draw the cursor at that point.

```
($draw actor *sys obj *cursor
          loc &newcurs-srloc mode (nil) time (nil))
      —— SR ——
```

The result of the execution of the $draw script is unimportant, from the point of view of SR.

The result of the redrawing is a new location for the cursor:

```
(s-change actor *cursor
          attr (loc val &newcurs-srloc dir (to))
          mode (nil) time (nil))
      —— OSE ——
```

Since the state occurring is explicitly seen by the user, it is deemed important, and the state is selected by OSE for expression ("The cursor moves to a new location"). The actual perception of the event by the user is ignored.

The change in location of the cursor enables the user to detect the change:

```
(mtrans actor *user
```

```
mobj (s-change actor *cursor
            attr (loc val &newcurs-srloc dir (to))
            mode (nil) time (nil))
    to (*cp* part *user) from (nil) inst (nil)
    mode (nil) time (nil))
—— INITIATE / REASON ——
```

INITIATE/REASON ignores user mental actions/states.

The user perception presumably led to an *mbuild,* which then led to this *mknow,* but the initiate/reason link has allowed us to skip all that. Here the user either (a) knows that the cursor and the device he has decided to create overlap (since their locations overlap) and the *$move* script ends, or (b) the two do not overlap, so the satisfaction condition is not met, and the RUT begins again.

```
(mknow actor *user
    mobj (p-config con1 *cursor
                con2 &desr-cr-dev
                confrel (overlaps)
                mode (nil) time (nil)))
```

7.6 Summary

This chapter has sketched a simple algorithm for explaining knowledge structures encoded as feature scripts, based on a notion of explanation as summarization. The algorithm uses an analogue of the generator's sketch-ifiers to trace the causal links of a script, to discard any subconcepts not needing to be expressed (because the user can infer them), and to expand/sketchify any imbedded scripts. The algorithm is usable for any rigidly hierarchically/causally organized structure of knowledge, working with the conceptual generator to create a narrative mode explanation. Simple bookkeeping (not described here) allows the system to notice when it is reexamining a concept or relation in a context where it should not be reexpressed, and to arrange for a briefer expression of the associated content, or perhaps to suppress it altogether. The algorithm presented here is of course much too simple to serve as the basis for a general explanatory facility. It *can* serve, however, as a useful "subrou-tine" for such a facility.

Notes

1. Representation design issues for feature scripts were discussed in Section 2.10.

8

Knowledge-Base Management

8.0 Introduction

It has been stated repeatedly that, if the computer is to talk with its user about an application domain, it will need to know (i.e., have usable representations for) many things about the domain. Useful language-processing systems for explanation, database query, or conversational tasks will need rapid access to items in knowledge bases (KBs) containing tens or hundreds of thousands of facts, rules, beliefs, plans, and the like.

Despite this, relatively little attention has been paid to the engineering issues of how to set up and update such huge databases. (For example, see McDe73; McDe75; Rebo76; Forg79; Deer81.) This chapter describes SOT (Self-Organizing Tree), a general-purpose knowledge base organizing program that automatically computes an efficient discrimination scheme for accessing large numbers of items of knowledge expressed in the slot-filler representational format used in this book.

The design of SOT was motivated by the following observations about how real KBs are likely to be used:

1. The primary performance consideration is very fast access to the KB items as the system using the KB runs. (For example, the speed of the hardware supporting the inference/reasoning component of the projected Japanese "fifth generation computer" is expressed in "Megalips," or millions of logical inferences per second.) Therefore, the KB should be organized to support access even if setting up the KB in the first place entails a major cost.

2. Since the major portion of a real KB is likely to consist of permanent knowledge (i.e., real-time updates and revisions are likely to add, subtract or window only a very small percentage of KB items), a high one-time cost for computing an efficient accessing scheme will usually be acceptable.

3. It is unreasonable to expect human beings to handcraft accessing methods for the huge KBs that will be required. Some automatic configuring scheme is needed, although the user should be able to influence the discrimination pattern chosen in various ways.

4. To be generally useful, such a configuring scheme must be applica-

---

This chapter is adapted from the M.S. thesis of L. J. Joseph, as summarized in Cull83.

ble to as many of the available knowledge representation schemes as possible. It should be able to use both the "syntax" (formal rules) of the representation and user-supplied "semantics" (special information about relations among the units of the representation, constraints on particular components of the representation, etc.).

5. The scheme must also support a variety of search regimes. For example, a KB consisting of "complete" (fully instantiated) items should allow efficient search by "incomplete" (pattern-type) probes. A KB of patterns should be rapidly searchable by complete ("factual") probes. There should be arrangements for returning all matching items, ordered in a "best first" manner; or for returning the best candidate item first, with an arrangement to allow the search to resume (i.e., in generator fashion).

Since we wish to avoid a strong dependence of access time on the number of KB items, SOT attempts to provide a sequential discrimination scheme based on simple, uniform tests at each decision node, as search for the KB item(s) matching a probe proceeds. The result is a discrimination tree with the items at the nodes, whose access behavior should be logarithmic in the number of KB items. Since the computation of a truly optimal discrimination (i.e., a single test that yields the desired answer) would be expected to take an enormous amount of time if the KB is large, we have developed instead a heuristically "good" scheme based upon a limited (but user-influencable) examination of the KB items.

8.1 KB Organization

A KB formed by SOT is probed by a "key" item containing structural characteristics of interest. First all the KB items matching the key (under a given search regime) are found, then constraint expressions (certain Lisp formulas) associated with the KB items are evaluated, and the items whose expressions evaluate to non-nil are the result of the search. SOT organizes the search both according to the slot-filler structure of the KB items and to the structure of the constraint expressions provided.

8.1.1 The Slot-Filler Tree

SOT organizes the items in a KB into a discrimination tree called the slot-filler tree. This tree is based on tests for specified headers in fillers at the end of precomputed slot paths into subsets of the items. To store the five items

(a b (nil))
(a b (c) d (e))
(a b (c) d (f))

Diagram 8.1
Example SOT Tree

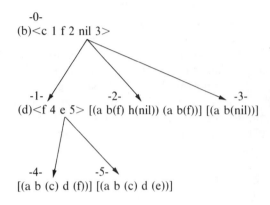

(a b (f) h (nil))
(a b(f)),

SOT might build a tree like the one shown in Diagram 8.1. Each numbered cluster represents a discrimination node in the tree. Each nonterminal node of the tree (0 and 1) has a "path," shown in parentheses, and an "index," shown in angle brackets in the diagram. Nodes 4, 5, 2, and 3, the terminal nodes, each have a list of one or more KB items, shown in square brackets.

Each nonterminal node path shows which header of the search key structure is to be extracted at this stage of the search. In each index are header values with a daughter node listed under each value. By comparing the extracted header to the index, the search process decides which of the daughter nodes to visit. For example, if node 0 is being visited and the search key is

(a b(f) j(k)),

the path associated with node 0, (b), would extract the key header f. The index

<c 1 f 2 nil 3>,

is scanned for the value f. Node 2, listed under f, would be the next node visited. Other nodes in the index might be visited also, depending on the type of search being conducted.

8.1.2 Slot-Filler Tree Construction

Slot-filler trees are built recursively. The tree starts as a root node with the complete set of KB items to be discriminated on the basis of an index.

In general, a wide variety of paths into the items could be used to compute an index. Suppose SOT had to distinguish among the following:

1: (atrans actor (person persname (Muhammed))
          object (ingobj ingtype (soda))
          to (poss part (person persname (Muhammed)))
          from (poss part (person persname (Olivia))))

2: (ptrans actor (person persname (Gerald))
        object (ingobj ingtype (soda))
        to (inside part (polity polname (Kentucky)))
        from (inside part (polity polname (Hartford))))

3: (ptrans actor (person persname (Gerald))
        object (person persname (Gerald))
        to (inside part (polity polname (Kentucky))
        from (prox part (polity polname (Storrs)))

Paths that might be considered include ( ), (actor), and (from part polname). The (actor) path is useless, since all of the substructures have the same header—person. The null path, ( ), would distinguish 1, atrans, from 2 and 3, ptrans. The headers for (from part polname) are nil, Hartford, and Storrs, respectively, and so this path would discriminate all three items. SOT has no advance information about what paths exist in the KB items other than that all of them have the null path ( ) and that any other paths will be nested inside ( ). It must find useful paths for itself.

SOT evaluates paths as it finds them in the items and stops searching when it finds one that satisfactorily discriminates among them. Candidate paths are created by extending preexisting paths by one slot name and examining the headers found at the end of the new path in the group of items to be discriminated. Thus, the path discovery process has the flavor of a breadth-first search of the header "contents" of the KB items. Since KB items typically have distinctive headers relatively near the "top" of their symbolic meaning structures, the paths thus computed tend to contribute to an efficient, overall search regime.

After choosing a path SOT divides the items into groups, discriminated on the basis of the path. Daughter nodes are created, and each of the node's daughters receives one of the item groups. The above process is then applied recursively to each daughter, and the tree is expanded in a breadth-first manner.

8.1.3 Index Quality

A path is tested for suitability by determining how many branches the node would have if its test were used, and how equal in size the item groups assigned to these branches would be. The number of branches below a node is important because it determines whether the tree constructed will be short and bushy or tall and sparse. Short and bushy is preferable, so the length of the searches can be short. The evenness of the branches is important so the tree will be balanced. Balance, like bushiness, affects the length of the search.

The path chosen to build the node is the one found, after a certain amount of effort, that discriminates the items into the largest number of, and most even-sized groups. Number of groups and evenness are the two components of *diversity*, a term used by ecologists to describe how rich ecosystems are in plant and/or animal species (Piel69). The user provides an indication of the minimal acceptable diversity at a given stage of the construction process, which SOT uses to control the amount of effort expended to calculate discriminating paths.

Several formulas have been developed for the measurement of diversity in different statistical circumstances. By applying one of these to the groupings of items produced from paths, the alternative paths can be compared, and the path that produces the most diverse grouping can be selected to build the node. The McIntosh measure (Piel69) was chosen as the best suited for this purpose. It is the easiest to calculate and can be applied to finite, exhaustively sampled populations. The equation for the McIntosh measure is:

$$\text{McI} = \left(N - \sqrt{\sum_j n_j^2} \right) \bigg/ (N - \sqrt{N})$$

where N is the total number of items and n_j is the number of items in the jth group. Note that this measure reaches a maximum of 1 when there are N groups, each of size 1. In this case, the discrimination tree is optimal: one test yields the matching form, if any.

8.1.4 Best-First Ordering of KB Items

When a search reaches a terminal node in a slot-filler tree it uncovers a set of KB items with identical slot-filler structures but different Lisp constraint expressions. Constraint expressions are Boolean combinations of predicates of the form (pred path key), where pred is a predicate on the filler at the end of the path in key. At this level, we would like to make the search yield the "best" candidates first, if possible.

Evaluating the quality of a match normally requires a complicated comparison of the probe and the KB item at the time of search. To eliminate this overhead, we have attempted to impose an a priori "best first" ordering of identical KB items at the time the KB is built. We have interpreted "best first" with respect to the constraint expressions as meaning "with the narrowest semantic requirements." A highly specific expression (one involving a complex combination of predicates) is one likely to be satisfied less often than other expressions in the KB. A simple numerical measure, based on elementary probability theory, has been used to estimate the specificity of constraint expressions.

Suppose two independent events x and y occur with probability $p(x)$ and $p(y)$. The probability that they will occur at the same time (x and y), is $p(x) * p(y)$. The probability that $p(x)$ will not occur (not x), is $1-p(x)$. The probability that x or y will occur (x or y), is $1-((1-p(x)) * (1-p(y)))$. Suppose we interpret the satisfaction of a predicate appearing in a constraint as an event. If there were an estimate of the probability of a predicate's being true with respect to a probe, the above relations would estimate the probability of yielding true of Boolean combinations of the predicates.

We crudely estimate p(predicate) to be proportional to how often that predicate appears in a KB. For example, for independent predicates x and y, we say $p(x) > p(y)$ if x appears in 10 constraint expressions and y appears in only 3. p(constraint expression) is then estimated as (#occurrences of the predicate + sum #occurrences of all predicates that imply the truth of the predicate) / (sum #occurrences of all predicates).

This measure is crude, especially since the predicates will not be independent, but is easily computed from the information available. Also it is consistent with some of the rules a specificity measure should follow:

1. (implies y x) -> $(p(x) > p(y))$

2. $p(x) >= p((\text{and } x \text{ anything}))$

3. $p(x) <= p((\text{or } x \text{ anything}))$

8.2 KB Search

Once the discrimination tree (or D-tree) for a given body of KB forms has been set up, SOT is ready to accept probes for which it can attempt to find matching forms among the KB structures, using the D-tree. If the probe happens to be one of the KB forms, SOT provides an *exact* discrimination for it in an "optimal" number of tests. If the probe form is not exactly the same as one of the KB forms, the discrimination is only *partial:* the KB forms may not really match the probe completely (i.e., we have a "false drop.") Thus, the use of SOT to find matches to general probe forms needs to be followed by a more careful, exact pattern-matching process on the KB items returned, to avoid false drops. That is, SOT is really a *filter,* which rapidly discards the great mass of the KB items and returns only those few that have a chance of actually matching.

The term "search" needs to be defined. SOT supports three general types of search: (a) a match of a general key against specific KB items, "instance search"; (b) a match of a specific key against general KB items, "template search"; and (c) search for items matching the key exactly. The first two types of search are converses of each other. To make the retrieval process faster, SOT can be told to organize the KB to support a specific type of search.

In instance search the emphasis is on the restrictions expressed in the key and finding items that fit the category defined by it. This kind of search is analogous to answering questions such as

"Tell me the names of all of the people in the CS department."
"What species of the family Vialaceae grow in Connecticut?"

A KB item is matched during instance search if all headers of the key that are non-nil are identical to the corresponding headers of the item. The key (a b (c)) would match any of the following:

(a b (c d (e)))
(a b (c) f (g)).

It would not match

(a)

because the item is missing a non-nil header, c, present in the key. It would also not match

(a b (d))

because the headers of the (b) path, d and c, are not equivalent. Items can have more information in their slot-filler structures and still match the key, but they must not lack information present in the key and must not have headers conflicting with key headers.

In template search the emphasis is on the restrictions expressed in the slot-filler structures of the KB items and recognizing the key as an example of some of them. Questions analogous to this type of search are

"What diseases could cause this symptom?"
"Is this plant a violet?"
"Whose modus operandi do these crimes fit?"

A KB item is matched during template search if all headers of the item that are non-nil are identical to the corresponding headers of the key. For example, the key

(a b (c d (e) f (g)) h (nil) i (j))

would match all of the following:

(nil)
(a)
(a k (nil))
(a b (c) i (nil))
(a i (j)).

It would not match

(x b (c d (e) f (g)) i (j))

because the header of the ( ) path, a, of the key disagrees with the corresponding header of the item, x. It would also fail to match

(a k (l))

because the header of the (k) path, l, has no counterpart in the key. An item's structure may lack information present in the key, but it can't have more information or conflicting information.

The exact match is a search for those items whose slot-filler structures are exactly like the key. The key in the above example

(a b (c d (e) f (g)) h (nil) i (j))

would match

(a b (c d (e) f (g)) h (nil) i (j))
(a b (c d (e) f (g r (nil)) i (j)))

but not

(a b (nil))
(a b (d d (e) f (g)) h (nil) i (j))
(a b (c d (e) f (g)) h (x) i (j)).

The requirements of the exact search are the intersection of the requirements of the template and instance searchs. Matching items cannot have less or more information in their slot-filler structures than is in the key, and their headers must be equal to the ones in the key.

8.2.1 The Tree Search Mechanism

Each non-terminal node in the tree has a set of KB items that are distinguished from each other using the index. The path of the node specifies which header to use for discrimination. KB items of the node are classified by the value they have for that header, and all items sharing the same value are assigned to the same daughter node.

The deeper a node is in the slot-filler tree, the smaller the set of items it will have and the more alike the items in this set will be. Comparing the header value of a key slot-filler structure to the index of the node determines which daughters have items with slot-fillers that "agree" with the key. These are the next nodes visited. The rest of the daughters, and with them a large portion of the non-matching items, are excluded from consideration. At each visited daughter node the above process is repeated until terminal nodes are reached. At this point the number of items still in consideration is much smaller, and the constraint expressions, if any, are evaluated to yield the retrieval set.

All varieties of slot-filler search use this same basic mechanism,

TABLE 8.1.
PERFORMANCE OF SOT KB SEARCH
(UNITS ARE IN CLICKS/ITEM FOUND, WHERE 1 CLICK = 16.7 ms)

No. of items in KB	SOT exact search		Linear exact search		SOT exhaustive instance search		SOT exhaustive template search	
	mean	dev	mean	dev	mean	dev	mean	dev
2	1.18	0.88	1.23	0.74	1.05	0.85	1.04	0.55
4	0.96	0.72	1.31	0.75	1.05	0.74	1.05	9.85
8	1.17	0.82	2.21	1.08	1.19	0.82	1.11	0.81
16	1.05	0.74	3.34	1.76	1.26	0.97	1.20	0.81
32	1.11	0.84	5.81	3.26	1.34	1.08	1.04	9.74
64	1.16	0.89	10.43	6.78	1.51	1.43	1.09	0.79
128	1.21	0.92	18.73	12.15	1.66	2.22	0.81	0.83
256	1.22	0.92	30.89	23.14	1.65	2.57	0.48	0.36

Note: dev = deviation.

starting at the top node of the tree and working downward. They differ mainly in their definitions of "agree."

8.3 Performance

The version of SOT described here, like the other modules of the NLP Toolkit, is programmed in Franz Lisp (Fode81) on a VAX-11/780 mini-computer system running under the UC Berkeley Version 4.2 of the UNIX operating system. To gain some idea of how well SOT was meeting the design aims, we created a toy KB of 306 conceptual structures representing the meanings of English sentences as output by the conceptual analyzer described in Chapter 4. These structures include examples of both assertions and rules and span a variety of knowledge domains. Thus they are crudely representative of the diversity to be found in a real KB. We were particularly interested in the relationship between KB size and speed of search for the various search regimes.

SOT was probed with key items drawn at random from the original pool formed into the KB. Table 8.1 shows time per item fetched from the KB (measured in 167 msec "clicks" by UNIX) as a function of the type of search. For comparison, results for a linear search using a symbolic pattern matcher are also given. The time of the SOT searches would be expected to grow with the logarithm of the number of items in the database, but we were unable to prove it because the fetch time per item did not change significantly for these KB sizes. Larger KBs are needed to clarify the relationship between search time and size, although the present results are extremely encouraging.

Of interest also is the relationship between the size of the KB and the time taken to compute the SOT tree, which might be expected to behave in an exponentially explosive manner. It turns out, however, that the relationship is only weakly polynomial for the current implementation, being expressed by

$$T = 2.0N^{1.3}$$

The first "real" application of SOT was as the retrieval component of the natural language generator described in Chapter 6. In this application, conceptual structures to be expressed in English are matched into a dictionary containing template structures corresponding to individual words spanning part or all of the input meaning. For the version of the generator provided with the NLP Toolkit, this process represents a template search in a KB containing more than 300 dictionary definitions (associations between meaning structures and words). In the course of probing this KB with concepts the generator could "say," SOT averaged 3.85 clicks per dictionary access (on a VAX 11-780). A linear search applied to the same task averaged 34.8 clicks per fetch. The order of magnitude speed-up achieved using SOT allows near real-time response for this application, a result which, from the above, is not expected to change drastically as the number of words known to the generator increases.

8.4 Summary

A vital component of any functional language interface to a large software system is a means of managing access to the items of information in the system's database. If the database is actually a knowledge base (KB) containing descriptions of the facts, rules, goals, etc., characteristic of the application domain, then the interface and KB share a representational vocabulary and can communicate directly. This chapter describes in overview terms the design of a self-configuring knowledge base manager for large numbers of symbolic items expressed in the ERKS formalism. The access machinery supports instance, template, and exact matching in KBs containing both factual and variabilized forms. The search may be exhaustive or resumable. Although the KB's discrimination-network scheme is set up according to a heuristic measure of "goodness," several empirical investigations indicate that the speed of access is sufficient to support real-time conversational interaction.

9

Commonsense Reasoning

9.0   Introduction: The Need for Reasoning in Language Processing

This book has promoted a model of language understanding that is *predictive* or *expectation-based*. If they are to cope robustly, systems that must deal with human users need to have strong expectations about the kinds of things users will say. For example, if such a system asks its user a question, it will need to have explicit structures representing the expected answers the user will give. These structures must be *conceptual* in form, rather than surface strings of, say, English. This is because the user may choose to express the same thought in a number of different surface forms, and for the system to anticipate all the possibilities would be difficult, if not impossible.

The problem with an expectation-directed understanding scheme is that the user's response, even in its conceptual form, may not (and usually does not) match up precisely with an expectation (cf., e.g., Cull79). Suppose, for example, that an academic counseling system has asked the question "What courses are you taking?" as part of an interviewing dialogue. Suppose the user has provided as part of the answer an underspecified description such as "Art." In attempting to fill out the description, the system may ask "What is the number of the Art course?" with the explicit (conceptual) expectation of an answer such as "The number of the Art course is 101." If the user responds instead "I'm in Art 101," there is a problem: the response, even in its conceptual form, looks nothing like the expectation.

Of course, one could store an expectation for this response, too, but such an approach really seems *unprincipled* and unworkable, in practice. The expectation presumably came out of a knowledge structure describing the current state of the interview, i. e., the knowledge that the interviewer wished to extract at this point. The user's reply, while true and even responsive, is, strictly speaking, irrelevant. To add all kinds of extra information to the knowledge structure to handle such cases seems *ad hoc*, at best.

What seems to be needed to handle situations where there is a responsive, but non-matching, answer is access to *inferencing* or *reasoning* power. A conversational system needs to be able to form the assertion "User is taking an art course numbered something" from the raw expectation "the number of the Art course is something." The inference step could be based, for example, upon a fuller paraphrase of the expectation "the number of the Art course *that the user is taking* is something," together with machinery to extract the subconceptualization and to use it to match the answer.

Note that the required reasoning apparatus cannot be purely deductive in nature. Deductive methods of reasoning have the characteristic that, if the premises are true in the world, then the inference rule guarantees that the conclusion will be true, as well. (That is, the rule is *valid*.) While people certainly use deductive methods in their everyday encounters with the world, it seems clear that rules whose conclusions are only *contingently* true are much more widely used. Moreover, people seem to be willing to admit premises that are not absolutely known to be true, in order to make a problem-solving process go forward. Often, these premises will be the result of a prior, contingent, inference step.

9.1 Deductive Retrieval

What is needed to solve problems caused by expectation mismatches is access to general-purpose reasoning power. One popular reasoning paradigm in AI, and the one I will briefly discuss here, is *deductive retrieval*. In this technique, formulas representing possible inference steps are kept in a database and retrieved when the reasoning process needs them. For example, the rule "All men are mortal" might be stored thus:

Rule 9.1:
(forall(?x)(implies (human ?x)(can-die ?x)))

This is a representation of the meaning of the sentence in a format typical of the first-order predicate calculus. The predicate calculus provides a means of reasoning about predicate forms, based on predicates such as "human" and "can-die," composed into more complex forms by connectives such as "implies." In addition, the forms may contain *quantified variables,* which can be used to talk about a group of objects or an unknown object. In Rule 9.1, the quantifier "forall" is the universal quantifier that is used to bind a *variable* (here ?x) to all instances of a certain set of objects. The existential quantifier "exists" is used to bind a variable to (one or more) unknown members of a set about which one wishes to make an attribution. Of course, the predicate-with-indexed-arguments form of Rule (9.1) has an analogous ERKS formulation.

The basic strategy of deductive retrieval is to reason or *chain backwards* through a collection of rules, in response to a query form. Suppose, for example, the query "is Socrates mortal?" is posed to the system. In an ERKS format, this might look like

Query 9.1:
(s-change actor (person persname (Socrates))
      toward (health val (-10))
      mode (modes mode1 *?* mode2 (:can)))

It is paraphrased as "can it be the case that Socrates can undergo a state change terminating in death?" The atom "*?*" at the end of the *(mode mode1)* path is a variable that the user wishes to bind to the truth value of a matching expression.

In attempting to answer such a query, a deductive retriever first directly attempts to fetch a matching fact from its factual database. Technically, matching facts are said to *unify* with the request. Two forms are said to be unifiable if one can find values for the variables in each form such that substituting those values makes the two forms identical. For example, a query such as "how old is Socrates?"

Query 8.2
(s-attr actor (person persname (Socrates))
      age (unit utype (year) umag *?*))

would unify with "Socrates is 80 years old" under the variable binding

? = (num numval (80))

If the direct fetch fails, the retriever then probes its rule database for forms such as Rule (9.1):

(implies con1 <antecedent>
    con2 (s-change actor "Socrates"
           toward (health val (-10))
           mode (modes mode1 *?* mode2 (:can))))

where the <antecedent> form may contain instances of the variable, as well. (The quantifier *forall* can be suppressed in the rule base by simply adopting the convention that all variables are universally quantified. Existentially quantified variables can be replaced by "constant symbols" standing for the unknown, but presumably extant, object.) That is, it looks for a rule that has the property that if the antecedent can be shown to be true (or plausible), then the consequent form can be inferred to be true (plausible). Note that the consequent part of the rule must unify with the query. If it does, the retriever *back-unifies* the rule by instantiating the antecedent form with the unifying substitutions found for the consequent form. It then attempts a direct retrieval of the instantiated antecedent form, searching for further back-chaining rules as required.

In our example, the back-instantiation step would yield the form

(s-attr actor "Socrates"
      attr (exist)
      mode (modes mode1 (:t)))

that is, "Socrates is alive," a form presumably already present in the factual database. In effect, the deductive retrieval process explicates parts of the *virtual* database implied by the actual facts and the available inference rules.

9.2   YADR, Yet Another Deductive Retriever

This section is a brief exegesis of YADR, a deductive retriever developed to support inferencing in the conversational program ACE. (The complete listing of a version of YADR is given in Appendix II.) Although YADR has severe performance problems, the program is simple in design and short and will serve nicely for illustrative purposes.

Actually, calling YADR "deductive" is a misnomer, since the system will readily construct reasoning chains based upon *cause, cancause* and *plausible* connectives, as well as simply *implies*. Such connectives are useful for expressing contingent causal relations (for example, "dropping a glass can cause it to break") and default conditions (such as "all birds fly"). The present system, however, doesn't attempt to assess the plausibility of chains constructed with contingent inference steps, so there's no real difference between it and a standard retriever (such as Char80). The assessment problem, the subject of what might be called "the calculus of plausibility," is one of the deepest and most difficult in AI. (See, e.g., Zade73; Doyl79; McAl80; McCa80; McDe80).

Before YADR is discussed, something should be said about its retrieval system. YADR works with ERKS forms, and thus the knowledge base manager SOT is very naturally used to organize efficient search for the relevant forms. The knowledge imbedded in the "expert" system YADR works with is kept in three SOT D-trees: one for facts and two for rules.

The facts are completely instantiated: all the required cases in the ERKS form are filled out. For example, one might record an instance of the "offered-course" *goalepisode* corresponding to "CS 110, Section 1, taught by Prof. Keith Barker, is held in the spring semester of 1984 in Engineering Building III, Room 217, on Tuesday and Thursday from 1 to 2:30 PM." A simplified representation for this might be:

```
($course actor "Keith Barker" teacher "Keith Barker" cno "110"
     department "Computer Science" section "1"
     building "Engineering III" room "217"
     abstime
     (abstimes
     semester "Spring" year "1984" day "Tuesday/Thursday" daypart
     "1-2:30PM")
     mode
     (modes mode1 (:t)))
```

(The *abstime* role in a concept is filled with an "absolute time" specification for the concept, consisting of subconcepts that are *tim(e)dur (ations)*. Instances of the concept are considered to occur within the shortest duration given.) A typical question form, or *probe* into the database, will be a less completely instantiated form of the above. Such a form can be thought of as containing variables at the locations where the requested information should appear. For example, one might ask "Is CS 110 being given in the spring semester?" or "Who is teaching CS 110 in the spring semester?" Both questions (in their ERKS realization) would match the fully instantiated form shown above under the SOT "instance match" search regime, as described in the last chapter.

The two rule D-trees, on the other hand, contain incompletely instantiated forms such as Rule 9.1. When back-chaining, YADR probes the rule database with forms such as

(implies con1 ?ante con2 <fact-form>)

where ?ante is a variable that can be bound to any form, and <fact-form> is a more or less completely instantiated (i.e., factual) concept that has been derived either from an input probe, or from other antecedent forms that have been unified with it. Rules of this kind are called *if-needed methods* (Hewe71), since they are called up only when needed to advance an inference process.

Another useful rule database is used in a *forward-chaining* manner; that is, with forms such as

(implies con1 <fact-form> con2 ?conseq)

Here, ?conseq gets bound to a new fact that YADR can deduce and add to the factual database, once it knows <fact-form> is true. Rules of this sort are called *if-added methods,* since they are typically used to add further forms when an external process adds a fact to the database. (The corresponding clean-up rules are called if-deleted methods.) In either rule database, the search of the rule D-tree is a species of "template search," as described earlier.

9.3   The YADR Interface

YADR reasons in a back-chaining manner. The first, and in many ways most important, design decision to be faced is the question of how to control the back-chaining process itself. Deductive retrieval can be thought of as a kind of search through the space of all possible inference chains constructable from the probe and the available rules. Some of these chains will terminate in facts known to the system (these represent solutions, answers to the probe question). Others will die out because no further back-chaining steps can be found.

Unfortunately, no good directed search scheme seems to exist for problems of this kind. Certainly, no obvious heuristic evaluators are available to allow optimal search in the sense of (Nils71). Such evaluators are typically composed of a function that estimates the distance of the current "state" from the goal, plus a function that estimates the effort that has been expended to push the search this far.

The goal states of this kind of search are characterized by sets of antecedent forms that happen to be among the known facts. It is difficult to see how to estimate "how far" one is from such a state when given only a collection of candidate chains, one of which is to be extended. Moreover, the length of a solution chain is not directly an issue in judging the "goodness" of a solution, if more than one can be found. Once we have them all, any of them is a good answer to the probe form. More to the point, perhaps, is the number of contingent inference steps a chain contains, since these presumably reduce our belief in the chain's plausibility. Thus, to get started, one is forced to use one of the blind-search paradigms, e.g., depth-first or breadth-first. For simplicity's sake, the design of YADR follows a depth-first regime. This is not as computationally expensive as might seem, since inference paths tend to die out quite quickly in application domains such as academic counseling.

A second design consideration is the nature of the interface to YADR. YADR itself can be used directly for question answering. Of more interest in a running system is the question of determining *the consistency of a probe form with known or hypothetical fact forms*. These facts are either those that exist in the long-term database of known things, or those that have been added temporarily to allow reasoning under the present real-world circumstances, or under hypothetical assumptions. An example of the former would be reasoning in a student record database in the case of the particular student being interviewed now. The latter might occur in a case where the student says "Suppose I took Physics 151 this semester." In either case, the factual database needs to be *primed* with some special circumstances.

Thus, one is naturally led to the development of the YADR interface function *consistent-with* shown in Figure 9.1. At [1], this function uses the helper function *prime-fax-net* temporarily to add the list of priming forms to the factual database, together with any other forms that follow from the primers through one or more if-added inference steps. The function *get-ifaddeds* (see Appendix II) computes the forms following from a given one in a forward-chaining manner at [5]. This function will need to call itself recursively to see whether further forms follow from the deduced forms. Obviously, one has the possibility of explosive forward inference here if the kinds of if-added methods allowed are not carefully controlled.

The function *qckanon-add* at [4] is a SOT interface function (not shown, but defined in the Toolkit) that "quickly" adds a set of forms to

Figure 9.1
YADR Interface

```
;CONSISTENT-WITH: is the probe (which must be variabilized) consistent
;          with the current factual/rule databases?
; ARGS: probe—a variablized assertion which is checked for consistency
;          in the face of ...
;          primerlst—a list of fact forms which are temporarily asserted,
;                    with if-added inferences too.
; RTNS: a list of instantiated forms, with the bindings of actual conatoms
;          from the database to the variables supplied with the probe

(def consistent-with (lambda (probe primerlst)

  ;[1]
  ;temporarily add primer list to Fax net, remembering names of added items
  (let ((tempfax (prime-fax-net primerlst)))
       (and *pau* (pause 'consistent-with))

    ;[2]
    ;let yadr find a connection, if one exists
    (let ((foundfax (yadr probe)))

      ;[3]
      ;discard the temp fax
      (mapc 'Delete-Fax tempfax)
      foundfax
      ))))

;PRIME-FAX-NET: stuff primers into Fax-net, along with additional
;          fax returned by if-added rules
(def prime-fax-net (lambda (primers)
  ; [4]
  ; add primers and if-added forms (if any) to the factual DB
            ; *FAX* is the global associated with the factual DB
  (qckanon-add (get-DB *FAX*)
            ; [5]
            ; if-added forms available?
            (append primers (rem-nil (mapcan 'get-ifaddeds primers))))))
```

---

a SOT tree discriminating "anonymous" leaf nodes, that is, a set of forms it has made up its own names for. Anonymous D-trees are useful for preserving database integrity. "Quickly" here refers to speed of insertion of the new forms, not to optimization of the retrieval through the heuristic methods discussed in the last chapter.

.The added forms are remembered in the variable *tempfax* and are erased, at [3], by the call to *Delete-Fax,* after the backward-chaining inference step at [2]. Any inference chain terminating in known forms in the factual DB signals that the probe form is consistent with what is known. If all chains die out, no conclusion can be drawn. (Note that one could ask for the consistency of the *negation* of the probe form with the primers, to test for inconsistency. I haven't bothered with this here.)

9.4 The YADR Top Level

A slightly simplified version of the "raw" interface to YADR is shown in Figure 9.2. The system first tries to fetch fact-forms directly that unify with the probe at [1]. Failing that, it checks to see whether the probe is a conjunction or exclusive-disjunction of simple forms at [2]. For example, YADR might be asked "Did student pass CS 110 AND CS 111?" Composed forms of this sort cannot be stored directly in the database. The function *prove-xor-and* (cf. Figure 9.3) uses YADR recursively to establish (one or all) of the composed forms. At [3] in Figure 9.2 the function *run-rule* is used to get if-needed methods to back-chain on. If this step succeeds, the function returns the fact-forms at which the search terminated, or else YADR fails.

Function *run-rule* computes the available rules in the let*-prolog at [4], using the SOT interface function *Fetch-IfneedRules* (not shown). If some rules are available, the necessary binding lists of data from the probe with variables from the rules are computed at [5]. At [6], YADR calls *filter-rules* (see Appendix II) to discard any rules being used with the same set of bindings as in a prior inference step. This is how YADR avoids inference loops. Then, YADR is called recursively at [7] to establish the antecedent parts of each of the instantiated rules in turn. Because of this recursion, the search is depth-first: each chain is pursued until it dies out. Note how, at [8], *run-rule* remembers the rule and binding being used in the recursive call (using *record-bindings;* see Appendix II) to prevent inference loops.

9.5 Logical Connectives in Antecedent Forms

In general, YADR needs to be able to establish forms containing arbitrary imbeddings of logically connected subforms, such as are typical of domain-specific rules. Of course, arbitrary forms have a canonical representation containing only (say) conjunction and negation.

Let's restrict our attention to antecedent forms containing only a toplevel *conj* or *xor*. (This version of YADR cannot handle negated forms.) These connectives are handled by the function *prove-xor-and,*

Figure 9.2
YADR Top Level

Note: This is simplified slightly for illustrative purposes;
See Appendix II for a more nearly executable version.

```
; YADR: Yet Another Deductive Retriever
; ARGS: probe—something which is to be shown to be true/plausible.
;      If probe is not asserted in the Fax db, the if-needed
;      rules (in ifn D-tree) are searched to see if a rule of the form
;      (<connective> con1 'something' con2 ,probe) can be found. If so, the
;      con1 is unified with the con2, and yadr tries to prove the con1
; RTNS: all available instantiated versions of probe, i.e., all factual
; forms which unify (perhaps after back-chaining) with the probe
; (which may contain variables)

(def yadr (lambda (probe)

  ;[1]
  ;get known fax that satisfy the probe and its variables
  (let ((found-facts (Fetch-Fax-w-vars probe))
       (proven-facts))

(cond (found-facts)

      ;[2]
      ;maybe it's an 'and' or an 'xor'?
      ((logical-con-p probe)
       (prove-xor-and probe))

      ;[3]
      ;if-needed step available?
      ((setq proven-facts (run-rule probe))
       proven-facts)

      ;pack it in...
      (t nil)))))
```

```
;               RUN-RULE
; ARGS: probe—the thing we're trying to prove using a rule
; RTNS: all available instantiated versions of the probe
; NOTE: rules look like (implies con1 'something' con2 ,probe)
;                 or (cause con1 'something' con2 ,probe)
;              or (cancause con1 'something' con2 ,probe)
;              or (plausible con1 'something' con2 ,probe)
; NOTE: a rule can only be used if the antecedent is known, so yadr
;      is called to determine this.
; NOTE: the above means we are operating yadr in a DEPTH-FIRST,
;                 CHRONOLOGICALLY BACK-TRACKING manner, which
```

```
;                     probably isn't the best thing to do; back-chaining paths tend to
;                     die out quickly, so the depth-first part isn't so bad; it's the
;                     "return to most recent option point" mentality that is suspect.
; NOTE: breadth-first, "best first" would be better; now, if we only knew what
;                     "best first" means!

(def run-rule (lambda (probe)
      [4]
      ;valid rules
(let* ((rule (make-rule probe 'implies))
      (matched-rules (Fetch-IfneedRules rule)) ; sot treeatoms
      ;cause rules
      (rule (make-rule probe 'cause))
      (matched-rules (append matched-rules (Fetch-IfneedRules rule)))
      ;cancause rules
      (rule (make-rule probe 'cancause))
      (matched-rules (append matched-rules (Fetch-IfneedRules rule)))
      ;plausible rules
      (rule (make-rule probe 'plausible))
      (matched-rules (append matched-rules (Fetch-IfneedRules rule)))
      (bindings)         ; the list of binding lists
      (inst-rules)       ; the instantiated forms of matched-rules + bindings
      (if-parts)         ; the antecedents of the inst-rules
      (proved-forms)) ; establishable versions of the then-parts


      (cond (matched-rules ; if we found some

            ;[5]
            ; get bindings from probe (which is inside rule)
            (setq bindings (get-probe-bindings rule matched-rules))

            ;[6]
            ;avoid loops
            ;Note: filter-rules returns a list of surviving rules
            ; and their corresponding binding alists
            (setq matched-rules (filter-rules matched-rules bindings))
            (setq bindings (cadr matched-rules))
            (setq matched-rules (car matched-rules))

            ; then use bindings to instantiate copies of rules
            (setq inst-rules (inst-new-rules matched-rules bindings))

            ; the if-parts are to be established
            (setq if-parts (mapcar '(lambda (mtch) (extract mtch '(con1)))
                        inst-rules))

            ;[7]
            ; Now call yadr on the if-part of each of the instantiated
            ; versions of the matched rules. If yadr returns non-nil, then,
```

Figure 9.2 *(Continued)*

```
; FOR EACH fact-form returned, unify that with the corresponding
; matched-rule. The result is a list of lists, each sublist
; containing the fact-form proved filled in w/ the variables from
; the if-part
(setq proved-forms
      (mapcar
          '(lambda (con mrule bdgs)
          ;[8]
          ; record that this rule was used with
          ; the corresponding bindings
          (let ((foo (record-bindings mrule bdgs))
                  ; and backchain merrily...
                  (prvd (yadr con)))
                  (mapcar '(lambda (x)
                               (inst-if-part x mrule))
                       prvd)))
          parts
          matched-rules
          bindings))

      ; knock out imbedded list structure
      (flatten proved-forms))

      (t nil))) ; if no matched rules, failure
))
```

---

shown in Figure 9.3. The do-iteration at [1] handles the case for
"exclusive-or".[1] Note how the *catch/throw* construct is used to exit from
the *do* when YADR returns the *xor* subconcept it has established.

The more complex case for "and" is handled at [3] by *merge-and*,
whose job is to show that *all* the composed forms can be established in a
consistent manner. First, at [4], *merge-and* uses YADR to find all the
possible instantiations of all the *conj* subconcepts. (The *catch/throw*
construct serves to terminate the iteration with the first subconcept that
fails to be established.) Next, the double *mapcar* at [5] computes an
association list consisting of each subform with its available variable
binding lists (one for each version of the form that YADR was able to
establish). At [6], *build-combs* (see Appendix II) computes the lists of
subconcepts representing a possible answer to the probe. Finally, at [7],
the function *consistent-combs* (see Appendix II) walks through the
binding lists, ascertaining for each variable that it is bound to the same
entity each time it appears, for example, that ?x is not bound to "Ronald"
in one subform and to "Walter" in another. The list of surviving

Figure 9.3
Composite Antecedent Forms

```
;           PROVE-XOR-AND
; ARGS: probe—concepts connected w/ "exclusive-or" or "and"
; RTNS: list of instantiated conjunctions of *all* the possible ways *all* the
;       conjuncts can be proved; or list of instantiated xor of *all*
;       the ways the *first available* xor disjunct could be proved

(def prove-xor-and (lambda (probe)
        ; get paths to imbedded and/xor concepts
    (let* ((conslots (get-conslots probe))
            ; isolate the imbedded subcons, making sure to give them a
            ; "variables" property for the recursive call to yadr
          (cons-to-prove
                (mapcar '(lambda (c)
                            (propagate-vars (grf (list c) probe) probe c))
                        conslots))
          ; what yadr will be able to establish
          (provable-cons nil))
      (cond
        ; [1]
        ; the case for xor
        ((xor-p probe)
        (setq provable-cons
                ;[2]
                ;wait for a result
                ; iterate on xor subcons...
        (catch (do ((nextcon (car cons-to-prove) (car restcons))
                    (restcons (cdr cons-to-prove) (cdr restcons))
                    (slot (car conslots) (car restconslots))
                    (restconslots (cdr conslots) (cdr restconslots))
                    (reslt nil))
                   ((null nextcon) nil)
                   ; until yadr establishes one...
                   (setq reslt (yadr nextcon))
                   ; then throw a list of the result up to [2]
                   (if (car reslt)
                       (throw (list (make-structure '(xor ,slot (,(car reslt)))))))))
                    ))))
        (t
        ;[3]
        ; the case for "and"
        ; merge-and returns a list of lists containing all ways
        ; all the conjuncts could be consistently established
        (setq provable-cons (merge-and conslots cons-to-prove))
```

Figure 9.3 (*Continued*)

```
    ; [8]
    ; convert to list of conjunctions
    (and provable-cons (build-multiple-con 'conj provable-cons conslots)))

)
    provable-cons)))

;               MERGE-AND
; ARGS: conslots, paths to...
;    cons-to-prove, conj subcons to be established
;
; RTNS: a list of all the possible instantiations of all the conj subcons

(def merge-and (lambda (conslots cons-to-prove)
  (let
    ;[4]
    ((known-cons
        (catch
          (do ((cns (cdr cons-to-prove) (cdr cns))
               (nextcon (car cons-to-prove) (car cns))
               (ydr-results nil) ; list of all the results
               (ydr-result nil)) ; just one result
              ((null nextcon) (reverse ydr-results))
              (setq ydr-result (yadr nextcon))
              (if ydr-result
                  (setq ydr-results (cons ydr-result ydr-results))
                  (throw nil)) ; if failure, throw nil
))))

    ; now, if any piece was not known or could not be proved, no need to
    ; go any further, stop here
    (cond
     ((null known-cons)
       nil)

     (t
      (let*
       ; [5]
       ; now, for each known-con (i.e., one that was proved), use the
       ; variables from the input cons to get the fillers in the proved cons
       ; cons&bindings will end up as a list of lists of:
       ; (known-con1 bindings1)
          ; It's a list of lists since yadr returns multiple facts
          ((cons&bindings
            (mapcar
             '(lambda (known-list-of-cons con-to-prove)
```

```
(mapcar
 '(lambda (proved-con)
    (cons proved-con
      (find-bindings proved-con
        (get-variables con-to-prove)
      nil))) ; end of inner lambda
  known-list-of-cons)) ; end of outer lambda
 known-cons cons-to-prove))

; [6]
; available conj-combinations
(pssbl-combs (build-combs cons&bindings))

; [7]
; consistently unifiable ones
(valid-combs (rem-nil (mapcar 'consistent-combs pssbl-combs))))
; end of let* prolog

; the result
valid-combs))))))
```

instantiations of all subforms is returned to *prove-xor-and,* where the *conj* forms are instantiated (at [8]), and returned.

9.6 Summary

This chapter has presented, in outline, an argument demonstrating the need for reasoning/inference machinery to handle expectation mismatches during understanding. A sample implementation for such a module was based on the deductive retrieval paradigm. While fairly limited in its power and subject to explosive computation because of its simple depth-first back-chaining policy, the retriever YADR does work well enough to support inference needs in simple conversational systems, as the next chapter will show.

Notes

1. I'm assuming that forms containing "non-exclusive or" antecedents, i.e., *disj* forms, will not occur in the rule DBs, but that these cases will be handled by separate rules, each having one of the disjuncts as its antecedent.

10

Putting It All Together:
A Goal-Directed Conversationalist

10.0 Introduction

This concluding chapter will argue that the most important remaining problem to be solved in the engineering of practical conversational systems is the *integration* of language analysis, generation, knowledge-base access, and inference into a complete system. I will argue for an explicitly goal-directed model of control, and will illustrate a form of this process in a particular conversational system. The system to be discussed does not directly confront many of the difficult problems that come up in discourse; e.g., judging conversational coherency (Hobb78), identifying false presuppositions (Kapl79), tracking user goals (Carb83), or modifying responses to avoid misleading the user (Josh84). But it does work well enough to suggest that extensions of this sort will eventually be possible within the goal-directed regime.

Conversation is one of the most striking characteristics of intelligent behavior. Keeping up with a conversation seems to require the application of enormous amounts of knowledge on the part of the participants. Thus, it is no surprise that the modeling of conversation in intelligent artifacts has run into extremely difficult problems, of which the main problem is the extreme mutability of natural conversation. The "topic" can shift at any time based on what a conversant is reminded of by what the other participant has just said. As a result, conversing requires nearly every language-processing and problem-solving skill possessed by humans. Until these skills are reasonably well understood, and can be effectively modeled and integrated *as processes,* there is little hope for usable, general-purpose conversational systems.

Certain types of conversations, however, exhibit much less variability than unrestricted discourse. For example, if one of the conversants is primarily in charge of the topic and can lead the other through a dialogue, the conversational swings are usually much smaller. A particular task of this nature is *interviewing.* Here, one conversant, the interviewer, attempts to extract some information from the other for the purpose of coming to some decision. Provided the person being interviewed is reasonably responsive, the course of the conversation can be controlled by the interviewer.

This chapter discusses a particular model of conversation based upon the interviewing task. This kind of task is best modeled as being *goal-based*. The activities of the system are directed toward achieving certain conversational goals: find out some information, answer a question, retrieve some data from the knowledge base, etc. Since such goals can be viewed as driving all the system's behaviors, including its language-processing behavior, the management of goals provides a useful means of *integrating* the language-processing and problem-solving capabilities of the system.

10.1   The ACE Microworld

ACE (Academic Counseling Experiment) is a natural language-processing system that was designed as a testbed for work in robust conversational interaction. The ultimate intention is for ACE to perform *in real time and in detail* the tasks of a faculty advisor to undergraduate engineering students who intend to be computer science majors. (The curriculum is the one used at the University of Connecticut.) The advisor works with students in a variety of tasks. He answers questions regarding course offerings and prerequisites, helps the student preregister for the coming semester, and counsels the student concerning career choices. Note that ACE's domain is open-ended in the sense that interactions of increasing complexity can be attempted in an incremental manner. Moreover, the system's robustness can be tested strenuously by the real users who are always available to work with the system.

To understand what it is told and to respond appropriately, ACE must bring to bear various kinds of knowledge, including (a) knowledge of the curriculum structure (distributional requirements, prerequisite requirements, professional elective choices, etc.); (b) knowledge about course-load scheduling (e. g., how many laboratory or programming courses should be taken in a given semester); and, most important, (c) how to conduct a *purposive conversation,* e. g., how to interview the student during a preregistration. Therefore, ACE addresses the concerns of earlier artificial intelligence conversational systems in its stress on the need for detailed domain knowledge (e. g., SOPHIE, in Brow75), for the explicit control of conversation (e. g., GUS, in Bobr77a), and for the capability of accommodating mixed initiative (e. g., SCHOLAR, in Carb70). The main new idea, is that of controlling a conversation based upon explicitly represented *goals*.

The version of ACE to be discussed here is a typical, multi-module AI system (see Diagram 10.1). The module labeled "NLP" in the figure consists of the conceptual analyzer and generator described in earlier

Diagram 10.1
Block Diagram of ACE

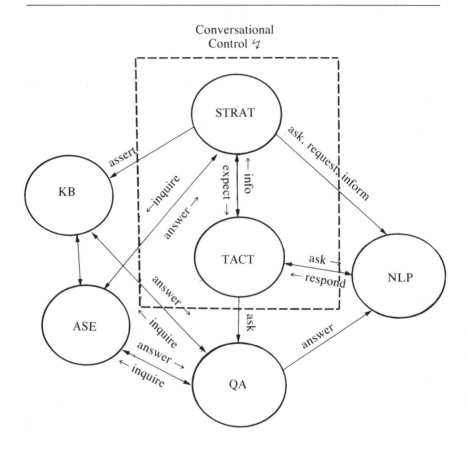

chapters, together with a *conversational context maintainer*. The knowledge-base manager, SOT, handles access to the generator's dictionary. The analyzer maps an English input from the user into the associated ERKS form, and presents it to the conversational control component of ACE. The generator performs the inverse mapping from an ERKS form of a concept the system wishes to express in English.

The main knowledge sources in ACE illustrate both the frame- and rule-based knowledge representation methodologies. The relatively rigid curriculum model gives a scriptlike account of the steps a computer science major must follow, including the important alternatives for achieving each subgoal.[1] For example, the introductory programming requirement can be met either by a single, intensive course worth 4 credits; or by a two-semester sequence worth 5 credits. Knowledge about scheduling, on the other hand, is much more flexible and thus is naturally encoded as a collection of rules. These criticize proposed courses to be added to the student's semester load on the basis of total number of credits, progress toward distributional goals, etc. One such rule will block the selection of the 4-credit introductory programming course unless the student has had experience with computers in high school or advanced standing in science or math. In ACE, both types of knowledge are stored in deductive retrieval databases (DBs) of the type described in the previous chapter. These are accessed by the conversational components of the system as needed.

Conducting a preregistration is currently the most difficult task handled by the system. Here, ACE's job is to set up a student's course schedule that will make sense in terms of the student's current standing. Thus, the preregistration dialog has the following prescribed steps, which amount to a simple "strategy" for this type of conversation: find out the student's identity; retrieve his course record if known, or interrogate the student; use the curriculum structure to propose the next set of courses; and let the scheduling rules criticize the choices. The Question-Asking Strategist (labeled STRAT in Diagram 10.1) controls the high-level flow of the dialog. At each point in this strategy, a question may be asked by the system that we hope will be answered in an incomplete or overspecified, but cooperative, manner. Dealing with cooperative, but unsatisfactory answers is the job of a question "tactician" process (TACT) in ACE. These modules are described in Sections 10.3 and 10.4.

Here is a fragment of a preregistration dialog between the system and a (simulated) first-semester freshman, which illustrates ACE's conversational capabilities:

1. ACE : What is your name?
   STUDENT : Ronald
2. ACE : What is your last name?
   STUDENT : It's McDonald
3. ACE : What courses are you taking
   at UConn in the Fall semester of 1983?
   STUDENT : 105, computer science,
   chemistry 130 and history 101.
4. ACE : What is the department of
   the 105 course?
   STUDENT : English
5. ACE : What is the number of the CS
   course?
   STUDENT : I am taking CS 110.
6. ACE : Have you completed Chem 129?

> STUDENT : I got credit for it by
> examination.

7. ACE : What other courses are you
   taking?
   STUDENT : I'm also taking a group 3
   course.

8. ACE : What group 3 course are you
   taking?
   STUDENT : Art 101.

9. ACE : Have you completed Math 133?
   STUDENT : I passed it in high school.

10. ACE : You will have to take Math 134
    next semester. You may take CS
    111, CS 207, a Group II course
    and a Group III course.

11. ACE : Do you agree to take CS 111
    and CS 207?
    STUDENT : ok

12. ACE : What Group II course do you want
    to take?
    STUDENT : Psychology 132

13. ACE : What Group III course would you
    like to take?
    STUDENT : I don't want to take a Group III
    next semester.

In this conversation the student exercised no initiative. There are two
ways for him to take some control of the conversation. First, he may ask
a question whenever a response is expected of him. For example,

9a. ACE : Have you completed Math 133?
    STUDENT : What is Math 133 called?
    ACE : Math 133 is entitled Introduction
    to Calculus I.

9b. ACE : Have you passed Math 133?
    STUDENT : I took it in high school.

Second, he may give information that is of use to the program later.

1a. ACE : What is your name?
    STUDENT : I am Ronald McDonald and I
    am taking 105, computer
    science, chemistry 130 and
    history 101.

4. ACE : What is the department of . . .

The above conversation pretty much circumscribes the system's conversational capabilities. ACE is not really *robust* in the way one would prefer. It knows about only one knowledge domain, and can carry on only a few narrowly focused conversations within that domain. I believe, however, that extensions of the current architecture are perfectly possible, indeed straightforward, both in the kinds of things the system can "talk" about and in more flexible interactions.

10.2 A Model of Purposive Conversation

ACE's model of purposive conversation is for the conversationalist to pursue a *strategy* during the conversation. The strategy is embodied in a data structure that is passed to the appropriate processing module as a goal for a conversation to be conducted. One such strategy is the interviewing strategy, given to the interviewing expert, the Strategist. This module is responsible for obtaining information from a user by asking questions until sufficient answers are obtained.

Different strategy modules are invoked for different tasks. For example, during explanation, the reverse strategy to interviewing, namely to *give* information, would be used. During question answering, the strategy is to determine an answer and respond in an appropriate fashion. A system that is intended to provide assistance to a user, perhaps a decision support system, would need both Interviewer and Explanation strategies, and our design would support this.[2]

Since ACE is conducting a conversation with certain purposes "in mind," a simple goal-achieving language, GAL (Mils83), was designed to allow the actions of the various parts of the system to be controlled in a goal-directed manner. This mechanism embodies an application of artificial intelligence subgoaling search techniques (see Nils71) to a conversational domain.

The mechanism is initialized with a single goal that represents a desired state of the world. A goal may be parameterized so that a general plan for achieving it may be used. When a goal is "finished," it returns a message of success or failure, perhaps containing some information needed for subsequent consideration. The use of *triggers* allows arbitrary constraints (preconditions) to be placed on the activation of a goal.

When a goal is processed, it is replaced by a plan for achieving it, where the run-time arguments of the goal replace the plan's parameters. In the ACE microworld, goals are simple enough to have ready-made plans available, so a planning mechanism is not needed. (Alternative plans for a given goal, however, will be retrieved if prior ones fail.) For example, if the Strategist wants to obtain some information, it uses the goal *find-out,* whose plan says, in effect, "First check memory for the information, and failing that, ask the user for it." Figure 10.1 gives the

Figure 10.1
Vocabulary of GAL, A Goal-Achieving Language

GAL is a specialized programming language which can be used to manage explicit goal-following behavior. Although the GAL interpreter currently has no planning capability, alternative goals can be set up for a given desired state of affairs; the system will automatically retrieve an alternative when one plan fails. A GAL expression is a form whose *car* is an atom chosen from the following vocabulary:

/goal
This is the top-level goal primitive. An instance of a goal has two arguments: the goal's name and its plan-body. The name can be *bound* to an ERKS form representing the desired state of affairs the goal-expression claims to achieve. Thus, a given goal may be retrieved in a pattern-directed manner [as in Hewe71] by other processes wanting the state of affairs to come about. More often, the goal-form represents a sequence of events that is so ritualized that it is essentially guaranteed to succeed. In these cases, the goal is directly invoked by name from other goals.

The plan-body is an s-expression based on one of the remaining primitive vocabulary items. It describes a set of alternative sub-goals, or a sequence of goals and actions, that may achieve the state the goal is defined for. The goal-form *returns* what the last form in the plan body returns.

/try
These forms encode sequences of activities for the system to try, in the attempt to achieve the goal. Failure of any subform does *not* terminate the processing of further sub-forms (i.e., a /try is like a *prog*). Side-effects are not undone, moreover, when the form returns.

/and
This form manages the interpretation of sub-forms *all* of which must succeed (i.e., return non-nil) for the form itself to succeed. The form terminates with the first failing sub-form, interpreted in a left-to-right order.

/or
This form specifies a set of alternatives, any one of which may succeed. It interprets the sub-forms left-to-right, and returns the first successful result.

/condgoal
This has a syntax reminiscent of the Lisp *cond*, where the cond-clauses correspond to lists headed by goals and having arbitrary sub-form lists as their tails. The first sub-clause whose initial /goal form succeeds has its tail sub-forms executed in the manner of a /try.

:=
This is the *run-time binding operator*, the function that is responsible for replacing every instance of a token (a symbol) with the value returned by a form. In the form (: = <token> <sub-form>), the value returned by the <sub-form> is substituted for the <token> everyplace it appears in the enclosing form; that form is physically modified. Thus, GAL can propagate intermediate results without having to bind up real variables in the run-time environment.

This operator is analogous to the operator of the same name in the analyzer. The only difference is that the GAL version *always* substitutes, rather than only in the cases where the <sub-form> returns non-nil.

/code
This allows the system to escape to Lisp for arbitrary computation. Usually, this is used to invoke the "primitive" operations of the system: generate a concept, analyze a sentence, summarize a knowledge structure, etc.

---

vocabulary available to the user who wants to set up goals and plans in the Goal-Achieving Language, GAL.

10.3   The Conversational Strategist

If, in processing the toplevel goal, *help-student-goal,* ACE receives an indication that the student wishes to preregister, the Strategist is given an initial goal, to conduct a preregistration interview with a student who wants a Computer Science degree. The plan to achieve this goal involves a conjunction of more specific subgoals. First, of course, the Strategist must get the student's name. (It should also inquire about the student's semester status and the particular curriculum being followed. The current system doesn't do this yet.)

Second, the Strategist should find out the student's previous courses and current schedule. Third, the Strategist should check the current schedule for completeness and consistency with course requirements. If it finds any problems, it must question the student for additional information. Fourth, the Strategist should consider the paths through the curriculum from where the student is now to completion of the lower (or upper) division requirements. It tells the student what courses must be taken and what electives are appropriate (by name or by category). Then it suggests a schedule for the next semester that embodies normal progress toward the degree. The student may assent, or propose other courses. The Strategist checks to see if they are permitted or would have adverse effects upon the student's program. If so, it informs the student. When enough courses have been agreed to by both parties, the Strategist will once again ask for agreement on the whole schedule. At this point, the subgoals implementing the preregistration task have been achieved, and the conversation ends.

This description of the conversation apparently shows all the initiative in the Strategist. In fact, the Strategist maintains a list of relevant topics that are passed to the Tactician whenever a response from the student is awaited. If the student's response touches on one or more of these topics, that information will be accumulated in short-term memory for use later. Thus, should the student, when queried "What is your name?" respond "I am Ronald McDonald and I simply must take CS 269 next semester," then the Strategist will remember, at the right time, what course preference was expressed.

The second way in which the student can take conversational initiative is to respond to one of the Strategist's questions with a question himself. The Tactician is not sophisticated enough to know that the answer to a question can be a question, or that questions can be rhetorical or ironic. If a response is analyzed as a question, the Tactician passes it on to QA, the Question-Answering specialist.

10.4   The Conversational Tactician

The Tactician is always called to check the user's response to a question posed by the Strategist. It is given two kinds of information with which to interpret the response, both of which are *expectational* or *predictive* in nature. The first kind is the ERKS representation of the question, including an indication of the slots that must be filled for the question to be answered adequately. The second kind is a list of ERKS forms used to interpret, if possible, the meaning of those parts of the response that do not bear on the question. The Strategist focuses the attention of the Tactician by the expectations passed.

The Tactician deals differently with the two kinds of expectations. In the case of the question expectation, its duty is to get a complete answer. If the user does not answer the question at all, the question just asked is repeated (in paraphrase). If the user answers part of the question, then two things occur. The information offered is accumulated as part of the answer to be returned, and a new question, a subquestion, is formed and posed about a remaining part of the original question. This procedure is repeated until the user has supplied all the information desired.

In the case of the expectations embodied in the list of ERKS forms, each individual form foreshadows a question to which the Strategist must know the answer to achieve one of its other subgoals. When the user's response includes semantic content beyond the original question, those "extra" parts are matched against the expectations. Any applicable information gleaned is associated with the matching expectation in a conversational short-term memory. All this "extra" information is re-membered by the Strategist at the appropriate time.

10.5   The Academic Scheduling Expert

The Academic Scheduling Expert (ASE) is responsible for answering domain-specific questions from both the Strategist and the user (via the QA module). Questions regarding individual students, potential sched-ules, individual classes, etc., are passed to ASE for an answer. These questions, ERKS forms, direct the path that ASE traverses through its goals. For example, the student may inquire whether he meets the requirements for a particular course or not. This causes ASE to activate a set of subgoals that determine if this student has achieved all the necessary requirements for that course. An entirely different set of subgoals would be traversed if the Strategist requested the "ideal" schedule the student should take the following semester.

ASE is closely tied to the knowledge structure of the KB module, since the KB contains all the known facts and rules pertaining to courses, schedules, and students. Example scheduling rules (expressed in pseudo-English rather than ERKS, for clarity's sake) present within the KB are

(&student must take CE 211)
(&student may take BIOL 107 instead of ENGR 150)
(&student may not take MATH 104 for credit)
(&student course load should be 18 credits or less)
(&student should take CS 130 or CS 110-111 and CS207 during his freshman—sophomore years)
(&student should not take more than 2 lab courses in any one semester)
(typical &student first-semester schedule is CHEM 127, MATH 133, ENGL 105, an ENGR course and a Group II or III course)

For example, when ASE is asked to calculate a new schedule for a student, it must consult the KB to determine the typical schedule for a generalized student. Guided by this data structure, ASE asks YADR more specific questions to complete the student's schedule (that is, take care of any idiosyncrasies in the student's schedule). Typically this would be done to ensure that all prerequisites are met before it schedules the student for a course.

10.6 More Problems in Language Understanding

As a system designed for the study of problems in real-world conversation, ACE must confront several non-trivial problems requiring robust understanding, such as word-sense disambiguation, reference specification, and ellipsis expansion. Solving these problems requires a complicated interplay among the system's language-processing, memory, and conversational processes. Consider, for example, some of the processing necessary to handle the preregistration dialog of Section 10.1.

First, of course, the system must find out with whom it is dealing. ACE can cope with any *responsive* answer, such as "I'm Ronald McDonald," "Ronald McDonald is my name," "My name is McDonald" (a partial answer), and "Ronald McDonald" (an ellipsed answer). Assuming that this student is new to the system, i. e., that his/her current schedule is not already stored in the database, ACE needs to know what the student is taking now. The second question in the sample dialog is designed to elicit this information. Since engineering students typically take five courses a semester (a scheduling rule), the response to this question is incomplete. ACE's understanding of the ellipsed answer to Question 3 depends upon the analysis of ambiguous terms such as "computer science" in the context of the question that was asked. (The term "computer science" could mean "the scientific field," "a department offering courses in the field," or "a course in the field.") After its first pass over the response to the first question, the analyzer notices that it has not been able to form a complete proposition or assertion. At this point, it attempts a process of *diagnosis* on the basis of the conceptual form of the question, including the part of the concept (viz., the identity of the courses) about which the question is being asked. The analyzer finds that the "target" of the question (i.e., the questioned subconcept) has the same conceptual form as the output of the sentence analysis (or one of the possible outputs, in the case of "computer science"). Therefore, the diagnostic process proposes that the output be imbedded in the question concept in place of the target. That is, the ellipsis is *expanded* to the proposed conceptual form for "I am taking a computer science course, etc."

After the diagnosis of the ellipsis has been passed to the conversational component of ACE, the Academic Scheduling Expert finds several problems with the response. First, the undergraduate chemistry requirement can be fulfilled in a number of ways, for instance by the sequence Chem 129/Chem 130. It is highly unusual for a first-semester freshman to be taking Chemistry 130, since it has a prerequisite. However, a student may obtain advanced credit by passing an examination based on the prerequisite's subject matter. ACE is "aware" of this possibility as it asks Question 6. As in the ellipsis problem, specifying the referent of "it" in the response to (6) is accomplished by examining the form of the question, which contains the conceptual entity (instantiation of the course script) for "Chem 129." This is proposed as a possible meaning for "it," allowing the analysis to be completed.

ACE determines the rest of the student's current schedule by asking the further questions shown in Section 10.1. It then invokes ASE to consult the curriculum to find out which courses are mandatory at this point and which are optional. The recommendations it generates at the end of the dialog are critically dependent on its understanding of what was said before.

10.6.1 Coordinate Constructions and Ellipses

ACE constantly asks questions that may elicit coordinated and/or ellipsed answers. Thus, answers of the following types can be expected and must be analyzable by the input module:

"I am taking CS 110, MATH 133, ENGL 105, and ANTH 106."
"CS 110, MATH 133, ENGL 105, and ANTH 106."
"CS and 133 and ENGL."

Handling coordinate constructions properly requires a sophisticated dictionary definition of the word "and." Even with such a definition, however, only the first example would be analyzed to a complete answer. The others are examples of ellipses, which require some knowledge of the ongoing conversation (e. g., the question which was asked) to be understood completely. Thus, the conceptual analyzer needs to be able to use *expectations* about the conceptual form of an answer generated by the conversational parts of ACE to diagnose incomplete answers and return complete concepts.

10.6.2   Defining "And" for the Analyzer

Some of the problems that arise in the analysis of coordinate constructions were discussed in Section 5.4. Here one can see the same kinds of problems in a more general setting.

Sentences in which entities and concepts are linked by "and" are expected to be analyzable into ERKS structures with the following general form:

(coord con1 (...) con2 (...) ... con[n] (...)),

This is a slot-filler structure based upon a "coordination" of concepts, which are stored as the fillers of the slots labelled *con1, con2,* etc. The real-world coordinate relation may be logical, temporal, causal, or intentional, although the same English word "and" may be used. For example, the sentence "John walked down the street and Mary cried" becomes a "coordinated" concept containing subconcepts for "John walked" and "Mary cried." The implementation of the "and" definition waits until the end of the clause before taking action. This avoids potential problems that could occur if "and" were to work on "Marie tutored Jim and Jeff" before the appearance of "took CS 110." The only immediate action "and" takes is to keep track of any adjacent entities as they are formed. This is simpler to do than finding them later when they may already have filled a slot in a concept.

The following are examples of sentences that can be successfully analyzed by the definition of "and" provided with the NLP Toolkit. Each of them involves special cases and problems that had to be considered in the implementation of the definition.

Case 1: I took CS 110 and I took MATH 133.

It should first be noted that in this sentence "CS 110" is a concept represented by the academic-course script, *$course*. As in the sentence "John took a beating," the definition of "take" recognizes that the following concept provides the main action and that its own role is limited. In effect, the sentence is "I CS 110'ed and I MATH 133'ed." This is a simple example where "and" appears between two well-formed concepts. The definition of "and" simply waits for the concepts to be formed and then inserts them into a *coord* as *con1* and *con2.*

Case 2: I took CS 110 and MATH 133.

The goal is to analyze this sentence into the same representation as that for the first sentence. As in Case 1, the sentence will analyze to two concepts, but here the second one will be incomplete and not well formed: it will be missing its actor, and other slots such as mode and time will also be unfilled. The solution lies in using the complete concept located on the other side of "and" for the missing information. The empty slots can be filled by copying them from the complete concept.

Case 3: I had to buy a textbook and a lab manual.

The result of the analysis, without any action from "and," would be a well-formed concept on "and" 's left but only an entity to the right. "And" has to be able to convert entities like "lab manual" into appropriate concepts. This can be done by realizing that "textbook," the entity on the other side of "and," has been consumed by a concept and that "lab manual" should be imbedded in a similar concept. This is achieved by copying the existing concept and then substituting "lab manual" for "textbook" in the copy. Such substitutions are supported by the bookkeeping that is done by the basic analyzer function *fill-gap*.

Case 4: John took CS 110 and MATH 133 and Richard took CS 130.
Case 5: John took CS 110 and Steve and Richard took CS 130.
Case 6: John and Steve took CS 110 and MATH 133.
Case 7: John and Steve bought a book and a pencil.
Case 8: I took CS 110, MATH 133, and CHEM 127.

Additional capabilities allow for the analysis of these sentences. In the version supplied with the NLP Toolkit, "and" can handle multiple "ands" or commas, can choose the correct concept to copy when there is more than one, and can convert three fragments into four concepts.

10.6.3 Using Expectations during Analysis

Two different types of expectations are used to aid the analyzer in handling answers involving ellipses. Both require information to be passed by ACE to the analyzer. One is intended to help during the parsing of the input, while the other operates on the analyzer's result.

As an example of the former, when ACE is expecting an answer involving a course name, it supplies an expectation to the analyzer that "knows" that an unconsumed 3-digit number in the range [100-600] probably designates part of a course name. As a result, "I took 130" is analyzable, although the department name cannot be filled in.

ACE also sends the analyzer a copy of the expected answer (which is usually nearly identical to the representation of the question that was asked). When the expectation program has an expected answer, it compares it to the analyzed input and tries to return a result having the expected form. It does this by considering each available concept and trying to find a place for it in the expected answer concept.

In the normal case, all available concepts from the analyzer are compared against the expected answer. Generally, an attempt is made to fill in the expectation using the result of the analysis. This is done by trying to find a slot in the expected answer that can be filled by something having the same conceptual type as one of the concepts from the analysis. Suppose the question "Who are you?" is answered with "Icabodia Aidobaci," where the words "Icabodia Aidobaci" are unknown to the system. First, the expectation for a named person handles the unknowns in the input, yielding the following parsing result:

```
(person persname (Icabodia) surname (Aidobaci)
      gender (nil) convrole (nil))
```

This is then compared to the expected answer:

```
(a-config con1 (person persname (nil)
              surname (nil) convrole (*other))
          con2 (person persname (nil) surname (nil)
              convrole (nil))
          confrel (equiv))
```

Since there are two potential slots that the *person* concept can fill, each alternative is considered before *con2* is filled with the names. (The reason the *con2* slot is chosen is that this is the subconcept that carries the *question focus:* the place where the requested information is to go.)

When ACE asks, "What are you taking this semester?" the expected answer is a concept representing

"I am taking <course> and I am taking <course> ... and I am taking <course>"

In this situation, the diagnostic process proceeds as described above, but for one concept at a time. The answer "CS 110, MATH 133, and 106 and English" results in a coordinate concept with four subconcepts, two of which are incomplete.

Finally, many questions can be answered with a simple yes or no. In this case, the expected answer passed to the analyzer will still be in the form of a complete answer, since it must handle the possibility that the student will avoid the simple answer. ("Did you take CS 130?" "I took CS 110" or "CS 110" or "Last semester.") Whenever the answer is a simple yes/no, however, this is detected and the mode in the expected answer is modified appropriately.

10.7 More Problems in Language Generation

The other half of the natural language interface to ACE is responsible for generating the questions used to elicit information from the student, as well as to express responses to student questions. Whereas the analyzer must expand ellipsis and produce referents for entities mentioned in an input, the generator must produce concise, understandable output from a concept.

Question analyzing and answering are standard tasks that knowledge-based systems perform, since users usually want to obtain information or test the system's understanding. Since the answers to questions are usually not full concepts, the generator should be able to produce sentence fragments. For example, an answer to the question "When is CS110 being taught?" might be "At 3:00 on Mondays." The generator described in Chapter 6, a version of which is used by ACE, does not require a full concept as input (i.e., it has no notion of beginning generation from a category such as "sentence"). In ACE, the generator itself does not make the decision to produce the elided forms as answers to questions; that task is performed by the module responsible for determining the answer to a question.

Unlike question answering, question asking is a less common task for knowledge-based systems. In ACE, questions to the user come from the Strategist, STRAT. In the current version of ACE, the ERKS representations for the questions the system needs to ask are prestored and are associated with particular goals STRAT pursues. The kinds of questions STRAT needs to ask the user are of two general types. One type is designed to elicit specific information from the user when ACE knows the *type* of entity it needs to know about but not the *identity* of the entity. Examples of these questions are those ACE asks of the user regarding who he is or what courses he is taking. This kind of general information-seeking question can be distinguished from those that specifically attempt to find a slot filler for a case frame in an ERKS structure (cf. Lehn78). The question "What is the number of the CS course that you are taking?" is an example of the latter. As will be seen below, the generator treats these different types of questions in the same manner.

In a system like ACE, which makes no distinction between the conceptual forms used for reasoning and language processing, the generator is often faced with the task of having to perform reductions on some of the complex concepts it is handed, in order to produce acceptable English. STRAT, for example, must explicitly represent the concept that an actor is simultaneously participating in five courses, using five *different* concepts. These five separate actions, however, may have an economical English expression, such as "five courses", "CS 110, MATH 133, CHEM 128, ENGL 105, and HIST 101", or "five courses that you haven't flunked." (The process of reducing complex concepts in this way is discussed in Section 10.7.2 below.)

In the ACE microworld (and in most others), further complexity is added by the need to use possessive constructions and relative clauses to identify entities. Also, the system must be sensitive to the assumed location and absolute time (here, semesters) of events. A major problem is that the conceptual representations that seem to make sense for a reasoner do not always have an obvious mapping to surface English form (see, for example, the discussion of attributes in 10.7.3). Most of this complexity can be seen by consideration of the processing necessary for the expression of a typical question from the academic counseling domain:

> What are the names of the courses that you are taking in the spring semester of 1985 at UConn?

As we shall see, generating this question in a principled manner is very complex, indeed.

The following subsections will discuss the additions made to the generator described in Chapter 6 to enable it to handle problems like these. The basic task was to add sketchifiers for phenomena such as *wh-movement* for question generation, and *factoring* to reduce complex coordinate-concept relations. Sketchifiers were also devised to handle more cases of the possessive construction, as well as ones for handling absolute time and location expression. Being able to use the generator of Chapter 6 directly in ACE reinforced our belief that its overall design is quite robust.[3]

10.7.1   Asking Questions

Question asking begins when ACE, in order to elicit information from a student, fills out a question template as part of a goal achievement. The STRAT module has (a) a concept representing the information that must be known and (b) a set of paths into the concept that must be filled (usually by the answer to the question) in order for the goal achievement process to continue. For example, when a preregistration task is begun, the STRAT module "knows" (i.e., has a prestored concept) that to determine who a user is, it must find out his/her name. Also, when a student unknown to ACE attempts to preregister, ACE must determine his current schedule. Students, courses, teachers, and semesters can all be identified uniquely by their names.

For finding out who a user is, the STRAT module has a prestored concept represented as

```
(s-attr attr (tag tag1 (persname val (nil))
              tag3 (surname val (nil))
        actor *other))
```

that can be paraphrased roughly as "You have an attribute 'tag' with some unknown value." The focus of the question (i.e., the paths that must be filled for the question to be answered) is on the attribute value, namely on the *persname* and *surname* of the *(tag)* filler. If either of these fillers is known, such as the personal name, an attempt to determine the *surname* will result in the same concept being sent to the generator, this time with the question focus on the *surname* of the *(tag)* filler.

The job of the generator when presented with a concept containing a question focus is to find a question word and then to move it to the beginning of the sentence, i.e., to "front" it. (It does not have the capability to produce double questions, as in "Who ate what?"). The fronting process is performed by the *qfocus* (question focus) sketchifier, unless question focus is on the mode, in which case the verb-kernel routines discussed in Section 6.3.4 handle it. The operation of this sketchifier is simple. First, it pushes the current parent concept back onto the C-LIST, since the questioned part is going to become the current focus. It also marks, in that concept, that the filler of the slot that is the question focus need not be said later. (This prevents, for example, "How many cats do I have cats?"). Next, the *wh-phrase* that expresses the question is determined. This computation uses the slot that is pointed to by the question focus, the contents of the questioned slot, and the concept it is part of.

The first part of the wh-phrase is the *wh-word*. The qfocus sketchifier determines the wh-word using information about the slot where the questioned concept occurred and the questioned concept itself. Sometimes the questioned concept in a particular slot is spanned by one wh-word, as in "Who ate the pasta?" In this case "who" spans the meaning of person, i.e., it expresses "which person." Notice, however, that the slot where the questioned subconcept occurs can influence the choice of the wh-word. For example, if the concept for "which person" occurred in a *possby* slot, the appropriate choice would be "whose."

Some wh-words do not span the entire questioned concept, so the wh-word must be followed by a concept that further identifies the thing being asked about, as in "Whose cat is this?" This second part of the wh-phrase is the expression of the concept containing the slot pointed to by the qfocus. For example, "Whose cat is on the table?" begins

(p-config con1 (animal animtype (cat) possby (nil)) ...)

where the question focus is on the *(con1 possby)* slot. The wh-phrase "whose cat" is formed by saying "whose" followed by the expression of the filler of the *(con1)* slot.

The following illustrate how the wh-phrase is selected.

1. If a *possby* is being questioned, use "whose," followed by the possessed concept. Example:

   "Whose cat is on the table?"
   (p-config con1 (animal animtype (cat) possby (nil))

    con2 (support supptype (table))
    confrel (topof))

A concept with question focus on *(con1 possby)* creates a C-LIST item containing

"whose" (animal animtype (cat))

as the source of the wh-phrase.

2. If an *attr* slot is being questioned in an *s-attr,* just use "what." As we shall see in Section 10.7.3, this prevents "What name is your name?" from being generated.

3. If the filler being questioned can be expressed by the dictionary as "person" or "someone," use "who."

"Who goes to the city?"
(ptrans actor (person persname (nil))
       obj (person persname (nil))
       to (inside part (polity poltype (city))))

A concept with question focus *(actor)* creates the wh-phrase "who."

4. If a *compnum, grpnum,* or *tnum* is being questioned, use "how many," followed by the concept containing the slot. For example,

"How many oranges are in the bowl?"
(p-config con1 (group typmem (ingobj ingtype (orange)) grpnum
               (nil))
      con2 (container conttype (bowl))
      confrel (inside))

Thus, for example, a concept with question focus on *(con1 grpnum)* is expressed with a wh-phrase:

"how many" (group typmem (ingobj ingtype (orange)))

5. If a *ref* role is being questioned, use "which" followed by the concept containing the slot. For example, the form

"Which student took the exam?"
($exam actor (person eprole (&student) ref (nil)))

with question focus on *(actor ref)* leads to the C-LIST state:

"which" (person eprole (student) ref (nil))

6. If an empty *abstime* or *locale* slot is being questioned, use "when" or "where," respectively. For example, the concept

"When did you take the exam?"
($exam actor (person convrole (*other)) abstime (nil))

with question focus on *(abstime),* yields the wh-phrase "when."
7. The default case is to use the word "what," followed by the concept the question focus slot occurred within. This would produce, for example

"what city" (non empty locale)
"what idiot" (if question focus not on ref)

There are several things to note here. One is that this method of generating questions ties generation of the wh-phrase to the fronting of the wh-word. As a result, our generator cannot produce so-called "echo questions" such as "John went where?" as well as double wh-questions. Handling these cases, however, would require simple modifications to the sketchifier.

10.7.2 Producing Coordinate Constructions

In ACE, the reasoning system frequently constructs complexes of concepts that are related by temporal ordering, causality, or contrast. For example:

1) What courses have you flunked?
2) Mary and John are teaching CS 111.
3) You must take CS 207 then MATH 133.
4) Have you taken CS 110 and CHEM 128?
5) You should take CS 242 and EE 201 but not CS 383.

The generator must produce these concise forms from complex concepts, such as the following one for Sentence (5), above:

```
(coord con1 ($course actor *other
                 cno (num numval (242))
                 deptname (CS)
                 mode (modes mode1 (:t) mode2 (:urge)))
          con2 ($course actor *other
                 cno (num numval (201))
                 deptname (EE)
                 mode (modes mode1 (:t) mode2 (:urge)))
          con3 ($course actor *other
                 cno (num numval (383))
                 deptname (CS)
                 mode (modes mode1 (:neg) mode2 (:urge))))
```

This bit of advice would be constructed piecemeal by the Academic Scheduler, ASE, and it is up to the generator to recognize that this can be shortened to Sentence (5).

The *coordinate* sketchifier is responsible for recognizing and reducing such concepts. The recognition part is the most difficult, and the current implementation of the coordinate sketchifier handles only a fraction of all possible reductions. Recognizing that a reduction is available involves determining whether the imbedded concepts are similar enough that the common parts can be "factored out." When the varying parts are determined, they are gathered into a special ERKS "group" type. This group is then placed into a concept that represents the common parts of the complex concept, in the same slot that the varying concepts filled in their individual concepts.

To find the varying elements, the coordinate sketchifier attempts to discover a *single* path (or in one special case, paths) over which the individual concepts vary. The sketchifier provided with the NLP Toolkit recognizes four distinct cases.

In one case, the identity of the varying path is known, i.e., the sketchifier is simply told what it is. In Sentence (1), above, for example, the varying path is the question focus, handed to the generator with the question ACE wishes to ask. The second case occurs when the path can be determined by simple matching of each pair of imbedded concepts (Sentence 2). The third case is like the second, except that one concept is negated while the others are asserted (Sentence 5). Finally, the coordinate sketchifier recognizes one special case where more than one filler varies, yet a coordinate reduction can still occur, as in Sentences (3) and (4). I shall examine each case in turn.

In the simplest case, the varying path is known and is actually part of the ERKS representation. For example, suppose I know that you went to some cities on your vacation. The following (abbreviated) concept could be used to represent what I know about your vacation.

```
(coord con1 ($visit-city actor *other
                place (polity poltype (city) polname (nil))
                time (times time1 (:past)))
         compnum (!))
```

I've used *coord* here to connect the actions; they are coordinated in the sense that they all occurred on your vacation. Other possible connectives are *sequel, simul,* and *disj.* The *goalepisode, $visit-city,* represents the collection of things one does on a vacation in a city, such as staying in a hotel, visiting museums, and so on. The *compnum* (component number) filler is "!", which means that some unknown number (greater than one) of occurrences of *$visit-city* took place. This concept can be expressed as "You visited some cities," where the phrase "some cities" is derived from the coord and its "greater than one" component number. If I knew that you went to exactly three cities, I would have a representation for "three" in the *compnum* slot, and the corresponding assertion is "You visited three cities." In such cases, the coordinate sketchier expects that it will be told that the "varying" slot is *(con1 place)*.

Since the coordinate sketchifier has determined that a reduction is possible in this case, how is the concept modified to reflect this? In essence, the reduction process takes a relation among *full concepts* and changes it into a relation among *entities*. We have made up three special ERKS types to represent the common entity relations: *ent-coord, ent-disj* and *ent-sequel,* corresponding to the full concept relations *coord* (or *simul*), *disj* and *sequel.* So, our first example becomes

```
($visit-city actor *other
           place (ent-coord con1 (polity poltype (city) polname (nil))
                  compnum (!))
           time (times time1 (:past)))
```

and the dictionary entry for *ent-coord* produces the word "some," followed by the plural of "city." The "three cities" version of this concept is expressed without "some," since the cardinality of the concept is given by the component number in the *ent-coord* slot.

The simplest case in which the sketchifier recognizes a reduction on its own occurs when a concept obviously has one intrinsic role that varies. This can be detected by a factoring algorithm that tries to match each pair of imbedded concepts from the subconcepts of a *coord* or other composite *conrel* against each other, and discovers that they vary in one and only one role. Such a case occurs in

```
"John ate a bagel then a muffin"
(sequel con1 (ingest actor *john obj *bagel)
        con2 (ingest actor *john obj *muffin)
        compnum (2))
```

Once the *obj* slot is found to contain the varying element, this is turned into

```
(ingest actor *john obj (ent-sequel con1 *bagel con2 *muffin
                         compnum (2)))
```

Notice that in this case, the component number does *not* get expressed. The rule is that it is not expressed if the number of non-empty components is exactly the component number.

The next case is similar to the last except that, in one of the imbedded concepts, the *model* filler (which represents the truth or falsity of the concept) is negated. This produces reductions such as "John went to Hartford but not Storrs" from "John went to Hartford and John did not go to Storrs." If the coordinate sketchifier fails to find one single role in which a concept varies, it will try the pair matching again while ignoring the mode fillers. Then, if just one varying path is found, the negated concepts are collected and placed into the *con2* slot of a *neg-expect* concept (for negative expectancy). The asserted concepts are then grouped and placed into the *con1* filler of the same concept. The reduction of the concept given as the meaning of Sentence (5), above ("You should take CS 242 and EE 201 but not CS 383.") is

```
(neg-expect con1 (coord con1 ($course actor *other
                        cno (num numval (242))
                        deptname (CS)
                        mode (modes mode1 (:t)
                                mode2 (:urge)))
                 con2 ($course actor *other
                        cno (num numval (201))
                        deptname (EE)
                        mode (modes mode1 (:t)
                                mode2 (:urge))))
            con2 ($course actor *other
                    cno (num numval (383))
                    deptname (CS)
                    mode (modes mode1 (:t) mode2 (:urge))))
```

The concept that is now in the *con1* slot of the new concept is a *coord* (not an *ent-coord*), but observe that it does not vary on a single slot. We will see how the reduction of this imbedded *coord* is carried out, below.

In Examples (3) and (4) the reduction is computed based upon the *naming* roles of certain subconcepts. In the concept corresponding to the sentence "You should take CS 242 and EE 201,"

```
(coord con1 ($course actor *other
                cno (num numval (242))
                deptname (CS)
                mode (modes mode1 (:t) mode2 (:urge)))
       con2 ($course actor *other
                cno (num numval (201))
                deptname (EE)
                mode (modes mode1 (:t) mode2 (:urge))))
```

the varying roles are *(cno numval)* and *(deptname)*. Each of these is a naming role (or "surface slot") of the *goalepisode $course*. The generator knows to express these together to identify the course, and so a reduction is available on the basis of a coordination of names. (Section 10.7.3 discusses the method the generator uses to produce names such as "CS 242"). If the pairwise matcher finds more than one varying slot, it will check to see if they are all surface slots. If so, it will form a special ERKS structure called a *tag-coord* to represent the reduced name, as for example:

```
($course actor *other
        cno (num numval (tag-coord con1 (242) con2 (201))))
```

deptname (tag-coord con1 (CS) con2 (EE))
mode (modes mode1 (:t) mode2 (:urge)))

This description of the Toolkit's coordinate sketchifier represents only the beginning of a solution to the difficult problem of reducing similar concepts brought together in a complex concept. As mentioned before, the most difficult problem is recognizing when a reduction is possible. For example, how can the reduced form "John and Mary each ate a bagel" be produced? Compare this with "John and Mary ate a bagel."

10.7.3   Generating Attributes, Absolute Times, Locales, and Names

Some miscellaneous problems arose when we adapted the generator of Chapter 6 to the ACE microworld. These problems have to do with the expression of *attributes,* an alternative form of the *possessive* relation, the realization of *locale* and *absolute time* in context, and the generation of *named* concepts.

In English, it is common to express attributes of entities in two different ways: (a) as a predicate adjective, as in "Linda is sick," or (b) as a possessive form, as in "Linda's last name is Garrison." In the first form, the attribute *health,* together with its value, is spanned by the single word "sick," whereas in the second case the attribute "last name" must be mentioned explicitly. The second form is commonly used for surface slot attributes, i.e., for things such as names and titles. The *attribute* sketchifier is responsible for the possessive realization of certain very common attribute/value pairings.

Let's examine the generation of the sentence "Linda's last name is Garrison" to see how this works. This is represented as

(s-attr actor (person persname (Linda))
        attr (tags tag3 (surname val (Garrison))))

For the attribute sketchifier to be applicable, the attribute must have no other means of expression. That is, the dictionary cannot supply a spanning form such as "Linda is sick." If the dictionary cannot provide an entry, the sketchifier creates a new concept by placing the filler of the *actor* slot into the *possby* slot of the filler of the attr slot. Performing this on the concept above yields

(tags tag3 (surname val (Garrison)) possby (person persname (Linda)))

which is "Linda's last name Garrison." In this form, the generator would produce "Linda's last name Garrison is Garrison," which we clearly don't want! The solution is not to express the *value part* of the attribute. So the attribute sketchifier "empties" the attribute to produce

(tags tag3 (surname val (nil)) possby (person persname (Linda))) which is "Linda's last name." Now, since this concept should be said first, it is placed into the *actor* slot of the *s-attr,* yielding

```
(s-attr actor (tags tag3 (surname val (nil))
               possby (person persname (Linda)))
        attr (tags tag3 (surname val (Garrison)))
        mode (modes mode1 (:t))
        time (times time1 (:pres)))
```

There is a problem with the movement of concepts described above. If the *actor* is the question focus in the original concept, the question focus must be moved, too, since that concept has been placed in the role *actor possby*. This ensures that the question sketchifier will generate something like "Whose last name is Garrison?" from the question form of the above. Now we can see the rationalization for the question sketchifier's use of the wh-word "what" when asking about attributes, as described in Section 10.7.1. Consider the following form of the question "What is your name?" after the attribute sketchifier has modified it

```
(s-attr actor (tags tag1 (persname val (nil))
                    tag3 (surname val (nil))
               possby (person convrole (*other)))
        attr (tags tag1 (persname val (nil))
                   tag3 (surname val (nil))) ...)
```

Clearly, the generator should not produce "What name is your name?" from this!

Chapter 6 described how to handle the simple possessive forms that express "your name" and "her hand." An alternative form of the possessive uses the preposition "of," as in "the house of the king." This form is mandatory when the possessor concept is modified by a relative-clause subconcept, as in "the house of the man who would be king." Enabling the generator to recognize and handle this more complex case is a simple matter. The simple version of the possessive sketchifier shown in Figure 6.5 was modified so that it would not fire if the possessed concept contained a filled *rel* (relative clause) slot. Another possessive sketchifier was then added to handle exactly this case.

Suppose, for example, this sketchifier sees the concept associated with "the name of the animal that you own,"

```
(tags tag1 (animname val (nil))
      possby (animal rel (a-config con1 *other con2 "backpointer to
                          animal" confrel (poss))))
```

It first marks the *possby* filler in the *tags* concept as not needing to be said. The sketchifier then pushes a copy of the *possby* filler back onto the

C-LIST. The connecting word "of" is then added, which would make the resulting C-LIST structure look like

    (tags tag1 (animname val (nil)))
    "of"
    (animal rel (a-config con1 *other con2 "backpointer to animal"
                    confrel (poss)))

This would produce produce "the name of the animal that you own," in a straightforward manner. Relative clauses are generated by expressing the entity, here "animal," followed by the word "that" followed by the filler of the *rel* slot, less the entity mentioned earlier, i.e., "you own" rather than "you own the animal."

The sketchifiers that monitor the absolute time and location of episodes are equally simple. Since any action can have an absolute time or location, these sketchifiers watch for concepts in which these roles are included. The first time a location or absolute time is seen, it is extracted from the concept and placed after the concept. The sketchifier then "remembers" that it has expressed this and suppresses the expression of the time or location the next time through. So, for example, we get

Sherry went to the store yesterday. She bought lox.

where the absolute time ("yesterday") in the second concept is not expressed the second time. If the time or location changes, however, it will be expressed, as in, "Sherry went to the store yesterday. She went back today."

A final modification that was made for ACE was to enhance the generator's capability for expressing names (and to make it more efficient). Rather than letting the dictionary simply produce the standard ordering of the surface slots, as was described in Section 6.2, a "namer" sketchifier was added to monitor entities to see if they could be expressed simply by a name. The order of the surface slots as declared in the *def-ERKS-type* call for the underlying type dictates the ordering of the names. For the *person* type, for example, the order is *title, persname,* and *surname.* (Thus, "President Ronald Reagan.") If the namer finds a named entity that is not to be generated as a pronoun, it tries to form a name for it from the surface slot fillers. The namer gathers the symbols that fill all the surface slots, arranging to add "'s" to the last one if the name is to be used to express a possessor. If the fillers of the surface slots are not symbols, but some form of coordinate concept (e.g., *tag-coord,* from the operation of the coordinate sketchifier), the imbedded fillers are gathered from the respective coordinate concepts. So, for example, the following concept, which represents two named courses,

    ($course cno (num numval (tag-coord con1 (242) con2 (201))))

deptname (tag-coord con1 (CS) con2 (EE))
mode (modes mode1 (:t) mode3 (:nom)))

gets turned into

(tag-coord con1 (|CS 242|) con2 (|EE 201|))

which becomes "CS 242 and EE 201." (Actually, if the namer did not operate in this case, the result would be "CS and EE 242 and 201"!)

This general process of extracting the filled surface slots does not always work. In naming a course, for example, both the department name and course number must be present (or implied) for the course to be named properly. In the event one is not filled, the word "course" must be used, as in "the CS course" or "the 111 course." To prevent the namer from operating in these special cases, a "naming function" may be associated with a particular ERKS type (in this case, *$course*). If such a function is present, the namer will use it instead of simply gathering the fillers of the surface slots. The function may prevent a name from even being used by returning *nil*. For *$course,* then, we have the naming function

(lambda (ent) (if (or (empty '(cno numval)) (empty '(deptname)))
　　　　　　nil
　　　　　　(name-is ent)))

where *name-is* actually gathers up the naming symbols.

10.7　Putting It All Together: A Session with ACE

This penultimate section presents an annotated transcript of a session between ACE and a simulated first-semester freshman. The transcript has been edited slightly for readability. Lines beginning with ";" in the transcript are comments. The session is a typical preregistration, with inputs that are realistic, ellipsed, and ambiguous (at least in surface semantic terms).

Probably more detail is here than anyone wants to see. Its purpose is to illustrate forcefully the complicated interplay among language processing, knowledge base access, problem solving, and conversational control that must be managed in even the simple dialogs that transpire between advisors and students. The reader will thus understand how far we really have to go to produce robust, general purpose, intelligent computer conversationalists. I also will demonstrate that ACE, a typical huge, slow, and fragile AI program, contains rudimentary forms of many of the proper ingredients of that far-off system.

This is the third implementation of ACE, on a Pyramid 90x minicomputer running Berkeley 4.2 Unix. After some setup, the counselor is started with the *help-student-goal* as its top-level directive. DO-GOAL is the goal-achieving controller's main loop; it starts with the Strat(egist) process goal stack active. The steps in the plan for the *help-student-goal* are to "acquire" (i.e., wait around for) a student to talk to; decide on which task the student wants the system's help in; and actually to carry out that task, followed by the removal of the student from the active database and a re-invocation of the toplevel goal. (The ": =" operator in the second subgoal below is the Goal Achiever's analogue of the analyzer's run-time binding operator.) The "rest-of-and" construct is used to hold the remainder of the plan as the toplevel subgoal is pursued.

Script started on Fri Apr 5 14:25:39 1985
Franz Lisp, Opus 38
NLP Toolkit, Version 1.09...21 March 1985
TOOL-> (**)

Academic Counseling Experiment...Version 3.08
29 March 1985

DO-GOAL . . . . . . goal!Strat
(/goal help-student-goal)

DO-GOAL . . . . . . goal!Strat
(/and (/goal acquire-student-goal)
    (: = @task (/goal get-task-goal))
    (/goal do-task-goal @task)
    (/goal de-assert-other-exist-goal)
    (/goal help-student-goal))

DO-GOAL . . . . . . goal!Strat
(/goal acquire-student-goal)
(/rest-of-and (: = @task (/goal get-task-goal))
        (/goal do-task-goal @task)
        (/goal de-assert-other-exist-goal)
        (/goal help-student-goal))

Henceforth, I will show only the top of the active goal-stack. "Rest-of" type constructs hold the remaining plan steps. The first thing the system is told to achieve is to use the generator to announce itself to the world, and to indicate what it is prepared to do. Then, in anticipation that a student will soon arrive, ACE asserts the ERKS form bound to "sheshere!" in a SOT-managed per-session database.

DO-GOAL . . . . . . goal!Strat
(/code (speak start?)

```
     (setq :assert
        (append :assert (qckanon-add 'Fax '(sheshere!)))))
```

; The first form to be generated: a greeting noise
GEN: top of c-list
(greet actor (person convrole (*self)) to (person convrole (*other)))
assuming default focus actor for Dw142

GEN: using
(hello)

GEN:clist
(hello)

utterance is (hello)

GEN: top of c-list

; :parentcon stores the current top of clist; "p" is a pretty-printing utility
(p :parentcon)
(a-config con1
        (person convrole (*self))
        con2
        (person persname (ACE) surname (nil)
                ; the "episodic role" gives the system's role in this
                ; conversational episode, that of "counselor."
                eprole
                (person persname (nil) surname (nil) eprole
                                                (&acad-counsel)))
        confrel
        (equiv)
        time (times time1 (:pres)) mode (modes mode1 (:t)))

; As discussed in Section 6.3, the verb kernel routines in the dictionary
; lookup package have made the appropriate decisions about tensing
; and person/number agreement, by examining the form and the
; sentential focus
GEN: using
(am)

; The dictionary inserts the (con2) subcon following the lexeme...
inserting (nil c639 (c636 con2)) at:
((fo c636))

; ...and the (con1) subcon preceding
inserting (nil c637 (c636 con1)) at:
((pr c636))

GEN: top of c-list
(person convrole (*self))

; The entity reference demon arranges a pronominal form for the
; conversational role "self." It then places this entity into the NLP
; context of the current exchange frame.
entref pronizing conversational actor c637
entref updating nlp context with c637
(p c637)
(person ref (pron) case (subj) convrole (*self))

GEN: using
(I)
utterance is (I)
utterance is (I am)

GEN: top of c-list
(p :parentcon)
(person persname (ACE) surname (nil)
        ; This will be realized with an appositive
        eprole (person persname (nil) surname (nil)
                                        eprole (&acad-counsel)))

; Entref notices the unique named entity, "ACE"
entref def-izing unique entity c639
entref updating nlp context with c639

; The dictionary returns a zero morpheme to act as a pivot for the name
; lexeme, and arranges an appositive realization for the eprole filler.
; (This is a characteristic way in which appositives occur in English.)
; "cm" is the dictionary version of "comma," eventually realized as ",".
DICT result: Dw246 (nil)
((((nil c642 (c639 eprole)) (fo c639) (pr (funcword cm)) (fo (funcword cm)))
((((ACE) nil (c639 persname)) (pr c639) (pr (c639 surname)))))

GEN: using
(nil)
utterance is (I am ACE)
utterance is (I am ACE cm)

GEN: top of c-list
(person persname (nil) surname (nil) eprole (&acad-counsel))

; This undistinguished entity will be realized indefinitely
entref indef-izing entity as default c642
entref updating nlp context with c642
(p c642)
(person ref (indef) persname (nil) surname (nil) eprole (&acad-counsel))

GEN: using
(academic counsellor)

; The indefinite fragment goes first
GEN: top of c-list
(indef)

GEN: using
(a)

utterance is (I am ACE cm a)
utterance is (I am ACE cm a academic counsellor)
utterance is (I am ACE cm a academic counsellor cm)

I'M SAYING:
; This actually goes to the external terminal
Hello. I am ACE, an academic counsellor.

; Here, ACE asserts the student's presence. SOT builds a discrimination
; sub-tree for the form
do-Node: built node Fax21
do-Node: built node Fax150
do-Node: built node Fax149

Next the system needs to find out what the student wants. First it announces what it can do; then it asks what the student wants, and uses the form returned by the analyzer to conduct a pattern-directed search of its plan database. (The version of the analyzer running here is called APE, the Academic Parsing Expert.) The "registration" concept imbedded in the goal stative that the system "hallucinates" when it sees the user input "to preregister" triggers the *prereg-goal*.

DO-GOAL . . . . . . goal!Strat
(/rest-of-and (: = @task (/goal get-task-goal))
        (/goal do-task-goal @task)
        (/goal de-assert-other-exist-goal)
        (/goal help-student-goal))

DO-GOAL . . . . . . goal!Strat
(: = @task (/goal get-task-goal))
DO-GOAL . . . . . . goal!Strat
(/goal get-task-goal)
DO-GOAL . . . . . . goal!Strat

; The idea is to "brag" about what we can do, use the exchange manager
; to get a user response, and try to recognize that; failing this,

```
; "apologize," and try again
(/or (/and (/code (speak brag!))
      (: = @response (/code (ace-xchange 'task?)))
      (/goal recognize-task-goal task? @response nil))
   (/try (/code (apologize)) (/goal get-task-goal)))

DO-GOAL . . . . . . goal!Strat
(/and (/code (speak brag!))
      (: = @response (/code (ace-xchange 'task?)))
      (/goal recognize-task-goal task? @response nil))
DO-GOAL . . . . . . goal!Strat
(/code (speak brag!))

GEN: top of c-list
(p :parentcon)

; We can do two things:
(coord con1
      ; (1) answer the user's questions
      (mtrans actor (person convrole (*self))
            mode (modes mode1 (:t)    mode2 (:ablty))
      time (times time1 (:pres)) from (cp part c672)
      to (cp part (person convrole (*other)))
      mobj
      (s-goal actor c672 time (times time3 (:tf))
            mobj (mtrans actor c681 to (cp part c672)
                  from (cp part c681)
                  mobj
                  ; this dubious form represents "questions"
                  (infostruc itype (question) compnum (plural)
                        ref (!indef)))))
      compnum (2)
      con2
      ; or (2) be the student's agent in a goal-realization episode in which
      ; the university authorizes the student to take a course in the Fall
      ; semester, i.e., "preregister" the student.
      (grc con1
            (a-config confrel (agent-of) con1 (person convrole c673)
                  con2 (person convrole c682))
            con2
            (auth actor c698
                  semester (timdur durtype (semester) durname (Fall))
                  mobj ($course actor c698) time (times time1 c678)
                  mode (modes mode1 (:t)))
            time c704 mode (modes mode2 (:ablty) mode1 (:t)))))
```

; The toplevel coord gets realized as a zero morpheme, which positions
; the function word "and"
GEN: using
(nil)

inserting (nil c694 (c670 con2)) at:
((fo c670) (fo (funcword and)) (pr (c670 con3)))

inserting (nil c671 (c670 con1)) at:
((fo c670) (pr (c670 con2)))

GEN: top of c-list
(p :parentcon)
(mtrans actor (person convrole (*self))
      mode (modes mode1 (:t) mode2 (:ablty)) time (times time1 (:pres))
      from (cp part c672) to (cp part (person convrole (*other)))
      mobj
      (s-goal actor c672 time (times time3 (:tf))
            mobj
            (mtrans actor c681 to (cp part c672) from (cp part c681)
                  mobj
                  (infostruc itype (question) compnum (plural)
                        ref (!indef)))))

; The (mode mode2) filler "ability" gets realized as "can"
GEN: using
(can answer)

; The rest of the output follows straightforwardly
GEN: using
(I)
utterance is (I)
utterance is (I can answer)

; It would be better to say "your questions." Can't quite see how to do
; it.
GEN: using
(questions)
utterance is (I can answer questions)
utterance is (I can answer questions and)

GEN: using
(can help)

GEN: using
(I)
utterance is (I can answer questions and I)
utterance is (I can answer questions and I can help)

GEN: using
(you)

; The infinitival complement was created by the dictionary definition of
; "help." A sketchifying operation would have worked as well.
; Note, however, that the standard "sk-inf," as discussed in Section 6.4.1
; does not apply. The top-level concept is a goal-realization conrel,
; not a mental act. An analogous sketchifier could be written for
; these cases.
utterance is (I can answer questions and I can help you)
utterance is (I can answer questions and I can help you to)

GEN: using
(preregister)
utterance is (I can answer questions and I can help you to preregister)
utterance is (I can answer questions and I can help you to preregister for)

GEN: using
(semester)

GEN: using
(the)
utterance is (I can answer questions and I can help you to preregister for
    the)
utterance is (I can answer questions and I can help you to preregister for
    the Fall)
utterance is (I can answer questions and I can help you to preregister for
    the Fall semester)

I'M SAYING:
; The user sees...
I can answer questions and I can help you to preregister for the Fall
    semester.

; Now for a question and answer exchange with the user
DO-GOAL . . . . . . goal!Strat
(/rest-of-and (: = @ response (/code (ace-xchange 'task?)))
        (/goal recognize-task-goal task? @ response nil))

DO-GOAL . . . . . . goal!Strat
(: = @ response (/code (ace-xchange 'task?)))

DO-GOAL . . . . . . goal!Strat
(/code (ace-xchange 'task?))

; The question is "what episode is it your intention to carry out?"
; "Episode" will be loosely paraphrased as "task."
GEN: top of c-list
(p :parentcon)

```
(s-goal actor (person convrole (*other))
       mobj (episode actor c758 mode (modes mode1 (:t)))
       time (times time1 (:past)) mode (modes mode2 (:intnt) mode1 (:t)))
```

Next is the first question the system is asking, so that in addition to the standard sentential focus, we have to arrange for the proper realization of the question focus subconcept. The q(uestion) focus demon shifts the sentential focus to the *(mobj)* filler of the goal stative. It computes the appropriate wh-word for this concept based on semantic features such as higher-animate vs. physical object. This computation also uses the nature of the path to the focused-on subcon, so that, for example, "whose" can be used rather than "who" if the subcon is a "possessor" concept. The wh-word is fronted, i.e., said immediately. In some cases, the wh-word encompasses the entire meaning of the qfocussed subcon, e.g., "who" expresses "what person." Sometimes, as in this case, some meaning is left over. Here the demon needs to nominalize [(mode mode3) = :nom] a copy of the episode in the *(mobj)* slot so it gets the proper noun form. A similar process is needed for the movement of wh-pronouns in subclauses.

---

qfocus: examining question concept c757 with ((mobj)) qfocus

; Entref adds the nominalized "task" to the NLP context
entref updating nlp context with c768

```
(p :parentcon)
(episode ref (nil) actor (person convrole (*other))
        mode (modes mode3 (:nom)))
```

GEN: using
(task)
utterance is (what task)

; Now the goal stative reappears, with "do" left over in the (mobj) slot
GEN: top of c-list
(p :parentcon)

```
(s-goal actor (person convrole (*other))
       mobj (episode actor c758 mode (modes mode1 (:t)))
       time (times time1 (:past)) mode (modes mode2 (:intnt) mode1 (:t)))
```

; The infinitival sketchifier arranges for the appropriate realization of the
; imbedded complement
inf: pushing infized embedded sent

GEN: using
(want)

GEN: using
(you)
utterance is (what task would you)
utterance is (what task would you want)

; Here is the infinitive complement. Notice that the actor has been marked
; (by the entref demon, in an operation not shown) as having subjective
; case. The reason for this is that the focus demon has placed the
; sub-sentential focus on this concept.
GEN: top of c-list
(episode time (times time1 (:infize))
        actor (person ref (pron) case (subj) convrole (*other))
        mode (modes mode1 (:t)))

GEN: using
(to do)
utterance is (what task would you want to do)

; The query to the user...and the user's response
I'M SAYING:
What task would you want to do?
input:
to preregister

; I have edited out the initial pool consideration steps.
; After APE has read the words, and "to" has grabbed its prepconst, we
; have:
Available: (c791)
(p c791)
(prepconst prep (to)
        mynom
        (auth mode (modes mode1 (:t))
            mobj
            ($course actor (nil) student c799
                    mode (modes mode2 (:ablty))))
        canbuild
        (nil))

When we reach a clausepoint (e.g., at the end of a sentence) and the
pools become quiescent, "to" notices it's still available, and unilaterally
creates a goal stative in which to imbed its constituent. This is a (fairly
dubious) example of an ellipsis expansion carried out within the surface

semantics itself. The expansion could also have been done by the clausepoint diagnostic request (which we will see running shortly), by comparing the actual response to the goal-stative form of the query.

APE: repeat pool consideration at clp after quiesence

; "Register" is looking for an actor, an abstime, and a course
APE: considering gapreq pool: ap3 (ar5 ar6 ar7) register

APE: considering gapreq pool: ap4 (ar8 ar9) to

TO: hallucinating a goal stative
Executed ar9
Available: (c804 c803)
(p c804)
(s-goal mobj
    (auth mode (modes mode1 (:t))
       mobj
      ($course actor (nil) student c799
            mode (modes mode2 (:ablty))))
    mode
    (modes mode1 (:t)))

APE: repeat pool consideration at clp after quiesence

When the pools become quiescent again, the diagreq/shipreq pool of PR (the sentence-ending period) looks at the result in the context of the question form that was used to generate the query. It sees that they have the same form, and passes the result on to the conversational parts of the system.

APE: considering diagreq pool: ap7 (ar14) PR

CLP: examining parse result: (c804)
in expectation context task?
CLP: cons at same level
CLP: result con: c804
Executed ar14

APE: sentence:
(to preregister pr)
result: (c804)

At last, we have a user input we can use to find a plan that will yield what the user wants. The plan search yields the *prereg-goal,* and Strat gains control to execute it.

```
DO-GOAL . . . . . . goal!Strat
(/rest-of-and (/goal recognize-task-goal task? c804 nil) . . .)

DO-GOAL . . . . . . goal!Strat
(/goal recognize-task-goal task? c804 nil)

DO-GOAL . . . . . . goal!Strat
; Either the user has responded to our question with a question, or
; we have (we hope!) a responsive answer...
(/or (/and (/code (get 'c804 'qfocus))
        ; Here we call the QA expert, if necessary
        (/code '(/goal answer-question-goal c804)))
    ; This clause forms the database search state for the plan look-up
    (/and (/code
        (setq :searchstate (form-goal 'task? 'c804 nil)))
        (: = @ goal (/code (car :searchstate)))
        (/code (setq :searchstate (cdr :searchstate)) t)
        ; The resulting plan gets substituted and executed here
        @ goal)
    ; If we don't get a reasonable plan, iterate on other plans
    ; available from the database; there may be more than one plan
    ; which satisfies the expressed goal
    (/goal recognize-task-goal task? c804 :searchstate))

; Eventually, the form-goal process yields the prereg-goal
DO-GOAL . . . . . . goal!Strat
(/goal prereg-goal nil nil)

; This has the plan steps: set up the next schedule, tell the student what
; it is, then answer any further questions.
DO-GOAL . . . . . . goal!Strat
(/try (: = nextsched (/goal find-next-sched nil '*other))
    (/goal tell-student-sched nextsched)
    (/goal update-acad-record nil nextsched)
    (/goal field-questions))

DO-GOAL . . . . . . goal!Strat
(: = nextsched (/goal find-next-sched nil '*other))

DO-GOAL . . . . . . goal!Strat
(/goal find-next-sched nil '*other)
```

; Find-next-sched has these plan steps: find out who the student is (we're

; assuming he's a first-semester freshman); get his current schedule; ; and
use that to compute a reasonable next-schedule.
DO-GOAL . . . . . . goal!Strat
(/try (/goal get-student nil '*other)
    (/goal get-cur-sched)
    (: = @ next-sched (/goal new-schedule))
    (/code '@ next-sched))

DO-GOAL . . . . . . goal!Strat
(/goal get-student nil '*other)

DO-GOAL . . . . . . goal!Strat
    ; We can either already know who the student is (if we got his
    ; name as a side-effect of a prior task — that didn't happen here) or
    ; we need to "find out" the information by asking "what is your
    ; name?"
(/condgoal (/test nil)
       (/goal assert-student nil)
       (/test t)
       (/try (: = @ who (/goal find-out name? '*other))
          (/goal assert-student @ who)))

Eventually, we embark on the find-out goal. Find-out is a general-purpose information acquisition goal that attempts to get a form that has the data required by a template (i.e., question) form. Here, the find-out is directed at the user (*other). Find-out can also retrieve from the system's own memory of facts and rules.

DO-GOAL . . . . . . goal!Strat
(/goal find-out name? '*other)

; The steps in a find-out of this sort are to ask a user a question, then
; determine a complete response to that question, according to the
; demands for information encoded in the question
DO-GOAL . . . . . . goal!Strat
(/try (: = @ answer (/goal ask-goal name? '*other))
       ; This goal is the interface to the Tactician expert
    (/goal assure-complete-response name? @ answer))

DO-GOAL . . . . . . goal!Strat
(/goal ask-goal name? '*other))

```
; The plan steps for this ask-goal involve another use of the exchange
; manager
DO-GOAL . . . . . . goal!Strat
(/condgoal (/test (equal '*other '*other))
        (/code (ace-xchange 'name?))
        (/test t)
        (/code (call-expert '*other (/goal name?)))))

DO-GOAL . . . . . . goal!Strat
(/code (ace-xchange 'name?))

; This is a naming form, with qfocus on the (attr) slot
GEN: top of c-list
(p :parentcon)
(s-attr actor (person convrole (*other))
        attr
        (tags tag1 (persname val (nil)) tag2 (middname val (nil))
             tag3 (surname val (nil)) tag4 (title val (nil)))
        time (times time1 (:pres)) mode (modes mode1 (:t)))

; Sentential focus defaults to the (actor) subcon
assuming default focus actor for Dw193
```

Something very complicated (but principled) happens here! Attributionals are characteristically expressed in English by "<entity> is <attribute>" constructions, as in "John is sick." Unfortunately, not all attributes have simple adjectival realizations. For our current example, we would need something like "I am named John." In such cases, an alternative form is possible: "My name is John." Here, we break out the bare attribute, possessivize it with the entity, and make it the (actor) filler of the attributional. Then we can express the *attribute value(s)* separately. The operations I just described are not easily implemented in the simple dictionary look-up and insertion machinery we have, so we've implemented an *s-attr* demon that first probes the dictionary to see if the given *s-attr* form can be expressed. If this fails, the demon modifies the attributional concept in the characteristic way.

At the same time, it must arrange that the qfocus property is properly set, so the qfocus demon will work, and front an appropriate wh-pronoun.

```
s-attr: examining attribute concept c818
; The dictionary probe fails, so we form the alternative construction
PROBE-DICT: no entries exist for c818
s-attr: modifying qfocussed attr
```

qfocus: examining question concept c818 with ((attr)) qfocus
; As a result of the qfocus operation, the fronted (empty) attribute value
; concept is looked up first and maps into the zero morpheme, (nil).
; As discussed in Section 10.7, we don't want to say "what name is your
; name."
DICT to match:
(attrval ref (nil) tag1 (persname val (nil)) tag2 (nil)
     tag3 (surname val (nil)) tag4 (nil))
DICT result: Dw106 (nil)

GEN: using
(nil)
utterance is (what)

GEN: top of c-list
(p :parentcon)
(s-attr actor
     (tags possby (person convrole (*other)) tag1 (persname val (nil))
       tag2 (nil) tag3 (surname val (nil)) tag4 (nil))
     attr
     (attrval ref (nil) tag1 (persname val (nil))
       tag2 (nil) tag3 (surname val (nil)) tag4 (nil))
     time (times time1 (:pres)) mode (modes mode1 (:t)))

; The zero morpheme corresponding to "is" appears
GEN: using
(nil)
utterance is (what is)

GEN: top of c-list
(tags possby (person convrole (*other)) tag1 (persname val (nil))
    tag2 (nil) tag3 (surname val (nil)) tag4 (nil))

; The possessive sketchifier notices that the tags are possessed-by
; someone. This entity gets moved to the top.
poss rule forming possessive of
(person convrole (*other))

entref pronizing conversational actor c819
entref updating nlp context with c819
(person ref (pron) case (poss) convrole (*other))

GEN: using
(your)

GEN: top of c-list
(tags ref (nil) tag1 (persname val (nil)) tag2 (nil)
    tag3 (surname val (nil)) tag4 (nil))

GEN: using
(name)
utterance is (what is your name)

I'M SAYING:
What is your name?
input:
I am Ronald McDonald

; These are "named" requests which will turn certain ambiguous or
; incomplete concepts into things that the system desires.
; Such requests are stored with the high-level expectations (i.e., ERKS
; forms) that the Strategist placed in the exchange frame.
APE: activating memory requests (exppers expcourse expcoursenum)

APE: new word is i

Executed ar20
Available: (c876)
(p c876)
(person persname (nil) surname (nil) ref (pron) gender (nil)
        convrole (*other) case (nil))

APE: new word is be

; "Be" puts its vel on the CLIST
Executed ar21
Available: (c884 c876)
(p c884)
(vel v4
    ; "...is prerequisite"
    (nil)
    v3
    ; "...is in the pool"
    (p-config mode (modes model (:t)))
    v2
    ; "...is sick"
    (s-attr mode (modes model (:t)))
    v1
    ; "...is a student"
    (a-config confrel (equiv) mode (modes model (:t))))

; "Be" decides it isn't a question-form
APE: considering os-gapreq pool: ap13 (ar24) be
Executed ar24
Available: (c884 c876)

; The lexeme "McDonald" is unknown to the analyzer's dictionary.
APE: didn't find McDonald

APE: new word is Ronald

Executed ar34
Available: (c897 c884 c876)

APE: new word is symbol0

Executed ar38
Available: (c900 c897 c884 c876)
(unknown lexval (McDonald))

APE: new word is pr

; "Ronald" picks up the unknown as surname
Executed ar36
Available: (c897 c884 c876)
(p c897)
(person surname (McDonald) persname (Ronald) gender (masc))

; "Be" eventually sees that it is surrounded by cognate entities, so it
; posits an equivalence relation between them.
BE: equiv relation between c897 and c876
VEL: disambiguated c884 as c885
(a-config confrel (equiv) mode (modes mode1 (:t)))

; The compressed "be" concept:
Executed ar44
Available: (c903 c885)
(p c885)
(a-config con1
        (person persname (nil) surname (nil) ref (pron)
                gender (nil) convrole (*other) case (nil))
        con2
        (person surname (McDonald) persname (Ronald) gender (masc))
        confrel (equiv)
        mode (modes mode1 (:t)))

The clausepoint diagnostic notices that the form of the response (an
a-config) is nothing like the expectation (an s-attr). We expect trouble!!

CLP: examining parse result: (c885)
in expectation context name?
CLP: single unmergable result
CLP: result con: c885

APE: sentence:
(I am Ronald McDonald pr)
result:(c885)

; The controller continues, placing the Tactician in charge.
DO-GOAL . . . . . . goal!Strat
(/rest-of-try (/goal assure-complete-response name? c885))

DO-GOAL . . . . . . goal!Strat
(/goal assure-complete-response name? c885)

DO-GOAL . . . . . . goal!Strat
(/code
(let ((copyques (copy-con 'name?)))

    (check-response copyques
          'c885
          (copy-con 'name?)
          (get copyques 'expects)))))
CHECK-RESPONSE PARAMETERS:
; The question/expectation:
QUES:
(s-attr actor (person convrole (*other))
       attr (tags tag1 (persname val (nil)) tag2 (middname val (nil))
              tag3 (surname val (nil)) tag4 (title val (nil)))
       time (times time1 (:pres)) mode (modes mode1 (:t)))
; The user response:
ANS:
(a-config con1 (person persname (nil) surname (nil) ref (pron) gender (nil)
                convrole (*other) case (nil))
       con2 (person surname (McDonald) persname (Ronald)
                gender (masc))
       confrel (equiv) mode (modes mode1 (:t)))

Check-response is the Tactician's top level. It sees no direct way to reconcile the user response with the only expectation about that response it has been given, i.e., the form of the question. Here, we can see a need for general-purpose reasoning power. Is there any way the answer can be connected to the question? The Tactician calls YADR with this query, using the "consistent-with" interface as discussed in Chapter 9.

YADR: checking consistency of c952 with:
(c885)

; YADR starts by asserting the response "I am Ronald McDonald" to the

```
; facts DB.
do-Node: built node Fax151

; Next it computes any available if-added type facts
INFER: computing if-added facts for Faxw107
infer: found (ifaw1)

; One available if-added method, the so-called equiv-exist-rule, says:
; "if one person is asserted to be equivalent to another, then if the
; first one exists, the second one does, too."
(p (get-structure 'ifaw1))
(implies con1
        (a-config mode (modes model (:t)) confrel (equiv)
                con1 (person) con2 (person))
        con2
        (implies con1
                (s-attr mode (modes model (:t)) actor (person) attr (exist))
                con2
                (s-attr time (nil) abstime (nil) rel (nil) locale (nil)
                        mode (modes model (:t)) actor (person) attr (exist)))))

; From this method and the assertion "I am Ronald M." we get the
; assertion "Ronald exists," since we asserted "other exists" when the
; session started.
(p (get-structure 'Faxw108))
(s-attr time (nil) abstime (nil) rel (nil) locale (nil) mode (modes model (:t))
        actor (person surname (McDonald) persname (Ronald)
                        gender (masc))
        attr (exist))

; Assert "Ronald exists"
do-Node: built node Fax152

YADR: primers:(Faxw107 Faxw108)

; Now start the back-chainer itself; can we directly retrieve the probe?
YADR: looking for: c952

(p c952)
(s-attr actor
        (person convrole (*other))
        attr
        (tags tag1 (persname val (nil)) tag2 (middname val (nil))
                tag3 (surname val (nil)) tag4 (title val (nil)))
        mode (modes model (:t)))

; No. Are there back-chaining rules?
RUN-RULE: looking for:
```

(implies con1 (nil)
  con2 (s-attr actor (person convrole (*other))
     attr (tags tag1 (persname val (nil)) tag2 (middname val (nil))
      tag3 (surname val (nil)) tag4 (title val (nil)))
    mode (modes mode1 (:t))))

; Yes, there are two.
RUN-RULE: found rules
(ifnw34 ifnw33)

; This one, the equiv-attr-rule, says:
; "if two people are equivalent and one is named, the other has
; the same name"
(p (get-structure 'ifnw34))
(implies con1
  (conj con1
    (a-config mode (modes mode1 (:t)) confrel (equiv)
      con1 (person convrole (*other))
      con2 (person persname (nil) surname (nil)))
    con2
    (s-attr mode (modes mode1 (:t))
      actor (person persname (nil) surname (nil))
      attr
      (tags possby (nil) tag1 (persname val (nil))
       tag2 (middname val (nil))
       tag3 (surname val (nil))
       tag4 (title val (nil)))))
  con2
  (s-attr time (nil) abstime (nil) rel (nil) locale (nil)
    mode (modes mode2 (nil) mode3 (nil) mode1 (:t))
    actor
    (person persname (nil) middname (nil) surname (nil)
      title (nil) standing (nil) eprole (nil)
      age (nil) gender (nil) ref (nil)
      rel (nil) agent-of (nil) case (nil)
      convrole (*other))
    attr
    (tags possby (nil) tag1 (persname val (nil))
     tag2 (middname val (nil)) tag3 (surname val (nil))
     tag4 (title val (nil)))))

; The other, the exist-attr-rule, says "if a person exists, he/she has a
; name"
(p (get-structure 'ifnw33))
(implies con1

```
(s-attr mode (modes model (:t))
      actor
      (person gender (nil) persname (nil) surname (nil)
            middname (nil) title (nil) eprole (nil)
            convrole (nil))
      attr (exist))
con2
(s-attr time (nil) abstime (nil) rel (nil) locale (nil)
      mode (modes mode2 (nil) mode3 (nil) model (:t))
      actor (person gender (nil) persname (nil)
            surname (nil) middname (nil)
            title (nil) eprole (nil) convrole (nil))
      attr (tags possby (nil) tag1 (persname val (nil))
      tag2 (middname val (nil)) tag3 (surname val (nil))
      tag4 (title val (nil)))))
```

At this point, it should be clear that this is an illustrative example only: I have put in only what rules I need to build the (somewhat contrived) inference chain I want. Many other rules that would allow a conclusion about a name to be drawn can be imagined, and should be present in a general reasoning system. This rule set, however, will serve to indicate the main phenomena. YADR is called recursively from Run-Rule with the antecedent of the equiv-attr-rule. The system notices that the antecedent is a conjunction, and attempts to prove each conjunct in turn.

```
YADR: looking for: c969
(p 'c969)
(conj con1
    (a-config mode (modes model (:t)) confrel (equiv)
          con1 (person convrole (*other))
          con2 (person persname (nil) surname (nil)))
    con2
    (s-attr mode (modes model (:t)) actor (person persname (nil)
                                                surname (nil))
          attr
          (tags tag1 (persname val (nil)) tag2 (middname val (nil))
              tag3 (surname val (nil)) tag4 (title val (nil)))))
```

YADR: examining and/or concept

; First it looks to see if "other is equiv to someone" has been asserted
YADR: looking for: c970
(p c970)

```
(a-config mode (modes mode1 (:t)) confrel (equiv)
        con1 (person convrole (*other))
        con2 (person persname (nil) surname (nil)))
```

; It finds the "I am Ronald M." assertion
YADR: found fact(s) for probe:
(Faxw107)
(p (get-structure 'Faxw107))
```
(a-config con1 (person persname (nil) surname (nil) gender (nil)
               convrole (*other) case (nil))
        con2 (person surname (McDonald) persname (Ronald)
                                        gender (masc))
        confrel (equiv) mode (modes mode1 (:t)))
```

; Next it looks for "someone has a name"
YADR: looking for: c979
```
(s-attr mode (modes mode1 (:t)) actor (person persname (nil) surname
                                                        (nil))
   attr (tags tag1 (persname val (nil)) tag2 (middname val (nil))
        tag3 (surname val (nil)) tag4 (title val (nil))))
```

; No such concept is stored (naming concepts exist only for specific
; people), so Run-Rule is called again to see if we can find a rule from
; which we can deduce "someone has a name"
RUN-RULE: looking for:
```
(implies con1 (nil)
   con2 (s-attr mode (modes mode1 (:t)) actor (person persname (nil)
                                                    surname (nil))
        attr (tags tag1 (persname val (nil)) tag2 (middname val (nil))
             tag3 (surname val (nil)) tag4 (title val (nil))))))
```

Next something interesting happens. Run-Rule finds *exist-attr-rule* and *equiv-attr-rule* again. It notices that *equiv-attr-rule* is being accessed with a set of variable bindings that have been used before, that is, that it is in a loop. Back-chaining through this rule is thus suppressed, and the system picks up again with most recent available rule, the *exist-attr-rule*. This says to find all the persons that "exist." For ACE, the only people who exist are the members of the Computer Science faculty and the student it's talking to now.

RUN-RULE: found rules
(ifnw34 ifnw33)

; Reject ifnw34: it's being reused with the same bindings
RUN-RULE: avoiding loop with rule ifnw34
and bindings:
((?var14 (tags tag1 c947 tag2 c949 tag3 c951 tag4 c953)) (?var13 (nil))
                                                                    (?var12 (nil)))

; Search instead for the antecedent of ifnw33, the exist-attr-rule:
YADR: looking for: c1060
(s-attr mode (modes mode1 (:t))
       actor (person gender (nil) persname (nil) surname (nil)
                    middname (nil) title (nil) eprole (nil) convrole (nil))
       attr (exist))

YADR: found fact(s) for probe:
(Faxw108 Faxw79 Faxw78 Faxw77 Faxw76
Faxw75 Faxw74 Faxw73 Faxw72 Faxw71
Faxw70 Faxw69 Faxw68 Faxw67 Faxw66
Faxw65 Faxw64 Faxw63 Faxw62 Faxw61
Faxw60 Faxw59 Faxw58 Faxw57)

RUN-RULE proved:
((c1099 c1139 c1179 c1219 c1259 c1299
c1339 c1379 c1419 c1459 c1499 c1539
c1579 c1619 c1659 c1699 c1739 c1779
c1819 c1859 c1899 c1939 c1979 c2019))

(p (get-structure 'c1099))
;Ronald M. exists, and therefore has a name:
(implies con1
      (s-attr mode
            (modes mode1 (:t))
            actor
            (person gender (masc)
                    persname (Ronald) surname (McDonald) middname
                                                                    (nil)
                    title (nil) eprole (nil) convrole (nil))
            attr (exist))
      con2
      (s-attr time (nil) abstime (nil) rel (nil) locale (nil)
            mode (modes mode2 (nil) mode3 (nil) mode1 (:t))
            actor
            (person gender (masc) persname (Ronald) surname
                                                                (McDonald)
                    middname (nil) title (nil) eprole (nil) convrole (nil))
            attr
            (tags possby (nil) tag1 (persname val (Ronald)))

```
              tag2 (middname val (nil)) tag3 (surname val (McDonald))
              tag4 (title val (nil)))))
```

; ...but so does, for example, Yaron Gold, a faculty person:
```
(p (get-structure 'c1499))
(implies con1
     (s-attr mode
              (modes mode1 (:t))
              actor
              (person gender (masc) persname (Yaron) surname (Gold)
                   middname (nil) title (Prof) eprole (&teacher)
                   convrole (nil))
              attr
              (exist))
     con2
     (s-attr time (nil) abstime (nil) rel (nil) locale (nil)
              mode (modes mode2 (nil) mode3 (nil) mode1 (:t))
              actor
              (person gender (masc) persname (Yaron) surname (Gold)
                                                    middname (nil)
                   title (Prof) eprole (&teacher) convrole (nil))
              attr
              (tags possby (nil) tag1 (persname val (Yaron))
                   tag2 (middname val (nil)) tag3 (surname val (Gold))
                   tag4 (title val (Prof))))))
```

YADR deduced fact(s):
```
(c1112 c1152 c1192 c1232 c1272 c1312
c1352 c1392 c1432 c1472 c1512 c1552
c1592 c1632 c1672 c1712 c1752 c1792
c1832 c1872 c1912 c1952 c1992 c2032)
```

; So a possible conjunction of the "who is equiv to the *other" and "who
; has a name" is "Ronald McDonald," since that's the only pair of
; fact-forms for which the surname and persname unify properly
```
(provable-cons is: ((c876 c1112)))
(p c876)
(a-config con1 (person persname (nil) surname (nil) gender (nil)
              convrole (*other) case (nil))
         con2
         (person surname (McDonald) persname (Ronald) gender (masc))
         confrel
         (equiv)
         mode (modes mode1 (:t)))

(p c1112)
```

(s-attr time (nil) abstime (nil) rel (nil) locale (nil)
     mode (modes mode2 (nil) mode3 (nil) mode1 (:t))
     actor
     (person gender (masc) persname (Ronald) surname (McDonald)
          middname (nil) title (nil) eprole (nil) convrole (nil))
     attr
     (tags possby (nil) tag1 (persname val (Ronald)) tag2 (middname val
                                                                 (nil))
          tag3 (surname val (McDonald)) tag4 (title val (nil)))))

; Arggh
gc:[list:9096{34%}; *fixnum:2{13%};1 ; ut:76%]

Recall that YADR exhaustively searches for all possible inference chains, by chasing each one in a depth-first manner until it either succeeds or fails, then back-tracking chronologically to the next available chain. Much earlier, there occurred an instance of the *exist-attr-rule* that was "pushed" pending the completion of the chain through the equiv-attr-rule. YADR now attempts to pursue this (fruitless) path. Note that this path fails because there's no stored fact form where a NAMED other is asserted to exist.

YADR: looking for: c1020
(s-attr mode (modes mode1 (:t))
     actor (person gender (nil) persname (nil) surname (nil)
               middname (nil) title (nil) eprole (nil)
               convrole (*other))
     attr (exist))

; We can't backchain past "exist:" this is a "ground" predicate
RUN-RULE: looking for:
(implies con1 (nil)
     con2 (s-attr mode (modes mode1 (:t))
               actor (person gender (nil) persname (nil) surname (nil)
                         middname (nil) title (nil) eprole (nil)
                         convrole (*other))
               attr (exist)))
Run-rule: Failed to find rule(s) for probe: c1020

; So, at this level, one path succeeded, one failed
RUN-RULE proved:
((c2100) nil)

YADR deduced fact(s):
(c2127)

; The final conclusion: "other's name is Ronald McDonald," where the
; naming information was ultimately obtained from the if-added
; "Ronald McDonald exists."
Yadr: facts
(c2127)
consistent with
(c876)

; The Tactician examines this result...
CHECK-RESPONSE PARAMETERS:
QUES:
(s-attr actor (person convrole (*other))
          attr (tags tag1 (persname val (nil)) tag2 (middname val (nil))
                    tag3 (surname val (nil)) tag4 (title val (nil)))
          time (times time1 (:pres)) mode (modes mode1 (:t)))
ANS:
(s-attr time (nil) abstime (nil) rel (nil) locale (nil)
        mode (modes mode2 (nil) mode3 (nil) mode1 (:t))
        actor (person persname (nil) middname (nil) surname (nil)
                      title (nil) standing (nil) eprole (nil) age (nil)
                        gender (nil) ref (nil) rel (nil) agent-of (nil) case (nil)
                        convrole (*other))
        attr (tags possby (nil) tag1 (persname val (Ronald))
                    tag2 (middname val (nil)) tag3 (surname val (McDonald))
                    tag4 (title val (nil)))))

CMPLTANS—before rules:
QUES:(s-attr actor c912 attr c914 time c923 mode c925)
ANS:(s-attr time c2161 abstime c2162 rel c2163 locale c2164 mode c2165
        actor c2169 attr c2183)
RULES ARE:(now-p true-p s-attr-rule update)

; ...and sees that all the required information has been supplied. Note that
; the user might have said "I'm McDonald," in which case the Tactician
; would have to form the question "What is your first name?"
DO-RULES: MISSES . . . . nil
UPDATE DONE

; The goal monitor asserts the naming concept, in its canonical form.
DO-GOAL . . . . . . goal!Strat
(/rest-of-try (/goal assert-student c927))

DO-GOAL . . . . . . goal!Strat
(/goal assert-student c927)

```
DO-GOAL . . . . . . goal!Strat
(/code (setplist 'c927 nil)
      (setq :assert
          (append :assert (qckanon-add 'Fax (list 'c927)))))
do-Node: built node Fax152
```

Now we have to get the student's current schedule. We'll ask ASE if it's already known (it won't be). Failing that we'll ask the student directly.

```
DO-GOAL . . . . . . goal!Strat
(/rest-of-try (/goal get-cur-sched)
            (: = @ next-sched (/goal new-schedule))
            (/code '@ next-sched))

DO-GOAL . . . . . . goal!Strat
(/goal get-cur-sched)

DO-GOAL . . . . . . goal!Strat
(/try (: = @ cur-sched (/goal remember-or-ask-cur-sched))
     (/goal assert-sched-to-DB @ cur-sched)
     (: = @ reply (/goal inquire-ASE-sched))
     (/goal act-on-ASE-reply @ reply))

DO-GOAL . . . . . . goal!Strat
(: = @ cur-sched (/goal remember-or-ask-cur-sched))

DO-GOAL . . . . . . goal!Strat
(/goal remember-or-ask-cur-sched)

DO-GOAL . . . . . . goal!Strat
(/or (/goal remember-cur-sched) (/goal ask-for-sched))

; Perhaps the student already told us the schedule?
DO-GOAL . . . . . . goal!Strat
(/goal remember-cur-sched)

DO-GOAL . . . . . . goal!Strat
(/and (: = @ record (/code (call-expert Ase (/goal talktoase cur-sched?))))
     (/goal add-xtake @ record))

DO-GOAL . . . . . . goal!Strat
(: = @ record (/code (call-expert Ase (/goal talktoase cur-sched?))))

; Awaken the Academic Scheduling Expert to see if the current schedule
; is known (call-expert initializes a new goal stack for an expert):
DO-GOAL . . . . . . goal!Strat
(/code (call-expert Ase (/goal talktoase cur-sched?)))
```

DO-GOAL . . . . . . goal!Ase
(/goal talktoase cur-sched?)

DO-GOAL . . . . . . goal!Ase
(/or (/goal answer-inquiry cur-sched?)
    (/goal fix-sched cur-sched?)
    (/goal remember-fact cur-sched?))

DO-GOAL . . . . . . goal!Ase
(/goal answer-inquiry cur-sched?)

DO-GOAL . . . . . . goal!Ase
(/and (/code (get 'cur-sched? 'qfocus))
    (: = @ returns
        (/or (/goal find-sched cur-sched?)
            (/goal hunh? cur-sched?)
            (/goal new-sched cur-sched?)
            (/code '(hunh? val (hunh?)))))
    (/try (/code (treeatom-del 'Fax :asserteds t)))
    (/try (/code (treeatom-del 'schedDB :asserteds t)))
    (/try (/code (dv asserteds)))
    (/code '@ returns))

DO-GOAL . . . . . . goal!Ase
(/code (get 'cur-sched? 'qfocus))

DO-GOAL . . . . . . goal!Ase
(/rest-of-and (: = @ returns
                (/or (/goal find-sched cur-sched?)
                    (/goal hunh? cur-sched?)
                    (/goal new-sched cur-sched?)
                    (/code '(hunh? val (hunh?)))))
            (/try (/code (treeatom-del 'Fax :asserteds t)))
            (/try (/code (treeatom-del 'schedDB :asserteds t)))
            (/try (/code (dv asserteds)))
            (/code '@ returns))

DO-GOAL . . . . . . goal!Ase
(: = @ returns
    (/or (/goal find-sched cur-sched?)
        (/goal hunh? cur-sched?)
        (/goal new-sched cur-sched?)
        (/code '(hunh? val (hunh?)))))

DO-GOAL . . . . . . goal!Ase
(/or (/goal find-sched cur-sched?)
    (/goal hunh? cur-sched?)

```
(/goal new-sched cur-sched?)
(/code '(hunh? val (hunh?))))
```

DO-GOAL . . . . . . goal!Ase
(/goal find-sched cur-sched?)

DO-GOAL . . . . . . goal!Ase
(/and (/code (ques-match 'cur-sched? 'cur-sched?))
    (/code (fetch-current-schedrec)))

DO-GOAL . . . . . . goal!Ase
(/code (ques-match 'cur-sched? 'cur-sched?))

DO-GOAL . . . . . . goal!Ase
(/rest-of-and (/code (fetch-current-schedrec)))

; Here ASE fails to remember it.
; Thus, we must ask the student....
DO-GOAL . . . . . . goal!Ase
(/code (fetch-current-schedrec))

POPSTATE removing . . . nil

; Stuff left out here clears the student record database and sets up for
; the question to the student

. . . .

DO-GOAL . . . . . . goal!Strat
(/goal ask-student-goal)

DO-GOAL . . . . . . goal!Strat
(: = @ response (/goal find-out coursenames? '*other))

; here's find-out being used again, this time to get a list of courses
DO-GOAL . . . . . . goal!Strat
(/goal find-out coursenames? '*other)

DO-GOAL . . . . . . goal!Strat
(/try (: = @ answer (/goal ask-goal coursenames? '*other))
    (/goal assure-complete-response coursenames? @ answer))

DO-GOAL . . . . . . goal!Strat
(: = @ answer (/goal ask-goal coursenames? '*other))

; Eventually, we get into ace-xchange for an exchange with the user
DO-GOAL . . . . . . goal!Strat
(/code (ace-xchange 'coursenames?))

GEN: top of c-list
; The concept to be generated is: "what is the name of the course you are
; taking, for an indefinite number of such courses?"

```
(p :parentcon)
(simul con1
    (s-attr actor
        ($course actor (person convrole (*other)) student c2211
                dept (org orgname (nil) orgocc ($course) orgtype (dept))
                obj (infostruc itype (ks)) superset (nil)
                locale
                (locales prox
                    (prox part
                        (polity polname (UConn)
                                poltype (university))))
                abstime
                (abstimes semester
                        (timdur durtype (semester) durname (Spring)
                            durmag (nil))
                    year
                    (timdur durtype (year) durmag (nil)
                        durord (num numord (1983))
                        partof (nil) durname (1983)))
                time
                (times time1 (:pres) time2 (:prog))
                mode
                (modes mode1 (:t) mode3 (:nom))
                rel
                c2210)
        attr
        (tags tag5 (superset val (nil)) tag1 (deptname val (nil))
                tag2 (cno numval (nil)) tag3 (secno numval (nil))
                tag4 (title val (nil)))
        time
        (times time1 (:pres))
        mode
        (modes mode1 (:t)))
    ; This means an arbitrary number of cons in the simul
    compnum (!))
```

; The coord sketchifier notices that the simul of "what name" concepts
; can be succinctly expressed in a single "what names" concept; it
; rebuilds the topcon. See Section 10.7.2 for a discussion.
coord1: c2208 factorable as (nil ((actor) (attr)) (c2209) mult)
coord1: c2209 is now: (s-attr actor c2210 attr c2243 time c2254 mode
c2260)

```
(p c2209)
(s-attr actor
```

```
; This is a special "syntactic" type used to generate and-clusters
; of entities
(ent-coord con1
        ($course actor (person convrole (*other)) student c2261
                dept (org orgname (nil) orgocc ($course) orgtype
                                                        (dept))
                obj (infostruc itype (ks)) superset (nil)
                locale
                (locales prox
                        (prox part
                                (polity polname (UConn)
                                        poltype (university))))
                abstime
                (abstimes semester
                        (timdur durtype (semester)
                                durname (Spring)
                                durmag (nil))
                        year (timdur durtype (year)
                                durmag (nil)
                                durord (num numord (1983))
                                partof (nil)
                                durname (1983)))
                time (times time1 (:pres) time2 (:prog))
                mode (modes mode1 (:t) mode3 (:nom))
                ; "What course name such that you are taking that
                ; course?"
                rel
                ($course actor c2261 student c2261 dept c2263
                        obj c2267 superset c2269 locale c2270
                        abstime c2275 time c2287 mode c2290 rel
                                                        c2293))
        con2
        (nil) con3 (nil) con4 (nil) con5 (nil) con6 (nil) compnum (!))
attr
; This syntactic type is a cluster of attributes
(attr-coord con1 (tags tag5 (superset val (nil)) tag1 (deptname val
                                                        (nil))
                tag2 (cno numval (nil)) tag3 (secno numval (nil))
                tag4 (title val (nil)))
        con2 (nil) con3 (nil) con4 (nil) con5 (nil) con6 (nil)
                                                        compnum (!))
time (times time1 (:pres))
mode (modes mode1 (:t)))
```

; The s-attr demon sees that the simple adjectival form won't work
; and re-arranges the concept to a "(courses') names are what?" form.
; See Section 10.7.3.
s-attr: examining attribute concept c2209
PROBE-DICT: no entries exist for c2209

; Qfocus fronts "what"
qfocus: examining question concept c2209 with
((attr con1 tag1 val) (attr con1 tag2 numval)) qfocus
utterance is (what are)

; The "poss" sketchifier sees that "names" is "possessed."
; It sees that the possessor can't be expressed by a simple nominal (since
; it has a rel-clause corresponding to "that you are taking" attached to it).
; So the construction "<possessed> of <possesser>" is used instead.
poss rule forming possessive of
(ent-coord con1 ($course actor (person convrole (*other)) student c2261
                    dept (org orgname (nil) orgocc ($course) orgtype

                                                              (dept))

            ....))

GEN: top of c-list
(tags compnum (plural) tag5 (nil) tag1 (deptname val (nil))
        tag2 (cno numval (nil)) tag3 (nil) tag4 (nil))
GEN: using
(names)

GEN: using
(the)
utterance is (what are the)
utterance is (what are the names)
utterance is (what are the names)
utterance is (what are the names of)

; The "courses" pseudo-concept appears from where "poss" put it.
; The plural ending arises from the fact that the dictionary notices
; that it's looking up an ent-coord
GEN: top of c-list
(ent-coord con1 ($course actor (person convrole (*other)) student c2261
                    .....))
; The sayrel sketchifier sees the rel clause attached to "courses."
; It extracts the rel concept and pushes it back onto the clist behind
; "that"
sayrel: examining rel clause c2293

GEN: using
(courses)

GEN: using

(the)
utterance is (what are the names of the)
utterance is (what are the names of the courses)
utterance is (what are the names of the courses that)

; Now the rel clause comes back
GEN: top of c-list
($course actor (person convrole (*other)) student c2346
        dept (org orgname (nil) orgocc ($course) orgtype (dept))
        ....)

; The locale sketchifier pushes "at Uconn" back...
locale pushing locational c2355

; ...and abstime pushes "during Fall 1983" back. See Section 10.7.3.
abstime pushing absolute time c2360

GEN: using
(are taking)

GEN: using
(you)
utterance is (what are the names of the courses that you)
utterance is (what are the names of the courses that you are taking)

; The abstime filler reaches the top:
GEN: top of c-list
(abstimes semester (timdur durtype (semester) durname (Spring) ....))

; Here is the zero morpheme used to position the abstime's components:
GEN: using
(nil)

; The dictionary supplies the rest of the abstime's words..
GEN: using
(semester)
utterance is (what are the names of the courses that you are taking in the)
utterance is (what are the names of the courses that you are taking in
  the Spring)
utterance is (what are the names of the courses that you are taking in
  the Spring semester)
utterance is (what are the names of the courses that you are taking in
  the Spring semester of)

GEN: top of c-list
(timdur durtype (year) durmag (nil) durord (num numord (1983))
        partof (nil)
    durname (1983))

; The name sketchifier looks to see whether this concept can be expressed

; simply with its name. It succeeds, because the number "1983" can serve
; as the name of the unique "year 1983 AD."
Name Maker: examining
(timdur ref c2402 durtype c2366 durmag c2367 durord c2368 partof c2370
        durname c2371)

; The word the name sketchifier placed on the CLIST is popped off.
utterance is (what are the names of the courses that you are taking in
  the Spring semester of 1983)

; "At," which comes from the "prox" concept in the locales filler, gets
; looked up next.
utterance is (what are the names of the courses that you are taking in
  the Spring semester of 1983 at)

; Just as in the case of the year "1983," the name sketchifier sees that
; "UConn," the name of the university, is sufficient to express the
; polity concept
Name Maker: examining
(polity polname c2458 poltype c2359)

utterance is (what are the names of the courses that you are taking in
  the Spring semester of 1983 at UConn)

I'M SAYING:
; The user sees...
What are the names of the courses that you are taking in the
  Spring semester of 1983 at UConn?
input:
105, Chem 127, Math 134, CS 110 and Hist 1

This is a heavily ellipsed and problematical student input. "105" presumably refers to English 105, the introductory composition course. "Chem 127" and ":CS 110" are OK for first-semester freshmen, but "Math 134" is unexpected: we were assuming its prerequisite, Math 133. "Hist 1" is a typo. APE will form the individual course-concepts (a named request making "105" into a course with that number along the way), "and" will try (and fail) to build a composite concept, and the clausepoint diagnostic will form the proper concept: "the names of," using the question concept as a template.

APE: activating memory requests (expcourse expcoursenum)

APE: new word is number0

Executed ar50

Available: (c2458)
(p c2458)
(num numval (105))

APE: new word is cm

; Comma's peekreq notices "105:"
APE: considering peekreq pool: ap28 (ar53) cm
Executed ar53
Available: (c2458)

; A request looking for a bare number in the range 100-500 converts
; "105."
APE: considering gapreq pool: ap24 (ar46 ar47) MEM
EXPCOURSENUM: creating $course from num: c2458
Executed ar46
Available: (c2458)
(p c2458)
($course cno (num numval (105)) mode (modes mode3 (:nom)))

APE: new word is CHEM

Executed ar57
Available: (c2470 c2458)
; "Chem" is 3-ways ambiguous; it could be the course, the department,
; or the field of study. A vel is created to allow for the possibilities.
(p c2470)
(vel v3
     ($course deptname (CHEM)
            dept (org orgname c2472 orgtype (dept) orgocc ($course))
            obj (infostruc itype (ks) iname (CHEM)) actor (nil)
            teacher (nil) student (nil) time (times)
                ; :nom means this is a nominalized episode
            mode (modes mode3 (:nom)))
     v2
     c2475
     v1
     c2471)
; "Chemistry," the field, is rather inadequately rendered as an informa-
; tion structure of type "knowledge structure."
(p c2475)
(infostruc itype (ks) iname (CHEM))
; This is the organization whose occupation is giving Chemistry courses.
(p c2471)
(org orgname (CHEM) orgtype (dept) orgocc ($course))

; A velreq of "Chem" notices the following "127"

VEL: possible disambiguation: c2470 as c2478
(p c2478)
($course deptname (CHEM)
 dept (org orgname c2472 orgtype (dept) orgocc ($course))
        obj (infostruc itype (ks) iname (CHEM)) actor (nil) teacher (nil)
        student (nil) time (times) mode (modes mode3 (:nom)))

; There are no other readings available: the vel is compressed
VEL: disambiguated c2470 as c2478
($course cno (num numval (127)) deptname (CHEM)
        dept (org orgname c2472 orgtype (dept) orgocc ($course))
        obj (infostruc itype (ks) iname (CHEM))
        actor (nil) teacher (nil) student (nil) time (times)
        mode (modes mode3 (:nom)))

; Similarly for Math 134:
VEL: disambiguated c2491 as c2499
($course cno (num numval (134)) deptname (MATH) ....)
; CS 110:
VEL: disambiguated c2512 as c2520
($course cno (num numval (110)) deptname (CS) ....)

; and "Hist 1" (the surface semantics doesn't know this is an illegal
; course):
VEL: disambiguated c2533 as c2541
($course cno (num numval (1)) deptname (HIST) ....)

; Eventually, "and" gets in; it obtains the concepts to be grouped from
; commas that have been seen. Unfortunately, they're all entities,
; and none have been gobbled by concepts. "And" just throws its hands
; up (and throws itself away).
AND: available (c2458 c2478 c2499 c2541 c2520) unavailable nil
AND: all still available, giving up

; At the very end, the diagnostic gets in:
APE: considering diagreq pool: ap62 (ar105) PR

CLP: examining parse result: (c2458 c2478 c2499 c2520 c2541)
in expectation context coursenames?
CLP: fragments (c2458 c2478 c2499 c2520 c2541)

; It sees that each of the course fragments can be merged with a cognate
; concept in the expectation/question concept
CLP: subcon c2458 fits in name-cd c2552 at (con1 actor)
CLP: hallucinating a merge between c2603 and c2458
MERGE: updating conrel

CLP: subcon c2478 fits in name-cd c2552 at (con1 actor)

CLP: hallucinating a merge between c2603 and c2478
MERGE: updating conrel

CLP: subcon c2499 fits in name-cd c2552 at (con1 actor)
CLP: hallucinating a merge between c2603 and c2499
MERGE: updating conrel

CLP: subcon c2520 fits in name-cd c2552 at (con1 actor)
CLP: hallucinating a merge between c2603 and c2520
MERGE: updating conrel

CLP: subcon c2541 fits in name-cd c2552 at (con1 actor)
CLP: hallucinating a merge between c2603 and c2541
MERGE: updating conrel
CLP: perpetrated multiple merge
CLP: result con: c2458

Executed ar105
Available: (c2551 c2458)

```
; Here is the result
(p c2458)
(simul con5
     (s-attr actor "Hist 1"
             attr
             (tags tag5 (superset val (nil)) tag1 (deptname val (HIST))
                   tag2 (cno numval (1)) tag3 (secno numval (nil))
                   tag4 (title val (nil)))
             time (times time1 (:pres)) mode (modes mode1 (:t)))
     con4
     (s-attr actor "CS 110" attr (tags ....))
     con3
     (s-attr actor "Math 134" attr (tags ....))
     con2
     (s-attr actor "Chem 127" attr (tags ....))
     con1
     (s-attr actor "a course numbered 105" attr (tags ....)))
     compnum
     (5))
```

APE: sentence:
(105 cm Chem 127 cm Math 134 cm CS 110 and Hist 1 pr)
result:(c2458)

DO-GOAL . . . . . . goal!Strat
(/rest-of-try (/goal assure-complete-response coursenames? c2458))

; the Tactician is called as usual...

DO-GOAL . . . . . . goal!Strat
(/goal assure-complete-response coursenames? c2458)

....

; ...and it notices that one of the subcons is not complete: "the 105
; course"
RESPONSE:(s-attr actor c3126 attr c3159 time c3170 mode c3172)
QPATHS:((attr tag1 val) (attr tag2 numval))
RE-ASK with qfocus:((attr tag1 val))

; It arranges to reask the question with the qfocus on the missing info
GEN: top of c-list
(p :parentcon)
(s-attr actor
        ($course cno (num numval (105)) actor (person convrole (*other))
                student c3178
                dept (org orgname (nil) orgocc ($course) orgtype (dept))
                obj (infostruc itype (ks)) superset (nil)
                locale
                (locales prox
                        (prox part
                                (polity polname (UConn) poltype (university))))
                abstime
                (abstimes semester
                        (timdur durtype (semester)
                                durname (Spring) durmag (nil))
                        year
                        (timdur durtype (year) durmag (nil)
                                durord (num numord (1983))
                                partof (nil) durname (1983)))
                time (times time1 (:pres) time2 (:prog))
                mode (modes mode1 (:t) mode3 (:nom))
                rel
                c3175)
        attr
        (tags tag5 (superset val (nil)) tag1 (deptname val (nil))
                tag2 (cno numval c3177) tag3 (secno numval (nil))
                tag4 (title val (nil)))
        time (times time1 (:pres))
        mode (modes mode1 (:t)))

....

; The generation proceeds analogously with the "what are the names
; of the courses..." (This concept is just a specialized form of
; the concept imbedded in "what names")

; Locale sees it's re-expressing a locale:
locale shutting up location

; Similarly for abstime:
abstime shutting up about time

. . . .

; The result:
I'M SAYING:
What is the department of the 105 course that you are taking?
input:
English

. . . .

; APE's result, after clausepoint diagnosis:
; "The name of the department is English"

APE: sentence:
(English pr)
result:(c3359)

. . . .

; The Tactician is now happy with the roster of courses, so it creates a
; special schedule concept and sends it to the ASE module

. . . .

; Here ASE gets in
DO-GOAL . . . . . . goal!Ase
(/goal talktoase check-sched?)

DO-GOAL . . . . . . goal!Ase
(/or (/goal answer-inquiry check-sched?)
   (/goal fix-sched check-sched?)
   (/goal remember-fact check-sched?))

DO-GOAL . . . . . . goal!Ase
(/goal answer-inquiry check-sched?)

DO-GOAL . . . . . . goal!Ase
(/and (/code (get 'check-sched? 'qfocus))
   (: = @ returns
      (/or (/goal find-sched check-sched?)
         (/goal hunh? check-sched?)
         (/goal new-sched check-sched?)
         (/code '(hunh? val (hunh?)))))
   (/try (/code (treeatom-del 'Fax :asserteds t)))
   (/try (/code (treeatom-del 'schedDB :asserteds t)))

```
(/try (/code (dv asserteds)))
(/code '@ returns))
```

At length, the "hunh?" goal gets invoked for ASE; this is a general-purpose goal that locates problems in proposed schedules and points them out to the Strategist. Here are the plan steps of "hunh?"

1. retrieve the schedule currently proposed
2. make sure all the courses are OK; for example, that they are all legal: existent and currently being offered
3. make sure the student has the prerequisites for the courses being taken (scheduling and plan of study difficulties may come up if the prereqs aren't in order)
4. are all the distributional requirements (engineering science, engineering design, social science, etc.) being met by the schedule in the context of the student's plan of study?
5. does the number of credits proposed meet the requirements for a full-time student?

```
DO-GOAL . . . . . . goal!Ase
(/goal hunh? check-sched?)

DO-GOAL . . . . . . goal!Ase
(: = @ sched (/code (fetch-current-sched)))
(/rest-of-and
 (/or (/goal okcourses? @ sched)
     (/goal prereqok? @ sched)
     (/goal allcoursesthere? @ sched)
     (/goal fullsched? @ sched)
     (/code 'oksched!)))

; Here is the currently asserted schedule:
; (The current student is the implied actor)
(p c4050)
(schedule compnum
     (5)
     con5
     ($course time (times time3 (nil)) cno (num numval (1))
            deptname (HIST) actor (nil)
            mode (modes mode1 (:t)))
     con4
     ($course time (times time3 (nil)) cno (num numval (110))
            deptname (CS) actor (nil)
            mode (modes mode1 (:t)))
```

```
con3
($course time (times time3 (nil)) cno (num numval (134))
        deptname (MATH) actor (nil)
        mode (modes mode1 (:t)))
con2
($course time (times time3 (nil)) cno (num numval (127))
        deptname (CHEM) actor (nil)
        mode (modes mode1 (:t)))
con1
($course time (times time3 (nil)) cno (num numval (105))
        deptname (ENGL) actor (nil)
        mode (modes mode1 (:t)))
; First semester, ongoing
semester (|+0|))
```

DO-GOAL . . . . . . goal!Ase
(/goal okcourses? c4050)

; Okcourses? just invokes check-courses...
DO-GOAL . . . . . . goal!Ase
(/code (check-courses 'c4050))

; ...which consults the knowledge-base manager about each of the listed
; courses. "Hist 1" comes up as undefined...
del-facts : no match found for c4098

; ...and ASE fails this time around.
POPSTATE removing . . . nil

```
(p c4098)
($course time (times time3 (nil)) cno (num numval (1))
        deptname (HIST) actor (nil) mode (modes mode3 (:nom)))
```

POPSTATE removing . . . nil

; We return to the Strategist with a reply indicating a problem:
; "Hist 1 is not an instance of a course"
DO-GOAL . . . . . . goal!Strat
(/goal act-on-ASE-reply c4188)
(p c4188)
(a-config con1
```
        ($course time (times time3 (nil)) cno (num numval (1))
                deptname (HIST) actor (nil)
                mode (modes mode3 (:nom)))
        con2
        ($course mode (modes mode3 (:nom)) obj (infostruc itype (ks))
                dept (org orgocc ($course) orgtype (dept)))
```

```
        time (times time1 (:pres)) mode (modes mode1 (:neg))
        confrel (instance))
```

; The Strategist sees that ASE wishes to make a comment to the user
; (or whoever it was that proposed the schedule)
DO-GOAL . . . . . . goal!Strat
(/goal field-ASE-assertion c4188)

; Maybe the schedule's OK?
DO-GOAL . . . . . . goal!Strat
(/test (car (cdmatch 'oksched! 'c4188 nil)))

; No, there's some problem; express it.
; Then compute the question which will elicit the necessary answer
; (This will be a specialized form of the original "what names?"
; query)
; Then re-assert the updated schedule and restart ASE.
DO-GOAL . . . . . . goal!Strat
(/try (/goal speak-goal c4188)
    (: = @ new-ques (/goal get-ques c4188))
    (: = @ response (/goal find-out @ new-ques '*other))
    (/goal assert-courses-to-DB @ response)
    (: = @ return (/goal inquire-ASE-sched))

DO-GOAL . . . . . . goal!Strat
(/goal speak-goal c4188)

GEN: top of c-list
(p :parentcon)
(a-config con1
        ($course time (times time3 (nil)) cno (num numval (1))
                deptname (HIST) actor (nil)
                mode (modes mode3 (:nom)))
        con2
        ($course mode (modes mode3 (:nom)) obj (infostruc itype (ks))
                dept (org orgocc ($course) orgtype (dept)))
        time (times time1 (:pres)) mode (modes mode1 (:neg))
        confrel
        (instance))

; A straightforward generation run ensues...
. . . .

utterance is (HIST 1)
utterance is (HIST 1 is not)
utterance is (HIST 1 is not a)
utterance is (HIST 1 is not a course)
```
```

I'M SAYING:
HIST 1 is not a course.

; Express the corrective question:
DO-GOAL . . . . . . goal!Strat
(/goal find-out coursename? '*other)

DO-GOAL . . . . . . goal!Strat
(/goal ask-goal coursename? '*other)

DO-GOAL . . . . . . goal!Strat
(/code (ace-xchange 'coursename?))

; Coursename? is a bare "what is the name of the course?" concept.
; Unfortunately, ASE's arrangements for indicating problems is not
; fine-grained enough to be able to communicate that it is unhappy
; with the *number* of the course, though "History" is OK as a
; department. It will rely on the user's ability to infer which
; course is it is asking about from its comment "Hist 1 does not exist."
; Deep problems here!!
GEN: top of c-list
(p :parentcon)
(s-attr actor
        ($course actor (person convrole (*other)) student c4263
            dept (org orgname (nil) orgocc ($course) orgtype (dept))
            obj (infostruc itype (ks)) superset (nil)
            locale
            (locales prox
                    (prox part
                        (polity polname (UConn)
                            poltype (university))))
            abstime
            (abstimes semester
                    (timdur durtype (semester) durname (Spring)
                        durmag (nil))
                    year
                    (timdur durtype (year) durmag (nil)
                        durord (num numord (1983))
                        partof (nil) durname (1983)))
            time (times time1 (:pres) time2 (:prog))
            mode (modes mode1 (:t) mode3 (:nom))
            rel
            c4262)
        attr
        (tags tag5 (superset val (nil)) tag1 (deptname val (nil))
            tag2 (cno numval (nil)) tag3 (secno numval (nil))

```
        tag4 (title val (nil)))
    time (times time1 (:pres)) mode (modes mode1 (:t)))
```
; The usual generator run ensues...

....

; ...with the result:
I'M SAYING:
What is the name of the course that you are taking?
input:
History 101
; The usual vel compression/ellipsis expansion process follows.
APE: sentence:
(History 101 pr)
result:(c4441)
(p c4441)
(s-attr actor
        ($course actor (person convrole (*other)) student c4454
                dept (org orgname (nil) orgocc ($course) orgtype (dept))
                obj (infostruc itype (ks)) superset (nil)
                locale
                ....)
        attr
        (tags tag5 (superset val (nil)) tag1 (deptname val (HIST))
            tag2 (cno numval (101)) tag3 (secno numval (nil))
            tag4 (title val (nil)))
   .....)
; And the Tactician resumes with the answer:
DO-GOAL . . . . . . goal!Strat
(/goal assure-complete-response coursename? c4441)

; The answer seems to be complete, so a new schedule is asserted to
; the knowledge base, and ASE restarts.
DO-GOAL . . . . . . goal!Ase
(/goal talktoase check-sched?)

DO-GOAL . . . . . . goal!Ase
(/goal hunh? check-sched?)

; This time okcourses? succeeds: HIST 101 is a legitimate course
DO-GOAL . . . . . . goal!Ase
(/goal okcourses? c4733)

; Now we check the schedule's prerequisites.
DO-GOAL . . . . . . goal!Ase
(/goal prereqok? c4733)
```
; The plan steps are to get the student's transcript, and look for
```

```
; missing prereqs:
DO-GOAL . . . . . . goal!Ase
(/and (/try (: = @ trans (/code (gettranscript (student-name)))))
    (/goal findmissingprereqs c4733 @ trans))

DO-GOAL . . . . . . goal!Ase
(/goal findmissingprereqs c4733 nil)
```

```
; To do this, we assert an empty transcript (this is the first time
; we have talked to this student), then the schedule, then
; a roster of special courses (having no prereqs).
DO-GOAL . . . . . . goal!Ase
(/and (/try (/code (assert-trans 'nil)))
    (/try (/code (assert-sched 'c4733)))
    (/try (/code (assert-special-courses)))
    (: = @ returns (/code (noprereqs 'c4733)))
    (/try (/code (treeatom-del 'schedDB :asserteds t)))
    (/try (/code (dv :asserteds)))
    (/code '@ returns))
```

The function *noprereqs* is intended to check on the prereqs of each of
the courses in the schedule. The way it does this is by using YADR, to see
whether the student has actually taken the prereq, or whether there is a
reasoning path to a valid answer if he hasn't. The prerequisite relations in
the curriculum are stored as *cancause* forms in the rule database and are
therefore usable by YADR. Once again, general-purpose reasoning power
comes to the rescue.

```
DO-GOAL . . . . . . goal!Ase
```

```
; First, HIST 101:
YADR: looking for: c4944
(s-attr actor ($course time (times time3 (nil)) cno (num numval (101))
                deptname (HIST) actor (nil)
                mode (modes mode1 (:t)))
  attr (has-prereq))
```

```
; The student doesn't overtly have the prereq, so we go to Run-Rule
; to see if we can establish this fact:
RUN-RULE: looking for:
(implies
  con1 (nil)
  con2 (s-attr actor ($course time (times time3 (nil))
          cno (num numval (101)) deptname (HIST) actor (nil)
```

```
        mode (modes mode1 (:t)))
        attr (has-prereq)))
```

RUN-RULE: found rules
(ifnw3)

```
; This rule says a student has the prereq for a course if either the
; course has no prereqs (i.e., it is an entry-level course), or the
; student has passed the course's prereqs:
(p (get-structure 'ifnw3))
(implies con1
    (disj con1
        ($course cno (nil) deptname (nil) actor (nil)
                ; This says "anyone can take this course"
                mode (modes mode2 (:ablty)))
        con2
        ; Prereq explicitly taken
        (s-attr actor
                ($course cno (nil) deptname (nil) actor (nil)
                    time (times time3 (:tf)))
                attr
                (taken-prereq)
                mode (modes mode1 (:t))))
    con2
    (s-attr actor ($course cno (nil) deptname (nil) actor (nil))
        attr (has-prereq)))
; YADR is called recursively on the antecedent
YADR: looking for: c4960
(disj
 con1 ($course cno (num numval (101)) deptname (HIST) actor (nil)
        mode (modes mode2 (:ablty)))
 con2 (s-attr actor ($course cno (num numval c4775)
                    deptname (HIST) actor (nil)
                    time (times time3 (:tf)))
        attr (taken-prereq)
        mode (modes mode1 (:t))))
YADR: examining and/or concept

; It pursues the first disjunct...
YADR: looking for: c4961
($course cno (num numval (101)) deptname (HIST) actor (nil)
 mode (modes mode2 (:ablty)))

; ...and finds that HIST 101 is a course anyone in the University can take
YADR: found fact(s) for probe:
(Faxw14)
```

RUN-RULE proved:
((c4985))

YADR deduced fact(s):
(c5003)

; Similarly for English 105...
YADR: looking for: c4947
(s-attr actor ($course time (times time3 (nil)) cno (num numval (105))
                    deptname (ENGL) actor (nil) mode (modes mode1 (:t)))
  attr (has-prereq))

YADR deduced fact(s):
(c5053)

; ...and CHEM 127.
YADR: looking for: c4950
(s-attr actor ($course time (times time3 (nil)) cno (num numval (127))
                    deptname (CHEM) actor (nil) mode (modes mode1 (:t)))
  attr (has-prereq))

YADR deduced fact(s):
(c5103)

; Now we get to Math 134:
YADR: looking for: c4953
(s-attr actor ($course time (times time3 (nil)) cno (num numval (134))
                    deptname (MATH) actor (nil) mode (modes mode1 (:t)))
  attr (has-prereq))

RUN-RULE: looking for:
(implies con1 (nil) con2 (s-attr ....))

RUN-RULE: found rules
(ifnw3)

YADR: looking for: c5110
YADR: examining and/or concept

YADR: looking for: c5111
($course cno (num numval (134)) deptname (MATH) actor (nil)
  mode (modes mode2 (:ablty)))

; This time the database denies that this is an introductory course
; Run-rule attempts to back-chain further...
RUN-RULE: looking for:
(implies con1 (nil)
  con2 ($course cno (num numval (134)) deptname (MATH)
        actor (nil) mode (modes mode2 (:ablty))))

; ...and fails.
Run-rule: Failed to find rule(s) for probe: c5111

; So YADR tries the other disjunct:
YADR: looking for: c5117
(s-attr actor ($course cno (num numval (134)) deptname (MATH)
           actor (nil)
           ; mode "transition final" is the system's
           ; representation for "passed"
           time (times time3 (:tf)))
  attr (taken-prereq)
  mode (modes mode1 (:t)))

; The database doesn't have this fact either, so Run-Rule looks
; for a rule that would allow it to establish that the student has
; taken the prereq:
RUN-RULE: looking for:
(implies con1 (nil)
  con2 (s-attr actor ($course cno (num numval (134)) deptname (MATH)
                 actor (nil) time (times time3 (:tf)))
         attr (taken-prereq) mode (modes mode1 (:t))))

; This rule is just a translation of the (rather dubious) "taken-prereq"
; stative into the underlying goalepisode form:
RUN-RULE: found rules
(ifnw32)
(cancause con1
      ($course time (times time3 (:tf)) deptname (MATH)
          cno (num numval (133))))
      con2
      (s-attr actor
          ($course deptname (MATH) cno (num numval (134)))
          attr (taken-prereq)
          mode (modes mode1 (:t)))))

; Unfortunately, neither the antecedent form nor any other rules are
; available. Stalemate!
YADR: looking for: c5134
($course time (times time3 (:tf)) deptname (MATH) cno (num numval
                                     (133)))

RUN-RULE: looking for:
(implies con1 (nil)
  con2 ($course time (times time3 (:tf)) deptname (MATH)
        cno (num numval (133)))))
Run-rule: Failed to find rule(s) for probe: c5134

RUN-RULE proved:
(nil)

; Thus, ASE must return to the Tactician, and try to get the student
; to account for the missing prerequisite. This causes an invocation
; of an exchange with the user. We call the generator with the concept:
; "Did you pass Math 133?"

....

GEN: top of c-list
($course student (person convrole (*other))
   time (times time1 (:past) time3 (:tf)) mode (modes model (:t))
   actor c5176 obj (infostruc itype (ks))
   dept (org orgocc ($course) orgtype (dept)) cno (num numval (133))
        deptname (MATH))

....

I'M SAYING:
Did you pass MATH 133?
input:
I passed it in high school

This is a user input that requires a staged disambiguation. First the
referent(s) of "it" must be sought in the exchange context. Then, "pass,"
which can either mean "terminate taking a course" (our version of "pass
course") or "throw a football" must select the appropriate "it"-referent
to decide on the former meaning. "In" also notices that it has been left
dangling and imbeds itself and the "pass" concept in a *during* conceptualization.

; First, "I" and the past/perfective fragment put themselves on the
; CLIST
APE: new word is i

Executed ar141
Available: (c5242)

APE: new word is pastperf$
Available: (c5250 c5242)

APE: new word is pass

Executed ar145
Available: (c5251 c5250 c5242)
; Here is "pass:"

```
(p c5251)
(vel v3
    ; I passed a football
    (propel actor (person) obj (inst insttype (football))
          to (in-grasp-of val (person)))
    v2
    ; The teacher passed me in a course
    (cause con1
         (episode actor (person))
         con2
         ($course actor (nil) student c5297 time (times time3 (:tf))
                 obj (infostruc itype (ks))
                 dept (org orgocc ($course) orgtype (dept) orgname (nil))
                 cno (nil)
                 deptname (nil)))
    v1
    ; I passed the course
    ($course actor (nil) student c5266 time (times time3 (:tf))
          obj (infostruc itype (ks))
          dept (org orgocc ($course) orgtype (dept) orgname (nil))
          cno (nil) deptname (nil)))
; The "past" fragment selects the vel subcons it is willing to assert and
; tense. Unfortunately, all the subcons are concepts, so this
; operation really doesn't help. Note that if we had included a
; nominal sense of "pass," as in a "a pass for the theatre," we
; would have discarded it at this point.
APE: considering gapreq pool: ap86 (ar143 ar144) pastperf$

Executed ar144
Available: (c5251 c5242)
(p c5251)
    ; The time/mode info will be copied into the vel result later
(vel mode (modes mode1 (:t)) time (times time1 (:past))
    v1
    ($course ....)
    v2
    (cause con1 (episode ....) con2 ($course ....))
    v3
    (propel ....))

APE: new word is it
APE: considering topreq pool: ap90 (ar152) it

; "It" consults the NLP context that APE and GEN have been maintain-
```

; ing for this exchange...
APE: referent for c5325 is c5209

Executed ar152
Available: (c5325 c5251 c5242)
(p c5325)
(vel v1
　　; The standard "expletive" sense of "it," as in "it's raining"
　　(expletive)
　　v0
　　; The nominal "Math 133," expressed earlier by GEN
　　($course ref (indef) student (person convrole (*other))
　　　　mode (modes mode3 (:nom)) actor c5210
　　　　obj (infostruc itype (ks))
　　　　dept (org orgocc ($course) orgtype (dept))
　　　　cno (num numval (133))
　　　　deptname (MATH)))

APE: new word is in

APE: considering velreq pool: ap88 (ar146 ar147 ar148 ar149) pass

; "Pass" sees the imbedded course, and compresses the "it"-vel
VEL: possible disambiguation: c5325 as ac2

; "Pass" compresses itself, as well
VEL: possible disambiguation: c5251 as c5265
(p ac2)
($course ref (indef) student (person convrole (*other))
　　mode (modes mode3 (:nom))
　　actor c5210
　　obj (infostruc itype (ks))
　　dept (org orgocc ($course) orgtype (dept))
　　cno (num numval (133))
　　deptname (MATH))
(p c5265)
($course actor (nil) student c5266 time (times time3 (:tf))
　　obj (infostruc itype (ks))
　　dept (org orgocc ($course) orgtype (dept) orgname (nil))
　　cno (nil)
　　deptname (nil))

; Here is the result
VEL: disambiguated c5251 as c5265
($course time (times time3 (:tf)) ref (indef)
　　student (person convrole (*other))
　　mode (modes mode1 (:t) mode3 (nil))

```
      actor c5210 obj (infostruc itype (ks))
      dept (org orgocc ($course) orgtype (dept))
      cno (num numval (133)) deptname (MATH))
```

; "Pass" picks up "I." (This just duplicates the existing info.)
APE: considering gapreq pool: ap93 (ar155) pass

Executed ar155
Available: (c5265)

APE: new word is hs

Executed ar162
Available: (c5339 c5334 c5265)
; "High school" is either the building, the administration or the
; goalepisode:
(p c5339)
(vel v1
      (struc structype (building) possby (org orgocc ($hs)
                                        eprole (executive))))
      v2
      c5346
      v3
      ($hs actor (nil) time (nil) mode (modes mode3 (:nom))
         executive c5346 teacher (nil) student (nil) locale
         (inside part c5343)))

Leaving ng mode

; At end-of-noun group, "high school" sees that its (ref) slot
; hasn't been filled, therefore, it should resolve itself
; to the "episode" sense (cf., "in the high school," "the high
; school informed me...")
APE: considering velreq pool: ap97 (ar163) hs

VEL: disambiguated c5339 as c5349
($hs actor (nil) time (nil) mode (modes mode3 (:nom))
   executive (org orgocc ($hs) eprole (executive))
   teacher (nil) student (nil)
   locale (inside part (struc structype (building) possby c5346)))

; Here's the request:
(p (plist 'ar163))
(body ((test
         (and (eq (envmnt) 'end-ng) (empty '(ref) 'c5339)))
       (actions (p-assert 'c5339 'c5349)))))

; At the end, "in" sees it's still available. We have a dangling
```
```

; during-concept, which "in" now proceeds to create...
APE: considering gapreq pool: ap101 (ar170) in

Executed ar170
Available: (c5360 c5265)
(p c5265)
(during con2
    ($hs actor (nil) time (nil) mode (modes mode3 (:nom))
        executive (org orgocc ($hs) eprole (executive))
        teacher (nil) student (nil)
        locale (inside part (struc structype (building) possby c5346)))
    con1
    ($course time (times time1 (:past) time3 (:tf))
        ref (indef) student (person persname (nil) surname (nil)
                        ref (pron) gender (nil)
                        convrole (*other) case (nil))
        mode (modes mode1 (:t) mode3 (nil))
        actor c5367
        obj (infostruc itype (ks))
        dept (org orgocc ($course) orgtype (dept))
        cno (num numval (133))
        deptname (MATH)))

; ...and this is the eventual result:
APE: sentence:
(I passed it in high school pr)
result:(c5265)

; The Tactician notices that this concept matches up
; with one of the ways it has been told a student can pass a course:
; by taking it in a high school cooperative program.

....

CHECK-RESPONSE PARAMETERS:
QUES:
($course ....)
ANS:
(during con2 ($hs ....) con1 ($course ....))
QFOCUS:
((mode mode1))

; "Xtake-in-hs" is the "took-it-in-hs" expectation, which the
; knowledge base has provided:
EXPECTS:
(xtake xtake-in-hs xtake-passed-exam)

; The Tactician accepts the response, and asserts that the student

; has indeed passed Math 133.
DO-RULES: MISSES . . . . nil
UPDATE DONE

DO-GOAL . . . . . . goal!Strat
(/goal assert-courses-to-DB c5417)

; ASE is restarted; it picks up with "prereqok?"
DO-GOAL . . . . . . goal!Ase
(/goal prereqok? c5570)

; It (wastefully) recomputes that HIST 101, ENGL 105 and CHEM 127
; are OK. Then it pursues MATH 134:

YADR: looking for: c5799
(s-attr actor ($course time (times time3 (nil)) cno (num numval (134))
                 deptname (MATH) actor (nil)
                 mode (modes model (:t)))
  attr (has-prereq))

; Run-Rule finds the usual rule:
RUN-RULE: found rules
(ifnw3)

YADR: examining and/or concept
YADR: looking for: c5957
($course cno (num numval (134)) deptname (MATH) actor (nil)
     mode (modes mode2 (:ablty)))

RUN-RULE: looking for:
(implies con1 (nil) con2 ($course cno (num numval (134))
                                          deptname (MATH)
                 actor (nil) mode (modes mode2 (:ablty))))
Run-rule: Failed to find rule(s) for probe: c5957

YADR: looking for: c5963
(s-attr actor ($course cno (num numval (134)) deptname (MATH)
                              actor (nil)
              time (times time3 (:tf)))
  attr (taken-prereq) mode (modes model (:t)))

RUN-RULE: looking for:
(implies con1 (nil)
  con2 (s-attr actor ($course cno (num numval (134))
                 deptname (MATH) actor (nil)
                 time (times time3 (:tf)))
        attr (taken-prereq)
        mode (modes model (:t))))

RUN-RULE: found rules
(ifnw32)

YADR: looking for: c5980
($course time (times time3 (:tf)) deptname (MATH) cno (num numval
(133)))

; This time, the back-chain through ifnw32 succeeds, because the
; Tactician has asserted the needed form.
YADR: found fact(s) for probe:
(Faxw118)

YADR deduced fact(s):
(c6029)

; Now ASE works on CS 110:
YADR: looking for: c5802
(s-attr actor ($course time (times time3 (nil)) cno (num numval (110))
                deptname (CS) actor (nil) mode (modes mode1 (:t)))
    attr (has-prereq))

; The "proof" proceeds in the usual way...
RUN-RULE: found rules
(ifnw3)

YADR: looking for: c6036
(disj con1
  ($course cno (num numval (110)) deptname (CS) actor (nil)
      mode (modes mode2 (:ablty))))
  con2 (s-attr actor ($course cno (num numval c5576)
                  deptname (CS) actor (nil)
                  time (times time3 (:tf)))
        attr (taken-prereq) mode (modes mode1 (:t))))

YADR: examining and/or concept

YADR: looking for: c6037
($course cno (num numval (110)) deptname (CS) actor (nil)
  mode (modes mode2 (:ablty)))

RUN-RULE: looking for:
(implies con1 (nil)
  con2 ($course cno (num numval (110)) deptname (CS) actor (nil)
        mode (modes mode2 (:ablty))))

; The first disjunct fails; CS 110 has (co-)requisites.
Run-rule: Failed to find rule(s) for probe: c6037

YADR: looking for: c6043
(s-attr actor ($course cno (num numval (110)) deptname (CS) actor (nil)

                    time (times time3 (:tf)))
          attr (taken-prereq) mode (modes mode1 (:t)))

RUN-RULE: looking for:
(implies
  con1 (nil)
  con2 (s-attr actor ($course cno (num numval (110))
                      deptname (CS) actor (nil)
                      time (times time3 (:tf)))
          attr (taken-prereq) mode (modes mode1 (:t)))))

RUN-RULE: found rules
(ifnw25)

; YADR looks to see if the student has passed CS 110's prereq, MATH
; 133...
YADR: looking for: c6060
($course time (times time3 (:tf)) deptname (MATH) cno (num numval
                                                        (133)))

; ...and finds that he/she has, due to the previously asserted form.
; Note that if "CS 110" had come before "Math 134" in the original
; user input (so long ago!), ACE would have asked the student
; "did you pass Math 133" in order to establish CS 110's prereqs.
; Assuming the same user response, the later query concerning Math 134
; would find the previously asserted query, and all would be well.
; Thus, slightly different things can happen depending on the
; precise order of the input....
YADR: found fact(s) for probe:
(Faxw118)

YADR deduced fact(s):
(c6109)

; Now, ASE checks that the student has supplied enough courses to
; cover distributional requirements.
DO-GOAL . . . . . . goal!Ase
(/goal allcoursesthere? c5570)

; This function does the check. If more courses seem to be needed,
; ASE will ask for them, via the Tactician, at this point. If the
; student really isn't taking any further courses, ASE will use
; other scheduling rules (not shown here) to make various comments
; about the violated constraints.
DO-GOAL . . . . . . goal!Ase
(/code (check-for-all-courses c5570))

; Finally, ASE verifies that this is the schedule of a full-time student

DO-GOAL . . . . . . goal!Ase
(/goal fullsched? c5570)

; ASE uses YADR to establish that the schedule neither has less than
; 12 credits nor more than 18 credits (the allowable range for
; a full-time student in the School of Engineering)
; Here is the schedule:
(p c6264)
(s-attr attr (full val (10))
      actor
      (schedule compnum (5)
          con5
          ($course time (times time3 (nil)) cno (num numval (110))
                deptname (CS) actor (nil) mode (modes mode1 (:t)))
          con4
          ($course time (times time3 (nil)) cno (num numval (134))
                deptname (MATH) actor (nil)
                mode (modes mode1 (:t)))
          con3
          ($course time (times time3 (nil)) cno (num numval (127))
                deptname (CHEM) actor (nil)
                mode (modes mode1 (:t)))
          con2
          ($course time (times time3 (nil)) cno (num numval (105))
                deptname (ENGL) actor (nil)
                mode (modes mode1 (:t)))
          con1
          ($course time (times time3 (nil)) cno (num numval (101))
                deptname (HIST) actor (nil)
                mode (modes mode1 (:t)))
          semester (+0))))

YADR: looking for: c6264

RUN-RULE: looking for:
(implies con1 (nil) con2 (s-attr attr (full val (10)) ....))

RUN-RULE: found rules
(ifnw6)
(p (get-structure 'ifnw6))
; "Full schedule" means "greater than or equal 12" or "less than or equal
; 18"
(implies con1
    (conj con1
        (a-config con1 (schedule) con2 (num numval (12))
            confrel (ge))

```
            con2
            (a-config con1 (schedule) con2 (num numval (18))
                  confrel (le)))
       con2
       (s-attr actor (schedule) attr (full val (10)))
```

YADR: looking for: c6317
(p c6317)

YADR: examining and/or concept

YADR: looking for: c6318
(a-config con1 (schedule compnum (5) ....)
      con2 (num numval (12)) confrel (ge))

; This form will match one of ACE's "generic facts:" forms which
; match many actual facts. The generic fact is credits-ge-pfact,
; which counts up the number of credits assigned to each component
; of a schedule, and allows the match to succeed iff there are at least
; 12 credits there.
(p (get 'credits-ge-pfact 'preds))
(lambda (probe) (greaterp (credits (grf '(con1) probe))
                         (add1 (car (grv '(con2 numval) probe)))))

YADR: found fact(s) for probe:
(c6372)

YADR: looking for: c6323
(a-config con1 (schedule compnum (5) ....)
      con2 (num numval (18)) confrel (le))
; This one matches the analogous credits-le-pfact:
YADR: found fact(s) for probe:
(c6464)

RUN-RULE proved:
((c6574))

YADR deduced fact(s):
(c6586)

; Now the system must calculate a new schedule for the student.
; This job is performed by ASE (using YADR as a sub-routine, as usual).
DO-GOAL . . . . . . goal!Strat
(/goal new-schedule)

....

; Here is the result...
(p c6739)
(schedule con5
```
```

```
; a "Group 3" (social science) distributional course
($course dept
        (org orgocc ($course) orgtype (dept) orgname (nil))
        obj
       (infostruc itype (ks)) student (person convrole (*other))
        actor c6878 time (times time1 (:pres))
        mode (modes mode1 (:t) mode2 (:urge))
        superset (GRP3) cno (num numval (nil)) deptname (nil))
con4
; a "Group 2" (Liberal arts) distributional course
($course dept
        (org orgocc ($course) orgtype (dept) orgname (nil))
        obj
       (infostruc itype (ks)) student (person convrole (*other))
        actor c6838 time (times time1 (:pres))
        mode (modes mode1 (:t) mode2 (:urge))
        superset (GRP2) cno (num numval (nil))
        deptname (nil))
con3
; the successor of CS 110
($course dept
        (org orgocc ($course) orgtype (dept) orgname (nil))
        obj
       (infostruc itype (ks)) student (person convrole (*other))
        actor c6783 time (times time1 (:pres))
        mode (modes mode1 (:t) mode2 (:urge))
        superset (nil) cno (num numval (111))
        deptname (CS))
con2
; the successor of Math 134
($course dept
        (org orgocc ($course) orgtype (dept) orgname (nil))
        obj
       (infostruc itype (ks)) student (person convrole (*other))
        actor c6760 time (times time1 (:pres))
        mode (modes mode1 (:t) mode2 (:urge))
        superset (nil) cno (num numval (200))
        deptname (MATH))
con1
; the successor of Chem 127
($course dept
        (org orgocc ($course) orgtype (dept) orgname (nil))
        obj
       (infostruc itype (ks)) student (person convrole (*other))
```

```
            actor c6745 time (times time1 (:pres))
            mode (modes mode1 (:t) mode2 (:urge))
            superset (nil) cno (num numval (128))
            deptname (CHEM))
      compnum (5))
```

. . . .

; Now we must tell the student the new schedule.
(/goal tell-student-sched-goal c6739)

; The schedule is divided into two parts: one for named courses; and
; one for the Group 2/Group 3 courses. These are converted into
; coordination-of-events concepts, and placed in a "somerel(ation)"
; form, to allow them to be said as separate sentences. This
; is an inadequate stab at what are really paragraph-structure phenomena.

```
(p c6739)
(somerel con1
      (coord con3 "CS 111" con2 "Math 200" con1 "Chem 128")
      con2
      (coord con1 "Group 2" con2 "Group 3"))
```

; This gets handed to the Generator, one subcon at a time:
DO-GOAL . . . . . . goal!Strat
(/goal speak-goal c6739)

GEN: top of c-list
(p :parentcon)
(coord con3 "CS 111" con2 "Math 200" con1 "Chem 128")

; The coord sketchifier notices that this can be said as:
; "You should take <courses>" rather than
; "You should take <course1> and you should take <course2>, etc."

; The result for the first subcon:
utterance is (you should take CHEM 128 and MATH 200 and CS 111)

GEN: top of c-list
(coord con1 "Group 2" con2 "Group3")

; And the final result...
I'M SAYING:
You should take CHEM 128 and MATH 200 and CS 111.
You should take a GRP2 and GRP3 course.

The interview concludes with the advisor offering to answer any questions, storing the proposed schedule, and showing the student out.

Then, a new instance of help-student-goal, which was created way back at the beginning, is invoked.

I'M SAYING:
Can I answer any questions?
input:
no

Your schedule has been sent to the registrar

It's been real nice. Please close the door behind you.

10.9 Parting Words

And so the story ends. In this concluding chapter I explained a method of integrating the language-processing, inferencing, and knowledge-base management machinery described earlier in a functioning conversational system, ACE. The basic idea is that all of the system's activities, and especially its language behavior, should occur in the service of one or more *conversational goals*. In ACE, the top-level goal is the *help-student-goal*. ACE tells a potential user the kinds of things it is prepared to do for him (e.g., question answering or preregistration). It then attempts to decide what the user wants by examining his response. If successful, the goal-following control is initialized with the appropriate conversational goal. As we saw, for preregistration this leads to successive subgoals of identifying the student, checking on the current schedule of courses, and agreeing on the coming semester's schedule. The further pursuit of these subgoals leads, from time to time, to calls to the language interface to tell the user something or to ask a question; to the knowledge-base manager for retrieval of student facts, curriculum items, or scheduling rules; to the conversational tactician for help with incomplete or ellipsed user input; and to the reasoning module for help when problems arise in understanding an input or in deciding upon the next course schedule.

As the session just described demonstrates, the need for a practicable integration technique is of paramount importance in the implementation of systems such as those presented in this book. The integration problem remains one of the major outstanding problems of Artificial Intelligence. An expert reasoning system together with its language-processing interface can be thought of as a collection of *resources* to be used in different ways to meet the overall system's problem-solving and conversational purposes. As systems continue to be built that achieve more sophisticated performance by incorporating more kinds of knowledge and problem-solving capabilities, the need for effective integration can only grow. It is my hope that the style of integration illustrated in this concluding chapter will provide guidelines for the system designers of the future.

Notes

1. Actually, the prerequisite links that define the curriculum "script" are stored individually in a YADR-type assertional database, rather than as a frame-system. The two forms are equivalent in representational power (cf., e.g., Char81), and the assertional form allows uniform access (through SOT) to both scriptal and rules-type data.

2. A new conversational "expert" process, a *mixed-initiative explainer,* is currently being developed which will allow ACE to describe its curriculum and scheduling knowledge base (Bien85).

3. The generator was originally designed for use in the CADHELP system, discussed in Chapter 7.

References

References

[Abel85]
Abelson, H., and Sussman, G.J. *Structure and Interpretation of Computer Programs*. Cambridge, Mass.: The MIT Press, 1985.

[Alle80]
Allen, J.F., and Perrault, C. "Analyzing Intention in Utterances." *Artificial Intelligence* 15, no. 3, (1980).

[Alle81]
Allen, J.F. "An Interval-Based Representation of Temporal Knowledge." *Proceedings of the 7th International Joint Conference on Artificial Intelligence.* Vancouver, B.C., August 1981.

[Alle82]
Allen, J.F. "ARGOT: The Rochester Dialogue System." *Proceedings of the 1982 National Conference on Artificial Intelligence.* Pittsburgh, Pennsylvania, August 1982.

[Appe85]
Appelt, D.E. "Planning English Referring Expressions." *Artificial Intelligence* 26, no. 1 (1985): 1–34.

[BarH60]
Bar-Hillel, Y. "The Present Status of Automatic Translation of Languages." In F. L. Alt, ed., *Advances in Computers*, Vol. 1. New York: Academic Press, 1960.

[Barr81]
Barr, A., and Feigenbaum, E., eds. *The Handbook of Artificial Intelligence,* Vol. I. Los Altos, California: Kaufmann, 1981.

[Bien85]
Bienkowski, M.A., and Cullingford, R.E. "Goal-Directed Explanations." TR-342, Princeton University, Department of EE & CS, 1985.

[Birn81]
Birnbaum, L., and Selfridge, M. "Conceptual Analysis of Natural Language." In R. Schank, and R. Abelson, eds. *Inside Computer Understanding*. Hillsdale, New Jersey: Lawrence Erlbaum Associates, 1981.

[Bobr68]
Bobrow, D.G. "Natural Language Input for a Computer Problem-Solving System." In [Mins68], pp. 146–226.

[Bobr75]
Bobrow, D.G., and Collins, A., eds. *Representation and Understanding: Studies in Cognitive Science*. New York: Academic Press, 1975.

[Bobr77a]
Bobrow, D.G.; Kaplan, R.M.; Kay, M.; Norman, D.A.; Thompson, H.; and Winograd, T. "GUS—A Frame-Driven Dialog System." *Artificial Intelligence* 8., no. 1 (1977).

[Bobr77b]
Bobrow, D.G., and Winograd, T. "An Overview of KRL: A Knowledge Representation Language." *Cognitive Science* 1, no. 1 (1977): 3–46.

[Brac78]
Brachman, R., "A Structural Paradigm for Representing Knowledge." TR-3878. Cambridge, Massachusetts: Bolt, Beranick & Newman, 1978.

[Brach79]
Brachman, R., et al. "Research in Natural Language Understanding." TR-4274. Cambridge, Massachusetts: Bolt, Beranick & Newman. 1979.

[Brow75]
Brown, J.S., and Burton, R.R. "Multiple Representations of Knowledge for Tutorial Reasoning." In Bobrow and Collins, eds., *Representation and Understanding*. New York: Academic Press, 1975.

[Bruc72]
Bruce, B. "A Model for Temporal References and Its Application in a Question Answering Program." *Artificial Intelligence* 3 (1972): 1–25.

[Carb83]
Carberry, S. "Tracking User Goals in an Information Seeking Environment." *Proceedings of the National Conference on Artificial Intelligence*. AAAI-83. Washington, DC, 1983.

[Carb79]
Carbonell, J.G. "Subjective Understanding: Computer Models of Belief Revision." Ph.D. dissertation, TR-150. Yale University, Department of Computer Science, 1979.

[Carb81]
Carbonell, J.G.; Cullingford, R.E.; and Gershman, A.V. "Steps Toward Knowledge-Based Machine Translation." *IEEE Trans. on Systems, Man & Cybernetics* PAMI-3, no. 4 (July 1981): 376–92.

[Carb70]
Carbonell, J.R. "AI in CAI: An Artificial Intelligence Approach to Computer-Assisted Instruction." *IEEE Trans. Man-Machine Systems* MMS-11 (1970).

[Char72]
Charniak, E. "Towards a Model of Children's Story Comprehension." Ph.D. dissertation, TR-266. Massachusetts Institute of Technology, AI Laboratory. 1972.

[Char76]
Charniak, E., and Wilks, Y., eds. *Computational Semantics*. New York: Elsevier, North Holland. 1976.

[Char77]
Charniak, E. "Ms. Malaprop, A Language Comprehension Program." *Proceedings of the National Conference on Artificial Intelligence,* AAAI-77. Cambridge, Mass.

[Char80]
Charniak, E.; Riesbeck, C.; and McDermott, D. *Artificial Intelligence Programming.* Hillsdale, New Jersey: Lawrence Erlbaum Associates, 1980.

[Char81]
Charniak, E. "A Common Representation for Problem-Solving and Language-Comprehension Information." *Artificial Intelligence* 16, no. 3 (1981).

[Clan81]
Clancey, W.J., and Letsinger, R. "NEOMYCIN: Reconfiguring a Rule-based Expert System for Applications to Teaching." *Proceedings of the Seventh International Joint Conference on Artificial Intelligence.* Vancouver, B.C., August 1981.

[Cull77]
Cullingford, R.E. "Script Application: Computer Understanding of Newspaper Stories." Ph.D. dissertation, TR-116. Yale University, Department of Computer Science, 1977.

[Cull79]
Cullingford, R.E. "Pattern Matching and Inference in Story Understanding." *Discourse Processes* 2, no. 4 (November 1979): 319–34.

[Cull81]
Cullingford, R.E., et al., "Towards Automating Explanations." *Proceedings of the 7th International Joint Conference on Artificial Intelligence.* Vancouver, B.C., August 1981. Pp. 432–38.

[Cull82a]
Cullingford, R.E.; Krueger, M.W.; Selfridge, M.G.; and Bienkowski, M.A. "Automated Explanations as a Component of a Computer-Aided Design System." *IEEE Trans. Systems, Man & Cybernetics,* SMC-12, no. 2, (March/April): 168–82.

[Cull82b]
Cullingford, R., and Selfridge, M. "Purposive Conversation with ACE, an Academic Counseling Experiment," *Proceedings of the IEEE International Conference on Cybernetics and Society.* Seattle, Washington, 1982.

[Cull83]
Cullingford, R.E., and Joseph, L.J. "A Heuristically 'Optimal' Knowledge Base Organization Technique." *Automatica* 19, no. 6 (Nov-Dec 1983).

[Cull84]
Cullingford, R.E., and Pazzani, M.J. "Word Meaning Selection in Multimodule Language Processing Systems." *IEEE Trans. Pattern Analysis & Machine Intelligence* PAMI-6, no. 4 (July): 493–509.

[Deer81]
Deering, M.; Faletti, J.; and Wilensky, R. "PEARL: An Efficient Language for Artificial Intelligence Programming." *Proceedings of the 7th International Joint Conference on AI,* Vancouver, B.C., August 1981.

[Doyl79]
Doyle, J. "A Truth Maintenance System." *Artificial Intelligence* 12 (1979).

[Dyer82]
Dyer, M.G., "In-Depth Understanding: A Computer Model of Integrated Processing for Narrative Comprehension." Ph.D. dissertation, TR-219. Yale University, Department of Computer Science. 1982.

[Enge84]
Engelberg, J.; Levas, A.; and Selfridge, M. "A Robust Natural Language Interface to a Robot Assembly System." *Proceedings of the IEEE International Conference on Robotics.* Atlanta, Georgia, March 1984.

[Fill72]
Fillmore, C. "The Case for Case." In E. Bach and R. Harms, eds., *Universals in Linguistic Theory.* New York: Holt, Rinehart and Winston, 1972.

[Film79]
Filman, R.E. "The Interaction of Observation and Inference in a Formal Representation System." *Proceedings of the Sixth International Joint Conference on Artificial Intelligence.* Tokyo, Japan, August 1979.

[Fode81]
Foderaro, J.K., and Sklower, K.L. *The FRANZ LISP Manual.* Berkeley: Computer Science Division, University of California, Berkeley, 1981.

[Forg79]
Forgy, C.L. "On the Efficient Implementation of Production Systems." Ph.D. dissertation, Carnegie-Mellon University, Department of Computer Science, 1979.

[Gers79]
Gershman, A.V. "Knowledge-Based Parsing." Ph.D. dissertation, TR-156. Yale University, Department of Computer Science, 1979.

[Gins78]
Ginsparg, J. "Natural Language Processing in an Automatic Programming Domain." Ph.D. dissertation, Research Report STAN-CS-78-671. Stanford University, Department of Computer Science, 1978.

[Hasl83]
Hasling, D.W. "Abstract Explanations of Strategy in a Diagnostic Consultation System." *Proceedings of the National Conference on Artificial Intelligence,* AAAI-83. Washington, DC, 1983.

[Haye77]
Hayes, P.J. "On Semantic Nets, Frames and Associations." *Proceedings of the Fifth International Joint Conference on Artificial Intelligence.* Cambridge, Massachusetts, August 1977.

[Haye79]
Hayes-Roth, F.; and Waterman, D.A., eds. *Pattern-Directed Inference Systems*. New York: Academic Press, 1979.

[Haye83]
Hayes-Roth, F.; Waterman, D.A.; and Lenat, D.B., eds. *Building Expert Systems*. New York: Addison-Wesley, 1983.

[Hend76]
Hendrix, G.G. "Expanding the Utility of Semantic Networks Through Partitioning." *Artificial Intelligence* 7 (1976): 21–49.

[Hewe71]
Hewett, C. "Description and Theoretical Analysis (Using Schemas) of PLANNER: A Language for Proving Theorems and Manipulating Models in a Robot." Ph.D. dissertation, AI Laboratory TR-258, MIT. Cambridge, Massachusetts, 1971.

[Hobb76]
Hobbs J.R. "Pronoun Resolution." TR-76-1, Department of Computer Science, City University of New York, 1976.

[Hobb78]
Hobbs, J.R. "Coherence and Coreference." *Cognitive Psychology* 3, no. 1 (1979).

[Josh84]
Joshi, A.; Webber, B.; and Weideschel, R. "Living Up to Expectations: Computing Expert Responses." *Proceedings of the National Conference on Artificial Intelligence,* AAAI-84. Univ. of Texas at Austin, August 1984. Pp. 169–75.

[Kapl79]
Kaplan, S.J. "Cooperative Responses from a Portable Natural Language Data Base Query System." Ph.D. dissertation, University of Pennsylvania, Dept. of Computer and Information Science, 1979.

[Katz63]
Katz, J.J., and Fodor, J.A. "The Structure of Semantic Theory." *Language* 39 (1963): 170–210.

[Lebo80]
Lebowitz, M. "Generalization and Memory in an Integrated Understanding System." Ph.D. dissertation, TR-186. Yale University, Department of Computer Science, 1980.

[Lehn78]
Lehnert, W. *The Process of Question Answering*. Hillsdale, New Jersey: Lawrence Erlbaum Associates, 1978.

[Mann81]
Mann, W.C., and Moore, J.A. "Computer Generation of Multiparagraph English Text." *American Journal of Computational Linguistics* 7, no. 1 (1981).

[Marc80]
Marcus, M.P. *Theory of Syntactic Recognition for Natural Language*. Cambridge, Mass.: MIT Press, 1980.

[McAl80]
McAllester, D. "An Outlook on Truth Maintenance." MIT AI Laboratory TR-551, Cambridge, MA, 1980.

[McCa77]
McCarthy, J. "Epistemological Problems of Artificial Intelligence." *Proceedings of the Fifth International Joint Conference on Artificial Intelligence.* Cambridge, Massachusetts, August 1977.

[McCa80]
McCarthy, J. "Circumscription—A Form of Non-Monotonic Reasoning." *Artificial Intelligence* 13 (1980).

[McDe73]
McDermott, D., and Sussman, G. "CONNIVER Reference Manual." MIT AI Laboratory TR-259a. 1973.

[McDe75]
McDermott, D. "Very Large PLANNER-Type Data Bases." MIT AI Laboratory TR-339. 1975.

[McDe80]
McDermott, D., and Doyle, J. "Non-monotonic Logic I." *Artificial Intelligence* 13 (1980).

[McDe82]
McDermott, D. "A Temporal Logic for Reasoning About Processes and Plans." *Cognitive Science* 6, no. 2 (1982).

[McDo81]
McDonald, D.D. "Natural Language Generation as a Computational Problem." COINS TR-81-33. Department of Computer and Information Science. Univ. of Massachusetts, Amherst. 1981.

[McKe80]
McKeown, K. "Generating Relevant Explanations: Natural Language Responses to Questions about Database Structures." *Proc. of the First Annual Conference on Artificial Intelligence.* Stanford, California, 1980.

[Mill76]
Miller, G.A., and Johnson-Laird, P.N. *Language and Perception.* Cambridge, Massachusetts: Belknap/Harvard Press, 1976.

[Mill78]
Miller, L. "Has Artificial Intelligence Contributed to an Understanding of the Human Mind? A Critique of Arguments for and Against." *Cognitive Science* 2, no. 2, (April-June 1978).

[Mils83]
Milstein, J. "GAL—A Goal-Achieving Language." TR-83-5. EE&CS Department, University of Connecticut, 1983.

[Mins68]
Minsky, M., ed. *Semantic Information Processing.* Cambridge: MIT Press, 1968.

[Mins75]
Minsky, M. "A Framework for Representing Knowledge." In [Wins75].

[Nash78]

Nash-Webber, B.L. "Syntax beyond the Sentence: Anaphora." In G. Spiro, B. Bruce, and B. Brewer, eds., *Theoretical Issues in Reading Comprehension*. Hillsdale, New Jersey: Lawrence Earlbaum Associates, 1978.

[Neim82]

Neiman, D. "Graphical Animation from Knowledge." *Proceedings of the National Conference on Artificial Intelligence*. AAAI-82, Univ. of Pittsburgh. 1982.

[Newe72]

Newell, A., and Simon, H. *Human Problem Solving*. Englewood Cliffs, New Jersey: Prentice-Hall, 1972.

[Nils71]

Nilsson, N. *Problem Solving Methods in Artificial Intelligence*. New York: McGraw-Hill, 1971.

[Norm75]

Norman, D.A., and Rumelhart, D.E., eds. *Explorations in Cognition*. San Francisco: W.H. Freeman, 1975.

[Piel69]

Pielou, E.C. *An Introduction to Mathematical Ecology*. New York: Wiley-Interscience, 1969.

[Rebo76]

Reboh, R. "QLISP: A Language for the Interactive Development of Complex Systems." Report TN-120. SRI International, AI Center, Menlo Park, California (1976).

[Resc71]

Rescher, N., & Urquhart, A. *Temporal Logic*. New York: Springer-Verlag, 1971.

[Rich79]

Rich, E. "User Modeling via Stereotypes." *Cognitive Science* 3, no. 4 (1979).

[Rieg75]

Rieger, C.J. "Conceptual Memory." In [Scha75a].

[Rieg76]

Rieger, C. "An Organization of Knowledge for Problem Solving and Comprehension." *Artificial Intelligence* 7, no. 2 (1976).

[Ries75]

Riesbeck, C.J. "Conceptual Analysis." In [Scha75a].

[Rych76]

Rychener, M.D. "Production Systems as a Programming Language for Artificial Intelligence Applications." Ph.D. dissertation, Carnegie-Mellon University, Department of Computer Science, 1976.

[Scha73a]

Schank, R.C. "Identification of Conceptualizations Underlying Natural Language." In [Scha73b].

[Scha73b]

Schank, R.C., and Colby, K.M., eds. *Computer Models of Thought and Language*. San Francisco: W.H. Freeman, 1973.

[Scha75a]
Schank, R.C., ed. *Conceptual Information Processing*. Elsevier, North Holland, New York: 1975.

[Scha75b]
Schank, R., and the Yale AI Project. "SAM—A Story Understander." TR-43. Department of Computer Science, Yale University, New Haven, Connecticut, August 1975.

[Scha77]
Schank, R., and Abelson, R. *Scripts, Plans, Goals and Understanding*. Hillsdale, New Jersey: Lawrence Erlbaum Associates, 1977.

[Simm72]
Simmons, R., and Slocum, J. "Generating English Discourse from Semantic Networks." *Comm. ACM* 15, no. 10 (1972).

[Spir75]
Spiro, R.J. "Inferential Reconstruction in Memory for Connected Discourse." TR-2. University of Illinois, Laboratory for Cognitive Studies in Education, 1975.

[Stef80]
Stefik, M. "Planning with Constraints." TR-784. Stanford University, Department of Computer Science, 1980.

[Swar77]
Swartout, W. "A Digitalis Therapy Advisor with Explanations." *Proceedings of the 5th International Joint Conf. on AI*. Cambridge, Masssachusetts, 1977.

[Swar81]
Swartout, W.R. "XPLAIN: A system for Creating and Explaining Expert Consulting Programs." *Artificial Intelligence* 31, no. 3 (September 1983).

[Tenn80]
Tennant, H. *Natural Language Processing*. Princeton, N.J.: Petrocelli, 1980.

[Wein80]
Weiner, J.L. "BLAH, A System Which Explains Its Reasoning." *Artificial Intelligence* 15, nos. 1, 2 (1980).

[Weis84]
Weiss, S., and Kulikowsky, C. *A Practical Guide to Designing Expert Systems*, Totowa, New Jersey: Rowman & Allanheld, 1984.

[Weiz66]
Weizenbaum, J. "ELIZA—A Computer Program for the Study of Natural Language Communication between Man and Machine." *Comm. ACM* 9 (1966): 36–45.

[Weiz76]
Weizenbaum, J. *Computer Power and Human Reason: From Judgment to Calculation*. San Francisco: W.H. Freeman, 1976.

[Wile78]
Wilensky, R.W. "Understanding Goal-Based Stories." Ph.D. dissertation, TR-140. Yale University, Department of Computer Science, 1978.

[Wile80]

Wilensky, R., and Arens, Y. "PHRAN: A Knowledge-Based Approach to Natural Language Analysis." UCB/ERL TR-M80-35. University of California, Berkeley, 1980.

[Wile84]

Wilensky, R.W. *LISPcraft*. New York: W.W. Norton, 1984.

[Wilk73]

Wilks, Y. "An Artificial Intelligence Approach to Machine Translation." In [Scha73b].

[Wilk75]

Wilks Y. "A Preferential, Pattern-Seeking Semantics for Natural Language Understanding." *Artificial Intelligence* 6 (1975): 53–74.

[Wino72]

Winograd, T. *Understanding Natural Language*. New York: Academic Press, 1972.

[Wino83]

Winograd, T., *Language as a Cognitive Process: Syntax,* Vol. 1. Reading, Massachusetts: Addison-Wesley, 1983.

[Wins75]

Winston, P., ed. *The Psychology of Computer Vision*. New York: McGraw-Hill, 1975

[Wins81]

Winston, P.H., and Horn, B.K.P. *LISP*. Reading, Massachusetts: Addison-Wesley, 1981.

[Wood70]

Woods, W.A. "Transition Network Grammars for Natural Language Analysis." *Comm. ACM* 13, no. 10 (1970).

[Wood75]

Woods, W.A. "What's in a Link? Foundations for Semantic Networks." In [Bobr75], pp. 35–82.

[Zade73]

Zadeh, L. "Outline of a New Approach to the Analysis of Complex Systems and Decisions." *IEEE Trans. Systems, Man & Cybernetics* 3 (1973): 28–44.

Appendices

Appendix I
The ERKS Types

This Appendix documents the collection of ERKS types that is the basis for the example representational system used in the main text. For each type, we show the defining declaration and give some examples of its use. For those who have access to the NLP Toolkit software, it may be useful to know that this is basically an annotation of the file nlp/ERKS/ERKStypes.l, corresponding to version 1.09 of the NLP Toolkit distribution. We will be working our way down from the top of the ISA–hierarchy in a more-or-less breadth-first manner.

Please Note: this type system is oversimplified, incomplete, and probably inconsistent in spots; its only purpose is to support the representation examples of the book. Some of the type names are not especially mnemonic, but are preserved for historical reasons.

The Upper Levels

At the very top of the tree is *thing*, the superset of all the other types.

(def-ERKS-type thing
intrinsic-slots
((thingname symbol-p))
)

Next is a garbage type for stuff that doesn't fit anywhere else: e.g., *times, modes, prepconsts:*

(def-ERKS-type other
superset (thing)
intrinsic-slots
((lexval symbol-p))
)

Some kinds of things are substantive:

(def-ERKS-type entity
superset (thing)
intrinsic-slots
((entname symbol-p))
extrinsic-slots
((ref (def indef pron))

```
(rel couldbe-concept-p))
)
```

Some entities are self-willed and aware:

```
(def-ERKS-type animate
superset (entity)
intrinsic-slots
((animname symbol-p))
extrinsic-slots
((ref (def indef pron))
(rel couldbe-concept-p))
)
```

Some animate entities are "higher animate," i.e., capable of engaging in high-level communication and social episodes. The wh-word "who" can be rendered using *hianimate*.

```
(def-ERKS-type hianimate
superset (animate)
intrinsic-slots
((animname symbol-p))
extrinsic-slots
((ref (def indef pron))
(rel couldbe-concept-p))
)
```

Another kind of entity is a location for some characteristic action. "Place," "scene," etc., are examples of this type.

```
(def-ERKS-type place
superset (entity)
intrinsic-slots
((placename symbol-p))
extrinsic-slots
((ref (def indef))
(rel couldbe-concept-p))
)
```

Another kind of entity is a "mental object," *mobj*. This is an amorphous object that is considered to exist in mental locations such as people's long-term memory, or in physical entities such as books.

```
(def-ERKS-type mobj
superset (entity)
intrinsic-slots
((mobjname symbol-p))
extrinsic-slots
((ref (def indef))
(rel couldbe-concept-p))
)
```

As opposed to the mental objects, there are the physical objects, animate or otherwise. Words such as "object" or "something," when used to refer to an undistinguished physical item, can be rendered by *pobj*.

(def-ERKS-type pobj
superset (entity)
intrinsic-slots
((pobjname symbol-p)
(phase phase-p)) ;physical phase
extrinsic-slots
((ref (def indef))
(rel couldbe-concept-p))
)

Artifacts are man-made things, whether mental (e.g., book content) or physical:

(def-ERKS-type artifact
superset (entity)
intrinsic-slots
((artifname symbol-p)
(product-of couldbe-hianimate-p)) ;who made it
extrinsic-slots
((ref (def indef))
(rel couldbe-concept-p))
)

Aside from entities, the other broad class of types are "concepts," actions /states of the world (entities doing or being predicated about), or relations among these:

(def-ERKS-type concept
superset (thing)
intrinsic-slots
((conceptname symbol-p))
)

This type spans the simple and composite "action" type classes:

(def-ERKS-type episode
superset (concept)
extrinsic-slots
((entrole couldbe-entity-p)
(ref (def indef)))
intrinsic-slots
((lexval symbol-p)
(actor couldbe-animate-p)
(mode modes-p)
(time times-p))
)

Another kind of concept covers states of the world (entities being predicated about):

```
(def-ERKS-type state
superset (concept)
extrinsic-slots
()
intrinsic-slots
((lexval symbol-p)
(mode modes-p)
(time times-p))
)
```

Some concepts are primitive actions (entities doing conceptually primitive things):

```
(def-ERKS-type act
superset (episode)
extrinsic-slots
()
intrinsic-slots
((lexval symbol-p)
(mode modes-p)
(time times-p))
)
```

Other concepts are composite actions (entities doing conceptually complex things, e. g., scripts). These actions are characteristically carried out in service of a goal, and thus are called *goalepisodes:*

```
(def-ERKS-type goalepisode
superset (episode)
extrinsic-slots
()
intrinsic-slots
((lexval symbol-p)
(mode modes-p)
(time times-p))
)
```

The final major class of concepts encompasses relations among episodes (e.g., *cause, before, during).*

```
(def-ERKS-type conrel
superset (concept)
intrinsic-slots
((lexval symbol-p))
)
```

A "degenerate" kind of relation spans relations among entities (*nextto, topof, poss,* etc.) such as we see in *s-attrs* and *a-configs.* These are called *pprel* because they relate entities that were historically (in conceptual dependency) known as Picture Producers (PPs):

```
(def-ERKS-type pprel
```

```
superset (thing)
intrinsic-slots
((lexval symbol-p))
)
```

One kind of *pprel* is the *confrel*, a configurational relation among entities:

```
(def-ERKS-type confrel
superset (pprel)
intrinsic-slots
((confval confval-p))
)
```

A *locrel* is a *confrel* expressing physical configurations of location:

```
(def-ERKS-type locrel
superset (confrel)
intrinsic-slots
((locrelval locrelval-p))
)
```

The analogous relation for mental objects and their "possessors" is *in-mloc:*

```
(def-ERKS-type in-mloc
superset (confrel)
)
```

The other major kind of *pprel* is an attribution (predication) about an intrinsic property of an entity.

```
(def-ERKS-type attr
superset (pprel)
intrinsic-slots
((attrval (tags intelligence temperature age exist unit phystate partform
health)))
)
```

Entities

In alphabetical order, the first kind of entity *(abstimes)* is an absolute time specifier for episodes, which are considered to be occuring during smallest *timdur* filled:

```
(def-ERKS-type abstimes ;note: this is the canonical filler of abstime slot
superset (mobj)
extrinsic-slots
((hour timdur-p) ;at 3 o'clock
(daypart timdur-p) ;in the morning
(weekday timdur-p) ;on (an April) Tuesday
(week timdur-p) ;in 3rd week (of April)
(month timdur-p) ;in April
(semester timdur-p) ;during Fall semester
```

(yearpart timdur-p) ;during the Fall
(year timdur-p)) ;of 1983
)

Animate entities other than higher animate are handled with *animal:*

(def-ERKS-type animal
superset (animate pobj)
intrinsic-slots
((animname symbol-p)
(animtype (cat dog kitty mouse))
(age age-p)
(gender (masc fem neut)))
extrinsic-slots
((ref (def indef pron))
(rel couldbe-concept-p)
(convrole (*self *other))
(agent-of couldbe-hianimate-p))
)

The class *b(ody)part* encompasses the physical/functional pieces of various animate actors. They may not be removed without a grave negative change in the associated health scale.

(def-ERKS-type bpart
superset (pobj)
intrinsic-slots
((bpname symbol-p)
(eprole role-p)
(bptype (hand nose eyes ears legs leg beard foot hair lungs
stomach mouth tooth knee)))
extrinsic-slots
((ref (def indef))
(partform couldbe-attr-p)
(partof couldbe-animate-p)
(rel couldbe-concept-p))
)

Entities that contain (and constrain the movement of) other entities are of type *container*. For example, "beer can," "envelope," "swimming pool (?)."

(def-ERKS-type container
superset (artifact)
intrinsic-slots
((conttype (bottle can glass))
(contains pobj-p))
extrinsic-slots
((ref (def indef))
(rel couldbe-concept-p))
)

Artifacts that "close" containers, clothes, windows, etc., are called *fasteners;* for example, buttons, zippers, bottle caps, throwaway tabs on soda cans.

```
(def-ERKS-type fastener
superset (artifact pobj)
intrinsic-slots
((fastenername symbol-p)
(fastenertype (button zipper container-cap, throwaway-tab)))
extrinsic-slots
((ref (def indef))
(rel couldbe-concept-p))
)
```

Large geographical/geological objects or formations are covered by *geofeat(ure).* For example,
"Mt Rushmore," "Gulf of Mexico," "barrier reef."

```
(def-ERKS-type geofeat
superset (place)
intrinsic-slots
((geoname symbol-p)
(eprole role-p)
(geotype (mountain ocean)))
extrinsic-slots
((ref (def indef))
(rel couldbe-concept-p))
)
```

A collection of inanimate entities being treated together as a unit are of type *group* (animate groups are handled with *team*). For example, "3 rocks," "bunch of grapes," etc.

```
(def-ERKS-type group
superset (pobj)
intrinsic-slots ;inherent roles (s-attr concepts)
((grpname symbol-p) ;role name vs constraining pred
(eprole role-p)
(typmem nomconcept-p) ;typical member
(grptype yanks-p)
(grpnum number-p))
extrinsic-slots ;slots filled by external entities
((ref (def indef pron))
(rel couldbe-concept-p))
)
```

Structures of information or knowledge are handled by *infostruc*. For example, "content of menu/course", "a thought."

```
(def-ERKS-type infostruc
superset (artifact mobj)
intrinsic-slots
```

```
((itype (ks field major minor major-acad-ks
minor-acad-ks related-grp acad-rec)) ; some for ACE
(iname symbol-p) ; this is a name for it
(eprole role-p)
(content string-p))
extrinsic-slots
((ref (def indef))
(possby couldbe-hianimate-p)
(somerel couldbe-entity-p) ;garbage slot for "content"
(rel couldbe-concept-p))
)
```

The type *ingobj* is intended to cover ingestible objects; for example, "John snorted cocaine."

```
(def-ERKS-type ingobj
;some are manufactured, others not
superset (pobj artifact)
intrinsic-slots
((ingname symbol-p)
(eprole role-p)
(ingtype (marijuana soda aspirin cabbage apple dope)))
extrinsic-slots
((ref (def indef))
(rel couldbe-concept-p))
)
```

The class *inst(rument)* spans the set of physical objects that are manipulated by actors to carry out certain well-defined functions. These objects are often grasped while being used. For example, "scalpel," "pencil," "keyboard," etc. The characteristic activity is normally a *goalepisode*.

```
(def-ERKS-type inst
superset (artifact pobj)
intrinsic-slots
((instname symbol-p)
(eprole role-p)
(funcep couldbe-episode-p)
(insttype (book football key ball hammer pencil)))
extrinsic-slots
((ref (def indef))
(rel couldbe-concept-p))
)
```

The "paths" that connect places and which vehicles of various kinds traverse are covered by the class *link*. For example, "in the channel," "on the tracks," "on I-91," etc.

```
(def-ERKS-type link
superset (artifact place)
intrinsic-slots
```

```
((linkname symbol-p)
(eprole role-p)
(linktype road-p))
extrinsic-slots
((ref (def indef))
(rel couldbe-concept-p))
)
```

The class *locale* is intended for the places where things happen.
Episodes are considered to be contained in smallest *locale* filled:

```
(def-ERKS-type locales ;note: this is the canonical filler of locale slot
superset (place)
extrinsic-slots
((inside couldbe-locrel-p)
(prox couldbe-locrel-p)
(topof couldbe-locrel-p)
(beneath couldbe-locrel-p)
(rightof couldbe-locrel-p)
(leftof couldbe-locrel-p)
(behind couldbe-locrel-p))
)
```

The class *m(ental) container* is used to describe containers of information such as
books, clocks, and billboards. The information itself is covered by the type
infostruc.

```
(def-ERKS-type mcontainer
superset (artifact pobj)
intrinsic-slots
((mconttype pobj-p)
(info infostruc-p))
))
```

Here we define the mental locations *(mloc)*, places where thoughts can be. (Note:
certain bodyparts, the sensors, can also be places where mental information can
be stored.)

```
(def-ERKS-type mloc
superset (entity) ;isa superset
intrinsic-slots ;inherent roles (s-attr concepts)
((part couldbe-hianimate-p) ;whose cp?
)
)
```

The "conscious processor" *(cp)* contains the current focus of mentation.

```
(def-ERKS-type cp
superset (mloc) ;isa superset
intrinsic-slots ;inherent roles (s-attr concepts)
((part couldbe-hianimate-p) ;whose cp?
```

```
)
)
```

The "long-term memory," the repository of thoughts that can (sometimes) be recalled into the *cp:*

```
(def-ERKS-type ltm
superset (mloc) ;isa superset
intrinsic-slots ;inherent roles (s-attr concepts)
((part couldbe-hianimate-p) ;whose cp?
)
)
```

"Intermediate" memory, which resides between *cp* and *ltm:*

```
(def-ERKS-type im
superset (mloc) ;isa superset
intrinsic-slots ;inherent roles (s-attr concepts)
((part couldbe-hianimate-p) ;whose cp?
)
)
```

Here we handle dirty lucre, including credit cards, portable, 2nd-level preferred debentures, etc.

```
(def-ERKS-type money
superset (artifact pobj)
intrinsic-slots
((monname symbol-p) ; quarters, dimes, pennies
(eprole role-p)
(amount num-p)
(montype (currency credit-card check)))
extrinsic-slots
((ref (def indef))
(rel couldbe-concept-p))
)
```

Numbers (both cardinal and ordinal) are handled by the type *num:*

```
(def-ERKS-type num
superset (mobj)
intrinsic-slots
((numval number-p)
(numord number-p) ;for ordinals: e.g first, second
(numcomp (low medium high)) ; comparative numbers (bogose)
(eprole role-p))
extrinsic-slots
((rel couldbe-concept-p))
)
```

The type *org* stands for structured assemblages of people having a common (often commercial) purpose (roughly speaking), viz., organizations. The org(anization) occ(upation) is typically a script indicating what the organization does. An *org* differs from a *team* in that it has internal structure, an executive and managers, for example. It differs from *polity* in that the latter controls a large physical area and has coercive powers. Examples are "IBM," "Energy Department," etc.

```
(def-ERKS-type org
superset (hianimate)
intrinsic-slots
((orgname symbol-p)
(eprole role-p)
(orgtype (post-office university corporation dept college)))
extrinsic-slots
((orgocc script-p) ; kludged, like role-p
(agent-of couldbe-hianimate-p)
(rel couldbe-concept-p))
)
```

And, of course, we need *persons:*

```
(def-ERKS-type person
superset (hianimate pobj) ;isa superset
intrinsic-slots ;inherent roles (s-attr concepts)
((persname symbol-p) ;role name vs constraining pred
(middname symbol-p)
(surname symbol-p) ; symbol-p defines "tag" slots
(title symbol-p)
; (standing timdur-p) ;for ACE: semester standing
(standing (frosh soph junior senior))
(eprole role-p)
(age age-p)
(gender (masc fem neut))) ;list of allowed fillers
extrinsic-slots ;slots filled by external entities
;(normally, a-config relations)
((ref (def indef pron))
(rel couldbe-concept-p)
(convrole (*self *other))
(agent-of couldbe-hianimate-p)
(case (subj obj reflx poss nom )))
)
```

Assemblages of people who have legislative and coercive powers over a large area, i.e., sovereign political units, go under the type *polity:*

```
(def-ERKS-type polity
superset (place hianimate) ;can be a place or an actor
intrinsic-slots ;inherent roles (s-attr concepts)
((polname symbol-p) ;role name vs constraining pred
(eprole role-p)
(poltype (university state munic nation)))
extrinsic-slots ;slots filled by external entities
```

```
((ref (def indef))
(rel couldbe-concept-p)
(agent-of couldbe-hianimate-p))
)
```

A *set* is like a *group,* except that its elements may be explicitly given and selected:

```
(def-ERKS-type set
superset (pobj) ; not clear about this
numslot (compnum)
intrinsic-slots ;inherent roles (s-attr concepts)
((eprole role-p)
(typmem nomconcept-p)
(con1 nomconcept-p)
(con2 nomconcept-p)
(con3 nomconcept-p)
(con4 nomconcept-p)
(con5 nomconcept-p)
(con6 nomconcept-p)
(compnum number-p))
extrinsic-slots ;slots filled by external entities
((ref (def indef pron))
(rel couldbe-concept-p))
)
```

The type *struc* stands for structures, man-made and immovable. For example, "Room 307," "Empire State Building," "George Washington Bridge."

```
(def-ERKS-type struc
superset (place artifact)
intrinsic-slots
((strucname symbol-p)
(strucno num-p)
(eprole role-p)
(structype (room building house woodshed airport cabinet bridge)) )
extrinsic-slots
((ref (def indef))
(partof struc-p)
(rel couldbe-concept-p))
)
```

A *support* exists to keep another entity from falling down, e.g., hangers, table legs, chairs, coat racks, etc.

```
(def-ERKS-type support
superset (artifact place)
intrinsic-slots
((suppname symbol-p)
(eprole role-p)
(supptype (table chair)))
extrinsic-slots
```

```
((ref (def indef))
(rel couldbe-concept-p))
)
```

The type *team* is used for groups of animates who are considered to be acting as one, e.g., "the Yankees," "we," etc.

```
(def-ERKS-type team
superset (hianimate pobj) ;isa superset
intrinsic-slots ;inherent roles (s-attr concepts)
((tname symbol-p) ;role name vs constraining pred
(typmem couldbe-hianimate-p) ;typical member
(convrole (*self *other))
(eprole role-p)
(ttype ttype-p))
extrinsic-slots ;slots filled by external entities
((ref (def indef pron))
(case (subj obj reflx poss nom ))
(rel couldbe-concept-p))
)
```

Durations of time are handled by *timdur:*

```
(def-ERKS-type timdur
superset (abstimes)
intrinsic-slots
((durname symbol-p)
(durmag num-p)
(eprole role-p)
(durord num-p) ;test the numord slot of durord filler; see num
(durtype (hour daypart day weekday week month semester yearpart year)) )
extrinsic-slots
((ref (def indef))
(partof timdur-p)
(rel couldbe-concept-p))
)
```

If an entity can be measured, that measure is expressed in terms of the type *unit:*

```
(def-ERKS-type unit
superset (mobj)
intrinsic-slots
((uname symbol-p)
(eprole role-p)
(umag num-p)
(utype (mile dollar second grade grad-point)))
extrinsic-slots
((ref (def indef))
(rel couldbe-concept-p))
)
```

The following is a special class for picking up unknown words/phrases. We arbitrarily assign the type a superset of "entity" to make it convenient for other constructions such as *prepconst*.

```
(def-ERKS-type unknown
superset (entity) ;isa superset
intrinsic-slots ;inherent roles (s-attr concepts)
((lexval symbol-p)) ;role name vs constraining pred
extrinsic-slots ;slots filled by external entities
((ref (def indef))
(rel couldbe-concept-p))
)
```

The class *veh* stands for conveyances (many self-propelled) which move people and goods
around:

```
(def-ERKS-type veh
superset (pobj place artifact)
intrinsic-slots
((vname symbol-p)
(eprole role-p)
(vtype (car helicopter train plane skateboard)))
extrinsic-slots
((ref (def indef))
(rel couldbe-concept-p))
)
```

Simple Actionals

The simple actions of ERKS are basically those of conceptual dependency [Scha73a; Scha75a]. The type *atrans* covers acts of abstract transfer of possession, control, or ownership. The standard senses of "give," "take," "borrow," "return," etc. are classic examples of this type.

```
(def-ERKS-type atrans
superset (act)
intrinsic-slots
((actor couldbe-animate-p)
(obj couldbe-entity-p)
; put entry "into" infostruc (e.g., an academic record)
(to (infostruc
poss own control))
(from (poss own control))
(inst couldbe-concept-p)
(time times-p)
(mode modes-p))
extrinsic-slots
((abstime abstimes-p)
(rel couldbe-concept-p)
```

(locale locales-p))
)

Actions in which an intentional actor takes a substance inside the body, where is it is consumed (at least in part), are spanned by the type *ingest*. For example, "John snarfed a beer," "John breathed heavily," and "John smoked a stogey."

```
(def-ERKS-type ingest
superset (act)
intrinsic-slots
((actor couldbe-hianimate-p)
(obj ingobj-p)
;should really test for p-configs about bparts LATER
(to couldbe-locrel-p)
(from couldbe-locrel-p)
(inst couldbe-concept-p)
(time times-p)
(mode modes-p))
extrinsic-slots
((abstime abstimes-p)
(rel couldbe-concept-p)
(locale locales-p))
)
```

Events of information transfer between animate actors, or between an actor and his sensors or memory, are covered by *mtrans*.

```
(def-ERKS-type mtrans
superset (act)
intrinsic-slots
((actor couldbe-hianimate-p)
(mobj couldbe-mobj-or-concept-p)
(to mlocbpart-p)
(from mlocbpart-p)
(inst couldbe-concept-p)
(time times-p)
(mode modes-p))
extrinsic-slots
((abstime abstimes-p)
(rel couldbe-concept-p)
(locale locales-p))
)
```

Mental events in which a new concept (the (mobj)) is constructed out of some data (the (msubj)) according to some rule (the (mrule)) are handled by *mbuild*. The verb "decide" is the best example of this type.

```
(def-ERKS-type mbuild
superset (act)
intrinsic-slots
((actor couldbe-hianimate-p)
```

```
(mobj couldbe-mobj-or-concept-p)
(msubj couldbe-concept-p)
(mrule couldbe-concept-p)
(inst couldbe-concept-p)
(time times-p)
(mode modes-p))
extrinsic-slots
((abstime abstimes-p)
(rel episode-p)
(locale locales-p))
)
```

The type *move* covers events where an actor causes a bodypart to move. It often occurs instrumentally in *propel* and *ptrans* events.

```
(def-ERKS-type move
superset (act)
intrinsic-slots
((actor animate-p)
(obj bpart-p)
(manner manner-p);manner-p is like rapidly normally, .....
(time times-p)
(mode modes-p))
extrinsic-slots
((abstime abstimes-p)
(rel episode-p)
(locale locales-p))
)
```

Events in which an animate actor applies a force to an object, with the possibility of contact with another object, are covered by *propel*. For example, "Rose homered in the seventh inning," "The glass shattered in the fireplace," "John swatted the mosquito."

```
(def-ERKS-type propel
superset (act)
intrinsic-slots
((actor couldbe-hianimate-p)
(obj couldbe-pobj-p)
(to couldbe-confrel-p)
(from couldbe-confrel-p)
(inst couldbe-concept-p)
(time times-p)
(mode modes-p))
extrinsic-slots
((abstime abstimes-p)
(rel couldbe-concept-p)
(locale locales-p))
)
```

Events in which an animate actor intentionally causes a change in the location of an object are spanned by the type *p(hysical) trans(fer)*. Chapter 2 discusses this type in some detail.

```
(def-ERKS-type ptrans
superset (act)
intrinsic-slots
((actor couldbe-hianimate-p)
(obj couldbe-entity-p)
(to couldbe-locrel-p)
(from couldbe-locrel-p)
(via couldbe-link-p)
(inst couldbe-concept-p)
(time times-p)
(mode modes-p))
extrinsic-slots
((abstime abstimes-p)
(rel couldbe-concept-p)
(locale locales-p))
)
```

Events in which an actor utters a noise are encoded with *speak*. These events occur often as instruments of *mtrans*.

```
(def-ERKS-type speak
superset (act)
intrinsic-slots
((actor couldbe-hianimate-p)
(time times-p)
(mode modes-p))
extrinsic-slots
((abstime abstimes-p)
(rel couldbe-concept-p)
(locale locales-p))
)
```

Goalepisodes

Some example goalepisodes. There are certainly thousands of others. These are all scripts. Another subclass is Wilensky's *named plans* (Wile78).
Football games:

```
(def-ERKS-type $futbol
superset (goalepisode)
intrinsic-slots
((actor couldbe-animate-p)
(inst couldbe-episode-p)
(time times-p)
(mode modes-p))
extrinsic-slots
```

```
((abstime abstimes-p)
(rel couldbe-concept-p)
(locale locales-p))
)
```

The US snail:

```
(def-ERKS-type $mail
superset (goalepisode)
intrinsic-slots
((actor couldbe-animate-p)
(inst couldbe-episode-p)
(time times-p)
(mode modes-p))
extrinsic-slots
((abstime abstimes-p)
(rel couldbe-concept-p)
(locale locales-p))
)
```

Guess what?

```
(def-ERKS-type $phone
superset (goalepisode)
intrinsic-slots
((actor couldbe-animate-p)
(inst couldbe-episode-p)
(time times-p)
(mode modes-p))
extrinsic-slots
((abstime abstimes-p)
(rel couldbe-concept-p)
(locale locales-p))
)
```

A cultural event:

```
(def-ERKS-type $play
superset (goalepisode)
intrinsic-slots
((actor couldbe-animate-p)
(inst couldbe-episode-p)
(time times-p)
(mode modes-p))
extrinsic-slots
((abstime abstimes-p)
(rel couldbe-concept-p)
(locale locales-p))
)
```

Attributes

Here we discuss the stative types. The basic type is *s-attr*, which defines inherent attributes of entities ("John is 42") and nominalized concepts ("the course is named CS 110"):

```
(def-ERKS-type s-attr
superset (state)
intrinsic-slots
;see ERKSpred1.l
((actor nomconcept-p)
(attr couldbe-attr-p)
(time times-p)
(mode modes-p))
extrinsic-slots
((abstime abstimes-p)
(rel couldbe-concept-p)
(locale locales-p))
)
```

The class *s-change* stands for changes in inherent attributes of entities:

```
(def-ERKS-type s-change
superset (state)
intrinsic-slots
((actor couldbe-entity-p)
(toward couldbe-attr-p)
(leaving couldbe-attr-p)
(time times-p)
(mode modes-p))
extrinsic-slots
((abstime abstimes-p)
(rel couldbe-concept-p)
(locale locales-p))
)
```

The state of an actor's having a goal (a desired state of affairs) is handled with *s-goal:*

```
(def-ERKS-type s-goal
superset (state)
intrinsic-slots
((actor couldbe-hianimate-p)
(mobj couldbe-mobj-or-concept-p)
(time times-p)
(mode modes-p))
extrinsic-slots
((abstime abstimes-p)
(rel couldbe-concept-p)
```

(locale locales-p))
)

    Below are the fillers of the (attr), (toward), and (leaving) roles of the basic statives (i.e., *s-attr* or *s-change*.

Names of things:

(def-ERKS-type tags
superset (attr)
intrinsic-slots
((tag1 (title persname surname deptname cno))
(tag2 (persname surname deptname cno))
(tag3 (persname surname deptname cno))
(tag4 (persname surname deptname cno))
;to remember where name info came from
(possby nomconcept-p))
)

Level of intelligence. For example, we could have "John is a genius."

(def-ERKS-type intelligence
superset (attr)
intrinsic-slots
((val number-p))
)

Temperature of an entity or environment:

(def-ERKS-type temperature
superset (attr)
intrinsic-slots
((val unit-p))
)

The calendar age of an entity (durations are handled by *timdur.*)

(def-ERKS-type age
superset (attr)
intrinsic-slots
((ageval number-p))
extrinsic-slots
()
)

To assert an entity exists:

(def-ERKS-type exist
superset (attr)
intrinsic-slots
()
extrinsic-slots

```
()
)
```

To assert that an entity is not "broken:"

```
(def-ERKS-type unity
superset (attr)
intrinsic-slots
()
extrinsic-slots
()
)
```

For attributions concerning the physical condition of a pobj (including animates):

```
(def-ERKS-type phystate
superset (attr)
intrinsic-slots
((statetype (hunger thirst intoxication fatigue))
(stateval number-p))
extrinsic-slots
()
)
```

For attributions concerning an animate's health (obviously connected with *phystate):*

```
(def-ERKS-type health
superset (attr)
intrinsic-slots
((val number-p))
extrinsic-slots
()
)
```

To talk about the characteristic form of a part (this needs to be expanded!!):

```
(def-ERKS-type partform
superset (attr)
intrinsic-slots
((val (fist)))
extrinsic-slots
()
)
```

Abstract Configurational Relationships

The basic abstract configuration is, of course, the *a-config*. It can hold between entities or nominalized concepts:

```
(def-ERKS-type a-config
superset (state)
```

```
intrinsic-slots
((confrel couldbe-confrel-p)
;see ERKSpred1
(con1 nomconcept-p)
(con2 nomconcept-p)
(time times-p)
(mode modes-p))
extrinsic-slots
((abstime abstimes-p)
(rel couldbe-concept-p)
(locale locales-p))
)
```

Now we discuss a few of the possible fillers that can go in the (confrel) of an *a-config*. First, there is the degree of affinity/animosity between an animate and another animate or episode; for instance, "I loathe Mary."

```
(def-ERKS-type affinity
superset (confrel)
intrinsic-slots
((val number-p))
)
```

Configurations having a mental relation between an entity and a concept:

```
(def-ERKS-type mentstate
superset (confrel)
intrinsic-slots
((stateval number-p)
(statetype (fear anger ennui)))
extrinsic-slots
()
)
```

One mental state is *fear,* ranging from "terrified" to "secure:"

```
(def-ERKS-type fear
superset (mentstate)
intrinsic-slots
((val number-p))
)
```

The next two have to do with degree of angriness or boredom. Traditionally, these have been construed as ranging from 0 to +10; i.e., there is no symmetrical negative state.

```
(def-ERKS-type anger
superset (mentstate)
intrinsic-slots
((val number-p))
)
```

```
(def-ERKS-type ennui
superset (mentstate)
intrinsic-slots
((val number-p))
)
```

For assertions of equivalence between (definitely described) entities: "I am John's brother."

(def-ERKS-type equiv
superset (confrel)
)

An assertion of set membership: "John is a sailor."

(def-ERKS-type instance
superset (confrel)
)

The "marriage" configuration:

(def-ERKS-type wedlocked
superset (confrel)
)

The configuration of possession (where (con1) in the surrounding *a-config* is the possessor:

(def-ERKS-type poss
superset (confrel)
intrinsic-slots
((val couldbe-entity-p))
)

For "agency" configurations, where x acts in the service of y and is placed in the (con1) path of the *a-config:*

(def-ERKS-type agent-of
superset (confrel)
)

Configurations of containment as in x contains y, where y is in (con1):

(def-ERKS-type contains
superset (confrel)
)

Characteristic living place:

(def-ERKS-type inhabit
superset (confrel)
)

The relation between an entity and one of its essential parts (in (con1)):

(def-ERKS-type partof
superset (confrel)
intrinsic-slots
((val couldbe-entity-p))
)

Relations of physical contact:

```
(def-ERKS-type physcont
superset (confrel)
intrinsic-slots
((val couldbe-entity-p))
)
```

Physical Configurational Relationships

The type for physical configuration between (among) entities is *p-config:*

```
(def-ERKS-type p-config
superset (state)
intrinsic-slots
((confrel couldbe-locrel-p)
(con1 couldbe-entity-p)
(con2 couldbe-entity-p)
(time times-p)
(mode modes-p))
extrinsic-slots
((abstime abstimes-p)
(rel couldbe-concept-p)
(locale locales-p))
)
```

Now we give just a few of its possible (conrel) fillers:

```
;in my apartment
(def-ERKS-type inside
superset (locrel)
intrinsic-slots
((part couldbe-entity-p))
)
```

```
;on the refrigerator
(def-ERKS-type topof
superset (locrel)
intrinsic-slots
((part couldbe-entity-p))
)
```

```
;near Peoria
(def-ERKS-type prox
superset (locrel)
intrinsic-slots
((part couldbe-entity-p))
)
```

```
;under the bridge
(def-ERKS-type beneath
superset (locrel)
intrinsic-slots
((part couldbe-entity-p))
)
```

```
;to the right of John
(def-ERKS-type rightof
superset (locrel)
intrinsic-slots
((part couldbe-entity-p))
)
```

```
;to the left of Reagan
(def-ERKS-type leftof
superset (locrel)
intrinsic-slots
((part couldbe-entity-p))
)
```

;street ends on another
(def-ERKS-type T-junction
superset (locrel)
intrinsic-slots
((part couldbe-entity-p))
)

;street crosses another
(def-ERKS-type X-junction
superset (locrel)
intrinsic-slots
((part couldbe-entity-p))
)

Conrels

This (probably infinite) class of types is intended to cover the possible relations among episodes/states. First, the Boolean operators:

(def-ERKS-type neg
superset (conrel)
intrinsic-slots
((con1 couldbe-concept-p))
)

(def-ERKS-type conj
superset (conrel)
numslot compnum
intrinsic-slots
((con1 couldbe-concept-p)
(con2 couldbe-concept-p)
(con3 couldbe-concept-p)
(con4 couldbe-concept-p)
(con5 couldbe-concept-p)
(con6 couldbe-concept-p)
(compnum number-p))
)

The next two are the non-exclusive and exclusive or conrels, respectively.

(def-ERKS-type disj
superset (conrel)
numslot compnum
intrinsic-slots
((con1 couldbe-concept-p)
(con2 couldbe-concept-p)
(con3 couldbe-concept-p)
(con4 couldbe-concept-p)
(con5 couldbe-concept-p)
(con6 couldbe-concept-p)
(compnum number-p))
)

(def-ERKS-type xor
superset (conrel)
numslot compnum
intrinsic-slots
((con1 couldbe-concept-p)
(con2 couldbe-concept-p)
(con3 couldbe-concept-p)
(con4 couldbe-concept-p)
(con5 couldbe-concept-p)
(con6 couldbe-concept-p)
(compnum number-p))
)

Next some simple temporal conrels. For the type *during,* by convention, con1 is the enclosing concept; i.e., in X during Y, Y goes into con1.

(def-ERKS-type during
superset (conrel)
numslot compnum ;where no of subcons in a particular one are stored
intrinsic-slots
((con1 couldbe-concept-p)
(compnum number-p)

```
(con2 couldbe-concept-p))
extrinsic-slots
((rel couldbe-concept-p))
)
```

For the type *before,* by convention, con1 is the preceding concept; i.e., in X before Y, X goes into con1.

```
(def-ERKS-type before
superset (conrel)
numslot compnum ;where no of subcons in a particular one are stored
intrinsic-slots
((con1 couldbe-concept-p)
(compnum number-p)
(con2 couldbe-concept-p))
extrinsic-slots
((rel couldbe-concept-p))
)
```

For events occuring in sequence, use *sequel.* For example, "X then Y."

```
(def-ERKS-type sequel
superset (conrel)
numslot compnum ;where no of subcons in a particular one are stored
intrinsic-slots
((con1 couldbe-concept-p)
(con2 couldbe-concept-p)
(con3 couldbe-concept-p)
(con4 couldbe-concept-p)
(con5 couldbe-concept-p)
(compnum number-p)
(time times-p)
(mode modes-p))
extrinsic-slots
((rel couldbe-concept-p))
)
```

For co-occurring (simultaneous) events, use *simul:*

```
(def-ERKS-type simul
superset (conrel)
numslot compnum ;where no of subcons in a particular one are stored
intrinsic-slots
((con1 couldbe-concept-p)
(con2 couldbe-concept-p)
(con3 couldbe-concept-p)
(con4 couldbe-concept-p)
(con5 couldbe-concept-p)
(compnum number-p)
(time times-p)
(mode modes-p))
```

extrinsic-slots
((rel couldbe-concept-p))
)

To form a *conrel* about potential causation, use *cancause*. For example, "smok-ing can kill you."

(def-ERKS-type cancause
superset (conrel)
intrinsic-slots
((con1 couldbe-concept-p)
(compnum number-p)
(con2 couldbe-concept-p))
extrinsic-slots
((rel couldbe-concept-p))
)

Strict causation is handled by *cause*. The causation may be expressed explicitly, as in "I went because Mary asked me to," or "I made Roger go;" or may be imbedded inside a wordsense, as in "John killed Mary," paraphrased as "John performed some action that was the cause of a terminal negative state change in Mary's health."

(def-ERKS-type cause
superset (conrel)
intrinsic-slots
((con1 couldbe-concept-p)
(compnum number-p)
(con2 couldbe-concept-p)
(time times-p)
(mode modes-p))
extrinsic-slots
((rel couldbe-concept-p))
)

For closely coupled events that seem to be mutually causative, use *dual*. The classic example is "John sold the book for $100," where the co-occurring events "atrans money" and "atrans book" seem to be mutually supportive.

(def-ERKS-type dual
superset (conrel)
intrinsic-slots
((con1 couldbe-concept-p)
(compnum number-p)
(con2 couldbe-concept-p))
extrinsic-slots
((rel couldbe-concept-p))
)

Concepts that are being coordinated with one another in some unknown (possibly temporal or causal) way are handled by *coord*. Many of the standard uses of "and" refer to such constructs: "John and Mary walked down the street."

```
(def-ERKS-type coord
superset (conrel)
numslot compnum ;where no of subcons in a particular one are stored
intrinsic-slots
((con1 couldbe-concept-p)
(con2 couldbe-concept-p)
(con3 couldbe-concept-p)
(con4 couldbe-concept-p)
(con5 couldbe-concept-p)
(compnum number-p)
(time times-p)
(mode modes-p))
extrinsic-slots
((rel couldbe-concept-p))
)
```

A concept that expresses the relation between an action and the goal it is intended to achieve is covered by a *g(oal) r(ealization) c(onceptualization)*. For example, "I got a gun to rob the bank:"

```
(def-ERKS-type grc
superset (conrel)
intrinsic-slots
((con1 couldbe-concept-p)
(con2 couldbe-concept-p)
(mode modes-p)
(time times-p) )
extrinsic-slots
((rel couldbe-concept-p))
)
```

A type that expresses the repeated execution of a sequence of events until a threshold stative becomes true is the *r(epeat) u(ntil) t(hreshold)* For example, "I turned up the brightness until I could see the picture."

```
(def-ERKS-type rut
superset (conrel)
intrinsic-slots
((threshold state-p)
; as many coni's as you want
(con1 couldbe-concept-p)
(mode modes-p)
(time times-p) )
extrinsic-slots
((rel couldbe-concept-p))
)
```

An operator for VALID reasoning chains among concepts:

```
(def-ERKS-type implies
superset (conrel)
intrinsic-slots
((con1 couldbe-concept-p)
(con2 couldbe-concept-p))
extrinsic-slots
())
```

Other Types

Finally, we list the ERKS type that don't fit cleanly anywhere else. The meaning structure primitive, which holds MIFP information for words:

```
(def-ERKS-type ms
superset (other)
intrinsic-slots
((nuance1 couldbe-concept-p) ;nuances
(nuance2 couldbe-concept-p)
(nuance3 couldbe-concept-p)
(nuance4 couldbe-concept-p)
(nuance5 couldbe-concept-p)
(nuance6 couldbe-concept-p)
(kernel couldbe-concept-p) ;the basic meaning structure
))
```

Repository for tensing and aspective information:

```
(def-ERKS-type times ;note: this is the canonical filler of time slot
superset (other)
intrinsic-slots
((time1 (:pres :past :futr)) ;simple tensing
(time2 (:prog :perf)) ;aspect
(time3 (:ts :tf))) ;"transition start" and "transition finish"
                    ;fragments: "begin" and "end" of an
                    ;episode, respectively
)
```

The type *prepconst* covers prepositional constituents, <prep><noun-group> forms.

```
(def-ERKS-type prepconst
superset (other)
intrinsic-slots
((prep symbol-p)
;accept either an entity or nominalized episode (from running)
(mynom nomconcept-p)
(canbuild couldbe-concept-p))
)
```

The type *clp* is a "clause point," a pivot on the C-LIST before which a clause level concept can be expected to have been assembled. Periods and conjunctions typically create clausepoints.

```
(def-ERKS-type clp
superset (other)
)
```

An *expletive* is a garbage type for expletive constructions, e.g., the "it" in "it's raining."

```
(def-ERKS-type expletive
superset (other)
)
```

Modal fragments:

```
(def-ERKS-type modes ;note: this is the canonical filler of mode slot
superset (other)
intrinsic-slots
((mode1 (:t :neg))
(mode2 (:urge :oblig :pntnt :ablty :prmssn :intnt))
(mode3 (:q :nom)))
)
```

Mutually exclusive word sense possibilities:

```
(def-ERKS-type vel
superset (other)
numslot compnum ;where no of subcons in a particular one are stored
intrinsic-slots
((v1 couldbe-concept-p)
(v2 couldbe-concept-p)
(v3 couldbe-concept-p)
(v4 couldbe-concept-p)
(v5 couldbe-concept-p)
(time times-p)
(mode modes-p))
extrinsic-slots
((rel couldbe-concept-p))
)
```

Appendix II
Source for YADR,
Yet Another Deductive Retriever
Version of 29 May 1985

```
;;;;;;;;;;;;;;;;;;;;;;;;;;;;;;;;;;;;;;;;;;;;;;;;;;;;;;;;;;;;;
;;;;;;;;;;;                                         ;;;;;;;;;;;
;;;;;;;;;;;   PLEASE NOTE:                          ;;;;;;;;;;;
;;;;;;;;;;;   This Appendix does not document       ;;;;;;;;;;;
;;;;;;;;;;;   all the functions mentioned.          ;;;;;;;;;;;
;;;;;;;;;;;   You also need the SOT KBMS            ;;;;;;;;;;;
;;;;;;;;;;;   package supplied with the             ;;;;;;;;;;;
;;;;;;;;;;;   NLP Toolkit, V1.10 on.                ;;;;;;;;;;;
;;;;;;;;;;;   Note use of "defun," rather           ;;;;;;;;;;;
;;;;;;;;;;;   than Franz primitive "def"            ;;;;;;;;;;;
;;;;;;;;;;;;;;;;;;;;;;;;;;;;;;;;;;;;;;;;;;;;;;;;;;;;;;;;;;;;;
;CONSISTENT-WITH: is the probe (which must be variabilized)
;      consistent with the current KB and the primers?
; ARGS: probe - a variabilized assertion which is checked
;                  for consistency in the face of ...
;          primerlist - a list of fact forms which are
;                       temporarily asserted, together with
;                       any if-added inferences
; RTNS: a list of instantiated forms, with the bindings of
;       database items to the variables supplied with the
;       probe
;EX: (s-attr actor *other
;              attr (tag possby (person persname (nil)
;                                       surname (nil))))
;          variables ((?pn (attr possby persname))
;                     (?sn (attr possby surname)))
;     i.e., "Your name is what?", returns fax56,
;     (s-attr attr (tag possby (person persname c42
;                                       surname c43))
;     where c42 is "Tristan" and c43 is "daCunha", provided
;     primerlst contained an assertion: "I am Tristan daCunha"

(defun consistent-with (probe primerlst)
  (msg N "YADR: checking consistency of " probe " with: " N
       primerlst N)
  ;clear rules-used global, which prevents loops
  (init-yadr)
;temporarily add primer list to Fax net, remembering names
;of added items
  (let ((tempfax (new-info primerlst nil)))
        (msg N "YADR: primers:" tempfax N)
        ;back-chain yer brains out..
        (let ((foundfax (yadr probe)))
        ;discard the temp fax (see Toolkit/sot stuff)
        (mapc 'Delete-Fax tempfax)
        ;clean up yadr detritus
        (init-yadr)
        (cond (foundfax
```

379

```
                    (msg N "Yadr: facts " N  foundfax N
                        " consistent with" N
                        primerlst N)
                    (mapcar 'make-structure foundfax))
                (t
                    (msg N "Yadr: probe inconsistent with "
                        primerlst N)
                    nil))
        )))

; ASK-YADR: "raw" yadr interface
; NOTE: no external process should call yadr directly!!
(defun ask-yadr (probe)
    (init-yadr)
    (yadr probe)
    )

; INIT-YADR: clear any "rules-used" info (from prior runs)
(defun init-yadr ()
    (cond
        ((null (boundp ':rules-used))
         (setq :rules-used nil))
        (:rules-used
         (mapc '(lambda(rul) (remprop rul 'prior-bindings))
                :rules-used)
         (setq :rules-used nil))
    ))


; YADR: Yet Another Deductive Retriever
;        This is a first pass at a deductive retriever
;        of the Charniak, Riesbeck & McDermott type,
;        for ERKS slot-filler forms
; ARGS:  probe - something which is to be shown to be true,
;            i.e., stored with mode = :t in a factual database
;            If probe is not in the Fax db, the if-needed rules
;            (in ifn tree) are searched to see if a rule of the
;            form
;            (implies/cancause/plausible con1 'something'
;                                      con2 probe)
;            can be found.  If so, the con1 is unified with
;            the con2, and yadr (really run-rule at this point)
;            tries to prove the con1.
; RTNS: a list of instantiated versions of the probe, i.e.,
; if the probe contained vars, they will be filled in by
; real values
(defun yadr (probe)
    (msg N "YADR: looking for: " probe N (xpn probe) N)

    ; get known fax that satisfy the variable's requirement in
    ; the probe, unless it's a logical conjunction or xor
    (let ((found-facts (if (logical-con-p probe)
                           nil
        ; Note: Fetch-Fax-w-vars only rtns those that satisfy
        ; the variable's requirement in probe.
                           (Fetch-Fax-w-vars probe)))
          (proven-facts))

        (cond (found-facts
                    (msg N "YADR: found fact(s) for probe: "
                        N found-facts N)
        ; now, return the structure associated with
        ; the fetched forms
                    (setq proven-facts
                        (mapcar 'get-structurem found-facts)))
```

```
                 ; is it an 'and' or an 'xor' ?
                    ((logical-con-p probe)
                     (msg N "YADR: examining and/xor concept" N)
                     (setq proven-facts (prove-xor-and probe)))

                 ; try to backchain
                    ((setq proven-facts (run-rule probe))
                     (msg N "YADR deduced fact(s):"
                          N proven-facts N)
                      proven-facts)

                 (t nil))

              proven-facts)
       )


;                        (the infamous) RUN-RULE
; ARGS: probe - the thing we're trying to prove using a rule
; RTNS: a bunch of instantiated facts, which should fill out
;     any variables which the probe contains.
;     run-rule operates in a backward-chaining fashion.
;     rules look like (implies con1 'something' con2 ,probe)
;                  or    (cancause con1 'something' con2 ,probe)
;                  or    (cause con1 'something' con2 ,probe)
;                  or    (plausible con1 'something' con2 ,probe)
; NOTE: the rule can only be used if the antecedent is
;       known, so yadr is called to determine this.
; NOTE: the above means we are operating yadr in a
;       DEPTH-FIRST, CHRONLOGICALLY BACK-TRACKING manner,
;       which probably isn't the best thing to do.
;       back-chaining paths tend to die out quickly,
;       so the depth-first part isn't so bad. It's the
;       "return to most recent option point" mentality
;       that is suspect.
; NOTE: breadth-first, "best first" would be better.
;     now, if we only knew what "best first" means!!!!

(defun run-rule (probe)
         ; first get implies (valid) rules
  (let* ((rule (create-rule-instance probe 'implies))
         ; SOT treeatoms
         (matched-rules (Fetch-IfneedRules rule))
         ; then cause/effect rules
         (rule (create-rule-instance probe 'cause))
         (matched-rules (append (Fetch-IfneedRules rule)
                                matched-rules))
         ; then abductive (cancause) rules
         (rule (create-rule-instance probe 'cancause))
         (matched-rules (append (Fetch-IfneedRules rule)
                                matched-rules))
         ; finally, simply plausible (e.g., default) rules
         (rule (create-rule-instance probe 'plausible))
         (matched-rules (append (Fetch-IfneedRules rule)
                                matched-rules))
         ; the list of binding lists
         (bindings)
         ; the instantiated forms of matched-rules+bindings
         (inst-rules)
         ; the instantiated forms of each rule that was proved
         (proved-rules)
         ; the antecedents of the inst-rules
         (if-parts))


    (cond (matched-rules    ; if not, bug out
```

```
(msg N "RUN-RULE: found rules"
     N matched-rules N)

; find out what variables of the matched rules
; are filled by the new rule we formed from
; the probe
(setq bindings
      (get-probe-bindings rule matched-rules))

; filter rules that are being called with
; prior bindings
(setq matched-rules
      (filter-rules matched-rules bindings))
(setq bindings (cadr matched-rules))
(setq matched-rules (car matched-rules))

; then use bindings to instantatiate copies of
; surviving rules
(setq inst-rules
      (inst-new-rules matched-rules bindings))

; Now, get the antecedents of each of
; the instantiated rules, to send to yadr to see
; if they are known or provable.
; Extract will set the 'variables' property of
; the con1 fillers
(setq if-parts
      (mapcar '(lambda (mtch)
                       (extract mtch '(con1)))
              inst-rules))

; Now call yadr on the if-part of each of the
; instantiated versions of the matched rules.
; If yadr rtns non-nil, then, FOR EACH fact-form
; it returned, unify that with the corresponding
; matched-rule.
; The result is a list of lists, each sublist
; containing the fact-form proved filled in w/
; the variables from the if-part
(setq proved-rules
      (mapcar
        '(lambda (con mrule bdgs)
              ; record that this rule was used
              ; withthe corresponding bindings
              (let
                ((foo (record-bindings mrule bdgs))
                 ; and backchain merrily...
                 (prvd (yadr con)))
                (mapcar '(lambda (x)
                              (inst-if-part x mrule))
                        prvd)))
        if-parts
        matched-rules
        bindings))

(msg N "RUN-RULE proved:" N proved-rules N)

; Since proved-rules contains the entire rule
; that was proved, and we only want the con2's,
; only return those.  (Need to flatten the
; proved-rules since they are the result of
; potentially more than one rule applying)
(mapcar '(lambda (x) (grf '(con2) x))
        ; and remove those that failed
```

```
                    (rem-nil (flatten proved-rules)))
          )  ; end cond on matched-rules

     (t
      (msg
       "RUN-RULE: Failed to find rule(s) for probe: "
          probe N)
       nil)))   ; if no matched rules, fail
)

; Some helper macros for RUN-RULE

; CREATE-RULE-INSTANCE: the function creates, from the probe
; yadr wants to prove, the rule one can use to prove it.  It
; builds the rule up with the yadr-probe in the con2 slot,
; and then transfers the variables from the yadr-probe to the
; new rule
; ARGS: yadr-probe, variabilized probe form from yadr
;       conclass, class (type) of the rule to be formed
(defmacro create-rule-instance (yadr-probe conclass)
 `(let ((newrule (newsym 'Rul)))
      (set newrule
           (list ,conclass
                 'con1
                 '(nil)
                 'con2
                 (eval ,yadr-probe)))
      ; make sure we know what this new rule is supposed
      ; to fetch. Then, add-path-prefix adds the atom
      ; 'con2 onto each path obtained from the yadr
      ; probe, since we're now looking for that as the
      ; con2 of a rule `
      (setf (rule-variables newrule)
            (add-path-prefix (get-variables ,yadr-probe)
                             'con2))
      newrule))

;         GET-PROBE-BINDINGS
; ARGS: rule-probe - a rule with con1 nil and the thing yadr
;             called run-rule with to try to prove in the
;             con2
;       fetched-ruls - everything that matched the probe
;             from the if-needed tree
; RTNS: for each variable in each fetched rule, if the
;       variable refers to the 'con2' role
;       (which is where the rule-probe is filled in)
;       and if the variable is filled
;       in rule-probe, the value is returned.
;       Note that the binding list returned is suitable for
;       input to instantiate
(defmacro get-probe-bindings (rule-probe fetched-ruls)
 `(mapcar `(lambda (x)
              (find-bindings ,rule-probe
                             (rule-variables x)
                             'con2))
          ,fetched-ruls))

;         INST-NEW-RULES
; ARGS: mtched-rules -  rules matched by the
;               `(implies con1 (nil) con2 yadr-probe)
;               created by run-rule
;       bindings - bindings for that rule as computed by
;               get-probe-bindings
; RTNS: copies of mtched-rules instantiated by the bindings
(defmacro inst-new-rules (mtched-rules bindings)
```

```
` (mapcar '(lambda (rul binds)
             (let ((instrul
                    (instantiate (make-cd (structure rul))
                                 (rule-variables rul)
                                 binds)))
               (setf (rule-variables instrul)
                     (rule-variables rul))
               instrul))
          ,mtched-rules
          ,bindings))

;                       FILTER-RULES
; ARGS: ruls, a proposed set of rules to backchain through
;       bindings, a list of corresponding alists of variable
;          bindings
; RTNS: a list whose car is the subset of the ruls which
;          have not been instantiated with these bindings
;          before, and whose cdr is a list of the
;          corresponding binding alists
; HELPERS: rule-used?, rul-usdl
; NOTE: this has trouble when unification yields different
;    subsets of bindings in different cases, with some
;    overlap. It ain't clear that a loop is really occurring
;    in such cases.
(declare (special bindings))
(defun filter-rules (ruls bindlist)
  (let ((filtered-stuff
         (rem-nil
          (mapcar '(lambda(r b)
                     (cond
                      ; this rule used before with
                      ; these bindings?
                      ((rule-used? r b)
                       (msg ROUTINE-MSG N
                            "RUN-RULE: avoiding loop with rule "
                            r N " and bindings " b)
                       nil)
                      ; let 'em go
                      ((list r b))))
                  ruls bindlist))))
    ; split 'em back up
    (list (mapcar 'car filtered-stuff)
          (mapcar 'cadr filtered-stuff))
    ))

(defun rule-used? (rul bindings)
  (do ((oldbnds (get rul 'prior-bindings) (cdr oldbnds))
       (loop! nil))
      ((or (null oldbnds) loop!) loop!)
    (setq loop! (rul-usdl (car oldbnds) bindings))
    ))

(defun rul-usdl (old new)
  (cond
    ; if we run out of the proposed new guys, bad...
    ((null new) t)
    ; if next pair isn't in old, good...
    ((null (member (car new) old)) nil)
    ; bad so far...
    ((rul-usdl old (cdr new)))))


;                       RECORD-BINDINGS
; ARGS: rul, a back-chaining rule
;           (SOT treeatom from ifn tree)
```

```
;       bdgs, the bindings proposed for this use of the
;          rule, as we hand its "if" part to yadr
; RTNS: t
; SIDE-EFFECTS: update :rules-used, if necessary
;       add bdgs to prior-bindings attribute of rul
(defun record-bindings (rul bdgs)
   (consprop rul bdgs 'prior-bindings)
   (cond
      ((null (memq rul :rules-used))
       (setq :rules-used (cons rul :rules-used)))))
  t)


;                  PROVE-XOR-AND
; ARGS: probe - concepts connected w/ 'xor' or 'and',
;    to be proved
; RTNS: a concept consisting of the proper connective
;    (and or xor) embedded in which are all the things
;    it proved.
(defun prove-xor-and (probe)
             ; paths to embedded subcons
   (let* ((conslots (get-conslots probe))
             ; isolate the embedded subcons, making sure you
             ; give them a variables property for the
             ; recursive call to yadr
             (cons-to-prove
               (mapcar '(lambda (c)
                            (propagate-vars (grf (list c) probe)
                                            probe c))
                        conslots))
             ; will be what yadr could prove
             (provable-cons nil))
     (cond ((couldbe-conj-p probe)
            (setq provable-cons
                  (merge-and conslots cons-to-prove))
       ; make the thing look like a conjunction!
       ; (now it's just a list of lists)
            (build-multiple-con 'conj
                                 provable-cons conslots))
          (t    ; must be xor
             ; Stop at first one proved
             (setq provable-cons
                   (catch
                     (do ((nextcon (car cons-to-prove)
                                   (car restcons))
                          (restcons (cdr cons-to-prove)
                                    (cdr restcons))
                          (slot (car conslots)
                                (car restconslots))
                          (restconslots (cdr conslots)
                                        (cdr restconslots))
                          (reslt nil))
                         ((null nextcon) nil)
                       (setq reslt (yadr nextcon))
                       (if (car reslt)
                           (throw
                             (list (make-structure
                                     `(xor ,slot (,(car reslt)))))
                             )))
                     )))
         ))
    ))


;                  MERGE-AND
; ARGS: conslots - paths to subcons connected by 'conj'.
```

```
;         cons-to-prove - the associated subcons
; RTNS: nil if at least one of the embedded subconcepts
;         in the and-con couldn't be proved, otherwise it
;         returns a concept connected by a conj where
;         each of the subconcepts is an instantiated
;         version of a concept proved by yadr
(defun merge-and (conslots cons-to-prove)
  (let
     ((known-cons
         (catch
           (do ((cns (cdr cons-to-prove) (cdr cns))
                (nextcon (car cons-to-prove) (car cns))
                (ydr-results nil)   ; list of all the results
                (ydr-result nil))   ; just one result
               ((null nextcon) (reverse ydr-results))
               (setq ydr-result (yadr nextcon))
               (if ydr-result
                   (setq ydr-results
                         (cons ydr-result ydr-results))
                 (throw nil)))))) ; if failure, exit
     )   ; end let bindings

   ; now, if any piece was not known or could not be
   ; proved, no need to go any further, stop here
   (cond ((null known-cons)
          nil)
         (t
          (let*
            ; for each known-con (i.e. one that was proved),
            ; use the variables from the input cons to get the
            ; fillers in the proved cons
            ; cons&bindings is a list of lists of:
            ; (known-con1 bindings1)
            ; (this is becausee yadr returns multiple facts)
              ((cons&bindings
                 (mapcar
                  '(lambda (known-list-of-cons cd-to-prove)
                     (mapcar
                      '(lambda (proved-con)
                         (cons proved-con
                               (find-bindings proved-con
                                              (get-variables
                                               cd-to-prove)
                                              nil)))
                      known-list-of-cons))
                  known-cons cons-to-prove))

               ; all possible combinations...
               (pssbl-combs (build-combs cons&bindings))

               ;subset with consistent bindings
               (valid-combs
                (rem-nil
                 (mapcar 'consistent-combs pssbl-combs))))

              valid-combs)
            ))))
```

```
;         CONSISTENT-COMBS
; ARGS: a combination, of the form
;       ((cd1 . binding1) (cd2 . binding2) ...)
; RTNS: the cd's, if all the bindings are consistent,
;       else nil
; HELPER: consistent-bdgs       .
(defun consistent-combs (combs)
```

```
(let* ((bdgs (mapcar 'cdr combs))
       (vars
        (mapcar
         '(lambda (x) (mapcar 'car x))
         bdgs))
       (cons (mapcar 'car combs)))
  (if (forall vars 'null)
      cons
      (if (consistent-bdgs vars bdgs) cons)))))

(defun consistent-bdgs (vars bdgs)
  ; only check consistency of shared vars
  (let ((ivars (intersec (car vars) (cadr vars)))
        (bdgs1 (car bdgs))
        (bdgs2 (cadr bdgs)) )
    (catch (do ((ivar (car ivars) (car restvars))
                (restvars (cdr ivars) (cdr restvars)))
               ((null ivar) t)
             (cond ((fmatch (cadr (assoc ivar bdgs1))
                            (cadr (assoc ivar bdgs2))
                            ))
                   (t (throw nil)))))
    ))

; INST-IF-PART
; ARGS: if-part - a concept matching the antecedent portion
;                 of a rule that was proved by yadr.
;       rule - the rule used to prove it.
; RTNS: the instantiation of a copy of rule with if-part.
;       Essentially, all the con1 variables from the rule
;       are picked out of 'if-part', then the resulting
;       binding is stuffed back into the rule
(defun inst-if-part (if-part rule)
  (let ((bindings
         (find-bindings `(implies con1 ,if-part con2 (nil))
                        (rule-variables rule)
                        'con1)))
    (instantiate (make-cd (get-structure rule))
                 (rule-variables rule)
                 bindings)))

; BUILD-MULTIPLE-CON
; ARGS: conclass - the ERKS type of the multiple con built
;       proved-cons - a list of cons yadr has proved
;       (some may be nil, e.g. if the type is a disj)
;       conslots - the concepts proved-cons filled in
(defun build-multiple-con (conclass proved-cons conslots)
  ; want to create something of the form
  ; `(conj con1 ,(first proved-cons)
  ;        con2 ,(second proved-cons) ...)
  ; for all the conslots
  (let ((newcons
         (mapcar '(lambda (prvd)
                    (assemble conclass prvd))
                 proved-cons)))
    newcons))

;Utilities

; LOGICAL-CON-P
; Test for a Boolean form
(defmacro logical-con-p (con) `(or (couldbe-disj-p ,con)
                                   (couldbe-xor-p ,con)
                                   (couldbe-conj-p ,con)))
```

```lisp
;        GET-STRUCTUREM:
;  Retrieve the ERKS form associated with a symbol, if it
;        exists, else the empty form (nil)
(defun get-structurem (atm)
  (or (get atm 'structure) ; where SOT keeps it
      (if (boundp atm) atm '(nil))))


;                EXTRACT
; ARGS: con - an ERKS form
;        path - the path which is to be extracted.
; RTNS: the subconcept, with the 'variables' property copied
;        over, and properly modified to refer to paths in the
;        embedded concept (e.g. if we extract the "con2" slot,
;        and we have a variable pointing to
;        "(con2 actor persname)", we add "(actor persname)"
;        to the variables property of
;        the extracted con2 slot.
(declare (special path))
(defun extract (con path)
          (cond
            ((null path) con)
            (t (extract (extract1 con (list (car path)))
                        (cdr path))))))

(defun extract1 (con path)
            ;the embedded con
      (let* ((subcon (grf path con))
            ;the vars/paths list
            (variables (rule-variables con))
            ;the actual vars
            (vars (mapcar 'car variables))
            ;the paths they lie in
            (paths (mapcar 'cdr variables))
            (subcon-pth
              (mapcar
               '(lambda (pths)
                  (mapcan
                  ; path-prefix (in ERKSfns.l) rtns t if path is
                  ; a prefix of pth (e.g. (con1 foo) is prefix of
                  ; (con1 foo baz))
                   '(lambda (pth)
                            (if (path-prefix path pth)
                                (list (cdr pth))
                                nil))
                        pths))
                 paths))
            ;the variables needed
            ; (some may be irrelevant at this point)
            (subcon-variables
              (mapcan '(lambda (var pths)
                         (if pths `((,var ,@pths)) nil))
                      vars
                      subcon-pth))
            )   ; end let* bindings
        (setf (rule-variables subcon) subcon-variables)
      subcon))


;                BUILD-COMBS
; ARGS: lists - a list of lists of facts/binding pairs
; RTNS: all ordered combs of all elements of each list
; example: (build-combs '((a b) (c) (d e)))
;        ==> ((a c d) (a c e) (b c d) (b c e))
; Helper fun for merge-and
(defun build-combs (lists)
  (cond ((null lists) nil)
```

```
          ((null (cdr lists))    ; end of the line
           (mapcar 'list (car lists)))
          (t (let
               ((tail (build-combs (cdr lists))))
              (mapcan
               '(lambda (atm)
                        (mapcar '(lambda (lst)
                                         (cons atm lst))
                                tail))
               (car lists)))))))

; ADD-PATH-PREFIX: add the prefix onto each path
;     in var-list
; ARGS: var-list - alist of form ((?foo (path1) (path2)) )
;       prefix - atomic prefix to add
; NOTE: this is used to alter the variables property in
;   run-rule when a thing is being looked for as a rule
;   Since it well be in the con2 slot, its vars need
;   to be modified accordingly.
(defun add-path-prefix (var-list prefix)
  (cond
    ((null var-list) nil)
    (t
     (rem-nil
      `(, (cons (caar var-list)
                (mapcar '(lambda (path) (cons prefix path))
                        (cdar var-list)))
         ,@(add-path-prefix (cdr var-list) prefix))))
    ))

; PROP-VARS: propogate the vars from a conjunction to
;     all its subconcepts
; ARGS: subcon - the subconcept
;       and-cd - the cd from which the subcon came
;       role - the con(i) role which subcon filled
; RTNS: the subcon
; NOTE: needn't absolutely be a conjunction, of course!
(defun propagate-vars (subcon and-cd role)
  (setf (rule-variables subcon)
        (get-subcon-vars (get-variables and-cd) role))
  subcon)

; Helper functions for propogate-vars
; GET-SUBCON-VARS
; ARGS - vars a list of vars
;        role - the role to key on the var paths with
; var-list is alist of form ((?foo (path1) (path2)) ...)
(defun get-subcon-vars (var-list role )
  (rem-nil (mapcar 'get-subcon-var var-list)))

; GET-SUBCON-VAR
; sublist is of form (?foo (path1) (path2))
(defun get-subcon-var (sublist)
  (let ((var (car sublist))
        (paths (gsv1 (cdr sublist))))
    (if paths (cons var paths))))

; GSV1
(defun gsv1 (pathlist)
  (rem-nil
   (mapcar '(lambda (path)
                    (if (eq (car path) role)
                        (cdr path)
                        nil))
           pathlist)))
```

Appendix III
Glossary of Terms

Note: Words not defined in the glossary may be ERKS types or role names, described in Appendix I.

ACE—Academic Counseling Expert; a system using a goal-directed regime of processing to handle mixed-initiative conversations typical of a faculty advisor talking to a student.

actional type—any ERKS type used to express a basic element of classes of events in the world. (See *stative type*.)

activate—a Lisp function that invokes requests and request generators from the dictionary for the Conceptual Analyzer when a new word is "read" from the input.

actor-spot—the term used to refer to the syntactic constituent preceding the verb kernel in an active voice sentence or governed by "by" in the passive; so-called because it often ends up being represented in the *actor* role in the underlying ERKS meaning structure.

actspot-req—a request generator (q.v.) that places a request that wants to fill an actor-spot into the Conceptual Analyzer's request memory.

add-pair—the Lisp function used to add a role-filler pair to an ERKS form.

add-word-con—the Lisp function to add an atomized form derived from the associated word sense to the Analyzer's C-LIST.

adictdef—a Lisp function for adding a word definition to the Conceptual Analyzer's dictionary. (See *def-wordsense*.)

anaphora—use of a grammatical substitute (such as a pronoun or pro-verb) to refer to a preceding word or group of words (or an inferrable concept corresponding to such words).

atomized form—an ERKS form in which all of the fillers (as well as the top level structure) have been bound to names (Lisp atoms).

atrans—abstract transfer; an ERKS type used for representing events in which possession, ownership, or control of objects is transferred between animate entities.

attributional concept—an assertion in which an intrinsic state or attribute of an object is described, such as color, weight, extent, etc.

backward-chaining—a process of validating a conclusion by decomposing it into a chain of premises that might have led to that conclusion, and comparing these premises with ones that are known to be true.

C-LIST—the data structure representing the short-term memory of the Conceptual Analyzer or Conceptual Generator.

CADHELP—a system for computer-aided design that converses with the user in

390

English, guiding him through the steps of designing simple SSI/MSI digital circuits with the aid of a graphics display and tablet. The system can explain the operation of the CAD Tool, including the ways in which the user can go wrong, and recover.

cancause—an ERKS type describing a contingent (weak) causal relationship between two events (e.g., "smoking can kill you"). *Cancause* is a type of *conrel*.

causal chain—a list of causally connected inferences; i.e., each inference must necessarily follow from the previous one.

concept—an ERKS form. Sometimes used to refer to the name attached to such a form (e.g., "HUM0" or "c523").

Conceptual Analyzer—the component of an NLP system that maps natural language (e.g., English) strings into symbolic representations ("meaning structures") of their literal or *surface* semantic meaning (q.v.).

Conceptual Generator—the component of an NLP system that maps meaning structures into natural language strings.

conceptual similarity—the criterion used for grouping the sentences in a model corpus into classes, each based on a kernel form containing a single ERKS type (q.v.).

confrel—the name of the role slot used to represent the *configurational relationship* between two objects. For example, in the ERKS form

(p-config con1 NOSE con2 JACK confrel (partof))

NOSE is stated to be " physically part of" JACK.

conrel—conceptual relationship; an ERKS type used to express relations among episodes. The relationships can be temporal, causal or logical.

contrast set—the set of possible atomic filler values for a role in an ERKS type.

coord—an ERKS type for grouping (coordinating) multiple events for an arbitrary reason (perhaps temporal or causal). (See *group* and *team*.)

cp—conscious processor; an ERKS type referring to the current focus of attention. (See *ltm*.)

D-tree—a discrimination tree, set up by the SOT program (q.v.) to organize search within a collection of ERKS forms for matching items, for some species of match. (See *SOT*, *instance* match, and *template* match.)

def-ERKS-type—the Lisp function for defining new ERKS types. In addition to entering the new ERKS type into the ISA-hierarchy (q.v.), this function defines two new Lisp functions (predicates) for testing whether candidate fillers in other types correspond to this type, and one for creating instances of this type. For example, for the ERKS type *ptrans*, the predicate functions are *ptrans-p* and *couldbe-ptrans-p*; the function *ptrans-f* creates ERKS forms that are instances of type *ptrans*.

def-wordsense—a Lisp function for entering new word sense definitions into a dictionary; used by both the Conceptual Analyzer and Conceptual Generator.

diagreq—a request (in the request memory of the Conceptual Analyzer) that sends a fragmented or otherwise anomalous noun group or clausal constituent of a sentence to inference processes in order that they may *diagnose* what has happened, and hopefully return a well-formed unit. (See *shipreq*.)

discriminator—an ERKS form that expresses a distinction between the ERKS type that the form instantiates and other ERKS types.

disj—disjunction; an ERKS type used to represent that either one and/or the other of two events occurred. A *disj* is a type of *conrel*.

dual—an ERKS type used to indicate that two events are mutually causative of each other, as in purchasing a book for money. A *dual* is a type of *conrel*.

ellipsis—the omission of one or more words that are obviously understood but that must be supplied to make a construction propositionally complete: for example, the parenthetical words in the sentence "Our house is small, his (house is) large."

ellipsis expansion—the process of imbedding the conceptual form of an ellipsed input in a more complete (e.g., propositional) form supplied, in the form of an expectation, by the "deep" understanding portions of a conversational system.

episode—an ERKS type spanning both simple and composite "action" type classes of events.

ERKS—Eclectic Representations for Knowledge Structures; the meaning structures used by the NLP system described in this book.

ERKS form—instances of ERKS types, i.e., symbolic structures containing role-filler pairs that are characteristic of the given type. Not all the mandatory role names need have fillers, but any filler is itself another ERKS form or a member of a contrast set (q.v.). An ERKS form representing the meaning of a sentence is based on the MIFP (q.v.) of that sentence.

ERKS types—atomic symbols standing for the unanalyzed primitive meaning units of an application domain. These must be declared (using *def-ERKS-type*, q.v.) according to the mandatory set of role names and fillers (structures based on other type).

ERKS structure—see *ERKS forms*.

extrinsic-roles—a Lisp atom for specifying a list of roles that are not essential to the meaning of the ERKS type being defined by a call to *def-ERKS-type*, but which a given utterance may "add on" in the manner of a parenthetical comment. The contraints associated with the role names are predicate functions for checking proposed fillers for consistency with the type's requirements.

forward-chaining—a process of deriving inferences by starting with a set of premises and repeatedly applying deductive rules to attain a conclusion.

frame—see *script*.

function lexemes—lexical units in a natural language that do not directly have an associated ERKS type, but which serve to modify the meaning structure built by another word (for instance, the verb root). For example, forms of "be," "have" and "do" used as auxiliaries, morphological endings such as "-ed" and "-ing," and modal words such as "can" or "might" are function lexemes.

gapreq—gap request—a type of request that is attempting to fill a gap in a conceptual structure on the C-LIST of the Conceptual Analyzer.

gerund—a progressive-form verb used as a noun; a verb ending in "-ing" can be used either as a subject or an object of a verb, as in "*Fishing* is a bore, but I like *hiking*."

gdictdef—a Lisp function that adds a definition to the Conceptual Generator's dictionary. It supplies the generator with specifications of syntax for sequencing words.

grf—get role filler—the Lisp function that returns the filler that is present at the end of a role path in an ERKS structure.

goalepisode—an ERKS type used for representing composite actions (e.g., scripts). These actions are characteristically carried out in service of a goal.

group—an ERKS type used for grouping inanimate entities that are to be taken together as a unit.

imbedded sentences—clause-level constituents that form part of larger sentences. For example, the clause "Mary to give him the book," in "John wanted Mary to give him the book."

implies—an ERKS type for expressing that a consequent must necessarily be true if the antecedent is true. *Implies* is a type of *conrel*.

infinitive—a verb form normally identical with the root form that performs some functions of both a noun and a verb and is usually used with the word "to", as in "I'd like to go fishing."

inst—a role name intended to specify the means (or instrumentality) by which an action was accomplished. It is typically used in *ptrans* events. *inst* also stands for the primitive class of "instruments," usually graspable implements with definite functions.

instance match—a type of SOT pattern matching in which the probe form (the input) is expected to be less specific than items in the SOT database, i.e., the database forms are "instances." (See *SOT* and *template match.*)

intrinsic-roles—a Lisp atom for specifying a list of roles essential to the meaning of the ERKS type being defined by a call to *def-ERKS-type*. The constraints associated with the role names are predicate functions for checking proposed fillers for consistency with the type's requirements.

is-above-p—the ISA-hierarchy predicate for determining whether one ERKS type is above another in the hierarchy; implemented as a Lisp function.

is-among-p—the ISA-hierarchy predicate for determining whether an ERKS type is among a given list of types; implemented as a Lisp function.

is-linked-p—the ISA-hierarchy predicate for determining whether there is a path between two ERKS types consisting of only subset or superset pointers; implemented as a Lisp function.

ISA-hierarchy—the inheritance hierarchy of ERKS types. Most types (the *subset* types) inherit properties and relations from one or more *parent* or *superset* types. We say that the subset type "is a(n)" instance of the superset type.

kernel form—the part of an MIFP (q.v.) that represents the main concept being expressed by a sentence. For example, for a sentence describing an action, the kernel is often the part of the MIFP that contains the verb that names the action.

knowledge structure—an assemblage of causally, temporally, etc., linked *meaning structures* (q.v.), representing a significant component of the knowledge content of an application domain.

ltm—long-term memory; an ERKS type defining the repository of thoughts that can (sometimes) be recalled into the *cp*.

meaning structure—a symbolic representation of a concept that was (or can be) expressed using natural language. The representation is independent of how the concept was paraphrased, or even of which natural language was used. The meaning structures used in the NLP Toolkit are called *ERKS forms.* See *ms*.

MIFP—Maximal Inference-Free Paraphrase; a paraphrase of a sentence, expressed by sentences in the same language as the original sentence, yielding the most verbose rephrasing of the original that preserves its literal meaning. An MIFP is constructed by looking at what information is required by the primitive ERKS types. The MIFP should be based only upon what can be inferred from the definitions of the words in the original sentence; no inferences concerning the surrounding context may be made.

mobj—mental object—an ERKS type representing an object (e.g., a unit of information) that exists in mental locations, such as people's memory, or in physical entities such as books. *Mobj* also appears as a role name in ERKS types such as *mtrans* and *mbuild*.

mode—a role name used for specifying whether an event is asserted to have occurred, to not have occurred, of having the potential of occurring, to not be possible, etc. Modal specifications are typically associated with words such as "not," "can," "cannot" and "might."

model corpus—a collection of sentences or sentence fragments which, taken as a whole, sample as large a fragment as possible of the knowledge content of the domain of interest. A corpus can be used as a starting point for constructing a new set of ERKS types, or for defining new word senses.

morphology—the study and description of word formation in a language including inflection, derivation, and compounding; the system of word-forming elements and processes in a language.

ms—a special ERKS type that is used to link the kernel form and all nuances of an MIFP into a single ERKS form. For example, "(ms kernel KER nuance1 N1 nuance2 N2 ...)."

mtrans—mental transfer of information—an ERKS type used to represent actions having to do with mental acts of perception and communication.

NLP—Natural Language Processing; the analysis and synthesis of natural language (e.g., English) by computer. This book specifically addresses *textual* representations of natural language.

NLP Context—the component of an NLP system that maintains information about the current state of a conversation, including things spoken in the past and expectations about what may be spoken in the near future.

NLP Toolkit—the software implementing the concepts and algorithms presented in Part I of this book. The Toolkit is available from Rowman & Littlefield, Publishers.

nuances—the parts of an MIFP other than the kernel form (q.v.); details to be added to the main meaning of a sentence.

obj-spot—the term used to refer to the syntactic constituent following the verb kernel in an active-voice sentence, preceding it in the passive; so-called because it often ends up being represented in the *obj* role in the underlying ERKS meaning structure.

objspot-req—a request generator (q.v.) that places a request that wants to fill an obj-spot into the Conceptual Analyzer's request memory.

os-gapreq—a one-shot gap request; a type of request that gets exactly one chance to fill a gap in a conceptual structure on the C-LIST of the Conceptual Analyzer. (See *gapreq*.)

p-config—physical configuration; an ERKS type expressing location, orientation or contact relation between two objects.

path—see *role path*.

perfective—expressing action as complete or as implying the notion of completion, conclusion, or result. The word "given" is the perfective form of the verb "give."

phonology—the science of speech sounds and sound changes in a language.

plausible—an ERKS type used to express rules of the "other things being equal" or "in default assume" variety. *Plausible* is a *conrel* connective, less strong than *cause* or *implies*.

polity—an ERKS type representing self-contained political units such as municipalities, states, provinces, and nations.

pos—used in a dictionary definition to declare the (traditional) *part of speech* of a word.

primitive type—same as *ERKS type (q.v.)*.

production system—a system in which the units of processing are individual *productions*, or test-action pairs, maintained in a *production memory*, operating in concert with a *working memory*, which contains facts or hypotheses, usually describing the current state of a problem-solving process. A simple *interpreter* iteratively selects items from the working memory and attempts to perform transformations on them by applying rules from the production memory, and adds the result to the working memory. Production systems are used for performing tasks of deductive reasoning (typically forward-chaining, but also backward-chaining).

progressive—of, relating to, or constituting a verb form that expresses action or state in progress at the time of speaking or a time spoken of. The word "giving" is the progressive form of the verb "give."

ptrans—physical transfer of location—an ERKS type in which an animate actor intentionally causes a change in the location of an object.

representational continuity—the principle that small changes in meaning should not lead to large changes in the associated meaning structure assigned, for example, by ERKS.

request generators—Lisp macros that place specific, stylized requests into the request memory of the Conceptual Analyzer. (See, for example, *actspot-req* and *objspot-req*.)

role filler—the ERKS structure associated with a role name in an ERKS form (see *ERKS type*). This is always an ERKS form in its own right (i.e., a complete concept, surface symbol, or member of a contrast set).

role name—the name of a mandatory role in an the case frame of an ERKS type (q.v.) Also called "role slot" or simply "slot."

role path—a list of role names leading from the top level of an ERKS form to a filler nested somewhere inside it.

rut—repeat until threshold—an ERKS type describing a causal relation connecting a sequence of actions with a specific condition; it provides a meaning analogous to the DO-UNTIL construct in ordinary programming languages. A *rut* is a type of *conrel*.

s-attr—stative attributional—an ERKS type used to encode an assertion about the state of an object. Attributional statives often take values along a scale from -10 to +10, for instance, to represent one's state of health.

s-goal—goal stative—an ERKS form that asserts a relationship between a higher animate entity and a desired action or state of the world.

script—a description of a stereotyped sequence of events, actions, or situations that is used by the computer to help form inferences or expectations, or to help it choose goals. (Also sometimes loosely called a *frame*).

sentential focus—the primary focus of attention in a sentence; this will usually be the constituent expressed first.

shipreq—a request (in the request memory of the Conceptual Analyzer) that sends a noun group or clausal constituent of a sentence to inference processes in order that they may come to a deeper understanding of it. (See *diagreq*.)

sketchifier—a "demon" process that gets executed by the Conceptual Generator for the purpose of eliminating redundancies and superfluities in the text being generated. The goal of a sketchifier is to generate more concise, natural-sounding text than the literal expression of a concept would yield.

SOT—Self-Organizing Tree—a general-purpose knowledge-base-organizing program that computes an efficient discrimination scheme for accessing large numbers of items of knowledge expressed in the role-filler representational format used in this book.

srf—set role filler—the Lisp function that assigns a filler at the end of a role path in an ERKS form.

stative type—any ERKS type that describes attributes of entities, relationships among entities, or changes in these attributes or relationships. (See *actional type*.)

surface form—a string encoding a sentence or phrase of a natural language (such as English).

surface semantic representation—the ERKS form representation of a sentence or phrase, built only from the literal meanings of the words in the text at hand (before any inferences or links to the main knowledge base have been made).

superset—a Lisp atom used for specifying a list of ERKS types immediately above the one being defined (i.e., the parent type in the ISA-hierarchy) in a call to *def-ERKS-type*.

template match—a type of SOT pattern matching in which the probe form (the input) is expected to be more specific than items in the SOT database; i.e., the database forms are "templates" or "patterns." (See *SOT* and *instance match*.)

team—an ERKS type describing a collection of animate entities that are intentionally distinct, but thought of as acting together (e.g., mankind).

topreq—top request; a structure, containing a test part and an actions part, that drives the execution of a dictionary definition in the Conceptual Analyzer.

tri-constituent form—a form of a sentence that contains a verb with both a direct object and an indirect object, in addition to the subject. For example,

"Olivia gave Muhammed a book." (These are also called tri-valent or di-transitive forms.)

vel—an ERKS type indicating a possible choice of one of several mutually exclusive word sense possibilities.

velreq—vel request—a type of request that examines the Analyzer's C-LIST for features that will allow it to decide upon ("assert") one of the senses of an ambiguous word. It may fill a gap in a structure at the same time. (See *gapreq*.)

verb kernel plus constituents—a model of English sentence structure in which the sentence is presumed to be built around a core consisting of the main verb, its auxiliaries, and possibly some modal words or adverbs.

word sense—a set of associations between a word in a natural language and one or more meaning structures that the word could create or add to. In the NLP Toolkit, word sense definitions are procedural in form; the actions taken by a word sense create new ERKS forms or fill in roles of existing ERKS forms, depending on the current state of the NLP context.

Index

Abelson, R., xiv, 7, 9, 57
absolute time, 263, 270, 272, 305
Academic Counseling Experiment, 8-9, 14, 234, 239
academic curriculum model, 9
Academic Parsing Expert, 277
Academic Scheduling Expert, 299, 311, 314-15, 330
ACE microworld, 270
ACE. *See* Academic Counseling Experiment
activation of requests, 89, 91
active problem solving, 9
Active Structural Networks, 18
actor-spot constituent, 87, 123, 126, 131
actor-spot request generator, 91-92, 102
adages, 8
add-con, 99
add-phrases, 80
add-syns, 110
add-word-con, 99, 133
adictdef, 90
affix hopping, 83, 109
agrammatical inputs, 19
Allen, J.F., 8, 39
AM, 6
ambiguous concept, 140
ambiguous word, 133
analysis. *See* conceptual analysis
analysis environment, 95
analyzer dictionary definition, 90
anaphora, 8, 145
antecedent, 236
APE. *See* Academic Parsing Expert
Appelt, D.E., 181
appositive, 276
Arens, Y., 21, 57
ARGOT, 8
ASE. *See* Academic Scheduling Expert
assertional database, 334
association list, 171

asynchronous forward-chaining reasoning, 6
aton-eval, 70, 74
atomized forms, 26, 74, 171
attribute sketchifier, 270
attributional concept, 22, 31, 46, 270, 286
auxiliary verbs, 176

back-chaining reasoning rules, 291
back-tracking chronologically, 297
balance of SOT tree, 228
Bar-Hillel, Y., 5
Barr, A., xiii, 9
base sentence, 28
belief systems, 8
best-first ordering, 228
Berkeley Unix 4.2, 114, 232
Bienkowski, M., xv, 6, 334
Birnbaum, L., xv
Bobrow, D.G., 5, 8, 18, 249
BORIS, 7
bottom-up processing, 12
bottom-up representation design method, 27, 34, 59
Brachman, R., 18
breadth-first search, 239
Brown, J.S., 84, 249
Brown University, 7
Bruce, B., 175
Burton, R.R., 84, 249
bushiness of SOT tree, 228
"but" test, 29

CADHELP, 6, 14, 52-53, 55, 167, 334
CAD tool, 207
calculus of plausibility, 237
canonical meaning structure, 19
Carberry, S., 248
Carbonell, J.G., xv, 6-7, 59, 249
CATALOG command, 208

Italicized entries in this index give references to Lisp functions in the text.

Index